THE HIPSTER'S LEGACY

THE HIPSTER'S LEGACY

A STORY ABOUT A FAMILY

A Memoir

written and illustrated by

Lorraine Gibson Cohen

plumtreetales.com

Illustrations by Lorraine Gibson Cohen

ISBN: 979-8-9908456-2-6 (hardcover)
ISBN: 979-8-9908456-0-2 (softcover)
ISBN: 979-8-9908456-1-9 (eBook)
ISBN: 979-8-9908456-3-3 (audio)

Library of Congress Control Number 2024912353

Most photos from family and friends' albums.

Photographs taken by Shelly Plumb:
Lindee, Donnie, Laurie, and
Jeff in the park with a dog

Keyboard illustration on cover by L. Bagnoli
Cover photo by Emily and Juliet Willing (AKA Romeo and Juliet)

Edited by Lauren Alexander
Proofread by Kharysa Watt
Cover and book designed by
Jan Westendorp/katodesignandphoto.com

For Gayle

CONTENTS

PREFACE   ix
FOREWORD   xi

MAP OF HERMOSA BEACH   xvi
JAZZ TERMINOLOGY   xvii
MUSICIANS MENTIONED IN THE TEXT   xix

INTRODUCTION   1
PRELUDE   3

PART I   7

WINTER   9
SPRING   74
SUMMER   202
AUTUMN   306
WINTER   323

PART II   347

SPRING   393
SUMMER   454
AUTUMN   488

FLOOR PLAN OF CULPER COURT   542
FAMILY AND FRIENDS PHOTOS   543

EPILOGUE   563
ACKNOWLEDGMENTS   571

ABOUT THE AUTHOR   573

PREFACE

My story is set in the early 1960s. John F. Kennedy is president. Fidel Castro and Russia are stirring up trouble in Cuba, and Beatle Mania has already arrived from England. The 1960s is moving away from the uptight 1950s and Martin Luther King Jr. is revving up for his "I have a Dream" speech at the Capitol in Washington. As yet, the protests against the Vietnam War were not on most people's radar.

There will be some words in this memoir that were commonplace in an earlier part of the 20th Century that have now changed. Black people were called Negro or Colored. Native Americans or Indigenous people were known as Indians. Asian Americans were often called Oriental. There are expressions and stereotypes of that time that may offend today's readers. There are historical people who were honored then who we now have questions about their rightful place in history. I have kept the terms and words used in the 1960s in order to preserve that time accurately.

Some people's names have been changed or altered a bit to make for easier reading.

FOREWORD

WHEN JEFF MET BETTY WHITE

It all started sometime in 1950 or '51 when my father, better known to the world as Harry the Hipster Gibson, the wild and crazy jazz entertainer, decided that he was going to write a novelty Christmas song. It would make big bucks for him in perpetuity because if it became a hit like what happened to Gene Autry when he recorded "Rudolf, the Red-Nosed Reindeer," it would be played every Christmas. Just imagine the royalties he would get for both writing and performing in it.

Harry eventually came up with a tune entitled, "I Hope My Mother-in-law Don't Come for Christmas." It was about a man who dreads that his mother-in-law will move in permanently with his family if she comes on that one fateful holiday. I must admit it was a clever song. Harry, thinking of all the angles, decided that if he included his own family in the recording, it would be a nice touch and get a kind of "Good Housekeeping Seal of Approval" that would counteract the bad press of his being named "The Cause of Juvenile Delinquency" a few years before.

In 1950, I was a shy nine-year-old and my extremely introverted younger brother, Jeff, was just seven. As the two youngest, we were the quiet ones. My older brother, Bill, at eleven, was already honing his musical skills on the drums and perfecting his comic timing with stories and skits that he performed regularly for the family while my older sister, Arlene, who at the mature age of thirteen had set her sights on becoming a famous singer and movie star like Betty Hutton or Judy Garland.

Yet with even that going for us kids, we had never been part of show business in any way before this new undertaking of Harry's, unless you count the time when Arlene went on a radio talent contest and sang "The Trolley Song" from *Meet Me in St. Louis*. She didn't win. She was beat out by a soft shoe dancer doing "Me and My Shadow." You may ask how you could ever present a soft shoe dancer on a radio show, much less have him win the contest with it, but I don't want to get distracted about that enigma right now.

One afternoon after Harry had gotten together the musical backing of a guitarist and a drummer who would play alongside his piano, we all hauled off to a recording studio in downtown L.A. and spent a long afternoon cranking out the mother-in-law song. The kids' part, our part, started off the record singing "Jingle Bells." After the first bar, there is a knock at the door. The mother and we kids think it is our grandma. Harry breaks in and stops us and starts his own song of complaint about the mother-in-law that won't go home. The song lists all the different holidays she stays through. Our part after this was to make background noise like singing or laughing or, when the father sings "She's there to scare the kids on Halloween," we kids all screamed really loud.

We did the song over and over until Harry and the man in the glass booth were satisfied with how it turned out. On the flip side of the record, Arlene got to sing a song all by herself called "The Worm Song." It was the old song kids used to sing on the playground, and Harry wrote new lyrics for it. Finally, everyone was satisfied with both sides of the record. It was a wrap or a cut or print or whatever people said back then, and we got to go eat lunch.

After all that, we thought we were done with the project, but it was just beginning. When the record came out, Harry started taking us around to the local television studios to plug the song. At that time, TV still was pretty new and except for a few cowboy shows and old movies, everything was live. I remember going to the little studios and onto funny painted sets. We would have to have thick orange makeup applied to our faces so that we would show up on the screen looking normal.

One by one, we covered as many studios and shows as we could. Usually they were daytime shows with a host that would introduce Harry and us and the song. One show was called *The Al Jarvis Show*. Al Jarvis was a pudgy, old (to us) guy who used to be a disc jockey on the radio but had moved over to TV when it started. He had a sidekick sitting next to him at his desk. This "Girl Friday" was thirty-year-old Betty White. She had medium short brown hair and as I remember was not at all glamorous. Al Jarvis's looks were at best on the froggy side and he did not have much of a personality either, so I guess Betty was there to supply the femininity, wit, and cheer to the show.

We were introduced to the American public by the duo at the desk and then went directly into our routine. Maybe we kids, not being real professionals, were getting a little overconfident or lax in our part of the song, because right when all of us were suppose to scream out after the line "She's there to scare the kids on Halloween," we all forgot to scream except Jeff. He didn't forget. He yelled out all alone and that turned out to be his downfall.

You have to know that at seven years old, Jeff, or Jeffery as we called him then, was still deep into his introverted self. He would get embarrassed if anyone even looked at him. Mostly, he looked down so he wouldn't have to make eye contact with people, but he loved Harry, so he didn't balk when he was required to go on stage. He didn't mind as long as he didn't stick out too much. He thought if he could blend in with the rest of the Gibson bunch, it wasn't going to be so bad.

But when Jeff rang out all alone with his Halloween scream, he did draw attention to himself. He was horrified when he realized that he was the only one making noise. He promptly turned a bright red and ducked down as much as he could. He looked like he was trying to drop through the floor or become invisible. The rest of us were feeling our own chagrin. We had missed our cue, and Harry would ball us out when we left the studio.

The Al Jarvis Show was a kind of variety/music/talk/interview show—pretty low budget, no rehearsals, no scripts. They had to wing it and be spontaneous. I don't know whose idea it was, maybe it was Betty's, but a short time after we finished the song, someone came over and took Jeff over to Al and Betty sitting at the desk.

We kids were still huddled together where we had done our number. Arlene hissed, "They got Jeffery! Oh no, they're going to interview him!" We all knew Arlene would have aced an interview and now it was going to be a disaster. We almost felt sorry for Mr. Jarvis and his Girl Friday. They didn't know that Jeff didn't talk even in the best of circumstances. They didn't know, but they found out soon enough now that he was being broadcast out to all of the Los Angeles area and beyond.

We watched with a feeling of doomed fatality. Poor Al Jarvis and Betty White, they probably thought that if they took the cute little showbiz kid out of the pack and interviewed him, he might come up with some adorable childish remark about his wild and semi-famous father, but all that Jeff could do was look down and mumble something unintelligible whenever they asked him anything. Finally after several tries, they gave up and just talked all around him or to each other. By this time, Jeff just sat there frozen in a kind of stoic panic. At the end, they presented him with a genuine badge (I think it was cardboard) that said he was now a full-time member of the Al Jarvis fan club and then finally let him stumble away back to us.

In later years, I saw an interview with Betty White. She was talking about her early days in television, and she stressed the fact that it was all live and you never knew what was going to happen, especially with an interview. I almost expected her to tell of the time she had to interview a mute child, but she didn't. Maybe she just wanted to forget the whole thing.

MAP OF HERMOSA BEACH

JAZZ TERMINOLOGY

A gas: A fun or exciting thing

A hipster: Someone who is knowledgeable about the latest jazz trends and vocabulary

A square: Jive talk from the 1940s meaning someone who isn't hip

Axe: A slang word during the 1960s for musical instrument

Battle of the Bands: During the jazz, swing era the Roseland Ballroom had two bandstands on opposite sides of the room. Each night when one band finished their set, the other band immediately started playing their set, and it went on throughout the night with the music never stopping

Bebop: A style of jazz developed during jam sessions in the 1940s which featured fast tempos, complex chord progressions, and an emphasis on improvisation

Blow: To play any instrument

Boogie-woogie: A style of blues played on the piano with a strong, fast beat and a repetitive rocking left hand leaving the right hand to improvise around the left-hand structure

Bread: Slang for money in the 1960s

Cat: A person

Chops: The ability to play an instrument with either the mouth, breath, or fingers

Crashing: Slang for staying at someone's house

Dig: To like or understand something

DownBeat Magazine: An American music magazine devoted to "jazz, blues and beyond"

Fake book: Often used by professional jazz musicians, it is a simplified book of sheet music with the melody written in the treble clef and the chords written above

Jam session: An impromptu meeting of a group of musicians to play

Man: An excited expression

Pad: A slang word for house, apartment, or living space

Roseland: A ballroom in New York City on West 51 Street built in 1919 that became famous in the 1940s for its continuous music of big jazz bands such as those led by Count Basie, Chick Webb, Harry James, Tommy Dorsey, and Glenn Miller

Scatting: A singer improvising using sounds like a musical instrumentalist

Short: Slang for car in the 1960s

The Five Spot: A jazz club famous during the 1950s and 1960s, cheap and low-key with cutting-edge bebop and progressive jazz that attracted artists and writers

Woodshedding: Jazz slang for practicing

MUSICIANS MENTIONED IN THE TEXT

Art Tatum: A blind American jazz pianist regarded as one of the greatest in his field. Active 1920s–1950s.

Billy Higgins: An American jazz drummer of mainly free jazz and hard bop. Active from the 1950s–1980s.

Bobby Troup: Lived 1918–1999. A jazz pianist, singer, songwriter, and actor.

Cal Tjader: An American jazz musician of the vibraphone, drums, bongos, congas, timpani, and piano known for his Latino jazz sound. Active 1948–1982.

Charlie Haden: An American jazz double bass player, bandleader, and educator who played a vital role in jazz by revolutionizing the harmonic concept of bass playing during the 1960s.

Count Basie: An American jazz pianist, organist, composer, and bandleader. Active 1924–1984, known for his swinging percussive style of band leading along with his tasteful piano style of less is more.

Dave Brubeck: An American jazz pianist and composer active from 1940-2012, known for his cool jazz, unusual time signatures, and contrasting rhythms.

Don Cherry: An American jazz trumpeter during the 1970s who pioneered fusion music, drawing on African and Middle Eastern themes and called one of the most influential jazz musicians of the late 20th century.

Ella Fitzgerald: An American jazz and pop singer referred to as the First Lady of Song and known for her purity of tone, phrasing, timing, and horn-like improvisation scatting. Active 1929-1995.

Fats Domino: An American pianist, singer, and songwriter of early rock and roll, selling more than sixty-five million records.

Gerry Mulligan: An American baritone saxophonist, clarinetist, composer, and arranger of jazz. Active during 1946-1996, considered to be an important proponent of modern jazz in the 1950s.

Julian Edwin "Cannonball" Adderley: An American jazz alto saxophonist of the hard bop era of the 1950s and 1960s. He became an important innovator and wrote the music for "Work Song."

Kurt Weill: A German composer active from 1920-1950 who wrote the music for the Three Penny Opera and other shows and films.

Little Richard: Lived 1932-2020. An American musician, singer, and songwriter of rock and roll known for his pounding piano and raspy, shouted vocals.

Maria Callas: A renowned opera soprano of the 20th century known for her wide-ranging voice and dramatic style.

Nat King Cole a.k.a. Nathaniel Adams Coles: Lived 1919–1965. An American singer, jazz pianist, and actor. His trio found success as a jazz ensemble, but his singing brought more fame.

Oscar Brown Jr.: Lived 1926–2005. An American singer, songwriter, playwright, poet, civil rights activist, and actor. Brown wrote 125 songs, namely the lyrics to "Work Song" and recorded twelve albums.
https://www.cmgworldwide.com/clients/oscar-brown-jr/

Rahsaan Roland Kirk (born Ronald Theodore Kirk): Lived 1935–1977. Known earlier in his career as **Roland Kirk**, he was an American_jazz multi-instrumentalist who played tenor saxophone, flute, and many other instruments and was renowned for his onstage vitality, improvisation, comic banter, and political ranting.

Ray Charles: Blind since childhood, this American pianist, singer, and songwriter pioneered Soul.

Thelonious Monk: An American jazz pianist and composer with a unique improvisational and highly individualistic playing style. Active during the 1940s–1970s.

Thomas Wright "Fats" Waller: American jazz pianist, organist, composer, singer, and comedic entertainer, active 1918–1943, laid the groundwork for modern jazz piano with his stride style.

INTRODUCTION

For more than fifty years, I have been carrying, from place to place, from the West Coast to the East Coast, from apartment to apartment, a gray loose-leaf notebook. I started writing in it in 1963 when I was twenty-two years old. At the time I was living temporarily with my older sister, her three children, and my younger brother in a Southern California beach town. I wrote down things as they happened. There were short stories, character studies of people and things, even a poem or two. It was mostly handwritten in pencil or ballpoint pen with a few typed out pages of writing I thought had turned out well.

Then life happened and I stopped writing. Still, I kept the notebook, sticking it in the tops of closets, burying it in drawers. Several years ago, at the urging of a good friend who seemed fascinated by the stories I told of my family, I started dipping into the notebook again. I retyped a few of the more complete stories and showed them to my friend. She wanted more, and before I realized it I was writing a book.

It wasn't easy deciphering my handwriting from so long ago. The gray notebook was a mess. Things were out of order. There were ripped and crossed-out pages. Some of it was missing or unfinished. What was not written down I had to remember, and what I didn't remember I had to figure out. I would have to rewrite old episodes and write completely new ones and bring all the bits and pieces together into one continuous story.

I started at the beginning and wrote in chronological order as Dickens and the authors of old had done. After a while, I started to feel like Dickens because, although my audience wasn't large (it did grow from my one encouraging friend and my husband to several other friends and family), I felt obligated to provide a new chapter each week with the idea that they were waiting with bated breath for the next exciting episode.

It was hard to keep all the memories straight. Sometimes I had to ask myself if I could truly call what I was writing a memoir. Maybe I should say "based on a true story." But, no, that was not right either. Perhaps calling my book a dramatized memoir or a memoir/novel would be the most accurate way to describe what I have done.

When I originally started writing in the notebook, it was with the idea of telling all the funny stories and mishaps that happened while I was living with my sister. After it was finished, I realized I had also explained who I was and how I got to be me, to myself.

PRELUDE
FROM THE GRAY NOTEBOOK
EL CAMINO REAL

The road that runs parallel along the California coastline sprints through many small beach towns, and as it does, its name changes with each new town. In our town it is called Hermosa Avenue, but a mile or so later, it becomes North Harbor Drive and then Ocean Drive as if it can't make up its mind who or what it is.

I was once told that our modest avenue had possibly been part of an old historic trail called El Camino Real. I don't know if this is true, but in elementary school I learned the story of that road and of Father Junípero Serra, who forged it in the early part of the state's history, building his missions of God along the rugged coastline of California. The long trail he forged was variously called El Camino Real, The Royal Road, or The King's Highway. In time, the old mission trail was joined and obscured by other newer ones which also ran along the shoreline of California. After a while no one was quite sure where the original road was anymore. That is why I always prefer to believe that our own Hermosa Avenue might really have played some part in the history of

Old California. Even the words "El Camino Real" ("The Royal Road") hold a promise of romance and adventure.

CULPER COURT

If Hermosa Avenue somehow runs all the way to San Francisco, the street we live on, by contrast, runs only one block.

Culper Court is short and narrow with no sidewalk and is more like an alley than a courtyard, but people do not want to live in an alley—therefore, Culper Court. Our house at number 230 is tucked midway into the block. At the back of our cottage, is a vast open acreage used as a landfill. Well, let's face it. It's a dump! Beyond that a railroad track runs to unknown places. The whole time I have lived here, I never once saw or heard a train go by.

On the edge of the landfill are two oil wells. Not the kind with the big Eiffel-like towers but pumps chugging away night and day like sooty black birds pecking for worms. From the hill that is Culper Court, you can also see the electric factory a few blocks away. By day it looks innocent and quiet, but at night smoke belches out of its chimneys and lights flicker on and off through intricate tubings that make it look like a city of tomorrow run by robots with mechanical brains.

A short brick walk leads the way to the red-shingled house. A few neglected flowers and scrappy plants struggle for existence in the hard dirt. Three crippled bicycles, rusted together, are at one corner of the brick porch while a pile of firewood is piled at the other. A dripping garden hose, curled and snarled like a snake, has made a small reservoir of water in the dirt. Maybe some of it will reach one of the parched flowers.

At the front door, a piece of wood is nailed over a missing pane of glass, and on closer inspection you can see that the doorknob also has a problem. It is gone. You will knock on the door and knock again and then pound. You will have to pound very hard to be heard over the shouts of children playing and the wailing sound of a saxophone inside the house. Soon, an eye will peek out through a hole in one of the panes of the door and a voice will call out. "Why don't you come in through the window?"

PART I

THE FIRST CHINESE PICNIC

In 353 CE in China during the Jin Dynasty, calligraphers, philosophers, and poets had a tradition of gathering in a forest by a babbling brook or stream of water for a day of wandering and inspiration. It was called *qū shuǐ liú shāng*, or "Liquor cups floating on the winding brook." As they sat by the river, they drank wine and wrote poetry. A game evolved where one poet would write a poem, then fill a cup with wine and sail it down the river. If a cup stopped near a person, they would have to make up a poem immediately and drink the cup dry. If he failed to make up a poem, he had to drink three cups of the wine. Soon everyone was very drunk and sometimes they got loud and disorderly, but the poems they made were glorious and became known as the famous *Preface to the Poems Composed at the Orchid Pavilion.*

Conclusion: Out of chaos can come creation.

WINTER

CHAPTER 1
LORRAINE

FAILURE

Here I was in Culper Court again, lying on the couch that I had made up into a temporary bed this first night back. I wanted to sleep but my mind kept me awake, talking, talking, not caring that I was tired. I thought back to six months ago. I was on my own for the first time, fresh out of El Camino City College with an AA degree in art and living in Hollywood. My apartment was on the top floor of a mock-Spanish mansion. At one time, it had been owned by a silent screen star, but the star and the pink stucco had both faded, and now it was an apartment house with a weedy brick courtyard and huge empty pots where palm trees had once grown.

The perch from my attic apartment on the fourth floor reflected my feelings. I felt like I was sitting up on a flagpole seeing everything from a high isolated view. I wasn't a part of anything yet—certainly not the Hollywood scene of would-be starlets and wannabe leading men.

The girls were predictably blonde, from screaming brassy yellow to fluffy popcorn white. The guys, a perfect complement, were generally tall and dark haired. Each day, they paraded Hollywood Boulevard, the girls in toreador pants, spiked heels, and always something in a leopard-skin print. The guys, in their dark glasses and glistening hair, would stop you on the street with lines like, "Hey, didn't I see you at the *Lolita* audition?"

I had come to the city hoping to find work as a commercial artist, but it seemed I just found "work." My job as a receptionist in a fashion-buying office wasn't hard, but I just wasn't good at it. I put people on hold then forgot them. I couldn't remember who was in the office and who was out; if they were out, I couldn't remember where they had gone. I lost packages, never got a message right, and when I had to run the old mimeograph machine, I got one hundred smudged and crumpled copies of an important document and ink up to my elbows. Worst of all, I was afraid of my boss.

I cringed whenever I saw her. Large, squat, and sixty, she snarled her way into the office every day looking like a well-groomed bulldog in a designer suit. Most frightening were her hats. They were large and ornate with veils and flowers, wonderfully delicate, but hideous sitting on top of her bulldog head. I was nervous and unhappy, a complete bust at my job. Strangely enough, they never fired me.

At one point, probably to save face, I developed a bad case of laryngitis and couldn't talk. I couldn't talk on the intercom, I couldn't talk on the switchboard, I couldn't talk and make any more humiliating mistakes. Happily, I stayed home in my attic apartment to swathe my throat in rags soaked in Vicks VapoRub.

Nursing my sore throat, that week gave me time to think of just what I was accomplishing in Hollywood. It came down to a strange paradox. I hadn't become a commercial artist. Therefore, I was now working in a city I didn't particularly want to live in, for the express purpose of being able to afford to live in that very city that I didn't particularly want to live in. I worked to live; I lived to work. What was the point?

A few days later, I got a call that Mom had fallen and hurt her back. She would have to be in traction for a month in the hospital. Fate had taken a hand. I took my mother's accident and my frozen vocal cords as a sign from above to quit my job and move back to Culper Court.

Packing all my precious possessions—my paints, my art books, my brass gold towel rings shaped like fishes—and leaving my tiny apartment with its charming slanted walls, its kitchen I had so lovingly painted with red hearts and flowers just a few months before, and its living room with the one tasteful olive-green wall and kidney-shaped coffee table to match (also painted by myself), I called my brother, Jeff, to come and take me home.

HOME AGAIN

Culper Court wasn't quite as I had left it. In my absence, my older sister's marriage had broken up yet again. And again, she had come back home to her mother. Now Arlene and her three kids— Lindee, Donnie, and Laurie J.—along with a truck-load of flotsam and jetsam surviving seven years of on-again, off-again marriage, were added to the small cottage.

Jeff, my younger brother by two years, was comfortable anywhere as long as he could play his saxophone, but Mom, at last, seeking peace and less clutter in her life, left for a brand-new apartment in the next beach town. The move was surprising, but what astounded everyone was that in a short span of time, my quiet mother not only started a new life but had fallen in love with her next-door neighbor, a used car salesman from Alabama. Even more astonishing was that her new boyfriend convinced her to move in with him.

Mom may have been in love, but she was still Mom, and with her typical thoroughness, started immediately cleaning and shining up her new apartment. The very next day, she promptly slipped and fell on her newly waxed floors and as a result was now in traction at the local hospital.

And here I was back at home again. It would be different with no Mom to make life clean and orderly. With just my sister, my brother, and the kids, it would be something new—what, I didn't know. I was drifting off at last and slid silently into sleep.

CHAPTER 2
ARLENE

THE NEXT MORNING

I was sure my back was permanently bent from the old couch. It had been like sleeping on lumpy mashed potatoes—soft and hard at the same time. Finally, I got up and helped the kids with their breakfast. Since it was Saturday, they ran off to play at Betsy's house next door. They seemed to take my reappearance into their lives as nothing unusual—just the normal kind of thing that happened.

It was ten o'clock; I had been up for hours when Arlene finally poked her head out of her bedroom. Trying to focus through half-open eyes, she felt her way into the kitchen, yawning and scratching her head, her wide cheeks creased and puffy from sleeping on rumpled sheets.

My sister's nightgown caught my attention. It was one of her own creations, a black floor-length shift with lace ruffling high at the neck. In the back however, it dipped down to a flagrantly bare back. The gown could have been found in the pages of Vogue but now only appeared bizarre on my sleepy sister about to start sizzling bacon in the narrow kitchen.

After a desultory look around, she gave up the search for a match and attempted to light the dwarf-like stove from a twisted piece of paper lit from the nearby water heater.

It must be uncomfortable to sleep in that funny gown—and dangerous! I thought, suddenly becoming alarmed as I watched the still drowsy figure move the flaring paper torch toward the stove and turn on the gas. At last, it lit with a big whoosh of flame. Undaunted, Arlene reached for the gigantic skillet that covered the entire top of the two-burner stove.

Even after having three kids, my sister at twenty-six still had the body of a teenager, only now, except for the naked back, the only parts of her body not covered by the dark gown were her large, angular hands and strange, tiny, square-shaped feet. Soon, the bacon and eggs were done, leaving a greasy residue in the pan. Casually thrusting it aside, Arlene replaced it with a small pot of water for coffee. As she shuffled to the table, breakfast in hand, I thought again of how my sister looked so young with her wide face and her pink and white complexion. The water for the coffee boiled while she ate her eggs ravenously, wiping up the runny yokes with brown bread and licking at the pink debris of yesterday's lipstick with her tongue.

My sister was pretty like our mother and had a perfect profile except for the slight bump on her nose. Only her wispy blonde hair, in its usual tangled state, threw off that symmetry of perfection.

The bubbling water caught my attention and I salvaged two cups of coffee from what had not evaporated. A minute later, I sat down, placing one of the cups in front of my sister. Thus began the day's conversation of all I had missed by leaving Culper Court and living in Hollywood for six months.

CATCHING UP

Arlene was eager to talk, and even now, though she was just sitting down, her nervous energy kept her moving in quick, sharp jolts as she spoke. Soon she was leaning forward, intently gesturing with her hands.

"I'm in love!" she burst out. "I'm in love with a wonderful saxophone player."

Love, I thought. *That is new.* Love was not a word she flung around casually. Love was a serious thing. Why else had she returned to her husband, Don, over and over again with each try at reconciliation more disastrous than the last?

"Oh, he is so beautiful," my sister sighed. "And get that amused look off your face. Don't you laugh! This is different." Arlene sat back in her chair and looked almost pontifical, ready to tell a big story.

"You know how I always just have these men, these flunkies, around me like old Ray, and Jack the drummer, and poor effeminate Paul? And remember Tony with his tiki god statues and hangdog face? He wanted to save me spiritually and be my children's father. These guys hung around me and I let them. They were in love with me, even Paul in his own way (although I don't think he really loved me, he just maybe wanted to *be* me). Anyway, I let them do things for me like buy groceries, take me shopping and to the laundromat. Remember poor Oatmeal Face Steve, that friend of Jeff's, who lied compulsively all the time? I got him to help me knock out the whole ceiling. What a mess that was!"

And here she stopped but only to catch a breath.

"Anyway, Sid is different. I feel madly attracted to him, and I respect him so much too. Do you know that he supports his invalid father?" Arlene looked at me for signs of admiration. "Another thing, he's really intelligent. We believe in the same things about life and love. I just told him right out when I first met him that I hated dates—all that phony stuff that goes on—and that I wanted a real relationship."

I felt obliged to look a trifle more excited and asked, "And then what happened?" Now on a roll with her story, Arlene practically got up and did a waltz as she continued rapturously, "So we walked on the beach in the rain and talked and talked. He's so idealistic. He cries in movies. Oh, but now he is gone." Arlene drew a long, sad breath. "He is at the National Reserve camp in Georgia." A moment later she brightened again and even looked a little smug. "So far, he's already written me four letters. I just can't wait till he gets back in two weeks."

By this time, I was impressed too and happy for my sister. She needed someone who would make her feel special. Maybe this time it would work out but I had other questions on my mind and Arlene was still "Sid is this and Sid is that," until I broke in and asked what else was happening.

"Well, I might get hired at the Zanzibar. That's where Howard and Sid work. Just think," she said amazed. "If I hadn't of met Howard and if Howard hadn't wanted me to sing his tunes, then I never would have met Sid."

"Yes," I said, trying to get her mind off Sid for a moment, "but who is Howard, and what is the Zanzibar?"

THE MUSIC MAN

"Oh, well, Howard K. Small comes over every day and I'm learning all his songs," my sister continued, "but on the weekends I've been going to this club where he works, and I sing. The owner says he'll hire me if I can sing more commercial, but you know how I love way-out things and, oh, Lorraine, you've just got to hear Howard's songs. The chords are so ringing they vibrate—and the melodies—wow, sweet and bittersweet at the same time!"

"When did all this happen? How did you meet?" I still didn't know much about this Howard K. Small. My questions, however, set off another one of her animated stories.

"It was really a funny night, Lorraine. You know the Penguin Club?" (I didn't, but I let her continue.) "Well, Jeff and I hang out there sometimes. He plays his sax and I sing when they let us. The piano player, he is all about free jazz—he loves our baby brother's sax playing and my singing (he's about the only one too). The owner can't stand us."

Arlene didn't just talk; she acted out the whole episode impersonating each character just like she used to do when she and I were kids and she would act out a whole movie she had just seen. I could imagine the small smoky room, the piano bar and our shy brother blowing his horn self-consciously and my sister standing near, brazenly scatting a jazz riff.

"And then I met Howard," Arlene rambled on. "He came up to me, and he turned out to be such a funny guy like he would—" Arlene stopped. "Wait, wait, a minute." She put down her coffee cup and dove back into her bedroom. After rummaging around for a while, she came out with a folded piece of paper. "Here, read this. I wrote it. I even typed it before the typewriter broke. It's a character study. You didn't know I could write, did you? Neither did I, but it just came out. The whole meeting of Howard was so . . . well . . . he is bizarre but a real talent. I just had to write it all down."

I picked up the paper with interest.

"No, not now," Arlene said, folding it up again and stuffing it into my pocket. "We have so many other things to talk about. Go to the beach later and tell me what you think. He is a real character, like in a book."

MAN TROUBLE

"Well," I said, "seems like things are shaping up for you. But tell me, how is Mom doing in the hospital? I guess Jeff can take me to visit if his van is working."

"She is almost better, they say." Arlene's brief smile faded and she looked serious. "But guess what? That boyfriend of hers that she's living with never came to see her. Not one time! Can you beat that?" Arlene jerked the edge of the table fiercely, making her coffee slop over the rim of her cup.

"But I don't understand," I said. "They just moved in together. I thought he cared about her so much. The way you said he pursued her and pursued her until she finally went out with him."

"He is just a rat fink like all the rest of the men in her life," Arlene said vehemently.

I knew "all the rest of the men in her life" really meant just one, our father, Harry, but I didn't want her to get into all that now, so I changed the subject.

"Did the county come through for you? Are you set up on welfare yet?" I said quickly before she could go on one of her rants about how awful our father was and how he had ruined all our lives. "I know Mom was working hard to get you on it after Don left—all those forms."

"Yes, finally, finally, finally!" Arlene gave a comical, exasperated look then took a last swig at the dregs of her coffee. "Yeah," she sighed. "It took awhile, but things are better. They give us three hundred a month. Man, do we eat now—meat, pie, ice cream—and just in time too. For a while there I thought if I had to look at another pinto bean or spaghetti noodle on my plate again I'd . . . I don't know what I would have done without the aid with Mom in the hospital and all. She had been paying my rent, you know."

"Don't you get anything at all from Don?" I asked. "Where is he now?"

Arlene's face narrowed at the mention of her husband. She looked down, her mouth pinched together. "You know, Lorraine, *he* doesn't give us a damn cent! He just disappeared—no word, no money, no anything." Her rising anger was making her stand up. "Just don't speak to me about him. God damn it!" She stretched her hands out as if to stop her thoughts. "I want to forget he ever

existed," she sighed, sitting down again. "He doesn't give a flying fig about what happens to us. He thinks Mom will always
be there to care for me and the kids. Yeah, Mom who is flat on
her back in a hospital, Mom who works as a maid cleaning other
people's toilets."

I tried to interject some reality. "You know Mom doesn't do
that anymore. She is the assistant housekeeper now."

"Oh, you know what I mean! Mom still works like a dog, and
that bum (not her bum who won't even visit her in the hospital
but my bum) Don, is probably living with some woman waiting
on him hand and foot in Topanga Canyon, while he fiddles with
his stupid metal sculptures." Arlene paused briefly then continued. "The last time I saw him, he threw my iron and toaster
in the garbage just because I hocked his precious tape recorder.
Man, what was I supposed to do? We were starving and that was
six months ago, our last attempt at making a go of it." Suddenly
limp, my sister said quietly, "It lasted a week."

Strangely enough, I was relieved. Don seemed to be really
gone this time for good. Maybe now Arlene and the kids could
stay in one spot for a while. I never could understand the allure
of Don Brower. He was so quiet, except for when he was throwing things around and destroying anything Arlene cared about. I
was glad he was gone. It was cleaner this way, but to abandon
his family? "Come on," I said. "Let's clean up this mess. We
can't talk all day." And with that, The Saga of Arlene's Life was
stopped, at least for the time being.

CHAPTER 3
THE WALL

AND
FIRST ENTRY OF THE GRAY NOTEBOOK
LINDEE

LATER THAT DAY

It didn't take long for me and the kids to walk the four short blocks to the beach. I could already see people walking along the Strand, sometimes stopping by the long wall to look at the ocean. *Good old wall*, I thought as I comfortably settled myself near it. Lindee, Donnie, and Laurie J. ran ahead to play. It was already far into the afternoon, one of those crisp March days in Southern California, a bit windy but the sun was still intense. Some of the locals were already out trying to pick up the first warm rays.

So far, there were more people walking on the Strand in sweaters and light jackets than sunbathers down on the beach, mostly locals this early in the year. The few out-of-towners seemed to study the houses and cottages that faced the ocean and lined the Strand almost as much as they viewed the water. Some of the homes were impressive, like the stately Spanish two-story stuccos with red-tiled roofs and walled-in terra-cotta patios. Most of the houses, though, were tidy but unassuming cottages.

These good citizens on the Strand strolled along the wide sidewalk alone or in small groups, stopping now and then to take pictures, taking turns posing against the wall, then switching over to shooting the others with Brownie cameras. Small children peddled by on bright, jangly tricycles they got for Christmas. Sometimes older boys on thin racing bikes whizzed past, like jets, incurring anger from parents with toddlers. "Too fast, too fast!" they would yell out to the bikers' disappearing backs. The toddlers, unaware, continued to dart here and there, dodging their parents' desperate grasps, laughing at the game. Late-coming fishermen in windbreakers shouldering long poles and carrying metal buckets that clacked, headed south toward the Redondo Pier.

At the wall, the cement blocks had absorbed the heat of the afternoon and were now radiating its warmth into my back. I curled closer to its heat, pressing tight against the pores of the gray brick, legs outstretched, my eyelids bright pink and unseeing, closed against the sun. Opening them now, I picked out Lindee, Donnie, and Laurie J. on the tall iron swings—their silhouettes kicking high against the white sky. There was a breeze snapping in the air and a few kids and adults were flying kites. The paper flyers quickly rose high then suddenly dipped and dived, crashing into the wet sand at the edge of the ocean.

I watched as two surfers paddled against the choppy waters on their stomachs until they were past the breakers. Then, turning their boards around, sat up expectant and alert. They had the ocean to themselves, except for the lone swimmer far out. I could just make out a small dark head moving slowly parallel to the beach. Every few seconds a pale arm jutted out to take a stroke into the dark sea. A second later, another arm reaching out slowly pulled the swimmer forward a little more against the current.

Beachgoers were scattered here and there on the sand. A young couple, trying to have a picnic, turned their backs to the wind. An elderly man in a soft slouchy hat was painting a watercolor, his jar of water close beside him. He moved surreptitiously, not wanting to be disturbed. My watercolor teacher at El Camino College, Mr. Green, said no self-respecting watercolorist would ever use anything but a sable brush to paint with.

Once, in an art store, I found a thick sable brush in the watercolor section. It was wonderfully soft against my thumb, but it cost twenty dollars! Twenty dollars was an awful lot for one paintbrush! My friend Sara Lee or Sari, as she liked to be called, told me she could feed her whole family of four for a week on twenty dollars—but Sari made a lot of casseroles. Good old Sari, now that I was home again, I should look her up. We had had the same art teachers in college.

Close to the water a small boy of seven or eight was throwing out pieces of bread. A big gray seagull wheeled in the air and dived down, snapping up the pieces greedily. Other gulls noticed and soon there was a crowd of them making cawing noises and demanding food. Now, the original bird was running back and forth in a kind of outraged hysteria—striking and flapping at the others trying to re-stake his claim to the spot. He would no sooner make one gull skitter away when another dropped down. It was a regular melee as more birds joined the fray, pecking, squabbling, and snatching for food as the boy continued to throw out bread.

"Fight! Fight!" he called out gleefully, jumping up and down, letting out several high-pitched cackles.

What a funny little banshee, I thought, *but who says banshee anymore?* It must have been one of my mother's expressions from her childhood. She still called a refrigerator an "ice box" and her purse a "pock-a-book." She had probably said to us growing up "You're acting like a bunch of banshees" too.

By now the little banshee had run out of bread, and the seagulls drifted away, but I was still thinking of Mom. I guess I would be visiting her soon in the hospital. Was there a bus? Could

I depend on Jeff's truck not to break down? There was a lot to arrange now that I was back. I could see that, but right now I just wanted to relax in the nice sun by this nice warm wall for a while.

Like me, there were others enjoying the wall. A few were reading a book or magazine. One woman was getting a head start on her tan by holding a reflector made from cardboard covered with thin aluminum foil. It folded out like a three-part book, and she held it under her chin and stayed very still with her eyes closed.

HIM

The sun was making me groggy and my eyes closed again. *Yes,* I thought dreamily, *today is very much like when we all first came to live at the beach.* I got that job right away at the dime store on Pier Avenue (I always did like dime stores). On my breaks I used to sit on that cement bench right on the Strand and draw the people walking by. *I was quite the artist,* I thought, *and wasn't it just a week or two later that I met* him? I opened my eyes suddenly. Oh no, I was not going there. I was not going to moon about my ex-boyfriend anymore. Hadn't I gone off to Hollywood just to show him I was not going to sit waiting for him to come crawling back to me? Well, he didn't, and it was better not to dwell on the breakup and my broken heart. *I won't even say his name even to myself,* I decided. That would only make that area right below my breastbone ache. From now on I would just refer to my first—and so far, only—boyfriend as *Him. But soon,* I reminded myself, *I will be hearing his name said out loud, probably very often. I had better be prepared.* My body stiffened a little. *I will remain calm and show a composed face,* I vowed. I had my pride. Yet, now that I was living back home, it was only a matter of time before I would actually see him—on the beach, in town, in one of the stores, even at Culper Court. He had always liked my family—that was one of the reasons I liked him. I suddenly felt colder and realized a cloud had momentarily covered the low sun. I reached into my jacket and pulled out the paper Arlene had given me. Carefully I unfolded it and started to read.

HOWARD K. SMALL, A STORY BY LENA GIBSON

"Well, well," I reflected. "It looks like Arlene is giving up her married name of Brower and going back to her maiden name." I wasn't surprised by the change of Lena for Arlene though. My sister had always hated her name. It was our father, Harry, who was responsible for it. He was going to name her Lorraine after the romantic popular song by Nat King Cole until he was confronted with his daughter's big fat baby face staring up at him with its little fuzz of hair. "Oh no," he laughed. "With cheeks like these, this is no Lorraine. This little 'house Frau' should be called Arlene," and then, paradoxically, never called her anything but Lena. I was the one who finally got the name of Lorraine, and Arlene never let me forget it.

A PLAN TO HAVE NO PLAN

I was still smiling when I folded the Howard caricature and put it back in my jacket pocket. *What a character*, I thought. I couldn't wait to meet this guy—this burly, fortyish bespectacled man with his strange medley of facial tics—blinking eyes, head jerks, and asthmatic snorts. Yet, he was a kind of poet who wrote music and could talk about anything from jazz to philosophy. *I guess things will be very lively at Culper Court and hey, that story was pretty good—funny too.* I didn't know Arlene could write.

It was a bit overblown in some spots, like the line "He erupted forth like an infested boil masturbating with every idea . . ." Ugh, not something I wanted to visualize, but it was pure Arlene.

Maybe she should give up singing and be a writer? I thought. No, she was in a good place at the moment—working with a pianist who liked her voice and had new songs for her to sing, and she was in love—I didn't forget that. I was the one who was in Limbo—finished with college, just lost my boyfriend, and failed in my first attempt to leave home. What would I do now? I sat back against the wall. *Here's a thought*, I told myself . . . *Maybe it's time for a break—like when the referee blows his whistle and the game clock stops ticking? That's what I need, a "time-out."* I let this new idea jell for a while. One thing I shouldn't do, I told myself, was to feel that I *needed* to do anything. I would live one day at a time until I knew what direction to take. *It's my time-out, and I'm going to do whatever comes along*, I vowed triumphantly.

But what *would* I do? My art supplies were all tied up in boxes, and, in truth, there was no room. I didn't even have a place to sleep yet. My toes scrunched harder in the sand; already there was a hitch in my plans. OK, why not do like Arlene and write? Maybe I could turn my talent for art into a talent for words? I had a feeling things would be happening in a different way now that I was living with Arlene and company. I could be the one to tell the story of the Gibsons and Culper Court before it slid into the dump. I remembered something my mother liked to say when things were going crazy or wrong: at a certain point she would proclaim, "Someday we will look back on this and laugh." *Yeah, Mom*, I thought, *and maybe if I can put it all down right, we* will *laugh about it.*

The more I thought, the more I liked the idea. Yes, the story of *us* shall be written! I could explain everything that had happened since our father had left us to fend for ourselves. Speaking of Harry, he would probably have expected me to make the story all about him. After all, wasn't he the famous Harry the Hipster Gibson, jazz musician, recording artist, entertainer par excellence, and the personification of the hip jazz scene?

The public gobbled up these stories—even movies were made but one thing always bothered me. Nobody ever asked about what happened to the family of those celebrated people that got left behind. Now I had to stop and smirk at the idea that *I* would be the one to write that story. The book would start when we had to sell our house and move to the farmlands of Riverside. I thought for a moment. Ugh, Riverside, that was when our happy suburban life collapsed and Mom had to find work to support us all. Then, there were our teenage years with my sister's early marriage and children, my older brother joining the Navy, and my little brother dropping out of high school and spending time in Juvenile Hall. As for me, I had almost accepted the fact that I would have to live in Riverside forever.

Wait a minute! What am I doing! First, I say I am taking a time-out—one day at a time and the next thing I know I have given myself the assignment of writing another Moby Dick. Forget all that, I'm just going to keep a log and if a funny story happens, I will write it down. I really did have to relax about this "time-out" thing. No *Moby Dick*, but I thought I should at least try to write a little something now to see how it would go. I scrounged around in my pockets and bag for a working ballpoint and some paper and looked around for inspiration. Lindee was playing in the sand not far from me. I watched for a bit then started writing. *Remember*, I told myself, *just use words to paint a picture.*

LINDEE

Nearby, Lindee is sitting with one brown leg tucked under her—the fine white hairs forming patterns against her tan skin. She is quietly pouring sand crabs into a cardboard cup murmuring to them as she counts. The straight blonde hair-cut frames her face like a platinum moon. For a moment she looks up and the sun catches the blue-green sparks in her eyes. At six, Lindee has already decided to be a dancer. She can spontaneously improvise a dance, whirling and gliding to Stravinsky or bumping and grinding to the score of

Gypsy. Now, however, she is only concerned with singing to the crabs.

Not a bad start to my writing career, I decided, rereading it twice and making some corrections. The beach was almost empty now, the sun turning paler as it neared the water. A fishing boat was chugging in the distance toward the Redondo Pier. It was getting darker and most of the people had gone. The last of them were gathering bags and towels and dragging off tired children who weakly protested. Ruby-eyed pigeons, gray and quick, darted forward to peck at the few bits of sandwiches and potato chips left by the vanishing people. A sharp wind whipped up from nowhere. I shivered. "Come on, Lindee! Let's get everyone together and go home."

CHAPTER 4
LIFE FELL INTO A PATTERN

AND
FROM THE GRAY NOTEBOOK
THE MUSIC ROOM

I FIND MY PLACE

Arlene and I took care of the house together. She had a lot more tolerance for clutter and disorder than I did and, for the most part, wasn't exactly an inspired cook. To tell the truth, it was only after all the silverware was gone from the drawer, or all the clothes were unwashed and every bobby pin gone from her makeup kit, that my sister felt it necessary to straighten things up.

It would be my self-appointed job to put the milk back in the refrigerator, screw the lids back on the coffee, peanut butter, and mayonnaise jars; and too often it was also my job to turn off the flame left burning on the stove. Yet, it was useless to try to change my sister. Arlene was Arlene. "She was always a scatter-brain!" our mother would sigh in resignation. My sister ran hot and cold. She was either up or down. There were times she would be yelling frantically at the kids, then, moments later, be singing and dancing with them. While I could nurse a grudge for days,

Arlene could never stay mad for long because, two minutes later, she had forgotten what set her off in the first place.

If I was the one who put things in their places, Jeff was the carpenter and fixer-upper of clogged drains, frayed wires, and the builder of forts for the children. That is, whenever we could drag him away from practicing his alto sax. To accommodate me, my brother had moved out of the loft above the living room and made his bed temporarily on the floor of the music room. I gratefully left my mashed-potato couch and moved up into the attic space. A wooden ladder led to my new bedroom. I crawled into this dim triangle of slanted roof each night. It was not high enough to walk upright, but I managed to get around on my knees, which did make it pretty awkward dressing in the morning. A mattress on a box spring and an overhead light were the only objects inhabiting this tight space. I brought in some cardboard cartons containing clothes and artwork and lined them up along the wall under the pitched ceiling. My few dresses were hung on a short pole extended across the opening of the loft like a sort of curtain giving me some privacy. When I lay in bed at night, I could look down and see the living room and look up and see where the termites ate intricate patterns in the wooden beams of the roof. Every morning, a patch of sunlight woke me as it slanted in through the one tiny window where the roof peaked. Usually by then, I could hear the kids downstairs getting ready for school, and I would crawl down the ladder and fix breakfast.

Lindee was in the second grade. Donnie, younger, was in the first. Laurie J., at almost four, happily stayed home and played contentedly by herself. It was Lindee's self-appointed job, she told me, to wake Donnie for school. She would call and shake him and sometimes, she told me, even had to sock him in the eye before he finally got up. Even so, they were always late. At last up, they would rummage through a box of clothes and somehow dress themselves from the odd assortment they found there.

Many of their clothes were hand-me-downs, thrift store finds, or "Arlene creations" that she would whip up on the old sewing machine. Sometimes, it was a combination of items that made up their outfit to school, like a pair of Goodwill corduroy pants topped off with a velvet blouse with a lace collar Arlene had fashioned from an old doily.

Living on my own had sparked an interest in cooking. So, with the limited resources I had at hand (I looked on this as a challenge to my budding culinary skills), I took over morning breakfast for the kids. It had to be cheap and nutritious—oatmeal was the obvious choice. I tried to make it more interesting, adding raisins and cinnamon and nutmeg. At least, the kids ate it and it was the best thing to be in their stomachs to get them through the school day. Off they would go in their special outfits—holes in their twisted tights and elastic waistbands ready to give way at any time during a game of tag or dodgeball.

With the kids off to school, Arlene would wake up and we would have breakfast and sit around talking over coffee. Jeff didn't wake sometimes until noon. Almost twenty, he was already a night owl, prowling the town in the wee hours looking for places to hear jazz, scanning deserted spots to practice his horn or perhaps just romping through the alleyways, his eye out to find treasures people had thrown away.

I TAKE ANOTHER STAB AT WRITING

One day, after lunch, I took a break from sweeping the bedrooms and dining room and threw myself on my old friend Lumpy Couch. Putting my feet on the overstuffed arms, I leaned back and surveyed the rooms. Jeff was still honking away nearby in the music room as I looked around. *This would be a good time to document my surroundings,* I thought, so I rounded up a pen and some paper. *Perhaps I should just describe what I see? Would that work out?* I wondered. I wrote down INSIDE THE RED HOUSE then stopped to think.

Everything was so different from when I had lived here with my mother while I had been going to City College. Then, the little house was neat and tidy. There were no missing doorknobs or broken windowpanes around the door—no rusty bikes on the porch either. It was the living room that had drastically changed though. Before, the only focal point in the small, low-ceilinged room was the red brick fireplace with its wall-to-wall bookshelves. Now, the bookcases and that ceiling were completely gone.

After Mom moved out, the story goes, Arlene, on a whim, started knocking down the ceiling—just knocked it out without moving or covering anything below. For weeks, plaster dust and shards of dark splintery wood still clung to some of the furniture and rugs. Then, not satisfied, she continued on, demolishing the floor-to-ceiling bookcases. Suddenly, the whole space was opened up. By uniting the living room with what had been the largest bedroom, Arlene had expanded the entire area to twice its original size and the bedroom became the music room.

Looking up now through the open beams, I noted how, with the low ceiling gone, the living room rose into a high peaked roof. *A kind of wooden cathedral*, I thought dreamily. *Should I write about that?* After some thought, I decided to describe just one room—the new music room would certainly be enough fodder for a writing exercise. I crossed out "Inside the Red House" and put "The Music Room," then started writing. I even remembered to write in the present tense like I had decided to do at the beach that first day.

THE MUSIC ROOM

A step down past the fireplace brings you into what we now call "The Music Room." In former times, it had been my mother's bedroom. Now, there is no more green chenille bedspread and matching drapes on the French windows. Now, the room has a different purpose, dominated as it is by the large yellow-painted piano that leans heavily against the wall. An old-fashioned crank-up phonograph painted in the same buttercup yellow is nearby, and an upright bass rests on the floor.

That's a lot of yellow paint! Jeff must have come across a bucket of it in one of his nightly excursions and it looks like Arlene made good use of it?

In a far corner, a large black desk is piled high with boxes of art pencils, paints, and stacks of library books. The walls exhibit drawings, posters, and black-and-white portraits of the children.

Ah, yes, and "Taken by a real photographer too," my sister had proclaimed proudly to me just this morning.

The room has a slightly Oriental flavor due to a bamboo wind chime attached to a trumpet sculpture that is fastened on the ceiling along with the big purple parasol that hangs upside down, shading the light bulb. It casts lavender patterns of color on everything below. Also in an Oriental mood, are the two well-worn Indonesian wicker chairs with the curly scrollwork on top.

I could see the unsightly jumble of Jeff's bedding-mattress, blankets, and pillows, all in a tumble nearby but I decided to skip describing it because it was just temporary. Jeff had plans for his bed elsewhere, he said.

On a far wall, a collage is forming. A bowl with a paste of flour and water stands ready.

Unfortunately, it was now dry and crusty, having been mixed the day before.

The collage is shaping up nicely; several photos and pictures cut from magazines are emblazoned on the wall. More photographs and magazines overflow a box that sits on the already crowded desk. There is an interesting picture cut from a magazine of Rembrandt's "Socrates Contemplating the Bust of Plato."

Or is it "Plato Contemplating the Bust of Socrates" or "Aristotle Contemplating the Bust of . . ."? Oh, well, it doesn't matter they will all be on the wall soon.

Already pasted are photographs of us and pictures of musicians, actors, artwork, and poems.

Well, that should be enough, I thought and put down my pen. I remembered the night Arlene and I started the collage. Midway through, I caught her staring up at it in deep thought.

"I wonder," she reflected soberly, "whether the landlord will mind if we do this to his wall?"

I had to laugh. "You are worrying about a little glue stuck on the wall? My God," I exclaimed. "You tore out an entire ceiling and a wall, and Jeff knocked out the back bedroom and cantilevered it three more feet to make room for the kids, and now he says he has plans of building God knows what under the back porch for his new bedroom and suddenly you think the landlord might mind a collage?"

Arlene had a bemused smile on her face as she recalled her past carnage.

I continued, "Why, I haven't seen our landlord since Mom and I first started renting here three years ago. And as far as I know, he hasn't set foot inside since that time. My guess," I went on, "is that as long as you pay the fifty dollars rent, you have nothing to worry about. He won't care what you do as long as you don't bother him for anything!"

Now, relaxing farther into the couch, I had to smile at how funny my sister's mind worked. Stretching luxuriously, I took a final look around. From where I sat, I could almost see every room—living room, music room, and through the arched door-way, the dining room. I could even see part of the tub in the bathroom because the door was left open, as usual.

But getting back to the living room, I had always liked it—the fireplace and thick plaster walls. Even in my days with Mom, they were hung with original paintings and charcoal drawings— all mine of course. Now, some of my work was still here but other artists had joined them. A crayon drawing of a caterpillar by one of the kids and a big charcoal of a naked old woman with hang-ing breasts filled the wall in front of me. The big-breasted woman was by Sari, as she liked to sign them. Sari was also a friend of Arlene's as well as a good friend of mine. They both had kids about the same age and babysat for each other. I reminded myself again that I should get in touch with Sara Lee soon. Of course, there not being a telephone at Culper Court made contacting people diffi-cult. My sister had either never gotten the phone turned on in her name when Mom left or she had, and it had been turned off for lack of payment.

I guess I'll run into Sara Lee in due time. I reminded myself again, *I'm on a "time-out," remember?*

My mind wandered back to the living room. Gazing fondly at the window seat that housed the TV, radio, and record player, I slowly realized that a pair of Laurie J.'s shoes and one tennis shoe belonging to Donnie were wedged between the TV and the wall. *The kids are as bad with their shoes as we are with our coffee cups,* I thought. Empty mugs were everywhere—on the fireplace, coffee table, window ledges, and on the floor by the sofa and the Indonesian wicker chairs with the curly scrollwork on top. I made a mental note to gather them up when I went to the kitchen for coffee but I hadn't quite finished the survey of my surroundings yet.

Facing the fireplace was what I thought must be the pièce de résistance of the room. It was a gift from Paul Milner, a friend of Arlene's who worked in amateur theater helping with props and set designs. Apparently, one of their productions had been *Breakfast at Tiffany's* because an exact replica of Holly Golightly's bathtub sofa graced our living room. It was fun to sit in it and pretend to be Audrey Hepburn. Painted a luminous gold on the inside and furbished with a red velvet cushion, it squatted in front of the fireplace on its short legs like Buddha contemplating the meaning of life. As I looked closer, I noticed a small piece of charred wood stuck into the nylon fibers of the little green rug in front of the bathtub.

Alarmed, I thought, *We really do need a screen for that fireplace! Maybe Jeff can concoct it or find one in his nightly searches.*

CHAPTER 5
JEFF

MORE PATTERNS

Between the house, kids, and all of us taking turns bouncing to and fro to the hospital in Jeff's rattletrap van visiting Mom, time was somehow squeezed in for music. Arlene, after doing her scales and breath exercises for her singing, could be heard a little later plunking away at a big bass someone had loaned her, swearing and crying at her mistakes and sore fingers. Jeff almost never stopped playing his horn. He was wonderfully oblivious to everything going on around him, pausing only to eat and sleep. Not to be outdone, I got out my old beginner's piano book and started teaching myself to play all over again on the old yellow upright that Jeff had installed in the music room. Where he had found this relic was anyone's guess.

Lately, he had been skulking around in the evening with his friend Tad. Tad, short for Thomas A. Duke, was the newest of his acquaintances. They made a strange pair. Jeff, all shaggy and rumpled, Tad, immaculate in a sharp suit with narrow lapels and a thin sober tie.

Jeff picked up people the way he collected interesting junk, like the rusty bikes on the porch. He told me he figured when he gathered up enough parts, he would someday assemble them all into one complete bike. And like the leftover parts of junk, Jeff collected people. His friends fell into the same categories of misfits, outcasts, and oddballs. Many were musicians or wannabe musicians he would gather to make up an ad hoc band. He wasn't picky. If you had a harmonica or a bongo drum, you could join him in song. If you could only play four chords on a guitar, that was good enough to be in the ensemble at Culper Court. I truly believe that if Jeff had ever run across a guy sitting on a porch blowing a high C into a bottle, he would probably have snatched him up too. Jeff just wanted to play music.

When my brother was a little boy, he was extremely shy and hardly talked at all. Then, when he was thirteen, he found his voice in an old C melody alto saxophone in a hockshop. He scraped together his money and bought it, then taught himself how to play songs by ear. To learn more, he bought records of jazz saxophone musicians like Earl Bostic, Eddie "Lock Jaw" Davis, and Jeff's personal god, Charlie "Yardbird" Parker. In junior high band class, he learned to read music, but after dropping out of high school in his sophomore year, he was pretty much on his own as far as his musical direction went. His latest idol was the outrageous Ornette Coleman who preached the gospel of "Free Jazz," which threw out all the rules of music. There were no set chords or melodies, there were no scales or keys to adhere to, there were no wrong notes—it was a musical free-for-all, an anything-goes philosophy, and that suited Jeff just fine.

Most days, he happily honked and squawked along with Ornette records, although he still liked to play ballads and "woodshed," as he called it, by running scales and chord progressions.

THE MUSIC LESSON

At that moment, as if hearing his name, Jeff suddenly stopped his practicing and peeked around the fireplace that separated the music room from the living room.

"Want some ko-ffee?" he bleated out.

Wow, talk about mental telepathy! Wasn't I just thinking of Jeff?

When my brother and I were very young, people thought we were twins, "the two little blonde kids with the great big eyes," they would say. We were two years apart but the same size, and it seemed at times that we were twins. I knew what he was thinking or what he would say before he said it or what he would do before he did it. When I dreamed, he was usually there too. Jeff was closer to Arlene now that he'd been living here with her and the kids, but maybe the bond between us was still there.

It was funny how quickly I got used to his constant practicing. All those scales running forward and backward were mesmerizing. I was sometimes only aware when he *stopped* playing. I hadn't even included him in my written description of the music room, and he was right there all along. If I was unaware of Jeff, Jeff was unaware of everything else when he played his alto sax. He was oblivious to people knocking at the door, the kids running in and out, and probably wouldn't hear it if Arlene tore down another wall. He was the most dedicated person to his art that I had ever known. Practicing the sax, learning piano, writing, arranging, or just listening to music was his life. He would study his theory books at the beach, humming his lessons out loud, while the surfers stared at him. They called him "The Mad Beatnik." He'd practice continually, pausing occasionally to fix a loose key on his sax with a piece of wire or rubber band. I had often been lulled to sleep with major and minor scales and other strange patterns of notes he repeated faithfully into the night.

In the music room, Jeff took the record he had been tooting along with off the old Victrola and carefully put it away in its paper jacket. Jeff was a total slob about most things but not with anything to do with music. That done, he yawned and stretched noisily then staggered toward the kitchen. Jeff didn't walk like anyone else. He leaned forward, almost to falling, then at the last moment caught himself and stumbled ahead in his heavy black boots.

Stopping by me on the couch now, he asked again in his comical way, shyly looking at me through a forest of thick lashes. "Want some ko-ffee?" he said in a low soft voice, mumbling and slurring his words. Every now and then he'd clear his throat self-consciously. *He is like a big shaggy amiable dog*, I thought, *especially when the kids are hanging all over him.* You wanted to hug him then give him a bath or cut his hair.

Arlene said once, "If people don't like Jeff, there must be something wrong with them."

During this reverie, Jeff was still hovering by the couch looking at me with a questioning face. "Oh, no thanks, Jeff," I said quickly. "Not just yet, I'll make some myself in a little while."

One soon learned not to accept the coffee he brewed. Arlene said it always tasted like crankcase oil. Jeff must have been used to this rejection of his coffee and just shrugged and scratched at his chin, disturbing the outcropping of blonde hair that grew there. He called this thin bit of fuzz his Dizzy Gillespie goatee, but, in truth, it was more like a bit of Shredded Wheat left over from breakfast than anything else. After another scratch, Jeff moved on.

There was some rattling and clinking in the kitchen along with some humming. Soon Jeff was staggering back with a steaming mug in his hand. He sat down on the Holly Golightly sofa and put his cup of coffee on the brick ledge of the fireplace. He was still humming. Leaning forward, he stirred his coffee with a spoon. It made tinkling noises. Jeff stopped to listen then he hummed the same sound. Getting up he walked to the piano and plunked a note on one of the keys. He came back smiling. "B flat!" he said.

"I thought so." Then sat down again and took a big swig of his coffee.

Jeff's face was dominated completely by his large eyes—grayish-blue with sparks of yellow around the pupils. His lids were heavy, giving him a sad, sleepy expression. Most striking were his thick, dark, black eyelashes and eyebrows—eyebrows that ran above his strange eyes in one furry line.

"Ah," he said now, smacking his lips in pleasure and wiping with his sleeve at the excess coffee caught in the straggle of hair on his chin. "Now that's real coffee!" He thought for a moment, then, threw back his head and sang out "Deep, dark, delicious Yuban!"

"Actually, Jeff," I said, "I think the jar in the kitchen says Maxwell House coffee."

"I know." Jeff smiled his crooked smile and one cheekbone jutted out. "I was just practicing my intervals. Did you know that the first two notes in the Yuban Coffee commercial is a minor seventh backwards?"

"What do you mean intervals?" I said. "What are intervals?"

Jeff assumed a professorial air. "Intervals are the spaces between notes—like say, if we start from C it would be called the *first* note. Then, the next note D is called the *second* note or *interval*. And E would be the *third interval* and so forth until you come to C again.

"Oh," I said, getting the idea.

Encouraged, Jeff went on, "Yes, and I'm practicing what intervals sound like so I will know them when I hear them. I have developed a little trick. For each interval I have found a familiar song or melody that has the same two-note intervals. So now all I have to do is think of the melody of the song and then I can sing the interval. What do you think the song is for a whole octave? That would be, in this case, from C to the next C. Or, then," Jeff sang out, "from C to shining C." And shyly smiled at his musical joke.

"I don't know," I said, smiling a little myself.

"Aw, that's an easy one. It's the first two notes of 'Over the Rainbow.' You can never forget that can you? Go ahead, why don't you sing it?"

I quavered out the first two notes of the famous song from *The Wizard of Oz*. "Kinda hard to sing," I said, embarrassed.

"Well of course, it's a full octave. Judy Garland could do it when she was sixteen. I don't know about now though. She has lost a lot of her pure voice now that she is older and mostly quavers when she hits notes."

My brother didn't talk much, but when you got him started on music, oh boy! Now he pulled out a rumpled piece of paper and smoothed it out on the fireplace ledge next to his coffee.

"I haven't got a song for every interval yet, and then don't forget there are also all the minor note intervals to learn too." He took another swig of his coffee. "Sure you don't want a sip? I put oregano in it this time."

I shook my head no and let him continue the lecture.

"Now, guess what song this interval is." Jeff sang out two notes.

"I know! I know that one!" I said, excited. "It's from *Westside Story*. It's the first two notes of 'Somewhere.'"

Jeff nodded and took another glug of his coffee. "And now," he said, "you will always think of a minor seventh interval whenever you hear that song. And did you know that if you added a third and a fifth interval to that you would have a dominant seventh chord?"

"Enough, enough," I said. "I'm getting confused."

"OK—but you should learn chords. I hear you plunking on the piano, trying to play music. Here is the deal. If you just learn to play the melody of the treble clef with your right hand then also learned to play the chords with your left, you could be on your way to playing the piano again. You could take on any song written in a fake book. You could even play one of Howard K. Small's songs, and they are weird."

"Really?" I was getting interested. How hard could it be to learn a few chords? I also wondered what a "fake book" could be.

Jeff had gone back to humming intervals again. Every so often he would stop and write something down on the piece of paper. At last, he stopped for a cigarette. Reaching into his shirt pocket, he pulled out a much-handled pack of cigarettes and a twisted book of matches. Carefully, he lit up and sat back in the Holly Golightly bathtub sofa, alternating gulps of coffee with inhaling the smoke of the cigarette deeply into his lungs.

Sometime later, after finishing his coffee and puffing out many spectacular white smoke rings that floated up through the rafters, Jeff looked at the pack of Camels in his hand.

"Damn, only two left. These things are expensive—thirty-five cents a pack now!" He was quiet for a bit. "I think I'll have to take up the pipe or start to roll my own from now on." He looked sadly at the depleted package then at his cigarette. "This is almost my last one." His cigarette was burning low by now. "Well, anyway we can have a nice fire in the fireplace." And with that, he balled up some old newspapers and magazines and stuffed them and a cardboard box into the fireplace. With the last of his cigarette, he ignited the paper.

After a few seconds, the magazines and paper caught fire. Moments later the cardboard exploded into a great blaze. Huge flames reached up and out, licking the wood mantel above like a great red tongue. The bronze plates propped up there seemed to dance as they reflected the flickering light of the blaze. Almost as quickly as it arose, the flame died down, as did the roaring and snapping sounds. A moment later all flammable contents had subsided like one great sigh.

"That reminds me, Jeff," I said, looking again at the old charred piece of wood still stuck to the green rug. "Do you think you could get us a screen for the fireplace sometime?"

"Sure, sure, I'll keep my eye out for one, but right now I need to work on fixing up my digs under the stairs of the back deck. It will be a great cool place to be when summer comes. I figure I can use some of that wood on the front porch. It's not so cold anymore, so we won't need it for firewood."

"It hardly seems enough," I quipped.

"Oh, that's just for starters. Tonight, I thought I'd go down to that new construction site with Tad and pick me up a few two-by-fours and planks. That will do for a start. And I think I saw some large pieces of plywood in the dump."

Our conversation, or maybe it was the roar of the fire, must have awakened Laurie J. who had been asleep in the back room. She tottered out into the living room rubbing her eyes and made straight for Jeff. Without a word, except for a soft chortling sound in her throat that was more for herself than communication with others, she climbed into Jeff's lap and made herself comfortable. Jeff accommodated her by stubbing out his cigarette in a nearby mayonnaise jar lid. With his hand free now, he started to lightly tickle her stomach while she giggled, making little heh, heh, heh sounds, and reached up and played with his shaggy goatee. Jeff still continued his interval humming but now added a rocking motion for the benefit of Laurie J. Every now and then he stopped to add another interval to his list. *How peaceful it can be here sometimes*, I thought, almost drifting away until a knock on the door sounded. By the second knock we were ready. Jeff and I and even Laurie J. called out, "Just come in through the window!"

JIM BISHOP

The knocking stopped. A few seconds later, we heard heavy steps moving away and soon the sound of jiggling at the French windows outside the music room. It burst open, and a large man with a simple but sweet face and a quizzical expression stepped inside. He looked around until he saw us. "It's Jim Bishop here," he slowly drawled. "Hey there, Jeff, remember me? You came into Sandow's Swap Shop where I work." Jim was now pulling a guitar case into the room. "You said if ever I was nearby I should bring my git-tar and we could play some music." Mr. Bishop acknowledged me then. "Howdy, Ma-am," he said with a smile and a nod.

Jeff rose with difficulty because Laurie J. was still clinging to him. He set her down gently then moved into the music room picking up his sax along the way. "Hey, yeah," he said to Jim. "Great to see you! Do you maybe know the blues in B flat?"

"B what?" Jim looked a little confused.

"Well then any kind of blues," responded Jeff gallantly. "It just means a sad song."

Jim brightened. "Well, I'm not sure about the B flat part, but I got plenty of really sad songs." He sat down in the Indonesian wicker chair with the curly scrollwork on top and positioned his guitar in his lap. "How about this here one?" Jim strummed a few chords in a kind of um-pa um-pa rhythm. "Bet you never heard this one a-for." And after a few more bars of um-pas, he broke into a high nasal voice. "I got tears in my ears from lying on my back cry-ing over yoo-ooou!" The last part of *you* ended in a high note, and I noted proudly to myself that it was an octave just like "Over the Rainbow." Without missing another beat, Jeff licked his mouthpiece and started playing.

I got up and proceeded to collect the coffee mugs, starting with the one Jeff left on the fireplace ledge.

. . . and sometimes the red cottage can be a magic one.

CHAPTER 6
TO MARKET TO MARKET

SHOPPING ON PIER AVENUE

Donnie and Laurie J. dashed for the nearest shopping cart and clambered aboard. Lindee, being older, stood beside the cart they had claimed and looked thoughtful, as if she were their mother running over a shopping list. It was eleven o'clock. We had come to Safeway Market early, or rather early for Arlene, in order to take advantage of the day-old bread that got put out on a special table. Even with the welfare check, Arlene seemed to run out of money before the month was over, and we had to economize.

"Ah-ha!" Arlene cried happily. "There you are, my pretties," she cooed, sounding very much like the Wicked Witch of the West as she ran to the half-price table and scooped up some hot cross buns and bear claws.

"We'll need bread for sandwiches too," I said, always the practical one. I was beginning to take my job of live-in auntie seriously.

Along with the day-old bakery items, was a special table for slightly worse-for-wear fruits and vegetables. I considered carefully the few choices that lay in the bin. There was celery, a bit limp, along with some rubbery carrots and bruised peaches. Some potatoes, already sprouted, were nestled next to a bunch of spotted bananas. Shrewdly, I made some quick calculations.

Hmmm, now if I pick up a sack of graham flour, I can make banana bread and a peach cobbler out of the fruit and with a few pinto beans I can parlay the vegetables into a hearty soup. "A nice soup bone here would really add flavor to it," I found myself saying out loud.

Arlene was onto the idea in a flash. "Ah, meat—a nice juicy steak sizzling—I can almost smell it!" She was still using her Wicked Witch voice.

With Laurie J. sitting inside the cart Buddha-like with her legs crossed and Donnie in the child's seat pretending to steer, I headed over to the butcher's counter with Lindee trailing close behind. "Ahoy, make way for land!" Donnie said. "We have to stop for supplies!"

"We sure do, Captain," I said, as we pulled up before the meat section. "Do you have any soup bones today?" I asked the stocky man behind the high glass counter.

"Yes, ma'am," he said, and expertly wrapped some thick, meaty bones in pink butcher paper, tying it quickly with string. "That will be one dollar please!" he said, as he slapped the tidy bundle onto the counter.

"A dollar," I gasped. "My mother says soup bones are always free!"

"Well, your mother must not shop at this market," replied the butcher with a slight smirk. "She was probably talking about back in the horse and buggy days."

Arlene had ambled over to the meat counter by this time and had caught the gist of the conversation. She studied the prices for a while, then, looking up at the butcher, sarcastically quipped,

"Heavens, man, don't you feel guilty charging these outrageous prices? Why, you're taking the food out of poor children's mouths. How do you sleep at night?"

"Look, lady," the butcher said looking annoyed, "I just work here."

Pushing her point further, Arlene continued, "You ought to quit your job out of self-respect. Why, paying sixty-nine cents a pound for hamburger is . . . is . . . un-American!" Arlene raised her arm in a defiant gesture, then put her hand over her heart for a more patriotic emphasis. I stepped in next to her to add support. The kids merely gaped.

"Do you want to buy something or not?" the butcher said, but his eyes started to look a little wary. He was eyeing Lindee, Donnie, and Laurie J. "You're wasting my time here."

Sensing weakness, Arlene laid on her coup de grâce. "You poor man, you look so glum back there with all the sausages. What do you get out of life slicing bloody beef all day? Where is the beauty? Where is the poetry? Is your life just about denying us a little bone to chew on?"

"All right, all right, take the damn bones and get out of here," the man thrust the pink bundle at us and turned his back. "No charge," he mumbled, throwing up his hands and walking into the back room.

Arlene clutched the package to her chest and scooted away, giggling. "Works every time."

I smiled to myself. That old un-American line did work most of the time. But I had to admit that our family was really not patriotic or political at all. We did not grow up with talks around the dinner table discussing current events and national news. With our father gone on musical tours most of the time, the dinner conversations were always kid dominated—the themes being school, friends, and what we would do on the weekend. Our mother would sit by quietly amused at our chatter. Being a musical family, sometimes the dinner included spontaneous entertainment—rollicking singing accompanied by clinking glasses and pounding rhythms on the table. It was only then that Mom would call a halt to the bedlam.

MORE SHOPPING

An hour later, we were headed for home, loaded down with groceries. It wasn't long before I could feel the bottom of my paper bag growing soggy from the celery. I hoped it would hold up until we reached home and made a mental note to bring the kids' wagon next time we came to the market. Walking home, we looked into store windows, commenting and criticizing everything, as Arlene and I liked to do. Soon, we came to the Logan Fabric Store. Arlene looked at me. "What do you think? Should we go in? Maybe they have some good stuff in the remnant box today. I have an idea for a new dress."

"Or maybe," I said, "if you let old Mr. Logan give you a pinch on your behind, he will give you a markdown on a yard of velveteen."

"OK, let's move on," Arlene sighed, remembering the encounter with the little man and his rambling fingers, but as we moved passed, Arlene looked longingly back at the store.

Soon, we were passing the thrift shop. We tried to fight the irresistible impulse of rummaging. Usually, Arlene and I could never go by these stores without going in to see what goodies we could find. Much of our home accessories and wardrobe could be traced back to this store. A real find, according to Arlene, had been the day she had unearthed a child-sized lederhosen outfit, a perfect fit for Donnie.

As far as great finds go, Jeff was the supreme specialist. He took top honors for his discoveries during his nocturnal treks. Always keeping his eyes alert for wonderful riches in abandoned houses and alleyways, he had single-handedly provided the house with its most unique possessions. It was he who was responsible for the two Indonesian wicker chairs with the curly scrollwork on top. We liked them even though they were slightly dented, and the straw wicker was unraveling in places. And let us not forget that heavy, oak bed frame he dragged home for Arlene. It barely fit into her tiny bedroom but she loved it. Truth be told, Jeff always considered the crème de la crème find of them all to be the tiny antique Grandma Moses stove he carted home one night. Today, however, nothing struck our fancy, and searching around was pretty difficult with the groceries slipping, getting soggier by the minute, and Laurie J. and Donnie playing hide and seek under the dress racks.

"Maybe we will have better luck in the alleys," said Arlene puffing through the celery leaves sticking out of her bag. "I think I saw another great straw chair like the ones Jeff found in that abandoned house last year. Keep a lookout for it as we go home, guys," she said. "If we see it, we will have to send Jeff down for it later tonight."

"Hey, Mommy, here's something good!" shouted Donnie enthusiastically behind us. "Do you want this?" he said as he pulled an ugly lampshade out of a garbage can and waved it in the air.

"Donnie, stop that this minute! Don't be such a garbage picker," Arlene said, turning bright red and marching quickly away from him as if he had no connection to her.

"But, Mommy, you said . . ." Donnie looked bewildered, then shrugged and ran to catch up with us.

CHAPTER 7
RITA

AND
FROM THE GRAY NOTEBOOK
RITA'S KITCHEN

THE MACKEYS

We turned the corner on Eighth Street and walked up the hill toward Rita's house. The Mackeys were good friends, and her house was our usual pit stop when we had a shopping day. Rita had four children, the two youngest just about the same ages as Lindee and Donnie.

"Do you want to drop in?" I asked. "Maybe Rita will have a spare paper bag." My celery was now threatening to drop out of the bottom of my sack.

"I don't think we'd better right now," Arlene replied. "Rita has been pretty upset lately, ever since Steven D. suddenly up and married some girl from Inglewood."

"What?" I said. "But they were together for—"

"Three years," Arlene cut in. "And they fought the whole time."

My mind flashed to the last time I had seen Rita and Steven together. It was at the production of *The Taming of the Shrew* at El

Camino, my old alma mater. Rita and Steven had the title roles. There they were—our friend and her explosive boyfriend, dressed in lavish Renaissance costumes, battling it out.

I had known Rita was an actress, but had never seen her perform until that time. I soon realized she commanded attention the moment she stepped onto the stage—just by the way she stood and spoke or moved. She had a kind of energy. Now I knew what was meant by having stage presence, and when she and Steven were together in a scene it was truly electric as they battled for supremacy. Later, Rita told me that it was all too real, and she had the bruises to prove it. Maybe that was the beginning of the end for them, and now he had gone and married some girl from Inglewood.

"I think we should move on and let her recuperate," Arlene said, breaking into my thoughts.

"Gee," Donnie burst out plaintively, "I never get to play with Fallon anymore."

"Or me with Mary," added Lindee.

"Pu-lease!" Donnie entreated.

"And this bag will never make it home," I put in.

"Well, OK," Arlene said, "but if she is in one of her stormy moods . . ." Arlene tapered off in mid-sentence as we turned into the brick patio in front of the house and walked up to the door.

Rita and her children lived in a small bungalow with fading red shingles and white trim, the front flanked by beds of haphazard flowers hugging the sides of the house. We noticed that the front door was halfway open.

Tapping with the brass knocker, the children called out, "Rita! You home?"

A bright voice from within responded. "Come in. Come in, you little darlings!"

Inside, the entrance opened to a very short hall flanked by a sun porch on either side. The interior then spread wide like a grin into the living room—its straw hemp rug dotted with toys and encrusted peanut butter. Except for a gold-painted fireplace surrounded by three modern wire chairs and books that were stacked, piled, and stuck in every conceivable place, for our friend was an avid reader, the room was quite bare.

One of the sun porches housed a daybed with a pumpkin-colored throw on it. A young girl about twelve years old sat reading a book quietly. Of Rita's three daughters, Christine was the second oldest and the most serious. She wore glasses, and her uncooperative curly blonde hair was carefully pulled back in a low ponytail.

In the living room, a wooden bar with two battered high stools separated the kitchen from the main room, and there behind it stood Rita smiling. It was a bit startling to see that she was practically naked, wrapped only in a towel—her bare backside peeking out coyly.

"Come in, come in, my beauties and your little kiddies too," she called out gaily. "You are just in time for coffee." Rita turned and put a kettle of water on the stove, further exposing even more of her rear end. "Ohhhhh, I have so much to tell you, so much has happened. So sit down, make yourselves comfortable, and I will be back in a minute. I have just finished my sunbathing, so you caught me just at the right time for a tête-à-tête." And with that, she tripped away down the hallway, again exposing her behind. As Rita opened a back bedroom door, the high-pitched giggles and squeals of teenaged girls, along with loud rock and roll music escaped from the room. "Yeah! Yeah! Yeah!" bleated the record until the door slammed shut. Now only muffled sounds were heard.

"Here you are!" Rita set two steaming
mugs of coffee before us on the counter.

Lindee, Donnie, and Laurie J. started looking around, calling for Mary and Fallon, then stopped when they heard thumping going on upstairs. Christine looked up from her book and made a gesture with her finger. "Hey, guys, go up. They're playing in the attic." Then she quickly returned to her book. The kids happily rambled off, disappearing up the stairs where soon more thumping was heard.

Arlene and I settled on the old yellow stools and pleasantly leaned our elbows on the bar.

How like Rita all this is, I thought, looking around as my new interest in writing kicked in. *I should try to capture Rita's kitchen like I did the music room.* I felt I was getting better the more I wrote and had discovered after rereading my description of the music room, that it had inadvertently explained a lot about my brother and sister. I should try to do the same with Rita's kitchen. I started to imagine what I would write as I looked around.

RITA'S KITCHEN

The bar countertop of Rita's kitchen is never ever entirely empty. Today it holds a multitude of apothecary jars stuffed with nuts and raisins and other dried fruit for children to gobble when they are hungry. There are knives and spoons sticky with honey and peanut butter; there is one pink light bulb, an empty container of wheat germ, and one perky carnation in a cocktail glass.

Pinned up around the bar on every vacant wall space, is an avalanche of clippings and announcements for concerts and plays and ballets and lectures. These tell us that a very busy art lover lives here. Loads of just-washed dishes are draining on a rack by the sink. Pots and cooking utensils hang from nails on the walls while others balance precariously atop the refrigerator, a white enamel monolith that stands tall and blank against the beautiful clutter of it all.

Is that all? I wondered. Oh, I almost forgot the other side of the bar. I don't even have to look to know what's there.

The other side of the bar is for storage. Here, open shelves are filled with more of Rita's fascinating foodstuffs. Rita is an avowed health nut so in the depths of her cupboard you will find bottles of vitamins and minerals covering the entire spectrum of the alphabet and the elements. Along with boxes of wheat germ and jars of un-hydrogenated peanut butter, is a five-pound jar of clover honey. There would definitely have to be in there, too, a few loaves of one hundred percent cracked whole wheat bread on which to spread all the peanut butter and honey, and, if my memory is correct, there will still be room for a few boxes of enriched powdered milk.

Arlene gave me a sharp nudge with her elbow. "Hey, little sister," she said in a slightly peeved voice, "what are you staring at with that weird look on your face? Come back to earth, will ya? Where do you go when you zone out like that? What were you thinking about anyway? OK, OK, I know you won't tell me. You've always been my secretive sister. I tell you everything, you tell me nothing."

Arlene was right, she had always confided her every thought, daydream, and crush of the heart with me, whereas I had learned early on to keep my mouth shut about my own fears and desires. My sister, four years older, had towered over me until I was in high school and because of her hot temper and rapier tongue, I had to be careful what I told her. Before I smartened up, early childhood fights had ended with me crushed and angrily slinking off to nurse my wounded pride while Arlene would forget the whole thing and a few minutes later wonder why I was giving her the silent treatment. Today however, she didn't press me further. Together, we looked over some of the more interesting flyers and announcements on the walls while we listened for the boiling of the kettle and waited for Rita to come back. Before she could return, I leaned over to Arlene and whispered, "Rita seemed to have recovered nicely from the defection of Mr. Steven D. In fact, I have never seen her so blooming."

"We shall see, we shall see," Arlene whispered back, then smacked me on the arm. "Why are we whispering?"

JARED

A few moments later, Arlene started to squirm around in her seat. "Hmm, stopping here was a good idea 'cause I've gotta use the bathroom." She jumped off the yellow stool, trotted around the corner and down the hall. A few moments later, I heard a loud "Yeek!" and Arlene came hurrying back with a crooked grin on her face. With mock terror she sang out, "Rita, you have a strange man in your bathroom. I caught him in mid-pee!"

At this point, the bedroom door opened again, letting out another burst of girlish screeches and rock and roll before it closed. Rita appeared around the corner, now dressed. She rushed into the kitchen, puzzled at the fuss.

"Arlene says that you are hiding a man in your bathroom." I laughed.

"What? Oh, you must mean—" She was interrupted by the sound of the toilet flushing and the bathroom door banging open.

A young man walked sulkily into the room. "Doesn't anyone believe in locks around here?" he growled, not quite looking at us, his face red from anger or embarrassment. He was probably still in his twenties but looked older. His blondish hair was already thinning and he wore glasses. I felt sorry for him suddenly, standing there in his neatly ironed madras shirt and khaki pants (they might have been ironed too) not the sort of person used to being exposed in a bathroom.

"Jared," Rita called out, "come here. I want you to meet my dearest friends."

Jared seemed a bit reluctant but approached us as gracefully as he could under the circumstances.

"Arlene and Lorraine, this is Jared," Rita said. "He is a film student at UCLA. I believe that he is going to be a famous movie-maker someday."

I said hello, and Arlene apologized for the "break-in." Jared murmured a hello back but still looked a trifle traumatized. It was hard to know if he was still uncomfortable from his exposure in the bathroom or just embarrassed by the glowing introduction about his up-and-coming fame.

"We are just sitting down for some coffee. Won't you join us?" Rita asked.

"Thanks anyway," he said. "Another time maybe. I'll just finish up here and then I can make it back to UCLA for my classes." He turned away and wandered over to the fireplace, where he took out a notebook and pen and started writing. At the bar, Arlene and I looked at him with curiosity.

"All will be explained later," Rita said, smiling. "But first let's have some coffee." And she turned to the stove to check on the kettle. Rita had exchanged her towel for the bright yellow beach dress, cut off somewhere above the knees. The intense color against her dark tan and untamed platinum hair was quite dazzling. Rita had a rather elongated face and always held her head proudly erect. This combined with her hair and skin always put me in mind of a painting I once saw of a palomino horse prancing grandly along the beach.

The water was boiling furiously now and Rita reached into a cupboard and came up with three thick earthenware mugs. She lovingly admired them a moment before setting them down before us.

"Just look at these!" Rita said with a flourish of her hands. "They are fresh from the kiln. Aren't they great?" Arlene and I stared down at the unusual mugs.

"Last week," Rita continued, "I went to a pottery show in Los Angeles and I met this unique potter. Her name is Flavyn, and she is a genius. They call her 'the mud hen' because she is always covered in clay dust. I bought six mugs from her, and I'm thinking of going back for the whole set of dishes."

Arlene and I looked at our mugs again. They were dark and organic, like something a troll would fashion from the gnarled roots of his tree home. Rita swept them away and proceeded to make our coffee. With Rita's back turned, we snuck furtive glances at Jared, still by the fireplace. Now he was measuring it and the walls behind. Every so often he would stop briefly to write in his notebook.

"Here you are." Rita set two steaming mugs before us then rummaged behind the bar.

"Sorry, ladies," she called out, as she hauled up from below the five-pound can of honey and a white cardboard box with a cow on it. "I'm all out of fresh milk, powdered will have to do for today." We fussed with our coffee while Rita explained just why she was so delighted with everything of late.

"Well, it all started with Sara Lee, dear, dear, Sari. And by the way, you just missed her. She was just here to drop off one of her drawings for me. Oh, Lorraine, she asked about you and wondered how you were doing now that you are back."

Darn! I had just missed Sara Lee by a few minutes this time but we were bound to get together eventually if the fates allowed. I was leaving a lot up to fate these days.

"She is such a wonderful friend," Rita rhapsodized, "and such a gifted artist too. Just think, there I was out of work again, at my wits end with ever getting and holding a job. I guess I just wasn't cut out to work in an office, or a store, or as a telephone operator, or as a waitress. Arlene, do you remember when we both tried to become cocktail waitresses? What was the name of that place—something like the Gay Nineties or the Silver Saloon or the Horny

Honky-tonk? It was something slightly lascivious like that. We had to wear those ridiculous outfits—spike heels with fish net stockings and shimmery short skirts—"

Arlene interrupted, "And some kind of stupid velvet head-dress with a big plumy feather sticking out of it?" She broke into laughter. "I couldn't get the drinks straight," she giggled.

"And I was the same!" Rita cut in, also bending over with laughter. "We both got all the drinks so mixed up that we wound up in utter despair—crying in the cocktails!"

"Crying in the cocktails!" we all screamed together, laughing and holding on to our sides until we calmed down—then looking at each other, broke up all over again.

"And that, that, bartender," Arlene added, finally settling down, "was so angry at us. And mean too. He was sooo mean." Her face looked haughty and proud now. "And I just banged down my tray and quit!"

"No," Rita shook her head sadly, "the manager fired us. We were terrible!" There was a moment of silence as if to signify confirmation of that fact. "So it was Sara Lee," said Rita resuming her story, "who saved me from more bad jobs like that and the humiliations of being fired. She was always telling me that I would make a wonderful life-drawing model. Finally, I listened to her. She encouraged me—explaining and teaching me how to be an artist's model. She taught me so much about esthetics and the beauty of art. Because of her, I got set up with an agent who books for all the colleges—California State, UCLA, and guess what?" There was a big pause. "I am good at it! They love me! Students say that when I pose they always get a good painting or sketch. I am so happy. That's why I must get tan all over. It wouldn't do for a nude model to have a bathing suit line, ugh! And I can't thank Sara Lee enough." Rita paused, then continued, "Lorraine, I have a great idea, you should come with me sometime when I model and bring along your sketchbook and chalk. What fun we could have, driving to UCLA together in my station wagon." Here she stopped to think. "Speaking of my old clunker of a car, now that things are looking up, I might be able to get this Volkswagen I have my eye on. I love those little bug cars, don't you? Did you know that Hitler had them built for the masses?" (Rita was always coming up with interesting tidbits like this.) "Anyway," she continued, "the car is used but in good shape, hardly any mileage on it at all."

I nodded agreement that it would be fun to go to a life draw- ing class again even if it was in a car that had been inspired by Hitler. I wasn't surprised that any art class would have success with Rita as a model. It was back to that whole stage presence thing again. Rita just brought excitement.

"And then things just started opening up for me again," Rita said continuing her monologue. "Going to the colleges, meeting new people at UCLA—I just had to peek in on their drama depart- ment, and that of course led to my meeting the kids in the film- making courses."

We all turned and looked at Jared once more who was still writing in his notebook.

But Rita wasn't finished. "Oh, you better believe new things are happening in films, and it is all starting in the colleges. I have seen some of this 'new world' student cinema, as they like to call it. Fascinating! So when this young bunch of filmmakers gradu- ate, watch out world! Right, Jared?" Jared smiled coyly from the other side of the room.

Rita was on a roll now, "Why even now things are changing. I have just seen the most wonderful avant-garde British movie called *Tom Jones*. It's fun. It's uproarious. There is an eating scene that is so sensual and funny all at the same time . . . and the new theater happening now is so exciting and I became a part of it by getting to know these future Bergmans and Fellinis, and it wasn't long before I was offered a part in the student film that Jared is

making as his senior project." Rita nodded at Jared who looked
up momentarily hearing his name. "It's a sort of a Lolita story,"
Rita explained, "and they are going to shoot one of the scenes
right here, correct Jared?"

Jared nodded and added another figure to his notes.

"Of course, I am playing the mother, not the Lolita figure."
Rita was so vibrant that I often had to remind myself that since
her oldest daughter was sixteen, Rita must be somewhere in her
middle thirties.

Rita, who had still been talking during my calculations, now
paused with a thought. "Hey, Jared, why don't you use Lorraine
here for the Lolita part? She is beautiful, and she is still a virgin!"

Here Jared looked embarrassed again. He fiddled with his
tape measure and mumbled, "The part is already filled, and she's
supposed to be sixteen. We got an eighteen-year-old to play the
part."

I was a bit taken aback. Was this guy saying that I couldn't
pass for a teenager? I was twenty-two but most people assumed I
was much younger. Suddenly, I felt over the hill and hardly registered the embarrassment I usually felt when Rita broadcasted
my virginity to all and sundry. I took a quick gulp of my coffee
and bruised my lip on the sandpaper-like texture of the mug. I
looked quickly over at Arlene who had also taken a gulp of her
coffee. She was rubbing her lips with her little finger as she, too,
quizzically eyed her mug, then jerked her head toward Jared.

"Most people think my sister is still a kid!" she called sharply
across the room. She almost spat the words at him, then thumping down her mug, jumped off the stool. "I'll take this as my cue
to exit to the john again. Maybe I will have better luck this time!"
And with that, Arlene whisked around the corner, leaving Jared
looking mildly confused.

Good old Arlene, I thought, *defending me to the death.* She knew I
must have been a little hurt.

Rita remained unaware of this small altercation and was still singing the praises of her new life and the sterling character traits of Sara Lee, which also included some kudos for Sari's mother too.

"... and why Sari would waste herself with that artsy-fartsy prissy-pants husband of hers. She does all the work at home plus brings in more money with her artwork than he does. Of course, he did have something to do with her two wonderful children. Inger and Nichia are just beautiful, but now there is another one on the way. Oh!" Rita put a hand to her lips and put on a sheepish look. "I'm not sure if I was supposed to say that."

Arlene had come back just in time to hear, and she and I both said together, "Sari's pregnant again?"

"But where will they live?" I cried. "Their apartment is way too tiny already."

Rita was explaining something about Sara Lee moving into a wonderful old adobe house in Manhattan Beach that her mother had found for her, when there was loud thumping from above and then a clamoring of children as they rushed down the stairs.

CHAPTER 8
THE ODYSSEY

CHILD'S PLAY

One by one, they appeared. First, six-year-old Mary Mackey dramatically swished into the room. Right behind, Lindee too, made a theatrical entrance, boldly stomping into view. Four-year-old Fallon Mackey, Rita's youngest, crept cautiously behind the older girls, while Donnie intrepidly followed close behind. Laurie J. brought up the rear, trailing after them all. Each child was wrapped in a sheet that dragged behind them, and in their hands they carried parts of old curtain rods. They were singing a made-up, triumphant song somewhat reminiscent of *The Mickey Mouse Club* and the theme from Wagner's Valkyries. "Da-da-da-duh, da-da, da-da-duh da duh! M-A-C-K-E-Y! Forever we wave our bananas high!" They were pink and breathless and extremely happy as they raced round the living room thrusting their curtain hangers in the air. Finally, they sank onto the grass matting floor in a joyful heap. Only Donnie kept standing with a serious expression on his face. His curtain rod was stuck through a belt like a sword.

Arlene, Rita, and I couldn't help smiling at the animated group. Then Arlene piped up in a Brooklyn accent. "Hey! What's all dis ruckus about? Watta youse guys tink dis is anyway, a Chinese picnic?"

This was the second time today that Arlene had quoted our father. The first time was in the market with the bit about the butcher being "un-American." Harry had used that line on our landlady. We had rented an apartment in San Francisco, but after seeing our whole family—Mom, Harry, four scruffy kids, a dog, and a turtle—the owner reneged. Well, Harry let her have it but good. He was so elegant as he laid the guilt trip on her that by the end of his bit about being "un-American," she relented, welcoming us with open arms and practically begging Harry for forgiveness, and now Arlene was repeating our father's favorite expression about a Chinese picnic. Whenever he thought his children were getting too wild and rambunctious (usually when we were in the back seat of one of his newly bought cars), he would pull out this phrase and use the same Brooklyn accent that he grew up hearing.

Now, Harry really loved his cars, mostly the Lincoln Continental and then the new powder-blue Cadillac convertible, so whenever we got too loud or antsy, he would turn around in the driver's seat—maybe even give my older brother Bill a haphazard whack on the head, then accuse us kids of trying to have a "Chinese picnic." I didn't know where this expression came from, and I never heard anyone else use it, but apparently, I reasoned, Chinese children were very hard to control.

Growing up, I had seen many illustrations of them in my picture books. They always wore pajamas and pointed straw hats. So whenever Harry used this idiom about the "picnic," I would get an image of hundreds of little children with long dark braids hanging down their backs dressed in bright silk pants and jackets running amok—climbing up trees and scaring birds and squirrels, jumping into running streams, stepping on the fish, or tumbling over the picnic blanket and baskets—food flying all around. The picture in my mind made me smile, but it was no joke. Whenever Harry said "Chinese picnic," we knew we were getting on his nerves and we quickly settled down. Our mother never got mad and never raised her voice to us, but we had on several occasions seen our father blow up at other people, and we didn't want that directed at us. Harry was lots of fun until he got mad. Then look out!

But now, in Rita's house, the kids just smiled at Arlene's funny voice.

"It looks more like a Roman Forum to me," Rita quipped. "But where is Marlon Brando, I mean Mark Antony, when you need him?"

"Or maybe it is a ghost revival! Ohooooooo," I added.

Mary jumped up, giggling, "No, no you are all wrong. We are Greek gods and goddesses."

Of all of Rita's children, Mary looked the most like her mother. The same lean El Greco face, the same wild blonde hair. "I am Athena, Goddess of Wisdom," Mary chanted.

On cue, Lindee jumped up. Giving a flourish to her sheet by dramatically waving her arms, she recited her piece, "I am the Moon Goddess Artemis, Goddess of the Hunt. I have my bow and arrow, see?" Lindee proceeded to shoot an imaginary arrow from her curtain rod.

"Oh how wonderful!" Rita clapped her hands with joy. "I think someone here has been reading the Goldfinch *Mythology* to the little ones again." Rita called across the room to Christine who had momentarily stopped her reading to watch the kid commotion.

"I thought she was ready for it, Mom," Christine chimed loudly back, all the while smiling like the Cheshire cat. "And," she added, "it was a step up from *Wonder Woman* comics, don't you think?"

"Donnie," I prompted. "Who are you?"

Donnie stood taller and said, "I'm a soldier, and a sailor too, right Mary? I'm O . . . O . . ."

"Odysseus," Mary finished it off for him. "He is making a long sea journey trying to get home but it takes him so long in his boat and there are storms and he has to fight—"

Donnie interjected here, pulling out the curtain rod from his belt and making a sweep in the air. "I fight the giant cyclops. He only has one eye in the middle of his head."

Fallon tugged on Mary's sheet, crying. "Mary, Mary, I forgot who I am! Mary!"

Slight little Fallon also had the same sinewy family likeness of an El Greco figure with his golden skin, but unlike his sisters and mother, his brown hair was straight and flopped over his eyes.

"OK, OK," Mary said. "I told you before. Remember, you are a very important god of the—" she stopped expectantly.

Suddenly, Fallon shouted, "I know, I know! I am the God of the Pacific Ocean." He looked happily around him then.

"Almost, Fallon," Mary said trying to stay positive. "The Pacific Ocean wasn't discovered yet." Here she gestured dramatically. "You are Poseidon, God of the Mediterranean Sea!"

Fallon yelled, "I'm Poseidon, I'm Pis-ion, and this is my pitchfork!"

"Your trident," Mary corrected gently.

As the youngest, Laurie J. was having the most trouble with her sheet and now was tangled up in it. "I'm a fairy!" she called out gaily, rolling on the floor kicking her feet in the air. "I'm a sea fairy."

Lindee came over and helped her unravel. "You are a nymph, Laurie J. A sea nymph is like a fairy but she lives in the water." Lindee continued unraveling her sister until Laurie J. was up again.

"And what do I do again?" Laurie J. asked.

"You sing to the sailors, and you swim, remember?"

Laurie J. nodded vigorously. "I'm a fairy, I'm a fairy," she continued. Lindee looked at us and shrugged.

I peeped over at Jared to see how he was taking this impromptu Greek saga. Or was it a comedy? He was grinning a little, then went back to his notebook. When I looked back, Rita was smiling one of her brilliant smiles. "Oh, Mary," she said, "it is so perfect of you to make Fallon Poseidon, God of the Sea." She gave a conspiratorial wink at me and Arlene. "Did you know the whole time I was pregnant with Fallon, his father and I used to go skin diving every weekend in a special cove? I did it up until my ninth month. I even had a special diving suit made with a pouch in the front."

I could picture Rita pregnant in that special wet suit diving off a boat into the sea. I just couldn't picture her with her ex-husband Roger Mackey. I had met him a few times when he came to visit his son. He was a big man with brown hair. Was it my imagination or did he seem totally out of place in Rita's world, as he laughed just a little too loud?

Rita was still smiling at the young gods and goddesses dragging her bed sheets around the floor. "You kids must be hungry. It's after one o'clock, how about a snack?"

A chorus of "Yays!" went up from the children, who were lolling on the floor again. Rita moved to the refrigerator while calling out to Arlene and me that the Goddess of Good Health had to be Adelle Davis, who along with *Let's Have Healthy Children* also wrote the cookbook *Let's Eat Right to Keep Fit*. Rita opened the refrigerator and took out a huge bowl. She put five spoons in it and plunked it down in the middle of the kids. "Eat away, my precious dears. This is food for the gods."

In the bowl was a light brown mixture the consistency of a cobbled road. The kids attacked it with gusto. Rita returned to the kitchen. "It may look funny to you guys, but it's Adelle Davis's recipe for candy and is actually called ambrosia, only it's made from brewer's yeast, wheat germ, powdered milk, honey, and the key ingredient—peanut butter. Adelle's recipe calls for it to be mixed well, rolled into round balls then it gets a final coating of shredded coconut. But usually, like today, the kids eat it before I ever get that far." We looked back at the kids hungrily dipping their spoons into the bowl. They seemed to like it all right. Rita returned to her presiding place behind the bar, her back to the kitchen.

As I said before, Rita's kitchen reflected her personality and was the focal point of her home. She loved cooking and eating good food, which accounted for the fact of always finding her in the kitchen concocting great fragrant and spicy dishes her children usually left untouched.

We were all so busy sipping coffee, talking, and watching the kids busily licking up the final morsels of Adelle Davis's candy mix, that we were almost unaware of the student filmmaker packing up his notebook and measuring tape and getting into his jacket.

"OK, I'm all packed up," he said, giving a jaunty nod before he moved toward the door.

"All right now, children," Rita exclaimed, clapping her hands, "let's give a fine send-off to the nice man who is going to put me into his next picture!" The children started a clamor of goodbyes, waving their peanut butter spoons in the air. We at the bar joined in the fun with our own farewells, which included the blowing of kisses. The whole clamor of high-pitched voices and little hands waving reminded me of the scene in *The Wizard of Oz* where the Munchkins sing and wave goodbye as Dorothy and Toto start their journey on the Yellow Brick Road.

THE WIZ

I was twelve years old when my sister and her best friend took me to see *The Wizard of Oz*. Arlene and Nancy were sixteen and acted very important that day, telling me how lucky I was they were giving me this special treat. They knew I had read all the *Oz* books but had never seen the movie. I think they wanted to see it as much as I did. It was made back in the '30s but considered a classic and was now playing in an old theater in Hollywood. It had seemed like a long bus ride to get there, but it was worth it to see the Good Witch Glinda float down in her pink bubble and the green-faced Wicked Witch appear and disappear in a burst of fire and smoke.

I could still remember when after the Munchkins sing "Follow the Yellow Brick Road," the movie fades out then back in again on a cornfield where Dorothy meets . . . I was drifting off again until a door opened in the back bedroom and music blared out— "She loves me ya, ya ya!" before the end of the third *ya*, someone jerked the needle. It made a screeching noise, and wide awake now, I could imagine a large scratch across that record.

After some scuffling around, three teenage girls sauntered out of the room and regrouped in the living room proper. I knew Diane, Rita's oldest daughter, but not her two friends. All three were about sixteen years old and looked immaculately put together. I suppose that is what they were doing all that time in the bedroom.

The girls stood abreast of each other like the Three Musketeers. Diane, the most animated of the group and the tallest, stood in the middle. She had the same Rita features of face, although her chin was longer and broader and her hair, curly like her mother's, was a chestnut brown and was now carefully relaxed due to vigilantly applying giant rollers all night. Diane wore a powder-blue nylon blouse tied in a soft bow at her neck. It was tucked neatly into green stretchy pants pulled smooth by stirrups that attached under her feet.

Of the two friends flanking Diane, one was rather ordinary looking with nondescript taffy-colored hair. The other was slim with shiny straight brown hair and bangs cut just above her eyebrows. The bangs made you notice her large eyes, which were emphasized by dark eyeliner giving her a sleepy, bored look.

"How do I look, Mom?" Diane asked, stepping forward and doing a pirouette in front of her mother.

"Oh, Darling," Rita responded, "you look like a delicious lime Popsicle. Those pants are fantastic."

Diane, beaming, bounced back to her friends, and they sailed dreamily out the door. All of a sudden, I longed to be sixteen again like the three teenagers drifting out the door, so adorable so carefree. Then I had to slap myself awake. What was I thinking? As I remembered it, I was a miserable sixteen-year-old, a complete failure as a teenager.

Just then, Rita's bright voice rescued me from my gloomy thoughts. "Oh, it is so good you two dears happened to come over today. My special order just came in the mail. Christine, will you go into the bedroom and bring back that package that came today?" Christine put down her book and went into the back room. A moment later she came back with a fair-sized package already opened and something black peeking out of the tissue paper.

Rita smiled at her daughter. "Thank you, Chris dear," she said, as Christine put the ragged package on the bar top and moved back to her couch. Rita dived gleefully into the tissue and pulled out two small black lace bras. "I saw this in a magazine advertisement, and I couldn't resist buying them for you girls."

Arlene and I were touched by Rita's generosity and awestruck by the lacy underwear.

"Look, look right here," Rita enthused. "See these little pads in the cups. When you put your little muffin breasts into these, they will be uplifted and instead of little muffin breasts your cups will runneth over. Pushed up breasts are very in now that *Tom Jones* is such a hit movie. All you see are ripe round apple breasts everywhere these days."

"Oh, Rita, this is so nice. It's too much!" Arlene and I said, fumbling in our embarrassment and enjoyment, while fondly touching the lovely black fabric.

"No, no, don't be silly. I just couldn't resist ordering them for you, and I got one for me too." With a flourish Rita pulled another black lacy bra out of the package. It was somewhat bigger than ours, I noticed, as she waved it in the air.

Later, when the coffee mugs were empty and the candy bowl licked clean, it was time to leave. The kids dragged all the sheets upstairs again and put them back on the beds while Rita dug up a new paper bag for my damp groceries. Soon, we were all packed and ready to go—the new black underwear stashed in Arlene's roomy straw purse.

Just as we were trailing out the door, Rita called a halt to our caravan. "I almost forgot to give you something. Christine, my dear, will you get that book we were talking about? I want to give it to Lorraine."

Christine thought a moment then scurried to a pile of books near the fireplace. She quickly found one and brought it to me. As she handed it over, she scrutinized me seriously from behind her glasses and then said, "Yes, I think you are ready for this book, Lorraine," and tucked the copy of Nabokov's *Lolita* into my grocery bag next to the box of Quaker Oats.

Regrouped, our convoy started for home once again, doggedly trudging up the hill, before turning right onto Monterey Avenue. There, Arlene stopped to readjust her bag of groceries. With her free hand she rubbed her bottom lip again and, turning to me, said, "After using those cups Rita got from that pottery genius, I'm not sure if she should get a whole set of dishes, but don't you think Flavyn is a really cool name? If I ever have another girl, I would like to name her Flavyn. Yikes, what am I saying?"

CHAPTER 9
TAD AND MISS BEEK

DAISIES IN THE DUMP

The pages of *Look Homeward, Angel* were spread out on my knees as I sat on the top step of the staircase. The staircase led down to the patio area and to Jeff's new bedroom under the deck. The sun felt warm and comforting like the cup of coffee I balanced in my right hand.

"A cup of coffee—the sun—and a great book, what more could one want?" I murmured to myself looking out at the vast lot in back of our house. Today all was beautiful, even the landfill was lovely since it started sprouting wild daisies. White butterflies flitted above the flowers, making it look like some of the daisies had broken free and taken wing. Nearby the faithful oil pumps continued, uninterrupted, to dip and then rise, like giant birds pecking in the loamy soil. *The earth does look loamy*, I reflected. *Spring is here, all right.* I smiled in satisfaction. *Loamy* was one of my new words.

In the distance, I could see the kids playing in the white flowers. A few minutes later, Donnie emerged from the foliage and, climbing up the dirt incline, stepped onto the cement slab we loosely called "the back patio." The only thing on it, except for a few boxes, was the broken washing machine. Standing on bent legs, its wringer still attached to the tank, the old washer looked like an aged, one-armed soldier saluting the dump, as if to signal that it was protecting the back of the red cottage.

Wow, my imagination was getting very fanciful these days. *It must be the Thomas Wolfe influence*, I thought.

Donnie passed by the iron soldier and climbed the wooden stairs carefully, all the while protecting a small bunch of daisies gripped in his fist. He stopped on the step in front of me. "For you," he said, and presented the white bouquet.

"Thank you, Donnie," I said. "They are lovely."

"It's to make you happy." Donnie squinted at me with his serious face.

"Well, thanks again." I gulped and accepted the flowers. Was I walking around with a sad face? I jumped up quickly. "I'll look for a jar to put them in right now." I gave Donnie a bright smile to allay any fear that I was ever sad. I had better watch out and look a little less solemn from now on. Donnie was so perceptive and tenderhearted. Only a few days ago, he had gone to school in his authentic German lederhosen pants all chipper and bright only to come home in tears. The kids at school laughed and made fun of him.

His mother had comforted him by saying that the kids at school were not very bright if they didn't appreciate a gen-U-ine German lederhosen outfit when they saw one. Donnie smiled through his tears but never wore it to school again.

I attended to the flowers and arranged a bunch in a jelly jar on the dining room table. When I came back to the steps, Donnie was again out in the daisy field doing some kind of digging game with Lindee and Laurie J. Were they playing buried treasure again? I hoped they weren't using the kitchen spoons, or if they were, I hoped that they would bring some of them back. I watched for a while then found my place again in *Look Homeward, Angel*. It was one of the novels Howard K. Small had assigned for me to read and a whole new literary world had opened up. Wolfe's writing was so juicy and every sentence full of oozy life. I learned new words like *desultory*, *lugubrious*, and *loamy*. The Gant family he wrote about was as outrageous and full of life as his prose. I liked the sketchy illustrations too that were in my edition and made a mental note to start making my own drawings. My stories would need illustrations too.

THOMAS A. DUKE

There was a rhythmic tapping behind me, and I turned to see Jeff's friend Tad. His grinning face was pressed against the dining room window as his fingers rapped out a calypso rhythm on the glass pane. I waved for him to come out, and a moment later he peeked around the back door showing just his head. "Hey, man, what's happening?" he drawled in his sleepy way.

I couldn't help thinking each time I saw Tad that he had a head shaped exactly like a turnip—wide and flat on top then small and pointy at the chin. His short brown hair was combed forward like Julius Caesar, emphasizing the wide forehead. "Hey, man," he said again, this time fully emerging from the darkness of the house. He held a bongo drum protectively under his arm. Tad was able to have complete conversations in nothing but jive talk, and he looked the part of the cool jazz fan. Even today he wore a dark suit with a narrow tie, and . . . were those suede loafers? Tad peered at me from over his dark sunglasses or "shades," as he called them. "Is the man up yet?" He gestured down toward Jeff's new bedroom under the stairs. "I got some info he needs to know."

I looked up quizzically and Tad continued. "Well, the scene is like this. Last night, I decided to check out the sounds at the Lighthouse.

The Lighthouse was the only outstanding entity in our small beach town. Against all odds, an obscure bar and Chinese grill had become one of the most famous jazz nightclubs in Southern California.

"Cal Tjader and his quintet are headlining all this week," Tad was saying, "and you *know* what a big fan I am of old Cal and his cool vibes." Tad always seemed to speak as if we should infer that he was on a first-name basis with many famous musicians. "Tjader's sound is the greatest!" Tad continued, "I just can't get enough of that Cuban Latin sound." Tad tapped his bongos for emphasis making a th-wap, th-wap sound.

I waited patiently for Jeff's friend to get to the point of his story while I studied the shape of his head again, noting that his ears stood out a bit with the sun's illumination, turning them a pinkish red.

"But I wasn't going to wait outside like the rest of the crowd," Tad said, moving on with his story. "Man, the line was around the block and then some. What a drag!" His small eyes closed even smaller as he smiled at his dilemma then continued. "But I knew a shortcut I could use to get inside. Dig this, I went into the alley at the rear of the club thinking I could get in the back door and *wham*, I ran smack into this cat, Wong. He's the cook at the Lighthouse and he was emptying some trash in the back and swearing like mad banging the cans around. It's funny how you can tell when someone is swearing even if it is in another language."

I wondered just where this story was going, but I kept my peace and let Tad continue.

"So, I was smart like a fox and helped him with the cans then and just sort of followed him back into the club, I mean kitchen. Have you ever had the Chinese food at the Lighthouse?" He didn't wait for my answer. "Man, it is too much—Wong's egg foo young is like—well, anyway, that is beside the point."

I began to wonder just when the point was going to show up.

"The point is . . ."

Tad must have been reading my thoughts.

". . . the point is I had never met Wong before. No, the point is that even though we didn't speak the same language, this cat, Wong, and I hit it off like crazy. In sign language I told him that I really dug his food 'the most.' Now, Wong doesn't speak much of our lingo, but I gathered that he was doing his own dirty work because his dishwasher-busboy didn't show up. Right away, I thought of your brother. Wouldn't it be a gas for him to work at the Lighthouse? He could hear all the jazz greats that come there and also have the swingiest Chinese food every night and all for free and get paid for it to boot. I told Wong a new boy would be coming in tonight and then I just left him and strolled out into the club, super-cool-like snapping my thumbs in time to the music. Howard Rumsey, the manager, was standing by the bar and didn't even notice I had snuck in. I spent the rest of the night digging the bongos and congas and old Cal's vibes."

Well, wasn't that sweet of old Tad. I was impressed. Here I had been thinking he was just another wannabe hipster who hung out with us because he thought we were hip or with-it or what-ever word there was now for being cool these days, and here he was thinking of Jeff like a big brother, very sweet!

I moved over so Tad could go down the stairs to tell Jeff the good news. A few moments later, I heard Tad pull open the rug that served as a door to the room and heard him scrabbling in. Soon, the muffled sound of bongos started up, and a little later the thin quaver of an alto saxophone.

I went back to my book. *What I really need is a dictionary*, I thought. There were so many words in Wolfe's story that I had never even heard before. *Betsy, our neighbor, might have one*, I thought, although I wasn't sure, but yes, she would almost cer-tainly have a dictionary to help her children with their home work. That was like her, and I bet she probably even had a set of encyclopedias from A to Z enshrined in her living room too. Betsy was very well equipped, her house stocked with practical things like light bulbs, toilet paper, SOS pads, and laundry detergent, her kitchen cupboards filled with cans of Campbell's soup and Spaghetti-Os. The basement too, was complete with every size of socket wrench and screwdriver to an electric drill set that her husband was particularly proud of.

Betsy was a solidly built redhead and a no-nonsense type mother to her two girls. I don't know why she put up with us constantly borrowing her things and using her telephone, but she did. She was always ready, too, with a pot of coffee and some jelly donuts.

I was startled from my musings about Betsy's larder when Arlene suddenly burst out the back door. "Quick, Lorraine! You have to disappear!" My sister waved her arms at me as if to hurry along my invisibility. Confused, I continued to sit. Still waving, she let out some choice swear words, finally gasping out, "The welfare people are at the door! I told them it was stuck and to come through the window. You and Jeff are not supposed to be living with me. Quick, go down and hide in his room and stop them playing that music. Now hurry!" And with that, she tore back into the house.

JEFF'S ROOM

I clambered down the stairs in my bare feet, leaving Thomas Wolfe and my coffee cup on the top step. Pushing quickly past the rug door, I flung myself into the dim interior. Tad and Jeff were just beginning to get into a groove and pick up speed in their duet when I quickly muffled them. In a hushed voice, I explained what was happening upstairs and why they had to remain quiet. I felt like a criminal hiding from the law in a cave, and Jeff's room added to the cave-like feeling. It was dark and somewhat damp. It took a while before my eyes could make out Jeff's newly built "pad," as Tad would call it.

My brother wasn't a bad carpenter when you considered his lack of proper tools and building supplies. When Arlene first moved in with him and Mom, he gave his small bedroom to the kids and moved into the loft. Later, to get more space for them, he enlarged their room by several feet cantilevering a new wall, Frank Lloyd Wright style, over the back patio. Not finished, he added a large window as wide as a door into the new wall. Of course, that meant he had to actually hang a real door in the space, which unfortunately made the room very dark until you opened it and secured it to the ceiling with special hooks. Propped open, the window then let in wonderful light, air, and also a few bugs.

Directly below that was now Jeff's new sleeping quarters. It was tiny, barely big enough to contain a bed. With the cement patio for a floor, it was tucked between the foundation wall and the wooden posts that supported the staircase and the deck above. Looking around in the semi-darkness, I spotted something large hanging near the ceiling. A dim arm reached out and the room was suddenly flooded with light. The large object turned out to be an old box spring that Jeff had suspended from the ceiling with long metal chains—a sort of hammock in that it did not touch the ground. How he got in and out of it, I could only guess.

The switch on the wall not only turned on his light but also music since he had affixed a speaker to the ceiling that was wired to the upstairs. A flick of his finger brought instant music, that is, if someone upstairs had the radio on. At the moment, Jeff was comfortably lounging on his box spring hammock, cradling his horn in his arms. I realized he must have been playing all this time lying on his back. Given the compactness of the room, it seemed to make perfect sense since Tad and I took up all the floor space. I had only taken one step into the room and yet Tad, sitting on the only chair with his bongos still between his legs, was only inches away.

If I felt uneasy having to hide from the social workers, Jeff didn't care at all that he was an illegal tenant; he was more concerned that he had to stop playing his music. "Well," he said in a mock injured tone, "did you hear any of what we were doing before we were so rudely interrupted? It's an original composition I'm working on."

"A bit," I said, happy to have gotten his mind off playing music and onto just talking about it. "It did have a kind of cute rooty-tooty sound," I added.

Jeff smiled in his high roost. "It's not finished yet, but I call it 'The March of the Cockroaches.'"

"And I added an Afro-Cuban beat with my bongos," Tad broke in.

Speaking of creepy crawly things, looking up now, I noticed a few snails leaving silver trails behind them as they climbed up the cement wall. I hoped that some of them were not the crunchy things I had stepped on when I jumped into the room. Then again, maybe I didn't want to know. Surreptitiously, I checked the bottom of my feet and was relieved to find no mashed shell or slimy smashed body.

Jeff yawned and stretched. Only an arm's reach away was a shelf fastened to the wall level with his bed and on it his few essential things: a stack of *DownBeat* and *Playboy* magazines; a rack holding tobacco, matches, cigarette paper, and various strange shaped pipes. Next to it, a small cedar box held a single edge razor blade, a bright silver pitch pipe, and seven cellophane bags, each containing an alto saxophone reed. The single edge razor blade, it turned out, was to whittle the reeds into the proper shape for his horn, an art my brother was of late, learning to perfect. Jeff languidly reached out and selected one of the funny looking pipes and the tin of Prince Albert tobacco. With loving care, he filled the pipe and lit it while Tad and I talked in whispers and low tones below.

With the light on, I noticed that my brother had created a large, striking design on one of the walls. When I commented about the interesting non-objective artwork, he mumbled that he had done it but directed my attention to the real prize, a cigarette butt pinned alongside the artwork, the likes of which had once graced the lips of Thelonious Monk. According to Jeff, Thelonious Monk was the most innovative pianist in jazz history, so when the great man took a smoke break between sets at the club where he was playing, Jeff was wily enough to snatch up the discarded butt as a trophy. I couldn't help smiling; it was so like my brother to cherish a thing like that.

It wasn't long before the room was engulfed in a haze of smoke and odorous pipe tobacco. My bare feet were getting cold on the cement floor, although the rest of me was getting warmer and more and more claustrophobic in Jeff's bunker-like room. After several minutes of this, I decided to take my chances in the outside world. After all, how long was I supposed to hide out here anyway? *I should just go around to the front of the house, sneak in to pick up my sandals, and then head out to the beach*, I thought.

Leaving Jeff and Tad to their jazz talk, I quietly scrambled over to Betsy's patio. Betsy was surprised to see me at her back door and even more surprised to find that I just wanted to walk through her house, yet she shrugged it off as just another funny thing her neighbors did. And Betsy did have a dictionary, after all, so it was not a wasted trip.

WELFARE LADIES

Now if I was quiet enough, I could deposit the dictionary, retrieve my sandals, and tiptoe out again. *I'm home free*, I thought, but luck was not with me; the door rattled.

"Who's there?" Arlene was quick to call out.

"Oh, it's just me, your sister, come for a visit," I called back as nonchalantly as I could. Dropping the dictionary on the couch and quickly slipping into my sandals that were conveniently left at the bottom of the ladder to my loft, I walked into the dining room with what I hoped was a casual air.

Arlene was sitting across the table from two women, one, somewhere between thirty and forty and the other, older, maybe fifty or sixty. The younger one was dressed sensibly in a skirt and white blouse. She had brown hair and even features, but the expression on her face was set in a kind of way that said, "I take no nonsense!" A notebook was open in front of her and she had a pen poised in her hand.

The older woman was far less threatening. She sat erect in her chair, her slender hands clasped loosely in front of her on the table. She wore old-fashioned clothes that were thin and soft as if they were worn and washed many times. A web of fine lines covered her face. It was a nice face with a quiet grayness about it.

"This is my sister, Lorraine," Arlene said, introducing me to the two ladies.

"Hi," I said reluctantly, sitting down at the table trying to smile, not knowing what else to do.

"Do you live here too?" was the first thing the younger woman said to me. She was smiling but was looking straight into me.

"No," I said, a little thrown off, because her gimlet eyes continued to lock onto mine. "No," I repeated. "I live with my mother in the Riviera section of Torrance Beach. It's a few miles from here." The social worker smiled but this time to herself.

She doesn't believe a word of this, I concluded. *God, I hate lying. I'm no good at it.* I switched my gaze to the little jar of Donnie's daisies on the table. They looked a bit jammed in but appeared perky and bright. My spirits rose a little. Now that I think about it, I really don't feel guilty at all living with Arlene. With me here, the food lasts longer, and the house is in order. I started to do a little arithmetic in my head. *Now, when I lived in Hollywood I spent five dollars a week on food, which was twenty dollars a month, and fifty on rent. So Arlene's check for . . . minus . . . plus . . .* I gave up trying to figure out if I was a financial burden or not. *Well, I could always try to get a job and add to the coffers,* I concluded to myself lamely.

The thirtyish or fortyish social worker lady was still talking to me it seemed. "I said," she raised her voice a little and repeated, "how is your mother?"

"Oh, fine, fine," I murmured, still trying vaguely to add income and expenses in my head.

The social worker lady looked surprised, "I thought she was in the hospital?"

"What I mean is, she is doing fine and coming out of the hospital next week."

At least that wasn't a lie, I thought thankfully. *Wow, deceiving is a tough business.* I was relieved when the two ladies started packing up their things.

The thin older lady rose and turned to Arlene. Her tremulous smile was strangely engaging. "I am so sorry," she said in a soft musical tone, "that I did not meet your children Linda, Donald, and Laura today. I do so want to bring Jesus into their lives, but I'll be back another time." Arlene's mouth opened but she didn't say anything. Then the thin lady turned to me and held out her hand. "I'm sorry," she chirped, "we were not formally introduced. My name is Miss Beek, Miss Philomena Beek."

"I'm Lorraine," I said, feeling slightly embarrassed at the formality.

Miss Beek shook my hand and twittered, "Goodbye, ladies, I'll be back another time." Then leaning over, she touched the flowers in the jelly jar. She whispered something to herself then fluttered after the other social worker lady, who was halfway out the door.

When they both left, my sister, who had been holding the

door open, closed it securely behind them. For a moment, she fell back against it weakly and groaned. "That was just so awful!"

"Oh," I said, "that one woman was kind of sweet, I thought."

"You weren't here and it was the other one with the x-ray eyes. She looked at everything. She looked in at every room. You should have seen her face when she saw the music room—so disapproving and when she saw my room and the kids' room, she looked absolutely disgusted that they had no real beds just box springs and mattresses. I had to explain that three real beds could not all fit in that room."

Arlene came back into the dining room and dropped into her seat again. She held her head for a while. "I need some coffee!"

I put a pot of water on the stove and went back outside to get my coffee cup and book and to give the *all clear* to Jeff and Tad. Not too long after that, Tad peeked around the back door. "Is it safe to come in yet? Is everything copacetic?"

"Yes," Arlene and I said together.

"Very cool then," Tad said and the rest of him emerged fully. Tad never just walked into a room. He always seemed to slither in like a lizard or a sly little elf. Right now, he was carrying a large gray loose-leaf notebook. He put it on the table next to the jar of daisies.

"Jeff told me to give this to you, Lorraine. He found it out back of that car dealership in El Segundo. He thought maybe you could write your scribblings in it." Tad pushed the notebook nearer to me and without waiting for comment, glided toward the door. "Ciao, baby," he called back at us before sauntering out.

Arlene jumped up. "Hold the coffee. What I really need is a cigarette. Maybe Betsy will let me bum one off her, and while I'm there I want to call Howard and tell him not to come over today. That social worker lady really frazzled me."

Arlene did look unnerved. Her angular fingers were visibly trembling. That was not a good sign. This might be the beginning of one of her terrible migraine headaches. When they got really bad, Arlene would gulp down several Empirin tablets and "take to her bed" for the rest of the day with a cold wet washrag on her forehead.

"What was the social worker concerned about?" I asked as I followed her to the door.

"Oh, about the kids and school, and that just reminded me that I have to write notes to the teachers again about why the kids are always late. Maybe Betsy has an extra alarm clock and," she added, "some writing paper and . . ." Arlene was still mumbling as she went out the door.

CHAPTER 10
HOWARD K. SMALL

THE GRAY LOOSE-LEAF NOTEBOOK

When Arlene left, I went back to the table and idly thumbed through the gray notebook. Inside it said Automobile Invoice Services Company Inc. It was a very thick book covering all the different makes of cars and trucks. Finally, I came to the end and flipped it over. Jeff was right: using the reverse side of the pages, I had tons of pure white empty space to write on. The front and back covers even had pockets where I could store the writing I had already done.

I jumped a little when I heard a brisk knock on the front door and before I could even get up to open it, the ornery thing suddenly sprang open. There was Howard K. Small looking surprised, eyebrows up. Well, this was a new trick. Half the time, the knob would be loose or missing and the door wouldn't open. The other half of the time, we left it hanging open ourselves but this time the door seemed to open itself.

Howard stepped cautiously into the living room. "Hey, man, anyone here?" He looked around in a surprised way although his expression normally always did look a little surprised.

"Come in, Howard. I'm in the dining room," I called.

Howard's bulky frame filled the arched doorway of the dining room and stood there with his usual dazed expression. With his unkempt hair and tawny coloring, he always reminded me of a lion. Not a real lion but a costumed one like Bert Lahr, who played the Cowardly Lion in *The Wizard of Oz*. Finally, Howard walked into the room. He was carrying his big satchel and a bulky envelope of sheet music. He sat down and stored the big satchel under the table by his feet.

I remembered the first time I met Howard K. Small. It was one of those days when the front door was left hanging open. I was in the living room busy with something, so my back was to the door. Suddenly, I felt a heavy hand on my shoulder as in a hearty greeting. I jumped because it was unexpected, and Howard jumped even more alarmed because the small blonde he thought he was greeting was somebody else—a near look-alike.

We soon straightened it out and introduced ourselves. Having read Arlene's caricature sketch of Howard, I was prepared for him and all his strange mannerisms and tics, but Howard, having no prior knowledge of a sister, took a bit longer to adjust to me. Once adjusted, however, it was no time at all before he was grilling me about my musical tastes and reading habits. Who had I read? What was I reading now?

My answers were unimpressive. My recent reading had been books that had been made into movies like *Exodus*, *Giant*, and *Gone with the Wind*, books that didn't impress him much. To save face, I threw in *Huckleberry Finn* and *Gulliver's Travels*, which was really fudging, because I had to read Swift's *Gulliver's Travels* in high school, and my mother had long ago read *Huck Finn* to us kids when we were little.

Howard seemed mollified, however. Then asked if I had ever read Hemingway, F. Scott Fitzgerald, Steinbeck, or Thomas Wolfe. When I replied in the negative, he took out a small spiral notebook with blank musical lines on it from his large satchel briefcase and started to write the names of books.

I looked over his hairy arm and saw *The Great Gatsby*, *For Whom the Bell Tolls*, *The Grapes of Wrath*, and *Look Homeward, Angel*.

Howard said, "Just go to your local library and try to get these books or any by these authors. It's a start." Then he added the authors' names to the list.

That had been weeks ago and, taking his advice, I found some short stories by Hemingway, *Tortilla Flat* by Steinbeck, and *Look Homeward, Angel* by Wolfe. Right away, I could tell I was reading something different.

Today I was telling Howard about how excited I was about *Look Homeward, Angel*. Howard blinked his eyes in pleasure and jerked his head a little to the side. "Keep at it," he said. "If you can get Wolfe, you can read anything."

I was glowing with pride, so I mentioned another feat I had mastered. "And you know what, Howard? I taught myself to play every chord in the scales."

"On the black keys too?" Howard looked impressed.

"Yes, and on the black keys too," I said confidently. "Jeff told me that if I could do this, I would be able to play your songs, but when I tried, my left hand has to jump around so much!"

Howard looked perplexed. "Well," he said, "why didn't you use inversions?"

"Inversions, what are inversions?" I asked with trepidation. I had a feeling I was not the success I thought I was.

Howard screwed up his face and launched into a lecture. "Each chord can be played in at least three different positions that are called inversions. It seems like you only know one position, probably the first position, right, with the root note at the beginning of the chord or as the first note in the chord?" We moved to the piano, where Howard sat his large presence on the wobbly piano stool. "See, I'll show you. Let's take the simple major C chord. You only know it in the first position CEG." And he played it with the root in the first position. "But," he continued, "it can also be played as EGC or GCE. Get it?"

Oh, I got it all right. My heart sank as I realized all that I had yet to learn. Just then, Arlene banged into the house leaving the door swinging open behind her. She had a lit cigarette in her mouth but no alarm clock. She stopped when she saw Howard. "You're here?" she said, coming into the music room. "I was going to tell you not to come today." She sank into one of the wicker Indonesian chairs with the curly scrollwork on top. It was now painted a rich apple green. Arlene sucked morosely on her cigarette and curled up like she was retreating from humankind, withdrawing from the bright hard world into a dark place.

Howard looked around in that impatient way he had, yet he sensed too that Arlene's mood could become explosive so he didn't, for once, talk about his troubles with money or his car or his girlfriend, Gillian, or chide Arlene about how a singer shouldn't smoke. He just said, "OK, finish your cigarette. I got a new tune for you to work on." Arlene huddled even further into the chair. "It's called 'Woke up and Found Myself Dead,'" Howard continued, turning to the piano and starting to play a fast, jerky melody. "Hey!" he called out gaily. "You know, it could be cool as a duo with two people singing close harmony. Maybe you and Lorraine could work this up?" Without looking, he sensed that Arlene was still in her cocoon state and switched to another song—a lilting ballad he had written for her. Arlene was still taking long drags on her cigarette, but looking a little more relaxed. A small smile began to play around her mouth.

By now, Howard was on a roll as he moved from one song to another, calling out the names as he changed tunes. "Here's one that needs lyrics," he said. "It's called 'Wiggledy Waggledy Woo.'" It was a lively piece with an infectious air. As it ended, Howard moved on to a haunting melody. "'Lost at the Fair,'" he called out.

Arlene had finished her cigarette, drowning it out in the dregs of somebody's abandoned coffee cup. It made a little sizzle as it sank to the bottom. She listened a while to the song then got up

*Arlene curled up in the Indonesian wicker chair with the
scrollwork on top and sucked morosely on her cigarette.*

and started drifting toward the piano. Howard, sensing her approach, started the song again, and Arlene began to sing, looking over his shoulders at the lyrics on the piano. She sang quietly, almost sadly without her usual tricky phrasing.

I was caught up too in the story of a girl who goes to the fair looking for something or somebody that she never finds. When the song ended, we all were quiet for a moment, not wanting to break the mood it had created. The tender moment dissolved quickly though, when I looked up and saw my sister's face. Her eyes were crossed, her tongue was stuck out of the side of her mouth, and a lurid grin was spreading across her face. I suddenly exploded into laughter, all tender feeling dissolved. Howard swiveled his head, from the piano. "What, what?" He knew he was missing something and bounced a little in his seat, which threatened to destroy the piano stool.

"OK," Arlene said, turning back to Howard. "Now maybe we can try 'Woke up and Found Myself Dead.'" She took a breath to sing and then stopped. "Lorraine, I just remembered something I forgot to tell you." She had a quirky little smile on her face—a face that I had seen before. She was going to spring something on me. "Guess *who* came over yesterday and was surprised you were back from Hollywood?"

My heart started to beat faster *Was it* Him? I wondered.

Arlene waited a few teasing seconds before blurting out, "It was funny Old Lenny Glassman."

It wasn't *Him*, but it was close. My beating heart subsided. Lenny had been one of my boyfriend's best friends, as much as Lenny Glassman could be anyone's best friend. They were both singers trying to break into the music business.

"And, Lorraine, he said to tell you he would be seeing you soon. It seems he is back sleeping on his mother's couch again, licking his wounds from his latest try at stardom in Hollywood. He should be popping up soon seeing as that his mother lives just a few blocks away." Arlene turned her attention now back to Howard and the score on the piano.

My heart was under control again. Lenny had an outrageous personality, cocky and vain. Yet, I wouldn't mind hanging out with him. After all, hadn't I made up my mind to be open to whatever comes along? I left Arlene and Howard and was finally ready for the long-delayed walk along the Strand.

CHAPTER 11
THE SEA CALLS US

OCEAN BREEZES

A short time later I was at the beach. I stood for a while at the wall. There it was—that wonderful smell I never tired of—a mixture of salt and seaweed and maybe even a bit of dead fish. The very blue sky made for a very blue ocean. That was what was good about living by the water. The sky was always clear, yet just a few miles inland, a yellow curtain of smog colored the landscape as the exhaust from cars and industries got trapped in the valleys.

I remembered when we lived in Burbank, in the San Fernando Valley, the smog was just starting then. The ocean was only twenty miles away, but it might as well have been a hundred miles. We didn't have a car most of the time. We kids could ride our bikes, but Mom walked everywhere she had to go, pulling her shopping cart behind her, that is, until my father made one of his sudden appearances. He'd pull into our driveway unexpectedly one day with his latest new car; it was usually a convertible with windows that went up and down at a touch of a button. We were hemmed in no longer. Soon we were off on a whirlwind of distant adventures—hiking in the mountains, swimming in far-off lakes, spending the day at the zoo and Griffith Park Observatory, or, our favorite, a day trip to the beach. Mom would pack up food for the whole afternoon, and Harry would pile all of us into the car. In my excitement I always forgot we would have to travel over the Santa Monica Mountains and take the twisty Topanga Canyon Road in order to get to that special place Harry liked at the seashore.

The trouble started even before we stopped at the gas station. In the back seat, I was already queasy from the smell of new leather and my father's tendency to ride the brake and jerk the gear shifts. The fumes from the gasoline just added another level of car sickness, and we hadn't even left town yet. Later, it would be the mountain passes that really did me in. As we rounded and circled through the mass of crags and basins, our car would start to sway. First to the left as the car rounded one part of the mountain then to the right as we finished off the other side. It did no good to close my eyes. Finally, I would tug on the collar of my mother's corduroy jacket as she sat in the front seat. "Gotta throw up," I would choke out. Harry, grumbling something, would pull the car over to the side of the road. Mom, moving quickly, took me outside and rubbed my back as I vomited my breakfast into the dirt. Sometimes, Harry would have to stop the car two or three times before we made it over those mountains. By then, everyone in the car, except Mom, would be groaning, "Oh no, not again." Finally, the twisting and turning would stop, and my torture would be over. You could smell the ocean before you ever saw it, and we all cheered when we hit that final turn and the salty air burst into our nostrils.

A week or two later, Harry would disappear from us as abruptly as he appeared. I would come home from school and no powder-blue convertible would be in the driveway, and our lives would go back to what they were before.

ALONG THE STRAND

At the wall, I took another deep breath. Harry may have taken us to the beach, but it was my sister who brought us all here to live. She had nagged and nagged her husband, Don, to find a job in a beach town and then coaxed and coddled the rest of us to come join her.

With that in mind, I started to walk alongside the wall, still looking out to sea. *Somewhere out there is the island of Catalina only twenty-six miles away, and somewhere way out there is our Bill,* I thought. *Way out in the middle of the Pacific Ocean on Hawaii.* My older brother, rather than take a dead-end job in Riverside, had joined the Navy as soon as he graduated from high school. "Join the Navy and See the World." That's what the recruitment posters said. So, after being stationed for a year or so in San Diego, Bill was sent to live in Hawaii. How I envied him. I pictured him swinging leisurely in a hammock sipping piña coladas, the ocean waves rippling behind him as the sun slowly sank in the western sky. He was so lucky!

I had wanted to live on a tropical island since the third grade. The school library had a big picture book. I must have read it a hundred times. A young sailor carves a seagull out of walrus tusks. It brings him good luck, and he becomes a captain of his own ship and has wonderful adventures. I was mesmerized by the gorgeous colored illustrations—a clipper ship charging through the waves, her sails flying, while purple shadows and golden highlights tinted the billowing canvases. I copied that clipper ship picture many times, wishing I were on that boat headed for the South Seas or the Caribbean. My favorite picture was of an island where brilliant-colored parrots flew through the air and vibrant flowers crowded for space on the lush mountainside while waterfalls splashed into blue ponds. Best of all were the brown children riding the waterfalls and diving into the pools below. Oh, how I wanted to be one of those children, so happy and naked in that magical place.

And there was Bill living in that magical place who complains, Mom says, about all the humidity and the termites that eat his TV. I was still staring at the horizon as I wondered, *If a beautiful sail-boat suddenly appeared right now and offered to take me to Hawaii, would I drop everything and just go?* Instead of going anywhere, I stopped abruptly. I had been walking so fast and thinking so hard that I was now surprised to find I was already at the main shopping area on Pier Avenue.

OLD JOBS, NEW JOBS

It was just the place I needed to be, now that I had come out of my dream of faraway places. *I should pick up some things for the house.* We were all out of matches to light the stove. I didn't want Arlene making any more torches from the water heater. Turning into the dime store, I knew my way around; I had worked here for a month when Mom and I first moved to Hermosa. I remembered how the assistant manager had carefully explained my job to me. My most important role was to spot shoplifters. They were usually teenagers, I was told, and if I suspected one, I was to skulk behind them until they were driven out of the store.

One morning I was surprised to see my sister. The surprise was not seeing Arlene but seeing her ride right into the store on a bike. She coasted breezily up to me, stopping the vehicle at the register. We chatted awhile. Arlene fiddled with the sunglasses rack, trying on one pair after another, looking at herself in the mirror, using it to put on her lipstick. Then she bid me goodbye and merrily propelled herself out the door again. It was fifteen minutes before I realized she had blatantly swiped a pair of sunglasses right in front of my nose. Some house detective I was; maybe that accounted for the fact that I was fired or "let go," as they liked to call it, just a few weeks later.

Remembering Arlene now made me think about earlier when the social worker lady made her feel like a bad mother and me like some sort of sponger and parasite. A thought came. I could look for a job here on Pier Avenue to lessen the burden at the house. There was the drug store, a lunch counter at the bakery, and that Italian place. Maybe they needed someone?

A FAMILIAR SIGHTING

Twenty minutes later, I turned off Pier Avenue and onto the Strand again with a Pio's Pizza and Italian Restaurant menu tucked under my arm. They would try me out at the breakfast counter tomorrow and I was to memorize the menu tonight. I glanced at some of the prices as I walked along. A dollar fifty for two eggs fried or scrambled with a side order of sausage or bacon and toast, either white or wheat bread. I was on to the pancake special when I realized that my peripheral vision was picking up a familiar figure on the beach. Oh my gosh! It was *Him.*

He was sitting on the sand not twenty feet away, sharing a beach blanket with a redhead, his dark hair close to hers deep in intimate conversation. *Oh horror,* I thought, *please don't let my old boyfriend see me.* I covered my face with Pio's menu and moved quickly past. I didn't even have time for that feeling in my stomach to kick in. Safely past, I stopped and turned around. His back was to me now, and the girl was unknown so I could casually pretend to view the ocean while I checked her out. She wasn't a girl at all, I realized. She was a grown woman!

She must be at least forty, I thought, *and kind of blousy at that.* I studied her full figure and red hair, which I noticed was the color you get from a bottle of henna rinse. Finally, lifting my chin, I did an about face and marched away. An older woman! Somehow I was disappointed and more confused than heartbroken. *Well,* I further informed myself, stepping a bit more briskly, *I have pulled through the first sighting of Him, so Old Lenny Glassman, the great tease, will not shake me up in the least.*

CHAPTER 12
FROM THE GRAY NOTEBOOK
EXPOSITION

Howard told me that stories must have something called exposition. I had to ask him what the word meant. It simply turned out to be background information or events that happened before a story has begun. The reader needs it, he said, in order to understand character and plot, so I think I will give old exposition a tryout. When I first started writing on the beach that day, I thought I could skip all that, but maybe I should give it another go to explain how we got to be us.

SOME BACKSTORY ABOUT THE GIBSONS

Hard times came for my family in the early 1950s when my father, Harry, was suddenly arrested for drug possession. His nightclub act was all about the wild life of a hipster musician. He made up funny songs about drinking and drugs, so it was not surprising the vice squad had their eye on him until one day they caught him with enough drugs to put him in prison for a year.

With lawyer fees and no income, our mother had to sell our house and all the good-enough-to-sell furniture—even the piano had to go. Our lives were downsized from the suburbs of Burbank to a small two-bedroom bungalow ninety miles away in the farmland of Riverside County. Nine thousand dollars was all we had left, and three thousand of it went to buy the bungalow. The rest was tucked away in the bank to be used as a safety net when we needed it, like when Bill broke his arm and Jeff broke his foot all in the same week, or when Jeff and I both had to have our tonsils out. Mom suddenly became the sole support of four adolescent children and after several short jobs, she found steady work as a chambermaid at the big hotel downtown. Every morning six days a week, she stood out on the road to wait for the bus that took her into town eight miles away. She worked from eight in the morning to four in the afternoon at the swanky Mission Inn. It would already be getting dark when she finally stepped off the bus carrying a bag of groceries. Slowly she walked up the hill to our house. It was only after dinner and clearing up that she would sit down, resting her legs on a hassock as she watched a little TV and darned the holes in our socks until bedtime. This routine remained the same until Sunday. That was laundry day, cleaning day, and a roast for dinner day.

Somewhere during that first year, my mother and father got divorced. If moving to the boondocks was a sea change for us, the divorce didn't seem to alter anything. We had been used to having an off-again, on-again father who would be home only a few weeks between engagements.

The next year when Harry got out of jail, he visited us once and then we didn't see him anymore. I was thirteen, just starting my first year of junior high and finding the change from tomboy to teenager a bit difficult. The divorce just confused me. My brother Bill, two terms ahead in the ninth grade, shrugged off the divorce and concentrated on looking forward to starting high school the next year. As the oldest,

Arlene, at seventeen, was already a full-fledged, sophisticated teenager and after the initial shock and embarrassment of our father going to jail, brushed off the divorce as almost beneath her contempt. It was poor, introverted Jeff, only eleven and still in elementary school, who felt the breakup in our family the most.

I never knew why my parents divorced. The story goes that Mom divorced Harry after he stopped providing for us, but somehow this never rang true for me.

WHEN HARRY MET FLORENCE

My mother had once told me she had fallen in love with my father the first time she saw him. She was in high school when she spotted him going through the turnstile at the Parkchester Square Subway Station in the Bronx. He looked like nobody she had ever seen before. Yes, he was handsome with wavy blonde hair but there was something else, a certain zest and cockiness in the way he sauntered through the turnstile like he knew exactly where he was going and couldn't get there fast enough. He was young and should have been heading off to his classes like she was, but he wasn't dressed for school. He was wearing something more suited to the fashions of Harlem. His zoot suit was a striking green, and a long watch chain was draped out of the pocket of his baggy high-waisted slacks. The suspenders were a flashy red color, and his shoes sported bright canary yellow spats. He looked like danger and my mother was hooked. She soon found out the exciting guy in the subway was the older brother of one of her classmates at James Monroe High School, and soon, that classmate became my mother's best friend. It wasn't long before Harry noticed the sweet and pretty girl who was his sister's constant companion, and things just naturally took their course.

For Mom, love was forever. For Harry, he was to say later, Mom was his first girlfriend that wasn't a fast and loose, easy chick. He was and always remained a wild child, never faithful, a love 'em and leave 'em type, yet he always came back to his Florence.

That's why the story of Mom divorcing Harry just didn't ring true. She had stuck by him through his heroin withdrawals, and she had stuck by him and moved away from her large family of aunts, uncles, and cousins to live in California where there was no one to help her with four little kids and a big white house. Whenever Harry whistled, Mom would pack up everyone and everything and travel on trains, buses, and airplanes to wherever he was. Then, there were his affairs. If Mom put up with all that, she would not have been the one to sue for divorce.

RECOGNITION

Early in his career, Harry had been a rising star in the jazz world with his raspy voice and rollicking stride-piano playing. In his twenties, he had already recorded several hit records. At that time, you could walk down the street and often hear one of his original songs blaring out from someone's radio. With these triumphs under his belt, Harry was flying high. An offer to headline at a famous nightclub in California lured him west. Hollywood was also tempting him with possible parts in movies. They were interested in the young, talented, good-looking blonde man with the crazy laugh and the jive vocabulary.

Yet, by the early 1950s his career seemed to stall. Rock and roll was replacing jazz in young peoples' hearts. Things slowly fell apart.

RIVERSIDE

During the five or six years we lived out in the country, my mother put her head down and just worked—no social life or friends and she never dated—not ever. After a year at the Mission Inn, she got a week's vacation and used it to paint and wallpaper the entire inside of our tiny house. The boys got sports figures on their walls, my sister and I got pink roses, and the kitchen, a quaint farm theme. On her second vacation, Mom repainted the entire outside of the house.

For us kids, our adolescence consisted of quite a bit of petty bickering when we argued about whose turn it was to do chores. It ended usually with our mother doing everything herself while we sat back feeling guilty, but not guilty enough to help.

By the time I was in high school, I was sure my mother would end up alone. Arlene had already married and, of course, the boys, when they got older, wouldn't stay at home. That left only me. I wouldn't be going to college or art school, and had come to the conclusion that I wouldn't marry either. Most girls my age married their boyfriends right after high school, and I had never gone on a date. Yes, I would have to be the one who stayed with Mom and live in Riverside forever.

I could already picture it. I would get some sort of clerical or civil service job at the city hall after graduating from high school where I was majoring in secretarial training. Soon I would be taking the bus back and forth into town just like Mom. I was doomed.

RESCUED

Fortunately, it didn't turn out that way and Arlene was the person who shook us out of our lethargy. One by one, she brought all of us to this beach. Mom got a much better job as an assistant housekeeper at the newly opening Plush Horse Inn, and I was able to take art classes at the nearby City College and surprise, surprise, I did fall in love.

CHAPTER 13
MOM

THE JINX

The car gave a little lurch as it went over a bump, bringing me back to reality. I became aware again of the chugging engine and Howard K. Small's voice that had been droning out a tale of woe about his car for the last half hour. I was sympathetic but had heard it all so many times that his trials and travails had lulled me into a deep introspection about my mother.

Howard: "... so I took it in to the garage and asked the guy to listen to the motor because I could hear this kind of stutter squeak every so often like especially when I tried to take a hill and the guy said ..."

Why do the men in my mother's life always let her down? Take this Bob person, for instance. Like Arlene told me that first day, the whole time Mom was stuck in the hospital, he never visited, no phone call, no explanation. What was I to think?

Howard: "... the garage man was stymied and didn't know what to make of ..."

Mom was certainly swept off her feet in more ways than one, I thought morosely. After Bob entered the picture, our mother became girlish and glowing. Suddenly, she looked pretty again. Then, the very week she was installed into his apartment, she slipped on her newly waxed floor and fell smack on her back. Her alarmed boyfriend, I was told, frantically rushed her to the hospital where she was immediately strung up in traction and would be immobile for at least a month. Time went by, but where was Bob? Was he calling every day? Did he show up at her bedside bringing flowers and bonbons? No, there was just silence and an empty chair beside her bed. I didn't get it.

Howard: ". . . so the garage guy says to me that he couldn't hear anything wrong, but it could be anything from faulty gaskets to a crack or leak in the cylinders, which would be very expensive to fix but in the meantime a tune-up couldn't hurt . . ."

Is Bob one of those people who, as soon as they get something they really want, doesn't want it anymore? I sighed, Well it doesn't matter right now because Mom is being released from the hospital, and Howard and I are picking her up.

Howard: ". . . 'Forget a tune-up!' I said to him. 'What I need is a new car! This one is falling to . . .'" Howard leaned forward. "Oh, man! Did I just hear that squeak again? Maybe a tune-up would help if . . ."

Why does Mom let these men walk all over her? Why is she a doormat? And why, I wondered, am I getting annoyed and testy with her when my entire wrath should be aimed at her phony used car salesman of a boyfriend? We were nearing the hospital, and Howard stopped talking about his car and started to worry about finding a parking spot. With a sigh, I ended my analysis and started looking for empty spaces where Howard could park his problematic car.

THE PATIENT

When we reached my mother's room, my heart sank. She looked so weak and breakable lying there in that hospital bed surrounded by magazines, flowers, and a basket of fruit sent from the staff at the Plush Horse Inn. I kissed her cheek. It felt soft and thin. Even her hands were baby soft and white, gone were the usual calluses from constant work. The cheery nurse bustled around the bed in her crisp uniform. "So we are going home today?" she sang out, her hands deftly strapping my mother into a brace.

"Watch close, Lorraine, because you'll have to do this for me," my mother said in a small voice.

I moved closer and tried to appear interested, but all I could think was that my mother was in her underwear being laced into an iron bar. Mom was never the type to run around semi-dressed, so it bothered me to see her exposed. I turned away trying not to notice the blue varicose veins running up and down her legs. Veins she got from working hard and bearing four children. They were now especially visible against her pale skin. When at last the contraption was secured, I helped her into a light robe.

"All set to go?" Howard popped his head in. His eyes swept the hospital room in his usual indecisive way.

"Yes, in a minute, Howard. Here," I said, handing him a bag. "You can start bringing these things to the car, and I'll help my mother."

Howard took the bag, a few boxes, and an armload of clothes and staggered out with them, to return in a minute for more things. Meanwhile, with the help of the nurse, I eased my mother into a wheelchair. Although she tried to be strong, sitting up for the first time in a month had a dizzying effect on her, and it didn't help her spirits any. I tried to be cheerful and humorous, but it fell flat. I didn't blame her—being confined at the hospital, wondering why your live-in boyfriend hasn't come to see you— no word or explanation—must be defeating, and now she was being released from the hospital with no place to go. Things were messed up but good! Mom couldn't go back to Bob's apartment in Torrance and we couldn't take her to Culper Court. There were no proper beds, much less a bedroom there. No, we couldn't take her home. We would surely drive her insane like before. As a last resort, we were bringing her to Rita's who had offered her home and the daybed in the sun porch for a week until a better place was found. At least it was a plan. Arlene and I prepared to take turns at Rita's house caring for our mother. She would be bedridden, almost a total invalid who could do nothing for herself, for at least another month.

After a half hour's drive, we arrived at Rita's house. Arlene and Jeff were still arranging the sun porch into an impromptu sickroom. Of course, they had done it all wrong. The bed was facing into the sun and was piled with too many pillows and teddy bears. Arlene and Jeff were still trying to improvise a curtain to block the sun with a striped sheet and no one had thought to fix up a bedside table to hold a glass of water or a jar of Nivea body cream. Mom almost collapsed in exhaustion before the right kind of bed was erected. We all rushed around hysterically rectifying the bedroom to suit her needs while Mom slumped miserably nearby in a wicker chair. A few minutes later, a little plop was heard. When we looked around Mom had slipped out of the chair and quietly passed out.

A panic ensued from everyone after that as we tried to revive her with glasses of water and whiffs of ammonia. Finally, everything settled down to our satisfaction but not to Mom's. "The bed, it's too soft," she whimpered in despair against the white sheets, her blue eyes staring helplessly at the ceiling. Jeff slowly slunk out of the room embarrassed to see his mother helpless, while Arlene and I flapped our arms in exasperation. We knew it wasn't perfect, but it was the best we could do under the circumstances. Only Rita remained cheerful—the perfect nurse.

"Oh, how beautiful you look, Florence," soothed Rita, "just like Camille." All day Rita hovered lovingly over Mom and gleefully skipped to the bathroom to empty the bedpans but nothing we could do would change the whipped jellyfish expression on our mother's face.

"Would you like me to read to you?" I asked hopefully, sitting lightly on the bed and reaching for one of the many books on a nearby shelf. "Here's a good one. Do you like Steinbeck, Mom?"

"I guess so," she answered tonelessly, then after the second paragraph, "I, I don't like that story, Lorraine."

"Well, maybe there is something else." My patience, I knew, was slipping away from me. The words out of my mouth sounded harsh and clipped to my ears. I scanned the bookcase again. Mom interrupted my search.

"No, no, I'd rather not hear any story now, Lorraine."

"A game then?" I was still willing to do my bit.

"Not now!" Her head tossed from one side to another from pain or despair or both.

Giving up, I left the bedside to get a cup of coffee in the kitchen, and Arlene took over. Fifteen minutes later, she burst out of the sickroom completely exasperated and joined me at the kitchen bar. She had had no better luck than I did in making Mom comfortable and happy. Normally, Mom was so malleable and easy to placate.

"I couldn't do anything to please her," gasped Arlene, and here she mimicked a whiney voice. "'The room is too bright, the street is too noisy. The bed hurts my back.' I took it all with a smile but when she wanted me to call Bob to come and get her. That was it! I told her not to go crawling back to that big rat fink. And I told her that he must not love her if he didn't even visit or call all the time she was at the hospital."

"You didn't!" Rita gasped from the doorway. "Oh, Arlene, don't you know how weak your poor mother is and it is so important for her to have good spirits?" Rita clasped her hands in front of her. "You two get out for a while. You've done enough damage. I'll take care of your mother." She scooped us up and swooshed us out the door. As we turned back, we saw her tripping away into the bedroom to give cheer and witty spirits to Mom in the sickroom.

Walking around the block in the sunshine was a relief, but my conscience wouldn't stop flogging me with insults. *Imagine wanting to be away from your own mother when she is ill. You are an ungrateful wretch. Think of all the things she has done for you and given up for you and you begrudge a couple of hours of your day to your mother who is practically an invalid now. No, she is an invalid!*

Then another voice replied, *But why does she always have to be the martyr, always giving, giving, giving, never taking any joy for herself. Maybe she likes being stepped on.*

The other voice cut in again, *The whole time in Riverside, she worked so hard. She did it all alone too. You children didn't lift a finger to help her out.*

I'm different now, I thought, defending myself. *I am older and wiser.* But no, I shrugged that voice off. *I* am *the worst daughter of all!*

Arlene for once just walked along looking down at the road, not saying anything. Finally, she looked up with an evil bend to her mouth. "Wouldn't I love to corner that old fart, Bob? What a fake he is. It would be delicious to chew him to pieces by telling him off. Just watch out, Mr. Bob, you old rat fink, you can't hurt my mother and get away with it. You deserve a good tongue-lashing, you old phony with your stupid cornpone humor." She looked at me in a menacing way. "Don't you think so, Lorraine?" she demanded.

"Yes, of course," I said. When Arlene got this way, there was nothing to do but to agree and, of course, she was right. Bob needed to know that we were not going to let him walk all over our mother like that. He needed to take responsibility for his callous actions. Why did Mom have such bad taste in men's character? First our father, then this Bob.

When we returned to Rita's cottage, Rita was at the door. "Where were you guys?" She sounded frazzled. Her white blonde hair curled out statically around her head; she then told us what happened in jumbled sentences. "That man of your mother's . . . she said she wanted to die . . . and I had no idea . . . Arlene you upset her so much." Rita paused every now and then for a gasp of air. "Your poor mother was writhing on the bed . . . I had to hold her down . . . 'Nothing to live for!' She said that! Yes."

This was so new to me. I had never known my Mom to be upset like that about anything . . . to be hysterical. It was hard to believe. She was always the model of quiet self-control.

My mouth hung open in disbelief. "But why would she . . . ? He's not worth crying over," I said stupidly.

"She's asleep now," Rita continued as she ushered us over to the kitchen bar and started to make a pot of coffee. "She must really love him to have been so upset. Now, girls," Rita spoke emphatically, "I want to explain something to you. Bob is coming over tonight. Ah-ah!" Rita raised her hands as if to hold back a cattle charge. "Don't say anything when he comes. Let your mother make her own decision. Bob has conceded to come over and talk. I had to call him."

"*He* conceded!" Arlene practically shrieked. "*He* conceded to come over? He is a dirty rat. I would love to tell him off." Arlene's body stiffened as if ready to fight. "If I was in the hospital and my boyfriend or husband didn't come to see me, I would never speak to him again."

"Yeah," I broke in. "Where is Mom's pride to want to have anything to do with that guy?"

"Don't you two say anything when he comes tonight," Rita said in the controlled manner of a teacher to schoolchildren. "Let your mother make her own decision. She needs him. We all need a man and she's got one, so for heaven's sake, don't torture her anymore by telling her he is no good. She knows that already. Promise me that you will leave her alone!"

THE CONFRONTATION

As agreed, Arlene and I said nothing to Mom, but that night when Bob arrived, I waited for two hours outside the house right by the door in the cool darkness while he and Mom talked.

I wondered what they could be saying and why were they taking so long. I wondered too where Arlene was and why wasn't she here with me to ambush and lambaste Bob when he came out to go home. Finally, I heard sounds and movements that told me Bob was getting ready to leave.

As he was ducking out the front door, I blocked the doorway, my five-foot-two frame against his six-foot-four. "Would you please explain your actions for the past month to me?" I managed to say icily.

"There's nothin' to say, girl," twanged Bob, shaking his head slowly and looking at me with his sincerest "honest used car salesman" expression.

Well, that did it! I exploded totally! I let Bob have every insult ever stored up in my brain. All the anger and resentment, all the unfairness of the weak against the strong, all the pent up fury of the treachery to be said against men, I took and threw at Bob who, strangely enough took it all without flinching, his hound dog expression intact. When I called him a phony, self-centered egomaniac that milked and bilked people for what he could get, his appearance didn't change. When I accused him of callously dumping my mother and called him a slimy coward who left her with no word like the unfeeling egotist that he was, even then, his face remained blank.

That should have been enough, but I was on a roll and went on until I exhausted all my new vocabulary words like pusillanimous, malevolent, specious, and fecal matter. Yet, my tirade had no visible effect on the man. With his tall string bean figure towering above me, Bob's eyes still remained glued to mine in an apathetic look as if he were sorry for *me*. "When you are a little older, girl, you'll understand," he drawled, almost patting me on the head.

This was infuriating. "What I understand," I squeaked, "is that you won't even give me one little reason for abandoning my mother, but I know the reason," and here my voice squeaked even higher. "You just wanted to cut out because my mom was no good to you anymore. She was your cook, seamstress, and laundry woman and she was broken." I was running out of breath, but I couldn't stop, "and . . . and . . . you don't fool anyone with your simple homespun act. You are just a lowlife, selfish . . . interloper." I wasn't sure about the word interloper, but it sounded like an insult to me and that's what I was after.

Bob never broke character. He turned away, shaking his head slowly. "Well, little lady," he drawled, "I won't get mad at you." He was still very calm as he walked away, but I noticed that his hands were in tight fists close to his sides. After getting to the curb, Bob's long body collapsed into his car. He waited a moment then turned on the gas and pulled out fast in his shiny Chevrolet.

My little brawl had had no effect on the situation, but I had gotten a lot of hostilities off my chest. I was kind of proud of myself. I didn't know I had it in me to tell someone off like that. I must have gone on for at least ten minutes straight. I only wish he had broken down or shown how mad he was, but then that would have meant that I was right. He was trying to use the "old used car salesmen psychology" on me but it just didn't work. Well, Mom might go back to him, but it doesn't mean I have to like the man.

The next day Bob returned in his shiny Chevrolet to whisk Mom to his apartment home again. Within a few hours, nothing remained of my mother's short stay at Rita's. Now she was in the care of Bob Porth, honest, folksy used car salesman.

Later that night, three figures hunched over Rita's kitchen bar sipping coffee. "What women put up with," sighed Rita. "Men, they run around neglecting us but when they come back hurt and sad-eyed, we open up our arms again and again." She smiled in remembrance or expectation. "If Steve popped up," Rita continued in a melancholy voice, "I would do the same thing as your mother, only I hope he stays away this time."

"But why is it," I asked, "that some women can fall in love and if it doesn't work out they go on to someone else?" I was forgetting to sip my drink. "And why is it that others just keep going back to the same man or same kind of man over and over?"

"I think some women are just jinxed," murmured Arlene, squinting through the steam of her coffee. "They are jinxed because they can love only one person in their life." Arlene sat back in satisfaction with a grim look on her face. "Yeah, we are all jinxed; Mom, although she doesn't know it, and Rita, and me, and you too, Lorraine."

When she said that, I felt the imaginary thumb pressing against the sore spot on my ribs again, but Arlene was right. If *He* came and said he still loved me. I would take him back.

CHAPTER 14
LENNY

THE AFTERMATH

Following Mom's return back to Bob's well-appointed apartment in what the realtors called the "Riviera" section of Torrance Beach, she made a miraculous recovery. Within two weeks, she was back on her feet. She even felt ready to finish waxing the treacherous floor that had originally put her in the hospital, although Arlene and I dissuaded her from doing it—for a while anyway.

In those first weeks, my sister and I alternated in the task of Mom care. Every day, one of us would be there to make our mother lunch and keep her company. We stayed from twelve to four o'clock, being careful to arrive well after Bob left for work and to leave before (as Arlene would say) "Mr. Rat Fink" came home again.

It seemed to work out perfectly for all. Bob got free help, Mom got well faster, and Arlene and I got to feel that at last we were giving a little love and attention back to our mother instead of always taking it away, which was the usual case. Arlene decided later that we were the perfect team; I was good at straightening up and making Mom a tasty lunch, and she was good at keeping her laughing and occupied with talk. It was true, I could tempt Mom with a hearty sandwich, and Arlene's stories kept Mom smiling for hours. I could just imagine Arlene on her day with Mom, going out of her way to act out all the funny episodes at Culper Court: Arlene doing a parody of her own travails and mishaps, Arlene skewering the shortcomings of people, places, and things with her sharp observations.

After two weeks, our services were not needed, and Mom bid us farewell, although she said she would miss the gossip from Arlene and my tuna melt on toast.

After our bit as Florence Nightingale, my sister got serious about rehearsing Howard's songs, and I got down to writing in the gray notebook again. It didn't take long for me to finish writing up the drama of Mom's homecoming and my confrontation with Bob. It was the first time I had tried to write dialogue, yet the right words spilled out onto the gray notebook. I used up three whole pages in no time. Later, rereading the story, I realized how surprisingly fierce and brave I was that night, telling off Bob like that. *Now, why,* I suddenly wondered, *couldn't I stick up for myself that way?*

REHEARSING

Howard was coming over almost every day now to practice with Arlene. Most of his songs were love songs. He was a true romantic, falling in love with both Arlene and with me, writing and dedicating songs and poems to us. Even so, he was serious and professional about rehearsing. Most of the time the music room was used, but sometimes Arlene and Howard would tape a session at one of his friend's houses in Palos Verdes or Hollywood where they would have recording equipment. Then Jeff would go along. During playbacks, Howard was quiet for a change, listening, his brow furrowed. Arlene winced whenever she heard her voice, and Jeff grinned sheepishly when his solos came up.

*"A metal waste basket on the head is good for
hearing yourself sing,"* said Arlene. Jeff tried it too.

Arlene tried hard to sing all the weird and beautiful songs Howard wrote but they were difficult. His tunes, as he called them, had the wildest melodies with sharps and flats and strange ringing chords. "I can't . . . I can't do it . . . It's too high, Howard!" Arlene would wail in a hysterical voice, glaring at him all the while, opening her eyes big.

Howard would always have an amazed look on his face when this happened. As if he had never known her to be anything but dainty, sweet, and delicate—his ideal love. "Of course you can do it, man! What do you mean you can't?" He'd blink and jerk his neck in that familiar twitch and begin the song all over again.

Once, Arlene got so angry and frustrated she looked around the room for something to throw at him. There was nothing near except a piece of paper, so she picked it up, and with a scream, hurled it at him. The paper harmlessly fluttered in the air and Arlene burst into laughter. After much crying and bellowing, rehearsals would end. Howard would leave in his car and Arlene would crawl into her bed with the faithful wet washrag on her temples.

If I was finished with my writing, I would take their place in the music room for an hour or two. First, I practiced all the chord inversions I learned from Jeff and Howard, then and only then did I attempt to play some of Howard's songs. It was painfully slow work, but I *was* getting better. Finally, I ended the session by turning to my *Young Beginners First Music Book of Songs* and finished the session by playing a rousing version of "The Woodchuck Song."

EMPLOYMENT

Jeff was staying out later and later with his new job at the Lighthouse. When it closed for the night and he finished gathering up all the plates and glasses to be washed, there was still music going on. Some musicians stayed to jam, and there was always a line of young, up-and-coming jazz musicians who waited patiently for their chance to show off their chops. A session would start casually. Someone would climb onto the bandstand and start to tinkle on the piano. Others joined in until someone would call out a tune and the key, or someone else might start to play the blues. If you had an instrument and were brave enough, you would step up and join the song. Jeff always took his sax to work, waiting for the moment he was courageous enough to play. He wanted to be ready because at some point everyone on the stand had to take a solo. If you botched it, you were kicked off. So far, his alto had stayed in its case.

Another pattern was forming for us. As Jeff got home later and later, I started waking earlier and earlier. Sometimes Jeff would be tromping through to his room just as I started to wake up. I was not working anymore. My job at Pio's lasted all of two days. The bakery lunch counter was a bit longer at a month. The average time I estimated was a four-to six-week stint and then I was out again. *What is it about me?* I wondered. *Why can't I hold a job?* They were simple and easy enough, I thought, but eventually the day would come when I would be called aside and with a serious, half-sorrowful expression on their faces, someone in charge would fire me. They all used that same line. "I'm sorry but we *have* to let you go," they would soberly announce shaking their heads sadly, as if what they were doing hurt them but was the best thing for me. Almost as if they had been keeping me in a basement chained to a radiator and now they were releasing me.

"But why?" I would ask. "Did I make too many mistakes?" How many mistakes can you make serving someone a stack of pancakes or a toasted ham sandwich?

"No, not really too many," they would say slowly. "You're just not working out." That was another thing they always said, and here their expression deepened into even more sadness.

Sometimes I would push for more information. "*How* am I not working out? Why are you 'letting me go'?"

Their next line was again the same. "You're a good kid, but you are not cut out for this kind of work." That line always amazed me. Not cut out to give someone a cup of coffee, or sell a tube of lipstick or sunglasses, or serve a slice of apple pie? I always tried my best, so it hurt to be fired. I wanted to know more, but by this point, my eyes would be burning and I would turn away so they couldn't see my tears.

In consequence, for the last week or so, I had been taking a break from even trying to get work. Maybe when summer arrived, I could start again. For now, I would be a stay-at-home auntie. I would play with the kids, try out new recipes for graham flour, and concentrate on writing and practicing the piano. I was making good progress despite continual interruptions of people coming in and out of the house. Then, a few days later the pattern of my days changed again.

AN EARLY VISITOR

One morning, as usual, the sun was slanting into the small attic window in an effort to pry my eyes open. In defense, I tucked the covers over my head and tried to continue my dream.

"Oh yes, I was just beginning to fly. I was in a kind of hovering pattern, having only gotten a few inches off the ground by flapping my arms vigorously but—"

"Get up, Lorraine!" A male voice knifed into my dream. I burrowed deeper into the covers.

"Lorraine!" The voice pierced through again.

Reluctantly, I came out of my cocoon and opened one eye halfway to see the head and shoulders of Lenny Glassman, best buddy of my ex-boyfriend, protruding into my loft. We had been seeing a lot of him for the last few weeks since he moved back in with his mother.

"You want to ride down to San Diego with me?" His voice sounded like he was doing me a favor.

"Lenny," I groaned, now sitting up. "Don't you ever knock when you come into a girl's bedroom?"

"I never have to." He smirked, and his eyebrows went up and down like Groucho Marx. "They always ask me in. Besides, this isn't a bedroom, it's more like a mouse hole." He was running his finger in a dusty corner then looked up to grin sarcastically. "Don't worry. I wouldn't want your skinny little body anyway."

"That's a relief," I quipped back, now more awake.

"Well, do you want to go or what? I gotta leave right now." His tone implied sudden impatience.

"I guess so," I answered after thinking about it for a moment. I did feel a bit restless lately. A day's break from writing and practicing would be refreshing, and a long ride in an open car along the coast sounded especially good to me.

"Hurry up then," Lenny barked like a top sergeant. "Get out of that bed that you haven't changed the sheets on for a month and out of those pajamas you've been wearing for the last week and—"

"Look, Mr. Perfect," I interrupted, at last getting miffed. "These sheets are just washed. I can't help it if they came out gray." I brushed at the blue flannel of my pajamas. My voice was getting high and squeaky. "And if you think I am so terrible, why should I come with you to San Diego?"

But Lenny didn't answer. Ignoring my question, he mumbled, "Are you coming or what?" Then he fastidiously brushed his hands together to remove the dust and backed down the ladder.

"Do I have time to take a shower?" I called down.

"Don't bother, Lorraine." He grinned up mischievously. "Why break your record of avoiding soap and water for a month? Just throw something on."

This time, I just laughed and, twisting quickly out of my PJs, grabbed for a bright yellow shift hanging on my wardrobe pole overhead.

Exactly one minute later, my feet scrambled down the ladder, landing conveniently into my sandals lying under the last rung. I gave my face a quick wash and after combing my hair and taking a moment to put on a dab of lipstick, I was ready to go. But where was Lenny?

I found him in the dining room standing in a beam of sunlight by the back windows. He was stretching in ecstasy like a young giraffe, arching his lanky body and extending his long neck. This done, his fingers massaged his entire chest, ending by languidly pulling at the hairs that freely spurted out of the top of his shirt. Yet, like a real giraffe on the plains of Africa, Lenny was not aware of the dangerous predators that lurked nearby. I had once seen a travelogue of an African safari where an unwary giraffe was brought down by three tawny lions, and now a version of this scene was playing out before my eyes as our early morning visitor, lost in thought and self-admiration, was being stalked by three tawny-haired children.

Slowly, they crept up to the unaware Lenny, still preening in the sun. Then, Lindee gave the signal and the three children converged on their prey. Lindee caught the startled animal around the waist and Laurie J. grabbed somewhere around his knees, while Donnie made a tremendous leap and hung onto Lenny's bent arm.

I had to smile at this because Donnie had a habit of hanging onto the arm of any visiting male, and like Lenny, they were always a bit surprised when it happened. But here, I must admit that, although Lenny fell into the trap, he was a good sport about it.

"Hey, there! What's going on? Oh, no you don't," he snarled. "You are not going to capture me. It is I who will catch you and eat you because I am the big bad wolf, and you are the three little piggies!" Lenny had upended my African analogy when he adopted his wolfish character, but the three little pigs—or should I say lion cubs—hung on until their prey spun around and around, swinging Donnie in the air while also scooping up Lindee and Laurie J. with his other arm and spinning himself around until the centrifugal force pulled all three children from their victim and slid them onto the floor. They skittered across the linoleum, practically into the adjacent kitchen. A moment later, they were up laughing and giggling, ready for another foray, when a bedroom door opened and the rumpled mother of the three attackers slowly peeked out.

Arlene had been out late with Sid last night, and it looked like she hadn't gotten a lot of sleep. Sadly, all that was left of an elegant pompadour she had fashioned last night now looked like a squashed beehive. Stepping gingerly into the room, she blinked her blue-shadowed eyes several times while still trying to keep them closed, then finally gave up. Today my sister was wearing the same long black nightgown I had seen that first morning, except now the long sleeves had been removed; some loose black threads were still clinging to the armholes.

"What the . . . ? Oh," she groaned, "it's just you, Glassman. I should have known. Don't you have the decency to wait until a body is awake before you come a-calling?"

"Don't blame me," Lenny said. "I was as quiet as a mouse until these young guttersnipes attacked me, and I prefer that you use my stage name, Richardson. It sounds less Jewish."

"But of course. Mr. Richardson, I presume?" Arlene put her nose in the air and assumed the accent of an English butler. The children were giggling at the funny language the adults were using and fell down on the floor again. Arlene screwed up her eyes and looked at Lenny. "And how did you get in, may I ask?" She was still using the posh accent.

"Actually, your brother let me in. He was coming back from his job and invited me in for a jam session in his pad downstairs." As if on cue, the sound of an alto sax drifted up from below the deck then ended abruptly in a high squeak. There was silence then while Jeff, I presumed, was adjusting a new reed in his mouth piece. Lenny continued. "I hear he works at the Lighthouse now. Maybe he can put in a good word for me with Howard Rumsey?"

I had to laugh and butt in to the conversation. "I doubt if a busboy/dishwasher has much pull with the manager of a world-famous nightclub."

Lenny looked around, seeing me for the first time. "Hey, are you ready?"

"Oh, I forgot to brush my teeth." I said. "I'll be right back."

"Typical," Lenny murmured and gave a sardonic look. "And while you are at it," he called after me, "why don't you shave your legs too?"

"I don't have to!" I smugly replied back over my shoulder. "My legs are tan, and the hairs are blonde, almost invisible."

Lenny had this weird thing about women and hair in particular. Except for glorious long tresses, he could not tolerate any other type of hair on women. He wanted it gone and baby smooth. It was as if he was looking for the perfect female and nothing but perfect would do.

I had seen Lenny with many of his girlfriends, and they were all gorgeous, mostly actresses, but he was always picking out flaws, anything and everything. Their bodies weren't perfect— too thin, too fat, too tall, too short. Maybe they had rough elbows, or a funny mole or their teeth were not straight or white enough. One crooked tooth and he would point it out to everyone. The flaws were so minor, but even a hangnail was cause for concern. Soon, that girlfriend would be gone. Once he noticed some hair on the toes of another girlfriend. He made such a fuss and embarrassed her. It was not long before she was gone too.

I had stumped him with my retort about my legs, but Lenny recovered quickly and grabbed Arlene's arm and lifted it up in the air. "Ah-hah!" he said. "Look at this unsightliness." And he pointed to a pale stubble of hair under Arlene's armpit.

"Quit that!" Arlene swung her free arm into Lenny's chest, and he released his hold. "Look at this!" She pointed to the tuft of hair arising from his open shirt. "You have your gall to point out a little stubble under my arm and just look at you. Your chest! You are a hairy ape, so hairy that you could play the part of Tarzan's best friend. You could go bare-chested to the Arctic and not need a fur parka. You don't need a shaver there. You need a lawn mower." Arlene smiled, impressed with her own sharp tongue.

"OK, OK, Miss Fast-talker, but you don't understand that what is repulsive on a woman is manly on a guy. The hair on my chest is a sign of the stronger sex and is masculine. In fact, I was thinking of trying some lotion to make it grow even more."

Lenny and Arlene could have gone on all day sparing with quips and put-downs, but they were stopped by a shy tapping at the door.

ANOTHER VISITOR

All eyes turned toward the tapping. The door slowly swung open, and Miss Beek stepped gracefully inside calling, "Hello? Hello?" The elderly lady looked around until she saw us in the next room. "Oh, there you all are," she trilled, and gave a faint wave of her hand. It was obvious she had come many times before. "Oh, good morning to you all, good morning." Miss Beek's head bobbed up and down as she came into the dining room, smiling with her bright eyes. Lenny was speechless for once, taking in her fluttery pale clothing and her Victorian manners. It was like there was a big comic book question mark over his head which meant, "What in the heck is this?"

Miss Beek saw the children, who were still in a state of disorder on the floor. "Oh, there you are, children," she said. "I have a surprise for you. Now let's get off the floor and go into the parlor where we can all sit down." She glided around the room, swooping up Lindee, Donnie, and Laurie J. from the linoleum, then gently guided them into the living room and nestled them one by one onto a small, overstuffed sofa. "I have a wonderful Bible story to share with you. It's called 'Joseph and the Coat of Many Colors.' Now if I can sit in the middle of you children, you can all see the pictures." Her voice drifted off into a mellifluous murmur too soft for us in the other room to hear.

Lenny was looking after her with the question mark still above his head. "Who is that?" he finally asked.

"Oh, that's . . . we call her 'the Bird Lady.'" Arlene tossed off the comment with a shrug. "We thought she was a social worker, but she is just a nice do-gooder-church-lady who wants to save the souls of my children. We just let her come and go as she likes."

"I think she's sweet and mysterious too," I added, "the way she is always swooping in and then swooping out again without warning. We never know when to expect her."

There was a lull in the conversation, so before we got into another debate, I dashed into the bathroom and started brushing my teeth, leaving Arlene and Lenny to argue about nothing as they usually did, both trying to outsmart the other.

When Lenny first started coming around, he was set on teasing me about my broken heart. He'd swagger in saying, "Hey, guess whose ex-boyfriend I just saw?" And then he would look at me closely to see my reaction. I was ready and I just looked back at him blankly, but Lenny was not daunted and continued.

"Yeah, as I said, I just bumped into your ex. He asked me how you were getting along without him, so I thought I would stop by and cheer you up." Lenny threw me another deep stare.

"Thank you, kind sir," I would say tersely, trying to look casual with my insides churning. One of the worst things about having a breakup was the fact that I couldn't talk about it to anyone. Arlene or Rita could never keep it to themselves, of course Jeff was out of the question, and Mom was, well . . . She would just shake her head and say something like "Men are like that, and we have to accept it." So, I didn't tell anybody about the breakup and especially how I felt about it.

"No, seriously, Lorraine," Lenny had said, looking almost serious, "*He* did tell me to check up on you."

"*He* was checking up on *me*?" I railed against that idea. *His* concern was making me feel worse. What was I, poor Little Orphan Annie? I was getting madder by the minute and trying not to show it. Lenny, not noticing, was still going on about his duty to his friend. "Yeah, I've been told to cheer you up," he said brightly. "Remember how you always laughed at my jokes?" Lenny tapped his finger to his head. "But I must remember that I am not to ever, ever, ever '*hit on you*,' Lorraine. Your ex said he wouldn't take it kindly if *we* were ever to get together as a couple."

"What?" I gritted my teeth. Who was *He* to tell me who I could and couldn't get together with! Everyone was fair game. Yet, *His* precious ego need not have feared. I could never get serious about Lenny. He went through girlfriends like Kleenex tissues. That conversation had been several weeks earlier, and now I was used to Lenny popping up at any time day or night to tease me.

In the bathroom, I squeezed the last bit of toothpaste out of the tube and managed to work up enough foam to clean my teeth adequately. I was just putting some lipstick on again, when Lenny banged on the door to hurry me up. Moving faster, I finished, but when I opened the door, Arlene and Lenny were again deep in a verbal war, using their rapier wits to cut each other down to size.

A light knocking coming from the music room stopped their chatter. After a few more knocks, the French windows were pushed open and a large leg stepped over the sill. In another moment, a matching leg concluded the operation and the burly shape of Jim Bishop, complete with guitar, moved into the music room. Since that first time he had come to Culper Court, when the front door had been stuck, Jim had gotten it into his head that the French doors that served as windows to the music room were the official and proper portal of entrance, and, ever since, always made his appearance that way. Today, though, he was followed by a slight, dark figure. A young man with close-cropped black hair and a delicate, pointed chin followed close behind the massive back of Jim. The small figure turned and looked around briefly at the yellow piano and the apple-green painted Indonesian wicker chairs with the curly scrollwork on the top, before following Jim. As they stepped up into the living room, the Bird Lady, with the children still beside her, stopped her story of Joseph and his many colored coat right at the part where Joseph's brothers had thrown him down a well. Jim, ever the gentleman, or at least ever gentle, bowed his head to the little group with a hearty "Good morning, ma'am." If he had a hat, I'm sure he would have taken it off.

The Bird Lady, like the gracious lady she was, answered, "Good morning to you too." And at that point the children were pulling on her sleeve to continue the story so they could find out if the fall down the well had killed Joseph.

Jim, spotting the rest of us in the dining room, smiled broadly and signaled with a wave of his hand. "Morning y'all," he boomed cheerily as he tromped through to us. "Is Jeff up?"

Lenny looked up and down the burly form of Jim Bishop and his small sidekick then stepped forward with the air of a snooty butler that Arlene had earlier imitated. "I'm Richardson," he said in a pretentious tone, and gave a dismissive little bow. "And whom may I say is calling?"

Jim looked confused at first, then his face burst into a big grin and he grabbed Lenny's hand and shook it fiercely up and down. "Hey, I'm Jim and this here," he indicated behind him, "is Tim. We're here for the jam session."

Tim peeked out from behind Jim and squeaked out a "Hello," then looked terribly embarrassed and pulled out a harmonica from his back pocket and slid his mouth back and forth on it, making that sound (like going up and down the scales) as if to indicate that he did, indeed, have the qualifications to join in the jam. By this time, Jim had picked up the sound of Jeff's sax from below that had just started up again and was already shuffling out the back door with Tim close behind. *Is Jeff playing the "March of the Cockroaches" again?* I wondered. The tune sounded familiar. "Looks like he's started without us," Jim called cheerfully back at us. A few seconds later, the sound of his boots clumped down the back staircase.

Lenny was looking around in a kind of bemused stupor, first out the back where the two musicians had disappeared, then into the front room at the kids and Miss Beek in her old-fashioned clothing. He shook his head. "What kind of place is this? I feel like I must be in a Dickens time warp because . . . hey, didn't I just see Tiny Tim go by?"

Ignoring this jest, Arlene headed for the kitchen. "Well, no use trying to go back to sleep, I'd better make the kids some oatmeal," she mumbled to herself, then louder to Lenny and me, "Hey, who's up for a cup of coffee?"

"I am," I responded.

"Oh no you don't," Lenny said. "I'm in a hurry. We can get some coffee on the road." Lenny had snapped out of his reverie and was now eyeing me up and down. He took in my sandals and short yellow beach dress. Cocking his head to the side he singsonged, "Look at little Lorraine in the itty-bitty baby dress. The last time you wore that, everyone asked me if you were my twelve-year-old sister." In a flash, his long arms shot out, grabbing me by the waist. In a second, I was slung over his shoulders like a sack of potatoes. A few moments later he had me by the feet hanging upside down an inch or two from the floor. By now, I was well used to all of Mr. Glassman's, or I should say Mr. Richardson's, crazy antics. "Oh, Lenny," I whined wearily as the blood rushed to my head. "Now I have to brush my hair again."

Still holding onto my feet, Lenny lowered me down to the linoleum where he let me wriggle a moment like a prize fish squirming to be free, then suddenly let go and walked quickly to the door, "I'll wait in the car," he said in a low voice.

I sat on the floor a few moments trying to figure him out. He sure had a funny way of treating his friends.

CHAPTER 15
THE OPEN ROAD

THE WHITE MG

It took just one more minute to dash into the bathroom again to brush out the tangles Lenny had created when he hung me upside down. My hair was getting long, I noticed. I put on a bit of lipstick again, and ran to the car, brushing my hair with my fingers as I flew. It took five leaps to plunk myself down in the white sports car next to Lenny.

"What took you so long?" he said, using his top sergeant voice again, then not waiting for an answer, lurched the little MG down the alley of Culper Court, the wind whipping at my just-brushed hair and twisting it into my mouth as my feet kicked at an empty lunch sack on the floorboard. Eventually, I made room for myself and eased back into the leather bucket seat.

At the first stoplight, I turned toward Lenny. "Why do you have to go to San Diego?"

"Promotion, man! Big things! I got a smash record, and I'm taking it to all the disc jockeys in the Southern California area." He was using his big businessman voice now. I could see his eyebrows rising and falling beneath his dark sunglasses as he explained his newest venture. "I wrote the song and produced the record so when it is a hit, I'll clean up." He ran his hand across his chest pulling at the hairs again. "Someday I'm going to have lots of money. I know it." Lenny nodded his head as if to assure himself.

Joining in the game, I teased, "Why don't you just marry a rich, old bag?"

"I plan to, only she has to be rich *and* beautiful."

I laughed at his quick comeback as we continued to speed along the road. Hermosa Avenue was an ordinary two-lane street, but eventually it connected to the highway that ran all the way to San Diego. It was exciting to be on the open road in a white sports car speeding down toward Mexico.

We soon left the modest beach towns of Hermosa, Redondo, and Torrance and before long were winding up into the hills of Palos Verdes. For a short time we lost sight of the ocean, until it reappeared again as we motored down the other side of the cliffs. At Long Beach, groves of oil wells, their derricks like toy erector sets, obscured the view but they gave way to the more upscale Newport and Laguna Beaches. Later on, we came to long stretches of steep cliffs eroded by the wind.

Speeding along the unbroken highway listening to the humming of the convertible and the wind rhythmically rushing past, I didn't have a hint of my old car sickness and soon fell into a dreamy state.

Lenny broke into my thoughts. "You know," he mused, "I was really surprised when you and J____ broke up. I mean, he had it so good."

Immediately, my relaxed state disappeared. Was I really going to have to talk about my ex-boyfriend?

But Lenny didn't need my participation and rattled on. "Here he had this really cute girlfriend, who didn't demand a single thing from him, and in no way nagged because he never had any money to spend on you. You were so easygoing, never jealous, never questioned when he wanted to take off to Hollywood or wherever and then, after almost two years, what does he do? *He breaks up with you!*"

I thought that was the end of Lenny's soliloquy, but he wasn't finished.

"Why, I ask myself?" he continued.

Here I interjected, "And do *you* know the answer?" Suddenly I was interested to hear what he would come up with.

"Well for one thing," Lenny was smirking behind his sunglasses, "for one thing this girlfriend is a virgin so he is not getting any."

I was stunned for a moment. Did everyone know about the state of my sexuality or lack of it? I had never discussed this topic with anybody, yet everyone knew all about it—Rita, Arlene, Mom, Lenny, and probably the mailman by now.

Lenny, not hearing my angry thoughts, was still talking as the California coastline zipped by. "I think I know the answer," he asserted.

"Well then, why don't you let me in on it," I dared him.

Lenny plunged ahead, "When *he* first met *you*, you were nineteen and never been kissed!"

Now how did he know about that? I thought only girls gossiped about their love life, but apparently not!

Lenny continued. "And you see, since *he* was your first and only boyfriend, my good friend had to start from the very beginning with you. *He* had to teach you everything—how to kiss, how to make out, so by the time it came to that last thing, your virginity, he balked, he ducked, he chickened out."

"Chickened out?" I echoed, my voice thin.

"Yeah, don't you see? He didn't want the responsibility of being the first one to have sex with you because he knew that with a girl like you, well you know, you are the marrying kind."

There was a short silence while he let that sink in. What he said made sense, but before I had time to dwell on it, Lenny broke the serious mood by saying, "Now, I have no such qualms. I'm ready to deflower you at any time you want."

Glad that we were back to silly banter, I answered with a mock prudishness. "Thank you, sir, but I think I will pass on your kind offer."

"Well, don't wait and play it safe too long or you will wind up like that ditzy dame I saw at your house."

Suddenly, I was a bit alarmed; I had a picture of myself at sixty, looking a bit like the Bird Lady: unmarried, baking cookies for the kids on the block. Lenny was still harping on my pristine state. "You know, there should be some way we can cash in on your virginity. Like there aren't many of your age left. It's too bad you don't sing, with your waifish looks and big eyes, like those paintings of the sad kids—you know—with the huge eyes."

"You mean the Keane paintings? That isn't good art. My teacher Miss Walker—"

"Good shmood! It sells, and I bet I could sell *you* too. It's too bad you don't sing."

"I can sing, a little."

"'A little' is right. Your voice sounds like a baby chick just hatched out of its shell. With your high, breathy voice—but wait, that could work. Picture this—you standing there dressed like an angel in white or in blue like the Virgin Mary herself. Too bad your name isn't Mary. And then we'll have some backup singers. We'll call it—how's this?—The Virgin and the Three Saints. Hmmm, or The Virgin and the Father, Son, and the Holy Ghost. No, the Virgin is not quite right. Oh, oh, wait, this is good, listen to this, how about—Madonna and the Immaculate Conceptions?"

I was laughing out loud now.

"But seriously," Lenny said, "if I wasn't already pushing this girl group I just put together, 'Madonna and the Immaculate Conceptions' is a great name for a group."

"I don't think the Catholic Church would like it," I said.

"Yeah, yeah, it may be ahead of its time. I wouldn't want the Pope to excommunicate me or anything."

"I thought you were Jewish."

"Whatever."

With a jerk of the steering wheel, Lenny turned the car off the highway and into the first gas station, screeching to a stop. Immediately, an aluminum comb came out of his shirt pocket and was carefully run through his sandy hair. He looked intently into the car mirror touching at his hairline worriedly.

"Lenny," I said, "why don't you take off those sunglasses, they make you look like a fly with big black eyes." Obediently, he took them off, rubbing his aquiline nose. White rings of pale skin showed against his tan face, giving him a gaunt and haunted look. Suddenly, I felt sorry for him.

"Did I get a tan or what?" he asked seriously looking into the mirror again.

"You look like a raccoon in negative," I joked.

He laughed, then in a bogus German Gestapo voice barked, "You haf fife minutes for un bat-room break!"

Exactly five minutes later, I came back to the car. Lenny was sitting quietly and thoughtfully looking down, the little curves of his mouth in a frown as he delicately sat chewing a fingernail. His foot on the floorboard beat nervously to no music. Suddenly, he jumped up, unfolding his six-foot frame and leaped out of the car. "Wait, I gotta make a phone call."

THE SCAM

Ever since I had known Lenny, the phone booth had been a second home to him. For hours, he would crowd himself into one of those glass squeezeboxes to cook up his "big deals" and "make money" schemes. He must have been the telephone company's biggest nonpaying client. I will try to convey Lenny's system of "making a phone call." First, he borrows a dime from you, then enters the telephone booth. The monologue goes something like this: Lenny putting *your* dime into the telephone slot, dialing O until he gets an operator.

Lenny: (sounding a little desperate) Hello, hello, operator? (pause, as operator speaks.) Yes, yes, you *can* help me. (Lenny gulps and sounds a little out of breath.) There must be something wrong with this line operator. (Lenny's voice now rises a little higher.) I've been trying and trying to call Hollywood -573-57 and . . . (A pause as the operator talks.) Yes, yes, it rings all right but then it just clicks and then it just goes dead. (Lenny's voice is sounding almost desolate as he adds) I've lost fifty cents already. (Another pause as the operator talks.) No, no (Lenny's voice has a touch of hurt in it), I don't want you to send me my money back in the mail. I really don't care. (Here, Lenny gives a touch of the martyr to his voice.) You can keep the fifty cents I lost. I just want to get my party. (Bigger pause as the operator talks.) Oh! (Lenny, in grateful disbelief) You mean *you* can try to get the line for me? (Biggest pause as the operator explains.) Thank you! And you'll give me fifty cents credit on the call? (Another operator pause.) I can't thank you enough! Lenny then closes the folding door on the telephone booth and continues in private. After the call is finished, the original dime is returned in the chute by the operator, and as Lenny swaggers out of the booth he flips the borrowed dime back to you. I saw him even contact New York in this way.

BIG PLANS

Later, back on the Pacific Coast Highway, Mr. Richardson continued to run off at the mouth about his future in the rock and roll record business. I listened for ten minutes straight about all the strategies he had for his new snappy song and the trio of girl singers he had gotten to record it. "Yup," he said, "I have a good feeling about this one. It can't miss. It has everything."

"And what is the name of this song?" I finally asked.

"Operator, operator, can you help me? I've lost my dime!"

138

"Our Surfer Boys." Did Lenny sound a little apologetic?

"Well, of course it is," replied Lenny stoutly. "That's why it will be a hit."

"Isn't that a total rip-off of 'Little Surfer Girl' by The Beach Boys?" I demanded.

"I'm almost afraid to ask the name of your girl group," I said.

"OK, but promise me you won't laugh. They're called, er, The Surf Bunnies."

I struggled to stifle the laugh bubbling up, but it was useless. "Surf Bunnies? Ha!" I blurted out. It was ridiculous! "Did you find them at Hugh Hefner's Playboy Penthouse?" I choked out. "Or maybe, ha, ha, in last year's Easter basket or in Farmer McGruder's garden patch?" My laughter made muffled, sputtering noises as I pictured Lenny's singing group and my silly illusions. I wasn't sure Lenny had picked up on the Beatrix Potter reference, but he couldn't miss the Playboy one.

"All right, all right, I get it, you think it is stupid."

After getting myself under control, I asked seriously, "Don't you get sick of peddling crap?" I looked at him closely for a reaction.

His face was very straight and solemn when he replied, "Not as long as there is a lot of money in it. Remember, I plan to be rich."

"But you like beautiful songs, don't you?" I was digging for some sign of sensitivity.

"Like this?" Lenny suddenly burst into the operatic "Be My Love," made famous by Mario Lanza, only Lenny was singing in the high-pitched, nasal voice of Jerry Lewis.

Never serious for a moment, I thought. *He's probably afraid he might really think about what he is doing with his life.*

After finishing Jerry Lewis, Lenny ran through his versions of James Cagney, Jimmy Stewart, Marlon Brando, James Mason, Cary Grant, and even that old character actor, Walter Brennan. Lenny was just getting into his interpretation of President Kennedy singing a Nat King Cole song, when I interrupted again.

"But you really want to be a singer, a good one." I was still trying to get a straight answer.

"Can you do this, Lorraine?" Lenny let out a high vibrating sound like an air raid siren.

With my ears ringing, I had to give up my pursuit of Lenny's soul and just join in.

The rest of the ride went something like this: I leaned back in my leather bucket seat and listened and laughed while Lenny Richardson alias Lenny Glassman went through his repertoire of jokes, stories, impressions, and songs. "Sing this," he'd say. "Dum dum dum, duby du wa wa wa wa." While I "dum dummed," he'd chant in a high falsetto like a rhythm and blues singer. "Do I sound colored or what?" he'd ask at the end of each song. Sometimes I'd be laughing so hard I couldn't reassure him.

CHAPTER 16
FROM THE GRAY NOTEBOOK
HAPPY MOTHER'S DAY

I IMPRESS MYSELF

Sitting again on the top step, of the back stairs in the warm afternoon sun, I was reading, only this time it was not Steinbeck or Thomas Wolfe but something I had written myself. Up to now, I had only attempted short things—descriptions, a bit of dialogue. Some were pretty good, I thought—at least promising, but what I had just finished sounded an awful lot like a real chapter in a real book.

After weeks of listening to Arlene and Howard rehearsing, I finally got to hear them perform at the Zanzibar, the nightclub in Santa Monica where Howard's group had been playing for the last few months. Early this morning, I got up and after two cups of coffee, put down all the details, conversations, and everything I could remember from last night. I even thought of a good title.

HAPPY MOTHER'S DAY
PART I

Turning off the shower and pushing the plastic curtain aside, I step gingerly out of the bathtub and onto the swampy floor. Looking back, I shrugged at the gray enamel tub. Not much use trying to clean it, but it's better than when I first came back home. I remember scrubbing at the encrusted scum and rust stains without much success. At one time, it must have been one of those grand old-fashioned tubs with legs, but someone had tried to modernize by cementing a heavy box around it. Years of splashed water and pounding showers has eroded the grout leaving a gaping black crack around the entire rim. I half expect all will give way one day and plunge the heavy porcelain and cement monstrosity through the floor with me in it but now is not the time to worry about that. Tonight is special.

Hurriedly, I wrap the oversized terry cloth robe around me and open the door. "What time is Howard supposed to pick us up?" I call out to Arlene in the bedroom who must be just taking out the rollers in her hair.

"What? Jeff! Shut up for a minute, will ya?" Arlene bellows at the blasts of our brother's saxophone coming from the music room. He grunts and is silent.

"When will Howard come?" I repeat, after the vibrations cease.

"Well, he said eight o'clock so that means he'll probably pull up around nine."

Nine o'clock? That means we have a good hour yet before we can leave for the Zanzibar. I take a breath and silently hasten Howard to please hurry up! I have been waiting for weeks to hear my sister sing with a full group behind her. Arlene and Howard have been rehearsing torturously and have worked up some beautiful things, and tonight I can go. Jeff is babysitting.

My sister's room is in its usual avalanche state as I enter and rummage through the big box next to her bed for some underwear. Finding none, I settle for a bathing suit bottom. Beside me, Arlene is standing before her mirror, hair hanging in noodles from the curlers and (yikes) she is shaving her eyebrows with a razor blade!

"Arlene!" My eyes flinch just watching her. "You'll cut out your eyeball."

"Well, can I help it if I always lose the tweezers?" Her tongue is between her teeth in concentration. "Just forget about me and start dressing. Wear my red velvet," she says, trying to change the subject. "It will match me in my black one."

Finishing up on her brows, she starts on her makeup—equipment sprawled out before her in mixed array—caps missing on the lipsticks, the ends of eyebrow pencils, short and stubby. I pick out a few items of mine from the clutter and return to the bathroom to start the same procedure.

The room is still a little misty. As I wipe the mirror with the end of my bathrobe sleeve, my face appears and I study it. Will the makeup cover the brown freckled splotches under my nose that recently popped out from sitting in the sun? After dabbing on Max Factor, I start on my eyes. The black pencil draws its waxy line on my bottom lid then continues on to form a dark pointy tip on the outside of my eye. "Just like Elizabeth Taylor in Cleopatra!" I think, examining the effect in the mirror. Moving on, I pry open a little plastic box with my thumbnail. Nestled next to a small cake of black mascara is a tiny brush. Gingerly, I take it out before spitting onto the dark cake of mascara. Using my tiny tool carefully, the gooey pigment is applied to my eyelashes.

Now comes the tricky part. I have just captured my lashes in the eyelash curler. Clamping the device tight together for at least fifteen seconds is mandatory. It is also advisable to hold one's breath. And I think, as I always do when attempting this delicate procedure, that if I sneeze now, I'll be holding a fistful of lashes. Finally, lipstick on, I twist and pin up my hair, which finishes my version of a high fashion look.

Meanwhile, in the bedroom, Arlene is just starting to apply her lipstick. Swirling the brush in the fuchsia pigment, my sister carefully paints in her full lips. They are her best feature, and she always takes meticulous care. Come to think of it, it's the only thing she does with real patience. *Now be fair,* I correct myself, *Arlene has worked very hard on her singing lately, hasn't she?* That's true, but most everything else is done in her usual slapdash manner.

For example, when cooking a meatloaf, she has been known to take the ground beef straight from the freezer and with no more preparation, put it into a 500-degree oven, only to be surprised later to find a smoky football-like object charred black on the outside and still raw and icy on the inside. Or when making a dress, without benefit of pins, patterns, or basting stitches, half the time is spent sewing and the other half fixing all the mistakes. Arlene's creations often end up with one sleeve tighter than the other or a bottom hem sewn together like a sack. Yet, the final results are often dazzling, like the two velvet dresses we are wearing tonight.

Having finished being carefully outlined, Arlene's lips are now filled in with a bright pink color that somehow gives her baby face a sensual look. Pressing her lips together, she smiles now showing perfect teeth.

"Now, where is my other gold earring?" Her eyes survey the disheveled bedroom. That is another thing about my sister, she loses everything. It is almost a body reflex—twenty-dollar bills float through the house like green ghosts, popping up in coffee cups. Once, I found her screaming and tearing off fingernails. Two hundred dollars had strangely disappeared—the month's budget. After going through the house like the vice squad, we found the bills in one of Donnie's cowboy boots, where she had casually chucked them and then forgotten all about it. Now, standing by the mirror, Arlene's eyes are still looking for the missing earring. "Oh, I remember now. It's—in my shoe, of course, but where are my shoes?"

"I saw one in the bathroom," I say, trying to help, "and there's the other." My finger is pointing to a large straw bag from which a heel is hanging out.

Recovering earring and shoes, Arlene slips into the black velvet dress while I struggle into the red one, wondering why I fixed my hair before putting on my clothes. A moment later, we stand together in front of the mirror, grinning at the resemblance. Two short blondes with wide faces and pink lips smile back. We are ready, but where is Howard K. Small? It is already nine o'clock.

Sometime later his car, sputtering like a cement mixer, pulls up in front of the house. When we answer the nervous knock at the door, Howard bounds into the room looking around anxiously. "You ready?" he asks, as we stand with our coats over our arms and purses in our hands. "Man, oh man! I had trouble with my car. I couldn't get the ignition going and I don't have the bread to fix it! So what do you think?" he asks blinking. "Should I fix it?" Then quickly changing the subject, he comments, "Man, you two look crazy good!" And his eyebrows go up in approval. Howard's conversation continues to flood us nonstop all the way to the car.

A dark, silent figure sits in the front seat. Gillian is Howard's girlfriend. I met her once before, when he brought her over one night. After depositing her on the red cushion in the Holly Golightly bathtub, Howard rehearsed with Arlene for three hours straight while Gillian sat in the comical, cut-away couch, her bony shoulders hunched, her hands clasped, and her sad baby deer eyes, staring straight ahead. I was too afraid to approach her. Now, as we climb into the car, the line of her mouth spreads a little in a hello. I'm figuring she must be thirty-something, maybe even forty, I conclude a bit unkindly. The car lurches forward, and we start on our journey to the Zanzibar.

"Do you think Fiddler will hire me tonight?" Arlene asks hopefully from the back seat. "He said he would soon."

Fiddler is the owner of the Zanzibar. From what I hear, he got his name because at one time he had been a jazz violinist.

"Oh, man," wheezes Howard, "I don't know, I guess he will hire you if he says he will. What do you think, Gil?" Howard asks, pushing back his glasses. "Will Fiddler hire Arlene?"

"How would I know?" Gillian replies in a thin voice. "Don't ask me, I'm not a singer, remember? I'm just a lyricist, just ignore me."

"Now what did I say? What's the matter with you?" Howard gets his panicky look going. They talk back and forth like this while I gaze out the window at the flickering lights, thinking how the night disguises things. At night, the town is like an animated Christmas tree—sparkling and twinkling—by day a dull puzzle of buildings with garish signs hawking gas, liquor, and Dunkin' Donuts. Howard and Gillian are still talking as we pull into the back parking lot. A few moments later we are walking around to the main door, heels clattering on the rough asphalt.

HAPPY MOTHER'S DAY
PART II

A jukebox is playing a Frank Sinatra song as we enter the Zanzibar. Arlene, spying her new boyfriend, Sid, at the bar, immediately prances over to him while I look around, adjusting my eyes through the haze of cigarette smoke. The Zanzibar is decked out to look like a tropical island. Where is Zanzibar anyway, I wonder? I remember an old movie, *Road to Zanzibar* with Bing Crosby and Bob Hope, but I still have no idea where it is. Through the mass of posts, I spot the bar roofed with palm fronds and a mural behind it of swimming fish. Is it Polynesian? Yet African masks and shields decorate the other walls. The small dance floor by the bandstand is empty. A few Colored couples sit at tables while other dim figures hover about the bar. Gillian and I and, eventually, Sid and Arlene, drift over to a table nearest the bandstand while Howard paces nervously up and down in front of it.

The drummer is the first on the stand. He arranges his drum set, pulling the sock cymbal closer, tightening the snare, and testing the bass drum with a soft thump-thump. After tapping a quick staccato with his sticks, he is silent. The bass player mounts the stage from the back curtain and picks up his bass, which lies on the floor. His dark fingers pluck at the four strings while he listens closely before tightening the pegs. Howard stops pacing. He jumps onto the bandstand and slides seamlessly onto the piano bench. Only his eyes, framed in glasses, show above the piano lid. The instrument is old and streaked with scratches from many moves. At last, Sid breaks away from Arlene and steps onto the stage too. Picking up his sax, he hooks it to the strap around his neck, then fingers the keys. Howard introduces the band and the group swings into "Lover Man." The music rings and vibrates on the tabletops, and a few more people saunter into the club. I turn to Arlene. She is staring in rapt attention at Sid. Gillian, of course, is watching Howard or the top of his head. Feeling left out, I glance at the bass player. Our eyes meet and his face lights up and gleams eagerly back at me. Embarrassed, I turn away to the drummer and concentrate on the rhythm and his missing teeth. Is he an old man who looks young or a young man who looks old? It's hard to tell. Soon my attention wanders to the way in which people keep time. Some don't move at all, while others sway violently. Arlene, I notice, nods and beats time with her right foot, while Gillian only taps one finger lightly on her cigarette. I look back again to the bandstand and the pointed toe of Sid's shiny shoe as it moves ever so slightly to the music. In contrast, Howard has one foot working the pedals while the other madly dances back and forth. I can hear him start to hum as he takes his solo and watch fascinated as his brow wrinkles and unwrinkles. Sid stands by—silently cool—waiting to take his solo, his sax hanging loose from his neck, a cigarette between his fingers. *He looks a bit like a vulture,* I think—*but in an appealing way,* I quickly add, amending my judgment for my sister's sake. She is always attracted to these quiet types that never appeal to me at all. It's funny, how saxophone players are mostly the cool type and look as if they are performing only for their own amusement. Alert now, Sid licks on his reed then takes his solo. Arlene is in heaven.

After the set, Howard and Sid come back to the table. Like a wise spirit hovering above, observing all, I watch the conversations progress. Arlene and Sid try to talk to each other. Gillian attempts to get Howard's attention while he tries to interject comments into Arlene and Sid's discussion. Sid seems unaware of a problem but I see on my sister's face that she is torn between her new love and her older mentor. I also see the eager expression on Howard, and finally the worried glances of Gillian.

Suddenly there is a flurry of activity. A little man of about fifty struts into the club. He wears a sailor hat pulled low over his balding head and holds a cigar between clenched teeth. A woman follows closely behind him, then moves casually to the bar. The great voluptuousness of her body strains against her red dress as she leans against the counter.

"Hey, folks, let's liven up this place! You, musicians there," the tubby man with the sailor hat and cigar points to our table, "get up here and play something hot!"

"That's Fiddler," Howard says dully, seeing the question in my eyes. I watch, fascinated, as the owner of the club bounces onto the bandstand. I almost expect him to say next, "Is everybody happy!" like some cornball master of ceremonies, but he fancies himself as someone more hip.

"Hi, all you cats out there," he says, "we're gonna have a swinging ball tonight!" His voice quavers on the word tonight and his chin jiggles. He reminds me of an old vaudeville comic—blustering, flustering, and fluttering around the microphone. "Hey did you hear the joke about . . ."

Silence follows Fiddler's story, and the customers, looking bored, search for bugs in their drinks. That doesn't stop this master of ceremonies, and he tells a few more jokes, laughing at them himself. This guy is really bombing and it's painful to watch. Since I have a low threshold when it comes to being embarrassed for other people, tears start to fill my eyes while my toes curl—still, the man on the stage continues.

"We have for you tonight an exciting array of talent lined up," Fiddler remarks, thankfully dropping the comic act and now trying to be suave. "I know you will enjoy Howard K. Small and his quartet, but we have a special feature here that I would like to present." His voice rises in pitch. "Di-rect from Las Vegas, the beautiful and talented . . ." I wait for Arlene's name to be announced . . . "Vera, the Exotic Dancer of the East!" A few heads raise and clap sporadically. From the bar, the woman in the red dress smiles and nods. She is from the East all right. East L.A.

At the table, my sister's fingers are strangling her glass of wine. "Can't afford a singer, huh," she chokes out through gritted teeth, "but a stripper is OK." Her eyes close in anger. "All the weeks I've been coming here singing for no money. That does it!" Her eyes open. "I won't sing!" She is sitting very tight and straight, holding herself from bursting like a balloon—no, not a balloon, a volcano.

"Now, Arlene," Howard is getting his panicky look again, faced with what is quickly turning into another one of my sister's meltdowns, "don't be that way. What do you mean you won't sing? We worked on these numbers for weeks." His eyes are really blinking now, and he looks like he is ready to bolt from the table. "The experience will be good for you," he says, finally calming down a little.

"I think you should sing too," Gillian quietly murmurs.

"You have to, Arlene," I add, "or else I came all the way down here for nothing."

"Fiddler knows a burlesque act draws and he has to think of the bread," Howard further explains.

The break is over, and back on the stand, Fiddler has started introducing Howard's quartet. The band leaves their tables and drifts back up to the stage again.

". . . and," continues Fiddler, "we have in our audience, a little jazz singer. Welcome Miss Lena Gibson, a singer with a good set of pipes." He is using his best "this is show biz" voice.

Flinching at the cliché introduction, Arlene reluctantly stands up and after throwing a sarcastic smirk at Fiddler, steps brazenly onto the stand. Now, faced with the audience, my sister's personality quickly changes. Slipping off her heels to steady her trembling knees and clutching the microphone tightly in both hands, she turns and nods to Howard, who slides into the introduction of "Honeysuckle Rose" in an up-medium tempo.

Still grasping the mike, and moving her face closer, lips almost touching the metal, my sister closes her eyes. In a voice a cross between the intimate cracked tones of Billie Holiday and the intricate jazz styling of Anita O'Day, she starts to sing. The audience remains a bit detached throughout, but when my sister scats on the bridge, one head jerks up in the audience. "Work out, girl," he cries, twisting his long body in time. "Yeah!" He claps, hands together in syncopation. "Yeah!" Now, other heads start bobbing. The club is filling up.

A fairly good hand follows the end of her song and Arlene smiles impishly, forgetting her fear of performing and her anger at Fiddler, then, without introduction, plunges into the ballad "When Sunny Smiles." It is one of the original songs written by Howard that they had been working on all week. After singing the first bar alone, Arlene is joined by the rest of the group. Sid, playing soft arpeggios on his horn around the melody, the bassist, plunking a tasteful rhythm, and the drummer, caressing the snare with his brushes. Arlene starts to relax as she feels the song, her voice dipping into the notes, her body swaying. At this point, the piano is making lovely little tinkling sounds that make my stomach go all squishy. A few people listen intently, others restlessly turn in their seats.

After the second song, Arlene jumps off the stage, pausing only to slip back into her heels. She looks relieved and a little drained but smiles cockily at Fiddler again. Fiddler doesn't see the snub and bounces back to his mike excitedly waving his hands. "And now, for our special feature," (big pause) "I give you beautiful, seductive, Vera!"

Caught off guard, I almost spring out of my chair. My plan had been to leave before the strip act, but now I can't get up without being conspicuous and, besides, the dancer is already dressed and poised dramatically in the doorway waiting to go on. Trapped, I ease back into my seat.

Vera has changed from her red sheath into something royal blue. A bodice of azure sequins sparkle on her abundant bosom while her stomach, not to be outdone, overflows over the top of her harem pants of the same blue sparkly material. Veils are draped here and there flowing around her body while one large cerulean plume, swaying gently, is attached to her head. Dyed the same brilliant color as the gold rings that dangle from her ears, the dancer's hair bounces flirtatiously in curled ringlets around her face. Swishing her veils, Vera prances past our table. One plump hand snatches a scarf that billows in the air like a parachute landing over my drink. I sit staring at the Coke through the translucent material, wondering if I should touch it. Embarrassed, I look up cautiously, then scold myself, *Don't be such a chicken, Lorraine. Watch the dance, everyone else is looking. See!*

Gillian gazes in indifference through the smoke of her cigarette, and Arlene looks on in amused embarrassment.

I force my eyes to the dance floor. Madam Vera, all veils gone now, is in the middle of the floor, moving rhythmically to the drums and seductively sliding her eyes back and forth. Suddenly, she stops, and spinning around, faces the band with her back to the crowd. Her fingers struggle with the clasp of her top and then her bra falls clinking to the floor. Howard's eyebrows shoot up over the rim of his glasses, and Sid glances over casually.

Vera, now topless, turns dramatically back again to the audience for the big reveal. Moving slowly, she commences to perform her signature trick. Swaying leisurely at first, then faster and faster, the performer twirls her now exposed long ambidextrous breasts in opposite directions, at one point, almost flopping them on a man sitting at a nearby table. He turns red and giggles. At our table, we look at each other in amazement, more startled than embarrassed. Back on the dance floor, the stripper is slowly removing her harem pants. The faces of the audience show a sort of half-interested amusement, as if they have seen it done, and done better, many times before.

Now, almost completely naked, except for a tiny string-like panty, Vera has really nothing else to do. The rest of the number consists of just bouncing herself up and down while trotting in front of the bandstand, her ample behind jiggling.

Finally, to my relief, the number ends and the mass of quivering Jell-O hurries past me, grabbing at her scarf that still clings to my glass. With a swish she is gone, leaving me to blink after her, Coke running in a little river on the table top.

"Doesn't faze you after awhile," Howard says, coming to the table, his eyebrows still up.

I smile to myself at the comment. Then all the females at the table ask almost simultaneously the question on our minds. "How can she do that? How can she expose herself to a crowd of men dribbling at the mouth?"

"Well," says Howard, "some of the nicest people I know are strippers, man. Smart too, and good mothers." He jerks his head around, trying to talk to all of us at the same time. This makes him seem even more nervous than he is ordinarily.

*"And now for our special feature,
I give you the beautiful Vera!"*

"But how can they bear it?" we wail.

Howard is being put on the spot, and his foot is tapping unconsciously under the table—he rubs his hand over his mouth. Finally, he says, "It's an art to be able to do a good act, and some of these girls have real talent."

"Now don't tell me men go to these shows to see the dancing," Arlene quips sarcastically.

"Yeah," I say, "they don't really want to be entertained that way."

Howard is getting flustered. He sputters around, fishing for something to come back with. "I've seen some beautiful dances, seductive as hell but beautiful, man. Why do you think women go to see strip acts?"

"Why?" I ask. "Is it morbid curiosity?"

"No, man, they go there so they can go home and seduce their husbands. It turns them on. That's why women go."

Suddenly, Gillian, who has been pretty quiet all this time, jumps up, her sleepy eyes big. "I never heard anything so sick in my life," she hisses. "You wanna know what I felt when I saw that act? I was repulsed. The thought of sex now makes me sick. That's how turned on I am!" She is shaking with emotion. "You can stay here and talk about it all night, but I'm going." And with that, Gillian gets up and stomps out, her hair frizzling with anger.

Howard is stunned and keeps perfectly still for once. His eyes are bugged open and his mouth forms a little O of surprise. "Wha-, what'd I say?" He is silent for several moments. At last, not accepting the fact that his girlfriend had almost hit him, he looks innocently at each of us. "Now what do you suppose made her do that?"

Trying to dodge the obvious answer, that he had not given her any attention all night, we change the subject, and soon Arlene and Sid are deep in conversation, heads together. I am talking with Howard when the door to the entrance opens and two couples walk in. Seeing them, Sid jumps up rather quickly. He looks a bit flustered as he whispers something to Arlene then excuses himself and walks over to the newcomer's table just as they are sitting down.

"That's Jennifer," hisses Arlene, jabbing me in the ribs.

"Jennifer?" I question, not knowing why I am whispering.

"Sid's old girlfriend," Arlene replies. "He told me she was coming in tonight, and he's going to tell her they're through for good this time."

Curiously, I turn around, trying to look casual as my eyes search the room. I see Sid talking to a brunette. She is slender and pale, her long almond eyes slanted and the curves of her mouth smile in an accustomed way at Sid as she slides her hand up and down on his wrist.

"She's beautiful, isn't she?" Arlene's fingers are gripping my shoulder. "She looks like Elizabeth Taylor, huh?"

"Oh," I fluffed, "she's not really beautiful. Pretty maybe, but in a hard sort of way." Arlene doesn't look convinced. Her eyes are gray with worry.

A few minutes later, we turn again to watch Sid and his old girlfriend. My sister's fingers are digging harder into my shoulder. "Why is he staying so long?" she whispers tensely. Suddenly, Arlene jumps up, shaking with emotion. "You can stay here and watch all night but I'm going! On second thought, come with me. Let's get some coffee or something." She is halfway out to the street before I can catch up.

Two doors down is a coffee shop. Our high heels make their tapping noise again on the sidewalk as we head over to it. The figure of Gillian bent over her cup of coffee is the first thing we see as we enter the café. "Hi, we came to join you," I say, sitting down next to her.

"Hi," Gillian says, and does her thin smile.

I look around automatically as I usually do in new surroundings. One long green counter runs the full length of the restaurant. The ceiling and walls are also green, only smoke and grease have given them a more yellow tinge. Against a wall, papered in an ivy pattern, stands a silent jukebox. A Colored couple sits in a booth nearby. The seats of simulated leather are starting to rip. Two men sit at opposite ends of the long counter; one in an old brown suit looks straight ahead while his freckled hands curl around his coffee, the other has a bright pink face and white blonde hair. He is hungrily eating a stack of pancakes with sausage on the side. Periodically, he pours on more syrup and watches as it gets absorbed into the stack. I pick up the menu and study it seriously, knowing I can only afford coffee.

"Are you ready to order?" A large woman in her fifties is wedged behind the counter. She wears a black jumper under her white apron. I can see little dots of holes running down the sides of her dress where the seams have been let out, but her flesh still pushes against the fabric. Her face has an eagle-like quality and there are hard lines around her mouth. Her one glory is the long chestnut braid coiled round and round her head. It gleams darkly under the fluorescent lighting.

"I'll just have coffee." I smile apologetically.

"Coffee," Arlene echoes gloomily.

"More for me," adds Gil, pushing her cup forward.

After sliding two thick mugs in front of Arlene and me, the waitress refills Gillian's empty cup. "I got some nice pie," she pushes hopefully.

"I don't think so," my voice answers.

"No," says Arlene shortly.

Gillian shakes her head.

"Maybe a nice juicy hamburger? I make the best! Hey, Hal," she calls to the man with the white hair, "don't I make the best hamburgers?"

"You sure do, Ma," he replies, still inspecting his saturated pancakes.

Ma! I think, *Oh no, this is too much like an old movie, complete with the typical characters.* First a loudmouth nightclub owner named Fiddler, then this Ma, who runs the café next door. Maybe they've both seen too many B movies. I just bet the sign outside says "Ma's Place."

"No hamburgers either for us," I finally answer, feeling like I, too, am someone from a movie or dime paperback novel.

Undaunted by the hamburger rebuffs, the woman says, "I see you're all dressed up." Her eyes are moving from me to Arlene. "Bet you two sing at the Zanzibar. I know everyone there. They always come in for my hamburgers. I make the best," she repeats. "This thick!" Her fingers measure two inches in the air.

"Yeah," answered my sister sarcastically, "I'm their singer," she is remembering the stripper again.

The eagle face looks impressed. "Would you sing 'Malagueña'? It's my favorite."

Arlene looks embarrassed. "I don't know it. Sorry." She takes a sip of her coffee, then absently runs her finger around the rim of the cup.

Waddling over to the jukebox, Ma puts in a quarter and punches the buttons. The voice of Connie Francis whines out the melody of "Malagueña," backed by strumming guitars. The woman, satisfied, returns to us by way of a quick stop to pick out a glazed donut from a covered plate on the counter.

She reminds me of someone. I'm still thinking of old movies. *Oh yeah, she looks a lot like the actress in that movie about the women's prison.* The one who played the sadistic guard who got stabbed and killed before the end of the picture, but the plump lady before me looks pretty innocent munching on her donut and smiling at us in a motherly way.

"Say, those are real nice dresses you have on."

I motion toward my sister. "She made them."

"Oh, do you sew?" Ma leans one elbow on the counter also, resting her generous bosom there. "I need someone to alter my clothes. They keep getting . . ." The friendly look fades from her face and takes on a sad expression as she points to her expanding waistline.

"Sorry," Arlene looks almost embarrassed, "I can't alter. I only know how to make sack-like dresses that just hang loose. I can't even put in a zipper. My necklines always have to be big enough so people can wiggle themselves in. My mother thinks I need to have more patience to do things correctly. She thinks I rush into things. She thinks . . ." Arlene stops talking, suddenly aware she is rambling, but before the woman behind the counter can respond to my sister's sad outburst, a voice interrupts.

"Hey, Ma," yells the pink-faced man. "Do you have any more syrup?"

"Hold on, I'll get it." Ma plops the rest of the donut into her mouth and licks her fingers. "Here's some right under the counter. There you are!" she coos to the syrup-lover as she slides by him and returns to us. "C'mon," she says again, looking at Arlene, "why don't you try to sing for me?" The record has ended, but after a few clicks, "Malagueña" starts once more. Arlene joins in and tries a few notes.

"It's not in her key," I explain, after Arlene has faked an operatic voice and cracked on a high note.

Even so, Ma is impressed. "You have a wonderful voice!" she comments, reaching for more food—another donut. "Sing some more."

But my sister is silent after her brief outburst. She moves back into her seat, sunk in depression. I wonder what she is more upset about, the stripper getting her job or Jennifer getting Sid.

Ma still hovers over us. She looks first at Arlene and then me. "Which one of you is the oldest? You're sisters, I know."

Arlene raises her head and replies, "I am. She's twenty-two," she says, pointing to me, "and I'm twenty-six." Then she adds, "I have three children—six, five, and four."

"You do?" exclaims Ma. "Why, you look like a baby!" The waitress's round face smiles, making her hard lines soften. "I have five myself and twelve grandchildren." She looks at me then. "Are you a mother too?" I shake my head. "Are you then?" Ma's glance falls on Gillian.

Gillian, who hasn't said anything all this time, looks up. "Yes," she says. She actually smiles this time. "I have three."

"Well then, that makes all the difference!" The stout older woman chirps merrily, picking up the coffee pot and refilling our mugs with the steaming brown brew. "The coffee is on the house today because only good things should happen to you. It's your one special day, you know," and gestures above at a sign that reads:

HAPPY MOTHER'S DAY!

We hadn't even known or we had forgotten there was such a holiday, but now our cups are raised together in a mock toast and we take big gulps. The liquid burns down our throats, then settles warm in our stomachs. Just then, the door bangs open, and Sid and Howard walk into the café with anxious faces looking for their girlfriends.

CHAPTER 17
A WEEK OF LENNY

AND
DIALOGUE FROM THE GRAY NOTEBOOK

WHEELING AND DEALING

"Don't walk so fast," I cried. My feet were scampering as fast as they could on the sparkling sidewalks. Now and then I jumped over a star to keep up with Lenny's long strides.

I was back in Hollywood, at least for the day. Lenny Richardson had persuaded me to accompany him to his office while he drummed up interest in the "Bunny Record." There was a typewriter to be had at his workplace, he said, and I was told I could spend my time "Typing up your little scribbled notes."

Lenny's tall figure swerved sharply into a large stone building, and as the heavy glass door swung open, I trailed after him while he trotted up the wide yellow stairway, his straight back bouncing brightly up the steps. On the landing, my sandaled feet made flopping sounds on the polished floor as we walked to the end of the hallway. A door with a metal plaque on it said in capital Roman letters:

GOLIATH RECORDS
TONTO MUSIC

Inside, the office was not as imposing as the door implied. The ceiling was extremely high, which gave one the feeling of being at the bottom of a well. Two old desks on opposite sides of the room and one card table in a corner made the space appear bare except for the clutter of sheet music, magazines, cartons of records and bits of tapes, and scribbled notes that littered the floor.

In all this, Lenny's desk was a pristine island of order, holding only a phone, a new typewriter, a stapler, a jar of pens and pencils, and a neat stack of mustard-colored folders marked: *Important Letters*, *Great Ideas of Lenny Richardson*, and *Surf Bunny Songs*. The one colorful note was a box of El Producto cigars with a picture of a raven-haired lady in red on the lid playing a harp to a nearby peacock, but this too, was neatly lined up next to the jar of pens and pencils. A card table nearby held a tape recorder and more papers. Near it, an old brown record player sat on the floor.

The other desk was a huge pile of confusion: empty paper cups, unsteady stacks of papers, books on music, and more large yellow folders. A man of about thirty-five sat talking on the phone as we came in. His brow was wrinkled in thought, giving him the puzzled expression of a puppy dog cocking his ears. As we entered, his dark raisin eyes looked up. He swiveled around in his chair, waved his hand in greeting, then turned his attention back to the phone.

Later, after introductions to his partner, Bernie Low, and a lengthy speech to me about how their record company would become the next Capital Records, Lenny rounded up another folding table and chair and set me up in a corner of the room.

"See," he said, carrying a ream of white paper and the typewriter from his desk over to my shaky table. "I'm loaning you my new Smith Corona Portable."

"I'm really touched, Lenny," I said sincerely, smiling up at him.

"Yeah, yeah, yeah, well, maybe you can type me up a few business letters or two if you have time after writing the next *Peyton Place*," he mumbled.

That was Lenny; he never let things get sentimental. "I'll see what I can do," I said, grinning at his retreating back.

At first, there was a general settling in. Lenny sat at his desk and moved the cigar box and pencil container around for a while, then leaned back in his bendy swivel chair and closed his eyes. Bernie, at the other end of the room, finished another call and fooled around for several minutes looking for something on and under the litter of his desk. I put a clean white paper into the Smith Corona and in capital letters wrote *Happy Mother's Day* at the top of the page, then, hitting the return lever two spaces down, started typing.

Back over at the two desks, Lenny and Bernie were trying to come up with new ideas for The Surf Bunnies. I soon discovered that when their two heads got together, the most idiotic conversations ensued.

BRAINSTORMING

First there was silence. After a while, Lenny cleared his throat loudly and struck up a "La, la, la, me, me, me" in a contralto voice. Bernie scratched his head, then wrote a few things down on a piece of paper. They sat there in a kind of funk with their desks facing each other.

Suddenly Lenny jumped to his feet, eyes alight. "Smash idea," he said. "Forget everything! We'll make a Surf Bunny *album*. Stop talking. Listen to me. Believe me, every station will play it! The title . . ." Lenny paused dramatically. "*Songs for Surfers,*" another pause, "*in Love*! It would sell a million! Think of it—the Bunnies singing dreamy surfing songs like 'Surf Angel,' 'Little Surfer Boy,' 'Surfing in the Moonlight.' I'm a genius." Lenny collapsed back down in his seat again, amazed at his own brilliance.

Away in my corner, I was stifling laughter. *Oh, I have to get this stuff down*, I thought. *This is too good to miss.* Stopping mid-type and grabbing a pen, I hastily scribbled what Lenny had just said about the Bunny album.

"No, no," Bernie responded a second later, now getting excited himself. "It should be *Songs for Swinging Surfers* and have songs like 'The Surf Shop Stomp,' 'Come Surf with Me,' 'Sidewalk Surfing' . . . and . . . and . . . 'Surfing My Baby Back Home'!"

This ridiculousness lasted over an hour. On and off they would argue and nitpick and make fun of each other's ideas. Now and then someone would jump up again with an increasingly bizarre inspiration.

"How's this for an idea for a song?" one of them would say. "How about 'Octopuses Surfing in . . . China'? Or this . . . wait, this is better, 'I Was a Surf Bunny Spy.' Why don't we make a . . . hey, I know a guy and . . ."

All this time, the phone rang spasmodically. Usually, Lenny would answer, interrupting one of Bernie's soliloquies. "Hello, yeah this is Richardson . . . Yeah you heard about it too . . . We got the greatest group . . . The Surf Bunnies . . . Man, three blonde chick surfers, tan and beautiful . . . Yeah, in a week it will be a number one hit . . . Music City ordered fifty discs." (Long silence while the caller talked, then Lenny again.) "I tell you it's a hot thing . . . a guarantee, no! In one week, I tell you . . . Here's what's happening . . . We got calls, yeah, for three thousand orders . . . I'll tell you again it's a hot comer on KFWB . . . What do you mean you don't believe it? Everyone flipped over the Bunnies at the Dance Party Radio Show, they did . . . I said three beautiful chicks. Yeah, well, come up to the office, maybe I can help you with your records. Got some material, huh? Well, maybe we'll use it in the Bunnies next album . . . OK bye." Lenny hung up and shook his head in disbelief. "Boy, that guy is the biggest

BS-er." He leaned back in his chair and put his arms behind his head and smiled. "What a hyper that guy was. Says he has a number one seller record. He never had a hit in his life. He's the biggest BS-er," Lenny said, repeating himself.

I smiled at the irony of this as I put down my pen and turned back to my typing. Maybe what I just jotted down from Lenny and Bernie's conversation could become another chapter in the book. I didn't know, but it was funny stuff.

MORE HYPE

The rest of the week unfolded in a similar way, first the brainstorming ideas and then the rest of the afternoon devoted to connecting with contacts and, I guess, "winning friends and influencing people" via the phone. Naturally, I didn't understand much of what was said, but it must have impressed someone. Terms flew through the air (or should I say wires). When Lenny, the big promoter, started talking, I would promptly pick up my pen again and get ready to write.

"Yeah, man," he said again, leaning back in his swivel chair, the phone suctioned to his ear like a plunger. "We got a smash on our hands. Listeners are screaming for it. It has just this morning won the Listener's Choice, a week straight. I tell you it's a hot comer . . . What? Sure, it's an awful song, the worst. But man, it will still sell a million with me behind it! Write-ups have started—*Vanity* and *Billboard* . . . and listen to this . . . Warner, Dot, and Liberty Records all want to produce for us . . . Believe it now, we will even release in Europe . . .

*Everyone talked "hit record," "hot record,"
"gold record." Everything was fabulous, fabulous,
fabulous! I sat in my corner and typed.*

soon mark my words . . . sure it will only cost a few thousand . . . I imagine five thousand dollars or so for distribution in France and England . . . Ought to go over big in Japan . . . You can quote me . . . might even be a gold record . . . a real go-er . . . believe me!"

Lenny never thought he out-and-out lied, he only felt he exaggerated a bit. I even started to believe him. The superlative adjectives gushed on and on. All the week long, I sat in my corner typing, writing down conversations or sketching the people that wandered in and out of the office—eager young singers and guitar players, songwriters, recording engineers, and disc jockeys. They were all doing the same thing: making records and saying the same things back and forth to each other. Everyone talked 'hit record,' 'hot record,' 'gold record'—everything was fabulous, fabulous, fabulous!

"Man, have I got a smash record for you!"

"I've got a group with me that, well, they're geniuses!"

I wondered how many musical geniuses the world could use, especially, since they all sounded alike to me. They came and went all day, singing and playing and talking and squawking like excited turkeys full of bluster.

It was a few days later that Bernie Low burst into the office. "Man!" (That was the usual greeting.) "Man, everyone is congratulating me on the hit record! Do you realize we have a smash? Everyone is requesting the song. Man . . . think of it, our little company—a hit!" His voice was high, like a little kid that has just gotten a bike for Christmas, and with his ears sticking out he looked like a little kid too. "I knew we could do it!" Bernie burst out.

"What do you mean *we*," snarled Lenny, taking his feet off the desk and spinning around in his swivel chair. "*I'm* the one who does everything around here, and what do *I* get out of it? *I'm broke*! I live with my mother in a little beach shack. I have to bring my lunch every day. Hey, I'm a real artist and I have to come to this stinky, dinky office and push your records. Since I am only a part-producer, there is no money in it for me. You really kill me! You are starting to believe your own hype! No, make that *my* hype! Do you know why the record is number one on KFWB? It's because of *me*! I'm the one who gets up at four o'clock in the morning and rushes to this office to wake everyone and make them call the show, requesting our darling Surf Bunny record for the past week and you come in with this *we*? *No*! It's *me, me, ME*!"

I thought that was plenty to say, but Lenny was not through. "I'm a frustrated singer. I can put on more of a show than any of these guys tramping through those doors on any day of the week. Shit, yet I got nothing going and nothing going for me. I can sing, do the twist, play bongos, I do imitations. I could work right now but *nooo*. I'm trying to promote this Bunny record because it might help me eventually to get more connections!" Lenny really was on a verbal rampage.

"I don't even get credit for that," he continued, tearing at his hair. "I'm the best promotion man. I could really do things if we only had some money and a good office and real talent!"

"OK, OK, so you're great. Calm down. We appreciate you," said Bernie, trying to quiet the fierce storm that was Lenny. Lenny's anger slowly simmered down after finally getting the acknowledgment he thought he deserved, but somehow after his catharsis, the bubble was burst, and he was subdued from his usual brio. I guess poor Lenny had been starting to believe his own hype too.

From my small corner desk, I felt sorry for him. In my concern, I had even forgotten to write down this last diatribe. It was a new feeling: instead of wanting to deflate Lenny's ego and take him down a peg, I wanted to say something to make him feel better, but I realized that anything said now would only push him further and deeper into his own personal funk. It was sad, but I suspected that Mr. L. Richardson née Glassman was like a cork in a bottle of champagne—you could push it down but it would bounce up more bubbly than ever, you just had to wait.

After a few days, things got back to normal, and it wasn't long before Lenny and Bernie were back to thinking up great promotional ideas and trading insults again. I was making progress too and was almost finished with "Happy Mother's Day." Things were humming along. Every once in a while, Lenny would walk to my small spot and peek over my shoulder as I madly typed away. Then, without warning, grab me up like a rag doll flipping me out of my chair. Up I'd go over his shoulder. He let me flail there for a while, then, after I was thoroughly dizzy, plunge me forward again.

"There, put that in your book!" he'd say, plopping me back into my chair while taking a quick bite at my forearm.

"Lenny," I would say in an exasperated tone, "why in the world do you pounce on me like a cat?" I was aggravated by my complete helplessness. "Are you *that* frustrated for female bodily contact? I don't see how you can be so sexually frustrated when you are always telling me of all the many girls you can have. So why, pray, pick on me to bite?"

"Oh, I'm not frustrated," he said, always ready for a quick verbal comeback, "I just like a little mouse once in a while." With this repartee in place, Lenny might try to give me another bite on my arm, and I would block it and give him a poke in the ribs. Lenny always seemed to revel in these encounters of wit and allusions to sex. I wondered if he really was as lascivious and lecherous as he seemed or was it just a game to shock me. At this point in my thinking, however, my attacker would have turned serious and abruptly dropped my arm, and walked away. With a sigh of relief, I would turn back to my typing.

A few days later, I met the soon-to-be-famous
Surf Bunnies in all their glory.

THE TALENT

One afternoon, a few days later, I met the soon-to-be-famous Surf Bunnies in all their glory, when three pudgy teenagers, giggling and dribbling candy in their wake, burst through the door. They all had the same bleached blonde hair, cut, styled, and sprayed into hard platinum helmets. So these were the beautiful, blonde, and tan Surf Bunnies? They looked like they hadn't been to the beach in years and wouldn't know a surfboard from an ironing board, and as for beautiful . . . well.

They had come to sing another one of Lenny's songs on a demo tape but mostly they just talked. Even the loquacious Mr. Richardson could not get a word in. At the typing station, I paused mid-word and made a grab again for my pen and paper. I was now getting pretty fast at writing down the crazy dialogue I heard at the office. That course in shorthand that Mom made me take in high school was coming in handy.

Diane: Who did you say took you out, Patty?

Patty: John from my science class. He has a great car.

Diane: Yeah, but I wouldn't date him. He is fat and creepy.

Patty: (Turning to Lenny and changing the subject) Lenny what do you mean, we all have to go on a diet?

Diane: Yeah, Lenny, don't you know, that "All the world loves a fat girl"?

Shirley: Yeah, but not up close, Diane.

Diane: Gee, Lenny, we all dyed our hair, so what else do we have to do to be famous?

Shirley: Patty! Stop digging in my candy. You really have to diet.

Patty: Do we really have to?

Diane: We are doing everything else. Look (she shows a pink arm to Lenny) we are getting tan now, see?

Patty: Yes. (She shows a pale arm too, then shrugging) Ah, I guess I can diet, but first I have to finish this box of Milk Duds.

Shirley: Once I lost twenty-five pounds, so I can do it again, but, Lenny, you'll be sorry when I look like a stick.

Diane: (Wailing) But I'm always hungry!

Shirley: If we don't lose the pounds, Diane, they won't be calling us the "Surf Bunnies" they'll call us the "Three Tons of Joy."

Patty: (Changing the subject again) When do we go on the Wink Martindale TV show?

Diane: Does TV make you look fatter or thinner?

Shirley: Forget that. Are our pictures ready yet?

All: Oh boy, let's see! (They all gather around as Lenny slides photographs out of a yellow folder)

Patty: (Looking at the proofs) Oh, you both look awful!

Diane: You look pretty bad yourself, Patty!

Shirley: (Holding her hand up to her mouth) My teeth look all crooked!

Patty: Oh, and my legs look so . . . Oh, I guess I'll get those Metrecal diet cookies after all.

Lenny: (Finally getting a word in gruffly) C'mon, c'mon, ladies, (then in a serious voice) we got to get this tape done today. Look, it's all set up over here at this table. OK? Now . . . ready . . . let's record . . . and a one . . . two . . . three!

(Giggling followed)

Lenny: Quit it! (In an irritated growl) We gotta get these tapes done. Now (in a pleading voice) start from the top.

All: (Singing) Oh, Surfer Boy, I love you so . . . (More giggles)

Diane: Patty! You made me laugh.

Patty: What, it's not my fault you hit that sour note.

On and on it went into the night; I had long given up even wanting to capture their silly patter, blatant put-downs, whiny complaints, and cheesy gossip. Finally, the tape was made, and the session ended. The Bunnies happily scampered away to their rabbit homes.

After a final run-through of the tapes, a subdued Lenny and a weary me stumbled down the yellow staircase, which to my tired eyes now looked like a river of melted butter. At the heavy glass door, we broke out into the crisp night air. Gratefully, I climbed into the little white MG. I needed sleep. It had been a long, long day. Curling up near the soon-to-be warm engine, I made a bed for myself down on the soft rug of the floorboard, and clutching the completed typed version of "Happy Mother's Day," I turned and looked up at the dark sky.

The night is like a big dark blanket with pin holes to let in the stars, I thought dreamily. Hmm, that sounded pretty good. Maybe I could work that line into a story. The car took off with a jerk and sped into the night. Lenny was thoughtful for a while, "Yep," he said finally, "I've got the biggest hype in the world . . . I took three stupid teenagers and turned them into . . ." Then Lenny finished on a pleading note (I guess to the gods above), "Who knows? I might even have a hit!" The MG sped along into the night and from my warm cubby, I watched the stars bounce.

UPDATE FROM THE GRAY NOTEBOOK

Poor Lenny, unfortunately, after getting his record picked for "new record of the week," "Our Surfer Boys" by the Surf Bunnies fell to the bottom of the charts, never to rise again.

CHAPTER 18
BILL CONNELLY

HIGH HOPES

Jim Bishop and I sat together on the front porch of the red house watching an ant carrying a dead insect. It was trying to find its way back to its anthill a few feet away where a few other fellow ants were ambling in and out of the hole.

"I wonder, Jim," I said, "if he has eyes or maybe just feels around with antennas. How does he find his way home?"

"Some kind of communication code between themselves," Jim chuckled, entranced by the moving little red dot. "Look how strong! He is carrying twice his size," he added, amazed. "Hey, ant, you're passing up your hole, ha, ha!" The insect stopped suddenly and turned around, dragging his burden with him as if he had heard Jim's warning.

Just then, Arlene came out of the house in a red knit dress and high heels. She was followed closely by Lindee, Donnie, and Laurie J., trailing after their mother. Arlene looked down at Jim and me. "I'm sure glad you dropped by, Jim. Now *you* can take me to my first bass lesson instead of the bus. My, isn't it nice to have a friend with a car!" she added slyly. Jim looked up from the ants, and Arlene threw him one of her dazzling smiles.

"It isn't mine," he said, throwing an easygoing grin back at her. "A friend is letting me borrow it. Only working people can afford their own cars." He smiled wider at the thought of work. Jim Bishop lived in a junk shop. The owner let him stay as a kind of caretaker. He had his own cot and hot plate behind a screen, and he sat all day long strumming his amplified guitar surrounded by piles of bric-a-brac, old furniture, and automobile parts. If anyone came in to buy something, Jim would stop his guitar playing and say, "If you see anything you want, just holler." Then he would go back to his strumming. Now, he got up good-naturedly and lumbered over to the borrowed car, opening the door for Arlene with a little bow, as if he were her personal chauffeur.

"Good luck with the bass teacher," I called as they pulled away.

"Goodbye, Mommy," the kids yelled, waving madly from the porch in their usual Munchkin style. "Bye, bye, Jim Bishop!"

I turned my attention back to the ant. He finally had his kill before the entrance of the ant hole where he put it down. *That probably tuckered him out,* I thought. Soon, dozens of ants swarmed out of the hole surrounding the lone ant, touching him, gesticulating as if to congratulate him, and as if on cue, they quickly helped him pull his dispatched treasure inside the anthill home.

How simple and organized your life is, I thought. *You all know your place and what to do, not like us people who run around in confusion and indecision, working toward who knows what.* I got up. "C'mon kids, let's go for a walk," I called back, already strolling up the alley toward Fourth Street. The kids trailed behind me as I aimlessly drifted along, my thoughts still on the ants. It was hard to know what to do with oneself, and trying to find what you were good at is often difficult and disappointing. What was it all for anyway? Arlene didn't know what to do with her talent. She had wanted to be a singer her whole life, but now she was not sure.

The previous night, when she came back from an audition (a small nightclub needed a singer for a trio) and I asked what had happened, she gave a defeated sigh. "The manager said I wasn't commercial enough, and, Lorraine, I really tried to sing straight too—no jazzing it up at all." She plopped down hard on the green wicker chair with the curly scrollwork on the top and stared at the wall. "Oh, why do I kid myself," she said at last. "I'm just not good enough and never will be! I should take Mom's advice—go to beauty school, get a nice normal job in a hair salon, give up all this!" She motioned around the music room.

I didn't interrupt. I had had a similar conversation with Mom when I was in high school. She had steered me away from thinking about art as a career and nudged me into majoring in secretarial training.

"If I got just *one* word of encouragement from someone," Arlene wailed. "Just *one*." Later, when she went to bed, I knew she would have bad dreams and wake with one of her headaches, but I had persuaded her to at least keep studying the bass and not give up on that too.

I hope this teacher will help her, I wished abstractly as I walked on, my mind unconscious of where my feet were going. When my thoughts eventually cleared, I was not surprised that my plodding feet had carried me and the kids to Rita's house.

RITA'S NEW FRIEND

Rita's door was open as usual, and I could see her in the kitchen. Sighting me in her doorway with the kids behind, she called and waved us into the house. "Oh, Lorraine, come in," she enthused in her low musical voice. "I want you to meet Carlos."

A thin young man in his early twenties sat on a stool at her breakfast bar. In one hand he held an ink pen, in the other a glass of wine. A sketchbook lay open on the counter in front of him. As I took my place on the other stool, my art training kicked in as I automatically studied his features, the outstanding characteristic being the back of his head, which curiously merged directly into his neck.

My study, however, was interrupted by Rita's enthusiastic introduction. "Carlos is a wonderful poet and artist, Lorraine," she breathed, putting a hand on his shoulder and striking a dramatic pose. "Just look at the picture he drew of my house, and wait until you hear his poems. We met a few nights ago at the Insomniac!" The Insomniac was the local coffeehouse on Pier Avenue. Rita smiled her wonderful smile then, putting her other hand on my shoulder, crooned, "And this is Lorraine. She is an artist too, but doesn't she look more like a goddess with her flowing flaxen hair?" I knew how I looked today. My flaxen hair needed washing, and my feet were in floppy old sandals, but that was Rita, always describing her friends in glowing adjectives.

Carlos was looking at me curiously with his liquid brown eyes. "Didn't I meet you yesterday?" he asked.

"Oh," I said, aware now that I was trying to hide my feet, "that must have been my sister, Arlene, people get us mixed up sometimes. We are both blonde and short," I added lamely.

"I see," he said, looking closer, his liquid eyes getting more liquidy. "Gee, you do look alike; I spent a whole day with her even took her shopping too. She told me I could even draw your house. I think it is very interesting, especially from the back."

I smiled to myself. Arlene knew him one day, and already she had him taking her shopping. Arlene could make you do almost anything if you let her.

Carlos was looking at me closely again. "I see the difference now," he said, still inspecting me. "And I think maybe you are a bit prettier."

There it was again! Probably Arlene had people telling her that *she* was the prettier one too. Why did there always have to be competition? I responded with discomfort. "Oh, I think we are about even in the looks department."

I did actually believe what I had just said. My sister and I both had our good and bad points, but all and all they were evenly distributed as if the gods above had been judicious in handing out our features. My mind conjured an image of two baby girls sitting on a cloud before they were born and a Good Fairy floating above doling out attributes with her wand.

Fairy: (Speaking to both babies) Children of Harry and Florence Gibson, I give to each of you talent, a fair set of brains, and, oh yes, curiosity—that is the most important. As for looks, you two sisters will have blonde hair, blue eyes, and a small frame. I'm saving the tall genes for your brother Bill. You will both be considered pretty. (And now for the fun part)

Fairy: (Holding her wand over baby me) Lorraine, I give to you beautiful, large almond-shaped eyes with thick black eyelashes and eyebrows. Your nose and mouth will be so-so and your teeth a little large, but you will have great cheekbones. Don't expect a chin but your jaw line and long neck will make up for it.

Fairy: (Holding her wand over baby Arlene) Arlene, I'm sorry to tell you that the big eyes were all taken with your sister and little brother to come, and you will have to make do with some paler small ones. However, your skin will be like alabaster, no Clearasil for you in your teens. Your lips will be full and ruby-colored with small white teeth, and your nose, well, it will be near-perfect.

Fairy: (Holding wand over baby me again) Lorraine, we have already spoken of your lovely neck, so moving down I give you a small but feminine body with a nice trim waist. Unfortunately, your legs will be short and on the chubby side. However, your hands will be well shaped, and your feet small and dainty.

Fairy: (Holding wand over baby Arlene again) Arlene, I give to you a short neck, but you will have a cute boyish figure with small hips and killer slim legs that will never know the sorrow of cellulite, and your hands and feet will be angular and interesting.

Fairy: Oh, I forgot hair. You two will both be blonde but . . .

Fairy: (With wand over me again) Lorraine, hmmm, I think you need one more nice thing to even things out, so I will give to you platinum blonde hair that will grow down to your butt if you wish.

Fairy: (Now over Arlene) Arlene, you will have golden blonde hair, pretty, but it will always remain soft flyaway-baby hair that never grows much beyond your shoulders.

Fairy: There, I think I have done very well here and . . .

"Your sister is a singer, isn't she?" Carlos's voice broke into my fairytale. A little embarrassed at being caught daydreaming, I quickly recovered and blinked myself alert. "When I talked to her last," he continued, "she said she was going to an audition. How did it go?" Again his liquid brown eyes looked even more sincere.

"Oh," I said, my thoughts now fully back in the present, "she's ready to quit the whole thing. She didn't get the job. She says no one thinks she's good. She even said she'll never sing again. It sounds overly dramatic, but I think she is really hurt."

Carlos looked disturbed. "But she *is* good, that is, she sang for me in the car. She shouldn't feel that way about giving up!" In his concern Carlos forgot to sip his wine.

"It's nice of you to take an interest," I said, studying the back of his head again.

OLD FRIENDS

A timid tapping at the outside door caught my attention. A man about forty with dark wispy hair and owl-like glasses was peeping into the room. He was dressed in a white shirt and tie and carried his suit jacket over his arm. "Hello?" he queried in a soft voice, leaning against the door jam. "Anybody home?"

"Well, if it isn't Bill Connelly! What a surprise!" said Rita. "Come right in and have a glass of wine with us." Rita's new visitor navigated himself slowly and somewhat cautiously into the room, finally arriving at the kitchen bar where he stopped and leaned heavily against the counter. Taking off his black, horn-rimmed glasses, he cleaned them on his white shirt that up close, looked a bit wilted, then put them on again. With his eyes blinking, he finally focused on Carlos and me.

"It seems as if this is my day for introductions," said Rita, striking a pose like a master of ceremonies. "Folks, this is Bill Connelly, my very dear and very oldest friend. Bill, this is Carlos, he is an artist and poet that I met in the Insomniac three nights ago." Then, breaking in on her own conversation, Rita turned to me. "Oh, I must tell you, Lorraine, I'm filling in there as a waitress, when they are short on help. I told the manager that I knew of two other waitresses who could work on short notice too. So, Lorraine, isn't that great! You and Arlene can pick up a bit of cash if the manager needs you." Then, coming back to the present and her introductions, Rita exclaimed, "Sorry, Bill. I am forgetting my manners. Lorraine is part of that family I always talk to you about, so you almost know her already. They are all beautiful and talented, and Lorraine here is the artist of the family."

Bill Connelly, still blinking, looked at me intensely behind his thick glasses. "It's a pleasure," he said slowly, picking up my hand to his lips then kissing the air.

It's funny how some people are immediately called by their first names yet others fall into the category of full and proper names like Howard K. Small and now Bill Connelly. Maybe it was his suit and tie or his quiet but strange demeanor. Anyway, I decided to take Bill Connelly seriously and answered with a proper, "Glad to meet you!"

Bill Connelly gave me a shy smile then turned to Carlos and gave him a rather slapdash salute. Carlos gave a snappy one back and motioned for him to take a seat at the counter where Rita placed a goblet of white wine before him. He grasped it like an old friend and sat there nursing it quietly while Rita talked and bustled around, getting me a cup of coffee.

It was at this time that I noticed the kids were getting antsy and starting to push and shove each other around with nothing else to do. "Where's Mary and Fallon?" Lindee and Donnie at last burst out together.

Rita moved from the kitchen into the living room and hovered over them in a motherly way. "Oh, I am so sorry. Mary and Christine are playing at a friend's house, and Fallon is with his father today." Rita thought a minute, then whispered to them in a conspiratorial way, "Come with me, kiddies, I just happen to have gone to the library today and have some wonderful books for you to see."

"Do they have pictures?" Laurie J. lisped, following Rita to the sun porch.

"Oh, do they ever," Rita responded, taking Laurie J.'s hand and gesturing for her to sit down on the rug. There was a pile of four or five large, thick books scattered on the floor. The covers had colorful pictures of old buildings. One proclaimed in large English lettering, "Gothic Cathedrals of the Middle Ages."

Lindee and Donnie, following Rita and their sister's lead, moved into the sunlit alcove and plopped down on the shag rug, sitting cross-legged. Rita threw a few pillows on the floor and trilled cheerily, "Here are some beautiful pillows to go with the beautiful pictures of churches. Look, see how tall they are, the churches I mean . . . Everything is spiraling up to the sky, see?" Rita had the book open on the floor so they could all see a two-page spread of the famous Chartres Cathedral in France.

Laurie J. whispered in awe, "Look at all the sky pointers!"

"No, Laurie J.," Lindee said, "they are steeples. Remember how I showed you?" Here Lindee locked her fingers together into two closed fists. "Now, here is the church," she said, "and now here is the steeple." Lindee's two index fingers shot up and came together.

Laurie J. finished the rhyme by opening her sister's thumbs and saying "And open the doors and see all the people." Lindee obeyed and wiggled her fingers and they both laughed together.

"And don't miss the flying buttresses," added Rita, pointing to some arch-like structures on the outside of the cathedral.

"Can they really fly?" asked Laurie J. "Are they like angels or fairies?"

Rita smiled. "Sort of, they hold up the cathedral, so it won't fall down."

Donnie, turning to a page that showed the inside of the church and a soaring ceiling, murmured in a low voice, "Look how tall the inside is. I guess it has to be big enough for God."

Not to be outdone, Lindee, assuming a teaching role, scoffed. "Miss Beek says God lives in Heaven."

Lindee was a year and a half older than Donnie and thought she had an edge on him, but Donnie, the only male child, felt he was at least equal to his older sister and held his ground. "Well . . . well . . . she also said that churches were God's houses." Donnie asserted this fact with a confident nod that seemed to say, "So there, what can you say to that?"

Laurie J. added in her own theory. "And . . . and . . . maybe when he is not sitting on a cloud in Heaven, he comes and visits the church on Sunday."

"All the churches?" Now, Donnie was scornful.

Still competitive, Lindee came to her sister's rescue, "If Santa Claus can go to every kid's home in the world on Christmas Eve, it wouldn't be anything for God to show up at a few churches. And besides, Miss Beek says that God is everywhere!" At this point, the kids looked up a little fearfully. Maybe God wouldn't like them comparing him to Santa Claus.

Rita smiled and said, "Well, kidlins, that all makes perfect sense to me," and she moved back to the grown-ups at the kitchen bar.

"Sorry about the interruption," I said. "Thanks, Rita, the kids really seem interested in the cathedral books. I guess it's because of the Bird Lady, er, Miss Beek, who comes and reads them Bible stories."

"Ah," said Bill Connelly, nodding his head over his wine, "a proselytizer, an Apostle of God."

Rita brightened again, then proudly looking at Bill Connelly, said to Carlos and me, "And did you know that Bill is a defrocked priest?"

Bill Connelly shook his head slowly and smiled. "Well, almost, but not quite. I was never frocked in the first place. I left the Jesuit seminary before becoming a priest."

Bill Connelly was getting more interesting by the minute with his funny nebbishy voice (like that actor Wally Cox who played Mister Peepers on TV) and with his big sad, slightly bulging eyes like my childhood dog, Benny, a Boston terrier. My dog Benny got lost one day and never came home again. Bill Connelly, too, looked a little lost.

The almost-priest, as if aware of my sympathy, smiled and raised his glass. "Fellow brethren, I am here on a quest. I have a problem to solve and I am in a quandary of what to do."

"Oh goody," said Rita, "I love solving other people's problems, although I'm told I have enough of my own to keep me busy."

I, too, perked up at the word "problem." For some reason I

had a strange need to fix things—a need to organize, to clean, to find lost objects, maybe a need to fulfill everyone's wishes too. *It must come from some early training from Mom*, I reflected, and here I caught myself before I fell into another reverie. Two in one day wouldn't do, I concluded and quickly picked up the gist of the conversation again.

"Is your problem a puzzle or a mystery?" asked Carlos, sitting up a little straighter.

"Well, it's not all that obscure," said Bill Connelly. "The thing is this; my firm Smith, Johnson and Maxwell Advertising are having a gala party. It is supposed to make the employees feel closer and friendlier to each other."

"Why is that a problem? It sounds nice," interjected Carlos, taking another sip of his wine.

"The problem," Bill Connelly continued, "is that they want us to come in costume, and I abhor costume parties. Even so, I do have an idea of who I could be but not exactly how to pull it off."

"Can't you go as yourself?" said Rita.

"That is a no-no, they tell me, and I also have to dress as someone I admire."

"How about you turn your collar around and *be* a frocked priest?" Rita said, still harping on that theme.

"I have already decided to go as Clark Kent," said the reluctant Bill Connelly.

I looked at him then, with his gentle demeanor, dark hair, and thick glasses. Yes, he would make a perfect, mild-mannered Clark Kent. Even his pale, pasty skin and slight paunch added to the look of the mild-mannered reporter for a, for a—"How does it go?" I said aloud.

"How does what go?" asked Carlos.

"Oh, you know, it was at the beginning of that old fifties Superman show on TV. My brothers and I watched it every week. There was this announcer who said . . . Oh, yes, I remember now. I better start from the beginning," I said, jumping off the kitchen stool. To illustrate my point, I shot up my hand and pointed into the air, then exclaimed in an excited and exaggerated TV voice, "Look up in the air! Wait, no, that's not it." I started again.

"Look up in the sky!

"It's a bird!

"It's a plane!

"No! It's (pause) Superman!

"Faster than a speeding bullet!

"More powerful than a locomotive!

"Able to leap tall buildings in a single bound!

"And who, (pause) disguised as Clark Kent, mild-mannered reporter for a great metropolitan newspaper, fights the never-ending battle for . . .

"Truth!

"Justice!

"And the American way!"

On the last line, everyone joined in and clapped at the end, laughing.

My emoting caught the attention of the kids, who started pretending to be superheroes themselves. "I'm Superman," said Donnie, flexing his small muscles.

"And I'm Wonder Woman!" said Lindee, taking a stance with her arms akimbo.

Laurie J. just ran around saying, "I'm an angel. I'm a flying . . . but . . . but" (she couldn't remember buttress) and finally smiled in triumph and said, "but-ter-fly!"

The adults laughed until Bill Connelly broke in. "I think it is good that we are really getting into the spirit of this, but I haven't solved my dilemma yet."

"What's that?" asked Rita. We all looked watchfully at Bill Connelly. Even the kids stopped running around.

"My plan is to show up and then when anyone asks me why I am not in costume, I will say that I *am* in costume, and they will say, 'Who are you?' And then I'll say, 'I'm Clark Kent, mild-mannered reporter for a great metropolitan newspaper,' and then they will say, 'No fair. You look just the same as you do every day,' and then I will burst open my shirt and there they will see the Superman insignia underneath. Everyone will gasp or laugh, then I will say something like 'I have the strength of ten for my heart is pure!'" To illustrate, Bill Connelly pulled open his white shirt, which showed only his bare pale chest and a few dark hairs.

"You see," he said, "I don't know where to get a Superman shirt. That is why I am here today. Rita, you are so imaginative, and now," indicating Carlos and me, "I also have two artists to help."

Rita offered, "Can't you rent a Superman costume? There must be stores in Hollywood that have costumes galore."

"That's a possibility, but I only want the insignia. I already have a royal blue tee shirt."

"You could paint it on?" suggested Carlos.

"Or," I said, "you could go to the fabric store—it's just a few blocks from here—and buy some red and some yellow felt. It would be easy to then draw the insignia and cut it out. After that, just a simple basting stitch could sew it onto your tee shirt." I leaned back on the high perch of Rita's kitchen barstool, rather impressed with myself.

Rita gushed, "You smart girl! That would be perfect. Don't you think so, Bill? And I'm sure Lorraine will sew it on for you."

I groaned inwardly. Now what have I gotten into? It's not like I didn't have anything else to do! Out loud, I said, "Well, er, sure, I guess I could do it if you buy the material and then give me the tee shirt."

"I just happen to have it in the car," said Bill Connelly.

Rita perked up. "Well, now that *that* is cleared up, let's finish our wine," she looked at me, "and coffee."

Glasses and my mug were touched as a salute to a problem solved, and the wine and coffee were soon gone. For the past few minutes, the children had been hanging onto my legs and tugging at my hands. The excitement of Superman was over for them. They wanted to go. I spoke up through the cheer of the wine tasting group. "I'd better move on now. The kids are getting restless again." I explained that the children and I would be going off to the supermarket on Pier Avenue. I checked the money in my pocket. I had two dollars and a handful of change. I announced to the kids that I was going to buy some hamburger, and what was their pleasure for dinner, meatloaf or spaghetti?

The chorus was unanimous. "Pas-gettii, pas-gettii," all three cried.

"Pas-getti it is," I chorused back. Soon I was saying goodbyes to all, but as I was moving out the door, Bill Connelly struggled off his perch on the kitchen stool and insisted that since his car was right outside, he would be happy to drive all of us to Pier Avenue. "And," he added, "we could pick up that material you were talking about. You say the fabric store is only a few blocks away?" The kids were excited to ride in the car, and after a short stop to pick up the felt material, we were soon pulling into a parking space on Pier Avenue.

CHAPTER 19
A SUPER PARTY

A JAZZ GREAT

The street on the last block of Pier Avenue was used as a parking lot and was so close to the ocean I could easily see a wide expanse of sand from where we parked. The block was crowded with cars and shops and stores that looked busy on this sunny day.

Bill Connelly suddenly cocked his head, "Is that jazz I'm hearing?"

"Oh, yes," I said in what I thought was the nonchalant manner of a jazz aficionado. "Today must be the first day that the Sunday Concert starts at the Lighthouse."

"Let's check it out, shall we, kids?" said Bill Connelly, getting out of the car and pushing back the front seat so the kids could spill out. We crossed to the other side of the street—the music getting louder as we walked. The kids were skipping to the sound of the horns and conga drums. I knew that Howard Rumsey, who managed the club, had Sunday afternoon jam sessions when the weather got warm enough, but I had forgotten that it would be today.

We reached the brick building where a tall sign shaped like a lighthouse spelled out its famous name vertically in large letters on the roof. Below, was another sign that said, "Howard Rumsey's All Stars." The "All Stars" were the regular house band, but today there was a different sound coming out of the club. The Lighthouse had two heavy Dutch doors, the main entrance and another adjacent to the bandstand. The main entrance door was fully open for customers, and some people were already filing in. The other door near the bandstand was open on the top so pass-ers-by could see and hear the band. There was already a small crowd around it, but we squeezed through so the kids could see a real jazz group. I held Laurie J., and Bill Connelly alternated between boosting up Donnie then Lindee.

It was not the house band but a quintet led by no other than Dizzy Gillespie! Now I remembered that Jeff, hardly able to con-tain his excitement, had told me a few weeks ago that "Diz" would be playing at the Lighthouse soon. "Man, Dizzy is a giant," Jeff had said excitedly, and exploded into one of his rare soliloquies. "A giant of jazz, I tell you! Did you know he and Charlie Parker invented bebop, at Minton's—that's a nightclub in Harlem—way back in the '40s? They introduced great chord changes into jazz, like, they invented using the flatted fifth and developed a new kind of improvisation."

I knew what a flatted fifth was because Howard K. Small used it in his songs, but I was soon left way behind when Jeff went on into more intricate theories of bebop like asymmetrical phras-ing. Soon Jeff started talking about our long-lost father. "Harry was there too," Jeff murmured in a breathless voice. "You know how he always hung out in Harlem with all them jazz greats. He even told me once he used to play checkers with Charlie Parker between sets when they both worked at Billy Burgs. And did you know that he taught Art Tatum how to drive?"

I nodded. I had heard many of these stories, but I didn't know about teaching Art Tatum to drive though (wasn't Art Tatum blind?).

Mom had told me long ago about the young Harry when they were first married. He was just an eager up-and-coming musician. There were the musical duels at after-hours places. Harry would come home all excited; even wake her up just to tell her about how he had played that night in front of piano-greats like Art Tatum. Fats Waller had hugged him and called him "son" when he heard him play. *What happened to that eager young musician?* I wondered. What had gone wrong with all the dreams my mother said he had when they were young? Why wasn't he here, playing at the Lighthouse now, with Dizzy Gillespie? And poor Jeff, he hadn't had much of a father. I guess that's why he treasured those little bits of information he did have. Finally, pushing away the sad thoughts, I concentrated on enjoying Dizzy Gillespie. The great man himself was playing not ten feet away.

"Oh," breathed Laurie J. into my ear. "He looks like a big frog."

Lindee and Donnie heard and were nodding in agreement. They were right. When Dizzy Gillespie took a breath and blew into his strange upturned trumpet, the man's cheeks and neck swelled up like a great bullfrog calling for a mate, then, when the riff was over, his face deflated and he turned into a man again until the next intake of air when the bulges reappeared.

The kids were delighted with the music and the musician who turned into a frog. "It's like he's a frog then a prince without a princess kissing him," Lindee concluded.

He certainly was a character known for his talent but also his crazy high jinks, jazzy clothing, and singular goatee. Today he was wearing a rather loud yellow plaid sports jacket and a kind of colorful knitted beanie on his head. I couldn't see the goatee while he was all puffed up.

I looked at Bill Connelly, who was helping Donnie hang on the door, his head bobbing along to the music. *Funny, he looked too straight arrow and proper to be into jazz, but people will always surprise you,* I told myself.

The quintet was now playing the lively "A Night in Tunisia," an original composition by Gillespie. It was familiar to me because Jeff played it so often, and my head started bobbing around too. According to Jeff, after inventing bebop, Dizzy introduced an Afro-Cuban sound into his music and always liked to have a conga drummer in his group. Now the conga took a solo, and Mr. Gillespie put down his horn. At once, his face sank back into a normal man, and I could see the little black fuzz of a goatee under his lip. After the drum solo, the band swung into the last chorus, and I realized why Mr. Gillespie was called Dizzy. The man could play dizzyingly fast runs up and down the scales and hit high and low notes with ease. I was wondering if Jeff had heard him yet from his spot in the back kitchen. The song finished with Dizzy hitting several high notes and the crowd inside and outside burst into applause.

SHOPPING FUN

Laurie J. was getting heavy, and I noticed Donnie was starting to hang on Bill Connelly's arm. It was time to move on. I turned to Bill Connelly. "Thanks for the ride," I said, "but we have to go now and do our shopping. I can probably make the insignia for you in a few days."

Mr. Connelly thought for a moment, then pulled out a pen and a small notebook and started writing. "So, I was wondering," he said, still writing, "if you could help me by gathering up a few things? I . . . um . . . I am giving a party, and if you could, I will meet you at the market later, but first I want to treat Mr. Gillespie to a drink." Bill Connelly ripped the page out of the notebook and held it out for me. "This is just a start, after that, just get what you think is needed for a super party."

I took the small piece of paper, thinking that maybe one of the qualities of Bill Connelly was that he used people. First, I get stuck making a custom insignia for him and now I was his personal shopper. Another voice told me I should have just said no, but then I didn't know how to do that. It was a problem of mine but it was too late now to refuse. Bill Connelly was already at the bar shaking hands with Dizzy Gillespie. I walked a few doors down and entered the market with the kids trailing as usual. I got a shopping cart and put Laurie J. in the baby seat then looked at the list as I slowly moved down the aisles.

"Let's see," I said out loud, "it says here, nuts."

"I'll get them!" yelled Donnie, and raced down an aisle.

"What's next?" asked Lindee.

"It says chips."

In a flash, Lindee zipped away too. By then Donnie had returned and threw several bags of walnuts, pecans, almonds, and a can of roasted and salted mixed nuts into my shopping cart. Lindee was also back, adding a large bag of Lays potato chips and two smaller bags of Fritos.

"Next on the list, it says pretzels," I announced. Off they both ran, bringing back pretzels of all sizes and shapes, big, little, thin, thick, bent. I never knew pretzels came in so many varieties. Growing up, my mother did not stock snacks. An apple, an orange, or a peanut butter and jelly sandwich would have to do. It was only when my father came home that there would be anything in our cupboard like what was now filling up the shopping cart. I noted that this was the second time I had thought about my father today and with all the excitement of the kids, it was beginning to feel like a Harry moment too. I had to admit it was always thrilling when he came home from one of his tours.

By this time, Laurie J. had wiggled out of the cart and was running after Lindee and Donnie. "I want to have fun too," she called back at me. The last item had been crackers, and now all three kids were picking out their favorite. Next, I moved to the soda aisle. What a selection there was!

"Maybe we should get one of each," said Lindee.

"OK," I said, "but be careful. They are glass! Laurie J., I will help you carry yours."

There were so many different kinds of soda to be had and a virtual rainbow of colors and flavors. I recognized a bottle of wild black cherry that had been a favorite of my father's at our many picnics.

"Well, that looks like the end of the list," I said when the sodas were all carefully placed in the cart.

"But Bill Connelly said for us to make up the rest!" Donnie was adamant about this point.

"Yeah, and get what we thought would make a good party." Lindee backed him up.

"OK," I said, "then we will do just that." Soon the kids were running around gleefully adding goodies of their own choice. They plopped them into the cart then shot off for more.

I will also get what I thought a good party should have, I told myself, like some cheese and fruit. I strode over to the produce stand. *Oh, those grapes look delicious and so do the apples and pears. This will turn out to be an elegant party*, I was thinking as I started loading up the cart with my choices.

Lindee and Donnie and Laurie J., working together, came back with chocolate syrup, a bag of Oreo cookies, and packages of Ring Dings. Soon they found colored balloons, streamers, and paper straws. Finally Laurie J. toddled up to the cart with a small jar of maraschino cherries. It was time to stop, so I gathered the children together, declaring, "Kids, I think we must have everything now because," I held up the jar of maraschinos, "here are the cherries, and we all know that the last thing is the cherry on top." We were having so much fun making the perfect party, I had almost forgotten to pick up the hamburger for dinner, but soon all was done, and we headed for the checkout.

I spotted Bill Connelly standing by the register, squinting past into the store. He spotted us and waved. As I pushed the heavy cart up to the checkout counter, I felt a little embarrassed. What would he think of our extra purchases? But Bill Connelly hardly batted an eyelash as the woman at the register slid the merchandise across the counter, ringing up each price as she punched it in:

$1.25—ka-ching, $2.50—ka-ching, $3.75—ka-ching, ka-ching. It was endless.

Just before all the purchases were tallied up, Bill Connelly walked over to the frozen section and came back with two pints of ice cream, Rocky Road and pistachio nut. He slid them across the counter and the woman, without missing a beat, rang them up: $2.00, $2.00—ka-ching! Ka-ching!

I held on to my hamburger until the long receipt rolled out of the register and Bill Connelly pulled out a sizable wad of bills and counted them off to the cashier. She took the money, putting several bills into the twenty-dollar slot, then solemnly counted back the change. I wondered if we had bought too much, but Bill Connelly was sanguine as the cashier lady speedily collected and bagged all the items into two large shopping bags. The sodas required a special cardboard box.

My small purchase took only a few seconds to ring up. Lindee, standing next to Bill Connelly, tugged his sleeve and asked if he liked all that we had bought for him.

"Yes, thank you so much for your help," he said, putting the shopping bags and cardboard box back into the shopping cart. "After we get all this in the car, I hope you will have the kindness of letting me drive you all home." We agreed and soon were outside pushing our heavy load over the bumpy asphalt, the sodas making jingling sounds in their cardboard box. Donnie, who bounced along in time to the jingling, announced proudly, "I bet this will be the most best-est ever party!"

Bill Connelly agreed that he really *did* think it was going to be a "doozy," probably the best he had ever given, he added. After the car was packed, we maneuvered out of Pier Avenue. "Which way shall I turn?" Bill Connelly asked at the corner.

"Turn right. We live close to the electric company," I said, and then asked where he lived.

"I live in Manhattan Beach with my cat, Fang," he replied serenely.

"But it's the opposite direction," I said, concerned. "Your ice cream will melt if you go too much out of your way. Look we only have this package of hamburger meat and home is not far. We can walk."

"Don't worry about that," he murmured, hardly speaking above a whisper.

Well, I won't argue about a ride home, I told myself. I hoped for his sake that the ice cream would hold up until he got home to . . . what was his cat's name again? Oh, yes, Fang, funny name. Bill Connelly was getting more and more interesting. It wasn't long before we pulled into Culper Court.

At the red house, the kids and I jumped out. I was clutching the hamburger and the felt material, when I suddenly remembered the blue tee shirt. "Thanks for the ride," I said. "If you will just give me the tee shirt, I think you can have it back in a few days."

Bill Connelly turned to the back of the car. "Well, what do you know? The tee shirt must be under all the groceries. I'll just have a look." He got out of the car and started unloading the bags and the jingly box of sodas onto our front yard. Finally, he reached way into the back. "Aha," he said, and pulled out the blue tee shirt. "There we go!" he said in a delighted voice as he handed it to me. "Well, I got to be going," he said, as he slid back into the driver's seat and started the motor.

"But wait," Mr. Connelly, I said, running to the front of the car, "you're forgetting your party goods." I pointed back to the shopping bags and the big box of sodas still sitting on the ground. You can't have a party without them," I added, laughing a little at his absentmindedness.

"Oh, *I'm* not the one having a party," Bill Connelly said, putting his head out the window as the engine idled. "If you remember correctly, what I said was that I was *giving* a party, and I'm *giving* a party to you and the kids! And hey," he added as an afterthought, "you'd better put that ice cream in your freezer before it melts." And with that, he stepped on the gas and sped away down the hill of Culper Court before anyone could say anything.

The kids, who had been standing by the party goods all this time, were a little confused at first, but when they heard what Bill Connelly said, they started jumping up and down, cheering and waving at the departing car. "We get a party! We get a party!"

As I stood looking at the retreating back fender speeding away, I realized that Bill Connelly had left so quickly he didn't give us a chance to thank him. *Well,* I thought, *Bill Connelly may be dressing soon like Superman but his fast getaway seemed more like another heroic TV personality, more like that mysterious masked man of yesteryear, who at the end of every episode, rides off in a cloud of dust calling out, "Hi Yo, Silver—away!"*

As if on cue, the theme of the William Tell Overture started playing softly in my head as Bill Connelly's car barreled away down the alley, leaving me to wonder, like those Western townspeople who are left scratching their heads and saying, "Who was that masked man? He left before we could thank him." At this point in the TV show, the Lone Ranger, pausing for a moment on the top of a big rock, rears his horse, Silver, high into the air before they race away as the final notes of the overture end in a grand crescendo. And like the TV series, my grand crescendo of the William Tell Overture comes to a close just as Bill Connelly's car stops at the corner on Second Street, pauses for a second and then turning right, speeds away.

Gosh, I thought, *I wonder what Bill Connelly would have bought us if I had offered to sew him an entire Superman outfit?*

CHAPTER 20
ROSES FOR TOMORROW

LATER THAT DAY

Only one pint of ice cream could fit into the freezer compartment, so we had to have the party right away. The kids blew up balloons, and we each had an Oreo cookie, a soda of choice, and a dish of Rocky Road ice cream with a maraschino cherry on the top. The rest of the day I spent sketching and plinking at the piano while the spaghetti sauce simmered and the kids dug up the front yard. I was listlessly playing when a voice called, "Lorraine!"

It was Betsy, our neighbor from next door. What would we do without her? Betsy was our alarm clock, calendar, and general store. Every morning we sent the kids over to find out what time it was or even what day. The voice called again, "You are wanted on the phone!" I stopped playing and bounded out the door and across the yard.

"Hello?" I said, a little breathless, sitting down on Betsy's new tweed couch.

"Listen, Lorraine." It was Arlene. "I'm at Mom's house. She's all upset. Bob tried to kill himself. He took fifteen sleeping pills. Mom said all the way to the hospital he mumbled something about always being sick and then how her children didn't like him. He had his stomach pumped out and everything!"

Immediately, guilty feelings stabbed at my stomach. I had been the most horrible. Was it the tongue-lashing I gave him that night for abandoning our mother? Was that the final straw? Yet, I never thought Bob was the type to . . . to . . . Oh dear, if I had shown one sign of liking him or . . . "Will he be all right?" I asked, drawing worried scribbles with a pencil on the pad in front of me then stopped, realizing that it was Betsy's pad and not mine to scribble on.

"He's going to live, but Mom is pretty upset and wants me to stay overnight. By the way," Arlene added as an afterthought. "The bass teacher turned out to be a nothing. I knew more than he did. Lorraine! I've never had such a terrible week. Everything I've done has flopped and everyone and everything seems to be falling apart!"

"I know, Arlene, I feel the same way. Do you feel guilty about Bob too?" My fingers were twisting and untwisting the phone wire.

"Yes, I do. That's why I'm staying with Mom tonight. Well, I'll see you tomorrow," she finished, her voice low and quiet, which was unusual for her.

That night, I had bad dreams. Arlene was at the beach and started swimming out beyond the waves. Suddenly, she changed into a bass and then Mom appeared. "See," my mother said, "I told her to get a job and stop being a beatnik." From the waves Arlene was singing and . . .

Soft murmuring sounds woke me up. It really *was* singing I had heard through my dream. I sat up in bed a little confused . . . singing? Where was it coming from? Was it inside the house or outside? I listened again. It sounded like it was coming from outside. I hung my head out the tiny window of the loft. It was definitely coming from the back of the house somewhere out in the dump. I knew of maybe a half dozen people who were strange enough to vocalize at night. Maybe it was Tad on a binge or Lenny playing jokes or Jeff thinking up a song, but then why would he be outside?

By groping in the dark, I found the light and switched it on. Cautiously I crawled over to the ladder and crept down. My foot landed on an errant ashtray at the bottom and it turned over with a clang. I tried not to make more noise as I tiptoed into the dining room and peeked out between the bamboo shades of the back window. With a shock, I realized I didn't recognize the figure at all. A stranger was directly behind our house, in the landfill, crouched on a cement slab. His shadowy head was bent down, and something was in his hands. What could it be . . . a knife? The uncanny hymn he had been humming was louder now, and I could make out his head bobbing in time to his weird chant.

A sudden terror seized me. *Oh my God! He must be insane burbling like that out in an empty field.* My mind raced into overdrive. *He could be a madman, a murderer, a rapist—a mad murdering rapist!* I was now in full panic mode, fear filling my throat. *Oh God, he could have been following and stalking us for weeks and tonight was ready to creep in and attack us. What can I do, what can I do?* It felt like someone had reached inside my stomach and was turning it inside out as I had seen my mother do when she cleaned a just-killed chicken. Funny, how those chickens always had pebbles in their little change-purse stomachs; boulders, not pebbles, were crashing around in mine.

At last, my brain stopped thinking of change purses and chickens and finally started working. "The doors," I whispered to myself. *They are all unlocked.* Running silently on my toes, I dashed around locking up the front and back doors. *But he could still climb in at the windows, they don't lock at all.* I raced to the spying place again. The dark figure was still there but had stopped singing. It looked like he was studying our house now.

He's plotting his attack! *Why do I have to be alone?* I thought. *Where is Arlene? Where is Jeff? Where is anyone when you need them! A weapon, I need a weapon!* I was chewing on the bamboo shade in desperation. *A knife? Yes! No!* He would just take it away, and the police would find little pieces of me and the kids all over the house . . . *The police, of course, why didn't I think of that sooner?* I still needed a weapon though, so I ran to the kitchen, keeping low. Desperately rummaging through the drawer, my fingers curled around a rolling pin. Club in hand, I eased myself back to my watching post. Eeek! He was gone! My mind whirled with pictures of a figure crawling like some kind of slimy reptile up the side of our house and into an unlocked window. I imagined him hiding in a dark corner of my loft waiting for me to go to bed then—pounce! I needed help!

I would have to chance running next door to Betsy's to phone the police. I could imagine the reaction from them when they heard my story. "Help, Police, this is an emergency. I want you to arrest a man. Yes, he's singing in my backyard!" Yeah, that would go over really big with the cops, but the thought of the lurking figure bursting into the kids' room was stronger than the fear of being laughed at. Gathering my courage, I proceeded intrepidly to the front door. Holding my breath, I first peeked out one of the cracked windows surrounding the door to see if it was safe to make a dash for—

What's this? Something was attached to the door. I could see some kind of paper. All my courage vanished in an instant. What could the note say? "The Phantom strikes tonight!" or something horrible like . . . My brain stopped again. All I could think of was that my pajamas were wet with perspiration and dripping freely down my sides. It struck me then that fear had an actual smell. *It smells exactly like chicken soup,* I thought, surprised but I couldn't stop and linger on this great truth. I had to stop thinking about chickens and chicken soup and think what the letter could mean? Writing maniacs had to be the worst kind, sneaky and quiet.

Then, with great daring, I flung the door open and, acting fast, snatched up what was attached to the door. I remembered to relock it, then ran with my prize to the bathroom, the rolling pin still in my sweaty hand. I locked the bathroom door behind me before turning on the light. It was then I realized the letter was more like a bundle because, in my hand was a small bouquet of wild daisies tied with string and rolled up in a piece of paper. My free hand nervously put aside the little posey on the sink and carefully unfolded the paper message, my breath coming out in little gulps as I read . . .

Roses are born each day
So you, Arlene, don't give up.
Carlos

There was also a little sketch of the back of our cottage. I sat down on the toilet seat and laughed weakly. Here it was—the one word of encouragement Arlene had asked for. Taking the note and flowers, I placed them on Arlene's bed where she would find them when she came home tomorrow.

SUMMER

CHAPTER 21
SENTIMENTAL JOURNEYS

A FEW WEEKS LATER

I heard afterward from Rita that Carlos had left town. After getting an overhaul on his car, he set off for New York City and Greenwich Village in particular. It was where all artists, musicians, and writers had to go, he explained. Rita also related words from Bill Connelly. It turned out that his version of Clark Kent and Superman had kept his fellow workers in stitches during the entire party. "The problem now is, they expect me to be funny all the time," he told her.

In the weeks that followed, Bill Connelly became a regular at our house. Every few weeks he would show up at the red cottage bringing treats and surprises. He had taken our family under his strange wing. Without our knowledge, he would leave a cake on the counter or slip the children money for treats, and the only way we found out was by the accumulation of candy wrappers in their bedroom. Our new friend took us into Hollywood to see foreign films. Arlene could not stop raving about *The Virgin Spring* by Ingmar Bergman or Fellini's *La Dolce Vita*. We discovered these films were not like the Hollywood movies we grew up with. Some confused me. I wasn't at all sure what they were about, especially the French ones, but after a while, I got the hang of it. Each country had a certain personality: the Swedes were strange and serious, the Italians funny, and the French . . . well, I already said something about them.

Sometimes, Bill Connelly took us to the Lighthouse to see whatever jazz great was playing. Lenny was still coming over regularly too, to fight with Arlene or to tease the kids. I still got invitations to join him at his office where I could type up my latest stories, but there was no more before dawn rush to plug the Bunny songs. In fact, the Surf Bunnies were never spoken of again.

In time, Arlene lost interest in the bass, and one day it disappeared from the music room. She might have even stopped singing except that I would remind her of Carlos's poem, and then there was Howard, who wouldn't let her forget that she was his muse and main singer (well, she was his only singer really). He faithfully came over to show her new songs or to practice old ones.

RAILROAD TRACKS

May turned into June, and the days got hotter. One Saturday, Jeff and I found ourselves trudging off to the library. We were using the shortcut along the old railroad tracks that ran in back of the dump. Jeff usually took his truck for a trip like this, but it was "on the fritz" again, he said, and until he got new parts we'd be walking.

The fritz? Who says that word anymore? I wondered. It sounded like one my father would have used. He always liked to throw a little Irish, German, or Yiddish into his conversations along with funny expressions like accusing us of having a Chinese picnic, when we got too loud. Harry also used the word fritz when something was broken. He even had a dog named Fritzy—two, in fact.

My father had a thing about animals, especially dogs. He maintained they had an instinct about good character and since he claimed all dogs loved him, it proved his point. I must admit that many dogs did follow him home, and over the years he brought them home, plus many other pets for us to care for—even a horse once. As for dogs, let's see, there was Fritzy, then Fritzy II. Later there were three consecutive Boston terriers called Benny, short for Benzedrine (a word Harry used in his nightclub act). There was Butch, a Labrador puppy who chewed up all my sweaters with me in them, and a beautiful collie named Lassie, of course. I was just getting to our last dog, a mutt called Tif, when I heard a faraway cry. Lindee was running across the dump, waving for us to stop. She was barefoot and carried her sandals in one hand.

She was panting heavily when she caught up with us. "Can I come too?" she gasped between breaths, quickly sitting down on the track and slipping on her sandals. Without another word, she fell into step with us as we trudged forward. "Mom sent me," she began, "because . . ." and here Lindee had to do a little skip hop to keep up with us, "Mom said that the more people the more books we can check out." Arlene wanted something by Faulkner, and Donnie and Laurie J. wanted picture books.

As we walked along, we tried to match our steps, first to the wooden ties that held the rails together, then to the area between them, which caused dusty dirt to build up in my sandals. Every so often, one of us would jump onto the rail and balance there until our equilibrium wavered and we fell off. Lindee was the best, maybe because she was the lightest or because she danced her way down the steel track. "We're going to the library," she chanted happily.

We were not going to our usual library on Pier Avenue. It was dinky, little more than a converted storefront. Today we were going to the grand library in Redondo Beach, the next town over. For some reason, we had the idea that the train tracks were a shortcut. But, to be honest, it was just fun to walk on them.

"We's ridin' de rails!" Jeff sang out as he took a stab at his version of a pirouette, leaping suddenly onto the steel track with his thick clumpy boots. Whomp! He immediately fell, landing heavily on his butt. Jeff could still get embarrassed, even if he was almost twenty, and now his mouth got crooked and a pink flush started up his face.

"You sure did go *whomp*!" Lindee exclaimed.

"Yeah, whomp!" Jeff echoed, laughing now, all embarrassment gone. He chuckled some more then, dusting off his clothes, started humming a melody. "OK, you guys," he said after a while. "Here is a great song written by Cannonball Adderley and Oscar Brown Jr. Now when I sing the line, at the end, we all go '*Whomp*' together really loud! Got it?" Jeff started singing in the lowest register he could muster, doing his best to sound like a tired and broken man singing about working on a chain gang.

Whomp! We called out at the end of the line like we were landing a pickaxe to the ground. Jeff smiled and belted out the second line about how the man was serving time by breaking up rocks.

Whomp! Again we called it out, Lindee in her falsetto, me in my second soprano, and Jeff in his best interpretation of a sorrowful man. Jeff's voice was getting more gravely and sorrowful with each line of the song and again we shouted out the *Whomp!* as Lindee and I got more and more into the spirit of the song.

At the end, Jeff croaked out the last few lines about how hard the work was and how long his sentence had yet to go.

Jeff didn't know the other verses, so just repeated the whole thing over again. This time, Lindee and I joined in. After the song, we all got quiet thinking about the man. Would he ever be free? A short time later, Jeff pulled out his flute and started fiddling with it. Lindee hummed her own song, and my mind wandered back to the railroad tracks.

BACK IN THE GLORY DAYS OF TRAVEL

The sun was intense as I took another turn jumping between the railroad ties, dust flying in all directions on each impact. *Rather like a train puffing along*, I thought. I had never seen or heard a train on these tracks, but you never know! *One could come along and we had better be ready to spring out of the way at a moment's notice.* There was something romantic about walking the rails even if it was a defunct line with no train.

I thought of Rita's friend Carlos who was traveling across the whole country to New York. He would have left the palm trees of California far behind by now. I envied the adventures he must be having.

Maybe he had even taken the same route my family took when I was four years old. Only his would have been the reverse of ours. In 1945, my mother packed up four young children—ages two, four, six, and eight—and traveled by train from New York City to Los Angeles. I remembered the train and the outside that flew by in countless telephone poles. I remembered the sleeper cars, where daytime seats magically turned into bunk beds fully equipped with crisp white sheets. On the top bunk, it was fun to be up close to the ceiling and look down on the passengers in their pajamas walking through the cars to their tucked-up beds. It took three days to cross the country. Jeff and I shared the bottom bunk with Mom. It had a window to the outside, where the dark night flew by—dark nights that did not make me sick like the telephone poles. At every crossing, I could hear the signal dimly clanging and would be lulled to sleep, punctuated by that distant clang and occasional hoot-hooting of the train.

I loved the dining car with its crisp white linen, shiny silver pots of tea and coffee, white cups and dishes with the insignia of our train on it. A special surprise was a pat of butter on its own little white dish imprinted with a picture of a cat, dog, or girl in a sunbonnet. Every day was a different picture. Best of all was the ever-changing scenery out the window, the dark green of forests, the purple of mountains till you got close, the rusty orange of canyons, and the endless, pale beige of deserts. As we traveled west, the world got drier. On the third day, we woke up to green again.

In Los Angeles, our father was there to guide us through Union Station with its Mexican tiles, arched doorways, and mosaic floors. Outside was a brilliant blue sky and a yellow sun—sharp and bright compared to the gray winter of New York we had left just three days before. We drove away from the station in my father's convertible—palm trees swirling above my head—as we sped toward our new white stucco house in Burbank.

How could I remember all that? I wondered. I had only been four years old, but that trip was not the only time we took a train across the country. There had been other trips. I must have blended some of them together to come up with that memory. There were also travels by airplane and Greyhound buses, but I liked the train trips best. They were so grand.

Our travels always started in an all-of-a-sudden way. Mom would get a long-distance collect phone call. It was Harry. He had a booking for an extended engagement somewhere and he would want us to be with him. Mom would drop everything and pack us up (sometimes there was a dog), and we would be gone. We could start a school year in our home in Burbank and end it in Miami, Florida or San Francisco. From 1951 to 1954, I counted nine moves and five different schools.

JEFF DOUBLES ON FLUTE

During my train reverie, Jeff had ended his flute practice and was trying to teach Lindee the backup part to "A Night in Tunisia." He took up the melody on his new flute. Well, it wasn't exactly new; Jim Bishop had discovered it in a battered musical case inside an old bureau at the Swap Shop. Could there still be an instrument inside? Yes, there was, and Jim showed the flute to Jeff when he stopped by for some spare parts for his van. Like the van, the flute needed extensive repairs. The keys stuck, and it had lost most of its corking and pads. Even so, it was a good instrument, and Jim gave Jeff a good deal on it. Working enthusiastically, Jeff had finally gotten his new prize into reasonable shape and had started learning the fingering.

An unusual musician who had recently performed at the Lighthouse had inspired all this work and effort. When not washing dishes, Jeff peeked into the club to hear the music. This time it was the phenomenal Roland Kurt. I was dismayed at first when I finally got to see him with Bill Connelly one night. Roland Kurt played great jazz saxophone and, amazingly, could play several instruments at the same time and in three-part harmony. For emphasis, or whenever he got excited, he also snorted into a nose horn, which made a kind of crazy blaaaazzzz sound. The man was blind and couldn't know how odd he looked swaying back and forth, saxophones strapped to his body and another one stuck up his nose. Kurt may have looked bizarre, but the music wasn't. Jeff, of course, raved about him for weeks and was inspired to double up on another instrument himself, consequently, the flute came at just the right time.

So as Jeff piped out the melody of "A Night in Tunisia," Lindee and I sang the backup part. He was learning fast, but every so often there would be an ear-piercing squeak. Stopping on the tracks to fiddle with an errant key, he said, "You know, I think I can make my own nose horn with a sax mouthpiece and the end of a clarinet."

Oh no! I did not want to see Jeff with a horn up his nose. He was weird enough already. Changing the subject, I asked how his job was working out back there in the kitchen of the Lighthouse. There was a pause before he mumbled that it was great except for Wong. "He doesn't like me. He yells at me in Chinese. I don't know what he is saying but sometimes it sounds a bit threatening."

"Threatening? Oh, you must be imagining that. Remember when we lived in San Francisco and in Chinatown how the people there spoke? How their voices went up and down so dramatically? It is almost musical really, and I'm surprised that you didn't pick up on that being a musician yourself," I responded.

"Yeah, well, you could be right, but he calls me 'lazy boy' and 'no good boy.' He doesn't think I work hard enough. He is always hurrying me up. I have to go out in the club and pick up the glasses and dishes without making too much noise, and then I have to wash them and put them away. Just look at my hands. They are wrinkly and waterlogged by the end of the night and it's very important, according to Wong, for the glasses to be washed separately, first in suds with a bit of bleach, then rinsed in hot water and ammonia and only then, hand dried. The glasses have to sparkle. Wong is always examining them to see if they are spotless. I don't see that it matters so much. It's dark inside the club. Who is going to examine how spotless they are?"

I wasn't surprised Chef Wong thought my brother lacking in the cleanup department. None of us Gibson kids had ever been trained to do housework. Mom always said she would rather do it herself than nag. She had to do chores growing up in her strict family and wanted us to have more time to play so she didn't push, and Harry, well, he had a theory about raising us to be free—"to invent, to be individuals," he said. Therefore, it wasn't surprising we were not much help around the house. Mom could have used it after she had to go to work, but we were trained too well by then to change. I felt guilty about this now, but soon the lovely day put all thoughts of past deficiencies out of my mind. Before long, I joined Jeff in his version of "A Night in Tunisia."

Toot-in-toot-in-toot-in, toot-in-toot-in-toot-in, Lindee and I chanted while matching our steps to the rhythm until Jeff came in on the second chorus, piping the bebop melody. He hadn't figured out the bridge to the song yet, so again we just repeated what we knew. Our time passed pleasantly and before long we were able to turn off the tracks and make our way over to the library a few blocks away.

CHAPTER 22
THE LIBRARY

MORE REMEMBRANCES OF THINGS PAST

The Redondo Public Library was the perfect place to be on a hot day. It was set on a hill overlooking the ocean, in a green park with cool pools of shade. Elegant palm trees lined the cement path running up to the large stucco building. Even without air-conditioning, the rooms were cool, quiet, and restful. If you looked out the back windows, you could see the sand dunes and ocean waves breaking on the shore. A short distance away, the Redondo Pier jutted into the ocean.

The library was reminiscent of an old Spanish mission with its red-tile roof, arched windows, and heavy, oak doors. A large tree grew close to the building. *It looks ancient*, I thought, stopping on the staircase. *I bet it was already old when they built the library.* Maybe it was because I was at a library, but the tree made me remember a special book I read in grammar school. A cottonwood tree grows by a dirt trail. As it gets older, it becomes tall and wide. It sees many things like Indians and buffalo and pioneers in covered wagons going west. The people stop and rest under the shade of the great tree. The tree wonders what is at the end of the trail. When it dies, a man cuts it down and makes a beautiful carved yoke for his two great oxen that pull his covered wagon, so it turns out that the tree gets to go down the trail it used to wonder about. Is that book still being printed? I wondered as I followed Jeff and Lindee up the rest of the stairs to the entrance.

Opening the thick doors was like entering a church with its hushed atmosphere. I got that excited feeling I always got when I stepped into a library. Everything you ever needed to know was right here for the taking (that is, if you had a library card). I had so many memories of libraries, mostly about my mother. No matter where we moved, we always got library cards. When we were little, she pulled us there in a red wagon (Mom never did learn to drive). We got to take several books out apiece, so with four kids a lot of books got pulled home. Mom read to us every night. We all sat on her bed in our pajamas, two kids hugging one side of her, two kids hugging the other. My mother did not act out the characters or exaggerate her tone at dramatic parts. She read each story in a clear, level voice, and I came to the conclusion that her way was the perfect way to read because I could picture everything in my own way.

On a Sunday, in the backyard, my mother read us the newest Donald Duck comic book. Squeezed in around her on the very uncomfortable twig lounge chair, peering over her shoulder to see the pictures, we heard the adventures of Donald and his three nephews, Huey, Dewey, and Louie. Uncle Scrooge was funny too, the way he loved money and liked to dive into heaps of it. It was sometime later that I actually saw a Donald Duck cartoon at a movie theater. I was surprised when he opened his mouth and I didn't hear my mother's calm voice, only an unintelligible squawking. I have to say that I lost a bit of respect for Donald after that.

Except for the comics, my mother only read us chapter books—fairy tales, fantasies, and classics like *A Connecticut Yankee in King Arthur's Court* or one of the books from the Oz series. There were stories about animals, usually horses, cats, or dogs. Once there was even a pig who could talk. We especially enjoyed stories about kids our age who had adventures or solved mysteries or were inventors of things like flying machines. Yes, the library was a very familiar place.

Jeff shuffled away to look for a book about how to fix flutes. Lindee and I moved into the children's section where I kept my eye out for the tree book. Lindee stooped to a low shelf filled with picture books. She pulled out a few of the largest ones and started turning the pages.

"Oh, Lindee," I said, "aren't you too old to read those books? They are for babies. They hardly have any words."

Suddenly, my niece's face took on a crushed look. "I still like them," she said in a soft voice, her lip trembling.

Oh my gosh, I thought, as tears welled in her eyes. *Who am I to criticize? I was still reading fairy tales and Oz books way into junior high school.* I smiled then and told her that we could pick out some of these books for Laurie J. and Donnie. "They can't read yet," I said. "What do you say? I'll help you." Lindee smiled and wiped her runny nose on her sleeve.

Looking through the stacks, I couldn't believe it! All my favorite books were still here. I pulled out *The Little House* by Virginia Lee Burton and read "The little house was very happy as she sat on the hill and watched the countryside around her." In the story, the little house was eventually surrounded by a dark busy city.

"Oh look, Lorraine," Lindee cried, momentarily distracting my thoughts. "Here's *The Little Engine That Could*. Donnie and Laurie J. will like this one."

As we moved farther down the row, more and more books made their way to our pile. There was Robert McCloskey's *Make Way for Ducklings*, about a family of ducks, and *Blueberries for Sal*, about a little boy and a bear—another Donnie-type book for sure.

After that were several Dr. Seuss books for Laurie J. I looked for my favorites and continued handing books off to Lindee, lost in my own childhood until I looked around and discovered Lindee's overloaded arms. "Sorry," I said. "OK, let's stop and see what we have. Let's count the books."

"I have six," Lindee said, "and we are only allowed three books each."

"That's OK," I said. "I will only take out one for me and one for your Mom. I'll tell Jeff to just take one book too, so that will be three more for you kids." Lindee was counting it up on her fingers, silently mouthing the numbers.

I had come to another remembered book. "Lindee," I asked, "did you ever read *Little House on the Prairie?*" She shook her head. "It's great. It's about a family that goes west in a covered wagon and they build a log cabin." It seemed my mind was on traveling today. Wouldn't it be great to travel across the whole country in a Conestoga wagon?" Lindee nodded, not knowing exactly what a Conestoga covered wagon was. "Well, you might not be ready for chapter books yet." I put the Laura Ingalls Wilder book back on the shelf and let Lindee make her own choices from then on. She reached for *The Cat in the Hat* by Dr. Seuss.

As we moved along, the books got more sophisticated. Suddenly, I stopped and slowly picked up—could it be? Yes, it was my absolute favorite book in grammar school, and just as I remembered it—on the cover, a white seagull glides over blue pounding waves and the word *Seabird* written in large letters. I skimmed through looking at the colorful pictures I had pored over so long ago—images of tropical islands, fast moving sailing ships, and monster whales breaching the waters. The familiar longing for faraway places came back as I gazed at the—

All of a sudden, Jeff slipped into the room, trying hard to control a smile that was playing on his lips.

"What's up?" I said.

"Shhh, you'll know soon enough."

A moment later, a loud blast of jazzy music boomed out from one of the back rooms. The librarian at the front desk was practically jettisoned out of her chair. When she recovered, she rushed into a small room just off the entrance. A few seconds later, the lively dance music was cut short. There was dead silence again. Flushed, but under control, the librarian moved purposefully back to her desk, trying to convey with her precise movements to the company at large that an outburst like that would not be tolerated again.

Jeff was chortling silently. He collapsed onto one of the tiny chairs and held his stomach. Fizzy noises came out of his mouth as he tried to stifle laughing out loud. Finally, he got control of himself. I already knew what had happened. It was an old joke that my ex-boyfriend used to play at this very library. I guess *He* must have told Jeff all about it.

The trick was this. There was a special small reading room with large comfortable chairs. On a table was an old radio bought back in the days when families used to huddle around them for news and entertainment. It was so ancient the tubes in it took almost a minute to warm up and play. Knowing this, my ex would casually enter the room. If empty, he would turn the volume knob up as far as possible then turn on the radio and stroll casually out of the room knowing that he had plenty of time to be far away before the radio blasted out its music at full volume.

I had to admit the joke was funny but I did feel sorry for the librarian. After things quieted down, I explained to Jeff that he should only check out one book so he wandered off again to the adult section and over to the desk of the recently startled librarian to ask for music books. *Oh darn, I thought, why did Jeff play that trick and remind me of the very person I am trying to forget or at least not think about. Trouble is, so many things made me think about him.* Even this library brought back a story from the past.

LOVE?

There was another day here about three years ago. Mom and I were living on Lyndon Street at the time and I was still in my first year at El Camino College. It was a Saturday morning, I remember, and I woke up early even though I didn't have to. The sun was streaming through a high window. As I studied it, I realized that something was different, but I couldn't put my finger on what it was. All I knew was that I felt that everything was peaceful and beautiful—the golden sun coming in the window, my comfy bed, the room I slept in, even the soft clinking sounds my mother was making in the kitchen. Everything was caught up in a golden radiance. I was happy—very, very happy—*but why?* I asked myself. Slowly an answer came to me. *I think I am in love!* This must be what it feels like but I've never been in love, so I don't know for sure. I got up and ate breakfast and still the sensation was there, a delicious feeling. I dressed quickly and told my mother I was going to the library. I wanted to think about this new thing.

At the library, I wandered dreamily through the stacks. Should I pick out a book and take it outside and think under a tree? I considered the idea vaguely. Forget the book. This was big. Could I really be in love? I never thought it could happen. I thought it had passed me by, like smoking cigarettes. I didn't pick up the habit in high school like everyone else because I thought it looked cheap. It just wasn't my style and the same applied to love. Since I didn't date during my school years, I thought "the love window" must also be closed. I assumed I just wasn't wired the right way.

But then I met *Him*. From the very first, he had enthusiastically pursued me—insisting on picking me up after my classes at El Camino, driving me home every day in his old Packard and coming over every night with stacks of his favorite records, which would require us to dance together. Taking me on long walks on the beach, he would patiently try to teach me how to kiss.

For the first time, I didn't get nervous when someone liked me. I could even be mean to get rid of someone and make them go away, but with *Him* it was different. Even when, after only three days, he declared that he was in love with me, I didn't panic. His enthusiasm overwhelmed my caution, or maybe it was because he could make me laugh and we liked the same music and how could I worry about him falling in love with me when he had already done it? He didn't even go away when I told him we could only be friends. He just laughed.

From then on, whenever he tried to hold my hand and I objected, he would say, "Friends hold hands, don't they?" Then he would laugh and take my hand again and whenever he would try to hug me and I pulled away, he would laugh and say, "Friends hug, don't they?" Then he would hug me. And when he would leave for the night and try to kiss me and I backed away, he would laugh again and say, "Friends kiss goodbye, don't they?" And he would kiss me. Then came that day, when I woke up with the new feeling. *It has finally come*, I told myself. How delicious it was, and just as I was luxuriating in my new discovery, who did I see wandering around the library looking for me? It was *Him*. Mom must have told him where I was.

Instead of being happy to see him, I was annoyed. The wonderful spell was broken as he waved hello and crossed the library to join me. His actual presence was intrusive and disturbing. How had I not noticed before how awkward he looked when he walked? The way his feet slapped the ground and the way his body dipped with each step. And the dark five o'clock shadow even when he had just shaved. The special feeling I had been nursing all morning burst like a great pink bubble. It was gone with the wind, sunk to the bottom of the deepest well. I wasn't in love after all.

Eventually, I got over my disenchantment as he jollied me back into the friendship mode, and by the time we were walking home on the railroad tracks, singing songs and chatting, we were pals again. It was months later that I was finally able to say my first real "I love you" back.

OLD BOOKS, OLD MEMORIES

I felt a tug on my sleeve. "Lorraine, Lorraine! Why are you staring? Why do you look so funny? Are you still mad at me?" I looked down to see Lindee looking up at me with concern.

"No, no, of course not. I'm not mad . . . just . . . thinking hard."

Lindee looked relieved and went back to her book, then looked up again. "But you had such a strange look on your face."

For how long, I wondered, had I been standing staring at the wall without seeing a single thing? I was still holding *Seabird*. Looking down now, I read the cover—written and illustrated, it said, by "Holling Clancy Holling." On the back was a list of his other books, and I realized he had also written the *Tree in the Trail*. How about that? I felt as if I had just found a long-lost friend, this writer-illustrator who had made me yearn for adventure as a child. My thoughts of love and loss drifted away.

"Lindee, I'll just be over there in the next room to find a book for me and your mom," I called out as I moved toward the door. "After you pick out your choices, you can just sit with the other kids here and read all the books you want."

In the regular stacks of the library, I heard Jeff somewhere in one of the aisles humming a Thelonious Monk song. It was either "Well You Needn't" or "Nutty." In the fiction section, I looked for Faulkner. *A, B, C, D, ah, here he is.* I picked out the thickest one. *The Sound and the Fury—that sure sounds like an Arlene kind of book,* I thought. Next, I moved on to the S row and found *The Grapes of Wrath* and sat down at a table and started to thumb through the Steinbeck book. Years ago, I had seen the movie on TV. It had been cut severely to fit in all the advertisements, but the story was still impressive—a poor family leaves their farm in the dust bowl of Oklahoma and heads out for California in a rickety truck with all their belongings. It dawned on me then that the Joads' route from Oklahoma to California must have been the reverse of a trip my own family took in 1951. Only our trip was from California, past Oklahoma, and all the way down to Miami, Florida. The year 1951 had been an important year for my family and in my own ten-year-old life.

CHAPTER 23
THE LOST ADVENTURE, THE WAY HOME,

AND
FROM THE GRAY NOTEBOOK
CLAUDETTE

THE CAR TRIP

As usual, it all began when Harry wanted us to be together when he got the contract to star at the Say When Club in San Francisco. It started out great that summer when I was ten. The whole family took a one-hour plane ride to San Francisco. All our furniture, even the family upright piano and our entire household goods including, linen, kitchen utensils, Mom's almost complete set of Blue Willow Ware dishes, her beloved portable Singer sewing machine, and even Bill's mother-of-pearl drum set complete with bass drum, sock cymbal, and cowbell, were to be hauled out later by truck. Again, like he did at Union Station, Harry met us with a car, and we sped over the Golden Gate Bridge to a fantastic house in Marin County. Our fabulous two-floor rental clung onto a steep cliff overlooking San Francisco Bay. From our bedroom window, Arlene and I could see porpoises leaping gaily in and out of the water in synchronization and at night heard the foghorns mournfully blowing and watched the lights on the Golden Gate Bridge twinkle. In the morning, there was gray fog where the bridge used to be.

It was a wonderful summer. My older brother Bill fished off the pier at the bottom of the stairs. He even tried to build a boat. Arlene had a summer romance with a local rich boy who took her in his sailboat almost to Alcatraz. Jeff and I and our dog Benny followed Bill around as he explored the rocky hills of Tiburon and swam in the lagoon he had discovered.

In September, in order to start school, we set off again across the Golden Gate Bridge to the city. For the second time that year, we packed all our possessions—the furniture, the upright piano, Mom's almost complete set of Blue Willow Ware dishes, her beloved portable Singer sewing machine, and Bill's mother-of-pearl drum set including bass drum, sock cymbal, and cowbell. Harry was not only headlining at the Say When Club, but also appearing in a play called *Room Service*. Things seemed good. Harry bought a brand-new convertible, another Cadillac, and I even restarted piano lessons.

FROM THE GRAY NOTEBOOK
CLAUDETTE

San Francisco was different from the suburbs of Burbank. We lived smack in the middle of the city just across the street from Golden Gate Park. There were no lawns or backyards, just a sidewalk in front of our place on Lincoln Way. Our building had a bay window on the second floor over a ground-level garage. It looked very much like the house next door, and that building, with a slight variation, looked like the one next to it, and so on and so on, until the houses stopped suddenly at the ocean.

Jeff and I enrolled in the elementary school a few short blocks away, but Arlene and Bill had to take the bus to

Roosevelt Junior High School on the other side of the park. Mom didn't realize that San Francisco was not like Burbank and that Roosevelt Junior High School was not like the ones in the suburbs. The kids were tough. Bill told me he often got jostled in the hallways and his lunch bag snatched. Bill just put his head down and kept a low profile, but Arlene took a different direction.

One day Arlene brought home a new school friend. Claudette Sung wore tight skirts and tighter sweaters. Her mouth was a slash of dark red lipstick. At fifteen, she knew all about style and wore her saddle shoes with the socks tightly rolled down almost out of sight, and when outdoors, the knot on her headscarf was located precisely dead center of her chin. Claudette's hair was not long and straight like the Chinese children in my picture books. She kept her hair short and curled in the latest style.

Claudette also smoked. She would take a big drag of her cigarette, then slowly let the smoke drift from her mouth up into her nose. Her sentences were injected every so often with the S expletive and she called my sister Girl. "Shit, Girl! You got to come over to my house and hear some of my Louis Armstrong records. You can bring your little sister too. Shit, I'll teach you the steps to the dirty boogie."

Soon Arlene gave up Pixie Pink lipstick for a slash of dark red. She set aside her cotton dresses for black turtleneck sweaters and straight skirts. She even showed me how she learned to French inhale just like Claudette. Poor Mom was shocked at the new Arlene who now "swore and talked back." "Arlene Rita Gibson. Where did you get that fresh mouth of yours? What am I to do with you?"

One day we were going to Claudette's cousin's apartment in Chinatown. The streets were narrow, the buildings and stores squeezed together. A jumble of signs in Chinese were vying everywhere for attention—big and small, blinking and flashing in different colors. I pointed to one. "What does it say, Claudette?" I was finally going to be in on that special secret language while I had a real Chinese person with me.

"Man, I don't dig that kind of jive!" she said, brushing me off with a disgusted wave of her hand. Claudette sure knew how to be cool!

FROM THE GRAY NOTEBOOK: A FLASH FORWARD

A year later, when we finally did get back to our home in Burbank and the suburbs, Arlene reverted to wearing Pixie Pink lipstick and full cotton dresses again, but she never quite gave up her cigarettes or her favorite S expletive.

MORE ABOUT SAN FRANCISCO AND THE AFTERMATH

With us settled at school, Mom set out to conquer city living. She learned to walk our dog Benny on a leash instead of letting him run free. She got used to doing the laundry in the basement and soon found all the stores with the best prices. Our family was finally settling into our new life in San Francisco but, sadly, we were soon to be off again.

Christmas was only a few weeks away, but that didn't stop Harry. The plan, this time, was to sublet the apartment. All the furniture, even the upright piano, was to be left behind. The rest of our stuff was to be put in an open U-Haul, hooked to the new Caddy and ready to take off for the white sandy beaches, palm trees, and coconuts of Florida.

Mom would stay behind to tidy things up and get a sublease. Then, packing poor Benny in a crate, fly to the Sunshine State to meet up with everyone at our new rental in Miami. I don't know exactly when I realized that I wouldn't be going in the Caddy with Harry and everyone else. When I protested, Mom said she wanted me to stay with her. "You get carsick," she simply said.

"I wanna go! I don't get carsick on long drives," I pleaded.

"Well, I can use your help here. You can take care of Benny." Mom had this way of tightening up her face, and I knew it was of no use to beg. She looked a little hurt too that I didn't want to stay with her.

Thus, the whole family except me, Mom, and Benny, got to make the journey from San Francisco to Miami in the Cadillac convertible. Away they went one morning, pulling everything we owned, crammed to the brim, in the open U-Haul—linen, kitchen utensils, my mother's almost complete set of Blue Willow Ware dishes, her beloved portable Singer sewing machine, and Bill's mother-of-pearl drum set with the bass drum, sock cymbal, and cowbell. I felt bad about being left behind but even worse when we all finally met up in Miami and I heard all the funny stories Arlene told me about the trip. Finally, Arlene said, "Quit complaining about how you missed out. Really, Lorraine, the whole thing was a disaster from beginning to end." Then went on to describe in hilarious detail the whole thing as only Arlene could do.

I had missed the fight with the liverwurst sandwiches that Mom had so carefully packed. The liverwurst got all over the car. Mostly it stuck to the convertible top and they had to smell it for the rest of the trip. I missed the time they went through farm-land, and it smelled like manure for miles and miles and then, when Harry couldn't stand anymore complaining said, "Can I help it if the country smells like shit?" I missed the time when Bill's mother-of-pearl drum set with the bass drum, sock cym-bal, and cowbell flew off the top of the U-Haul and rolled down the hill. I missed the time Harry got mad at Bill (Willy, he called him) and pushed him into a mud puddle. I missed seeing what the whole rest of the country looked like, felt like, and smelled like, but what I missed most was not being there with them.

After all that, Florida turned out to be a disaster. Benny ran away on the third day we arrived and didn't come back. The

Caddy was pretty much destroyed, the engine burned out by the three-thousand-mile trip across the country. Harry lost the job he had come for (I learned later that he was coming off heroin), and everything fell apart.

Harry left and went back to California to find another job, and we were stuck in Florida with very little money. Mom moved us from our three-bedroom stucco into a tiny wooden house set behind a large gloomy Victorian manor that had seen better days. Our landlady owner of the manor, to my eyes, looked a hundred years old, and her brother was no spring chicken either. He had a crazy laugh, and I was terrified I would meet up with him when he came out to the little patch of grass between our houses to play golf with no ball.

Our little hovel didn't have hot water, but it *did* have mice. It looked exactly like the set for the Tennessee Williams play *The Glass Menagerie*. In the one small bedroom, Bill and Jeff shared a double bed that humped up in the middle. They were constantly rolling out of bed at night. Arlene and I shared an old-fashioned brass bed that sunk down in the middle. We were constantly rolling into each other. Our bedroom was cloaked off from the living room by a big tapestry curtain on a string. Mom slept on a daybed that served as our couch in the living room. It was months before Harry sent us enough cash to come home.

To save money, Mom booked us on a Greyhound bus back to Los Angeles. It had no air-conditioning, and we lost all the food she had packed in one of the suitcases, but we didn't care; we were going home. We didn't even mind that we had to live in a hotel in Hollywood until the lease was up for the tenants renting our house. It took a while before we got our furniture back from San Francisco but finally, just before school was to start, we were home again—our home at 118 South Lamar Street, Burbank, California. Yet, our happiness did not last. By the end of the next year, our lives had fallen apart completely.

This time I was the one to shake myself back to reality and stopped myself from rehashing all that followed when Harry was arrested and Mom had to sell our home and move us to the farmlands of Riverside. I was aware now that I had been staring again and was glad Lindee wasn't there to see me. *Memories have a way of getting out of hand*, I realized, then added defiantly, *Yes, we lost our home in Burbank, but we did finally get to Hermosa Beach.*

CHECKING OUT

The Sound and the Fury and *The Grapes of Wrath* were still in my hands when Jeff came whistling out of the stacks with *The History of Jazz* (1890-1955). Together, we gathered up Lindee and her chosen books and proceeded to the checkout desk where the librarian was kind and efficient. Soon we were out squinting in the summer sun. As we divided out the books to be carried home, Jeff started slapping his pockets. "My flute, where's my flute!" he cried, still slapping at the pockets of his pants and shirt. "It was in my hand!"

"When?"

Jeff looked down as if he was hoping the flute would appear in the grass like a surprise Easter egg. "No, no, no, this can't be happening! I worked so hard on that thing."

"Jeff, stop. Don't panic. Where did you have it last?"

"I was in the stacks looking for a book. It was in my hand. I remember 'cause I scratched my nose with it."

"Well, good, good. Go back inside and look in the stacks where you were."

Jeff bounded away, his boots making floppy sounds on the cement path. A few minutes later, he appeared holding up the flute and smiling. "I was going crazy," he said. "It wasn't in the stacks, so I finally asked the librarian. She had it. Someone had turned it in to her."

"You know what, Jeff?" I said. "I think you have just received your retribution." I had come upon that word the day before in a book. "It means," I continued knowingly, "that if you do harm, it will come back as something bad happening to you. I think you got off easy this time."

"What do you mean?"

"Well, remember that trick you played with the radio, scaring half the people in the library and embarrassing the nice librarian?" Jeff looked a little sheepish. "So, your retribution was that you lost your flute, if only for a short time, so then you became the one who was upset."

"Wow! So if someone does something bad, the fates will punish them for it?"

"Exactly."

"Cool! It's kinda like 'I'm rubber, you're glue; everything you say bounces off me and sticks on to you.'"

"Yeah, that is cool," added Lindee.

Jeff rolled the word around in his mouth. "RETRIBUTION, it's a great name for a tune." He started humming to himself and was off on one of his songwriting jags, happy again.

THE WAY HOME

We decided to take the ocean route along Harbor Drive to get home. Not far from the library lay the silhouette of the Redondo Pier, snaking out invitingly over the water. On the pier were shops and food stands jostling each other, selling seashells, bathing suits, and exotic snacks. A short stroll there would be fun, but we needed to get home. Moving past, we ran into the large construction site of the new marina being built. Caterpillar tractors were moving dirt and huge rocks around. Other machines were dredging in the water and piling up mounds of wet sand. I remembered when Arlene lived on Harbor Drive. Now the block of those old houses was gone, and the empty space waited for the great new marina to come.

Scrambling up from the beach, we continued home. Before long, the large gray Southern Electric Power Plant came into view. I took in the factory's belching smokestacks and round tanks surrounded by metal ladders—pipes and tubing squirreling everywhere. It seemed somber and out of place compared to the swanky marina that was coming. Trudging on, Harbor Drive turned into Hermosa Avenue once again and we were officially back home.

A few blocks more and we were turning up Second Street. The books were getting cumbersome, especially the thick fairy tale volume that Jeff and I had been passing back and forth. Lindee was having trouble with her stack too. For the last few blocks, they had been slipping from her fingers and falling onto the sidewalk. *The Cat in the Hat* was getting a real beating, but home was near and, sensing this, our tired troop picked up the pace. Just three more blocks to go.

We were on the final stretch of our journey. The old street sign that said Culper Court was still strangely twisted and pointing the wrong way as we turned in toward home. Our neighbor Betsy was standing outside her house watering her tidy patch of lawn. We nodded as we passed by like bedraggled desert recruits from the Foreign Legion. At last, we came to our own oasis, the red cottage.

There, far off, was a figure at the very end of Culper Court—that funny, loping, flat-footed walk, that dark hair—it was *Him*. *He* must have been visiting at the house. I could see now that he was just about to turn the corner. In a second he would be gone. I had just missed him. Or had he just missed *me*? I felt a great urge to drop my books and run after him, catch up with him, and . . . But what did I want? What would I say?

"How could you not love me anymore?" Or maybe I just wanted to box his ears.

CHAPTER 24
THE TRUCE

MR. RAT FINK

It was late afternoon but Bob looked like he had just gotten up. As he stood there in the doorway, I found myself staring at his white-ribbed undershirt that exposed his lanky arms and bony shoulders. My mother's boyfriend was a redhead, and his pale skin was speckled over with rusty freckles except for his bright pink feet that were now peeking out from underneath his blue silk pajama bottoms.

"You girls look purtier than a jar full of beetle bugs!" he twanged in an exaggerated drawl, a grin breaking out across his face. "What have you two been up to?"

EARLIER THAT DAY

For more than an hour, Arlene and I had been walking along the beach. We had decided over coffee this morning to finally visit our mother. We hadn't seen or talked to her since her return to the Rat Fink and subsequent recovery, but we knew sooner or later we would have to see them together, so today was as good a time as any to make the trip.

We had already searched the house for bus fare—on the floor, under the bed, and beneath the cushions—and had come up short, so we started the three- or four-mile hike to Mom's apartment with the idea that at least it would be good exercise.

PAULINE

The previous week, after school closed, Pauline, Arlene's mother-in-law, showed up at the red cottage. Ever since Don had left his family with no word and no money, his mother had decided to help out by taking her grandchildren to stay at her home in Riverside for a week every June. The first time, they came back remade into different children with fresh haircuts and new clothes often handmade by Pauline herself. Arlene hated the way they looked. Donnie's head would be shaved in a close crew cut, and Lindee and Laurie J. would have blunt bobs which Arlene dubbed their "village idiot haircuts."

Pauline had taken the kids three days earlier. She didn't even come into the house this time, and that was all right with Arlene. Her mother-in-law stood and waited outside next to her perfectly clean, sensible car, standing proud and straight in her perfectly ironed clothes, her tawny skin, tight across her high cheekbones, her cap of black hair shining in the sun.

There had always been an uneasy truce between Arlene and her mother-in-law. My sister had resented Pauline's attempts to train her to be an ideal wife to her son—her golden boy. Now, even though the gold had tarnished, Pauline still did not condemn or apologize for Don and never told us where he had gone either, but every June, after school ended, Pauline was there to "help out," as she called it.

BACK ON TREK

Now that we were on our own, a kind of lethargy and idleness took over. We lazed on the beach, nursing our tans, and splurged our sparse money on corn dogs and cream soda from the food stands. I didn't make an entry in the gray notebook for days. I had finished writing the story about the night I thought a prowler was about to break into our house and was having fun now mulling around for a good title. So much had happened that day but I hadn't made up my mind yet. I was playing around with calling it "Scary Night" or "Stranger in the Dump," but "Roses for Tomorrow" was a strong contender too. I also had plans to write about our trip to the library. The old railroad tracks had made me remember all the traveling we used to do following our father from one coast to another. I even had a title picked out in advance. I was going to call it "Sentimental Journeys," like the song by Doris Day.

The expected welfare check was late, and the food larder was down to a bag of potatoes, an onion, and a quarter box of Cheerios. Jeff ate his fill at the Lighthouse every night, but Arlene and I were getting tired of thinking up new ways to cook potatoes, so today was the day to pay Mom and Bob a surprise visit, and we soon found ourselves trudging by foot along the shoreline.

THE SAGA OF ARLENE AND DON

Seeing Pauline always brought back memories of Don Brower for my sister, and three days later, she was still grumpy as we stomped along the water's edge where the sand was wet but solid. Arlene could be a lot of fun to be around when she was in a good mood. I had better times with her than with almost anybody else, yet I also had some of the worst times when she was in one of her dark moods.

I left her alone today and tried to enjoy the water as it swirled around my feet when the suds-like tide came in and out. It was icy at first, then became deliciously refreshing. *She's probably thinking of Don now*, I reflected. Would she have married so young if we had stayed in Burbank? In Burbank, Arlene had gone to John Burrows High School just two blocks away from our home. She was in her glory days then, with a group of tight-knit friends:

Nancy, the leader and queen bee; Alice, dull but sweet; Marie, fun but kind of loose; and Janice W., aloof and sarcastic. Arlene found her place as the funny cut-up and screwball of the pack. She was popular with boys too, with one or two always hanging around our house. Arlene mostly dated Frank Marcello. He wasn't the captain or star, but he was on the football team and that counted for a lot. She was happy then; all she dreamed about was a cashmere sweater for Christmas. Her whole life fell apart and went down the tubes (as Arlene liked to say) when we had to sell our beloved home and "move to the sticks" (Arlene liked to say that too). There was no high school two blocks away. Only a big yellow bus that took her to school with all the other kids that lived in farm country. Arlene was mortified to have to stand out on the road while farm trucks and eighteen-wheelers whizzed by. It was a far cry from hooking up with her best friends before school and chatting about clothes and dates and what outfit to wear to the next dance, then meandering to school.

Arlene felt superior to the country kids on the bus, yet didn't feel accepted by the townies either. She was the new girl and pretty, and they didn't like her. Arlene was alone but defiant. "They don't even know the latest dance steps here and they dress in last year's fashion too," she whispered to me at night in the bed we shared.

Arlene filled her elective classes with chorus, modern dance, and drama. It was in drama that she met her husband-to-be, Don. Actually, at that time, he was called "Curly" because of his golden curls. After only three dates, they were both "madly in love!" They were "lost souls," who had found their "soul mates." "Yes, it was like that," Arlene said. They were both outsiders and when they met they knew they had found the missing part of themselves. She would be his muse and he would be her rock. Arlene described their third date in detail.

"After the movie, we went to the local park. Of course, it was empty because it was dark. We sat on the swings and talked and talked and then he came over and started pushing me on the swing. I went higher and higher, it was scary and thrilling, and then he came in front of the swing and said, 'Jump. Don't be afraid I'll catch you!' and I jumped into his arms. Then after he kissed me, he said he loved me and I said I loved him too. Just like that. Lorraine, it was so romantic and exciting I've never felt this way ever before!" It was true, she had big crushes on some of the boys she dated but she never really said she loved them for real.

I never knew what my sister saw in Don. He was so quiet. All those other guys that came to see my sister were funny and amusing. Don just sat there and looked down at his hands. I must admit that they made a handsome couple. Don with his golden curls and broad shoulders. Arlene, pretty and blonde too, looking small beside him.

Don, or I should say Curly, was nineteen and graduated that year. He got a job unloading potatoes that summer when he and Arlene told Mom they wanted to get married. Mom begged them to wait and managed to postpone the wedding for seven months. Yet, Arlene and Curly didn't waver and saw each other almost every night. Curly would arrive in his souped-up '36 Ford, tearing up the dirt road to our small house on the hill. Inside our even smaller living room, he sat quiet and brooding on the daybed-sofa until Arlene swooped out of our bedroom in some full-skirted cotton sundress, and they would leave. Again, Curly would gun his engine and they would roar and bounce down the other side of the hill, the car spitting up the dust of summer.

At night, a tapping sound on the bedroom window would wake me. "Lorraine! Psst, psst, Lorraine!" Arlene would hiss, her face pressed to the glass, motioning for me to open the window. I would help her struggle through into the bedroom while Curly, below, took away the ladder and put it back in the garage. "Sorry, kiddo," Arlene would whisper conspiratorially as she slipped into bed. "I didn't want to wake up Mom. It's three o'clock."

Mom slept on the daybed in the living room with the cardboard boxes underneath housing her clothes. The creaky screen door opening just a foot away from her pillow would surely wake her, and she would not have approved of the late hour her daughter was getting in. I'm not sure I did either. What were they doing that they stayed out so long? At thirteen, I really didn't want to think about it.

They married in December. Arlene was in her senior year of high school when she got pregnant and was beginning to "show." She was told she would have to drop out of school and never did get to graduate. After that, things fell apart. For one, Curly started losing his curly hair. He took to wearing a dark greasy cap and from then on, called himself Don. He hated being told what to do so he went from job to job. After work, he would go out with the boys and leave Arlene and the ever-growing family at home. And Arlene? Well, Arlene was Arlene; she was not going to be the silent helper, the "woman behind the man." She had always been the star of her own show, and she would not stand being ignored.

A wave slapped against my legs, catching me unaware and wetting the bottom of my rolled up jeans. Arlene gave a shriek and jumped toward the dry sand. "Where the hell are we anyway?" she said in exasperation. We passed the Redondo Library and the Pier ages ago!"

"Torrance Beach should be coming up soon," I said. Yes, Arlene had little patience and a short temper, and it didn't help that he, her brand-new husband, had his own short temper. All the things they loved at first in each other—Arlene's fire, Don's quietness—afterward, when they were married, those very things sparked ongoing fights that resulted in several breakups and reconciliations, and the kids kept getting born in between times. During the breakups, Arlene came home to us. Our two-bedroom bungalow was bursting at the seams trying to accommodate first Arlene and one kid, then two, then three. It helped a little when my brother Bill graduated high school and quickly joined the Navy.

Now, as I walked along the water's edge, I hoped again that Don wouldn't be coming back anymore.

FUN WITH TRUDY AND BOB

Another slapping wave broke around my ankles. The tide was coming in. I could tell that we were in Torrance Beach because it was starting to get rocky. After Torrance, the hills rose up into Palos Verdes, an upscale community of evergreen trees and red-tiled roofs.

"Hey," I pointed to a green apartment building, "let's go look at the number to see if it's Mom's house." We trudged toward the building, the dry sand sticking to our wet feet like a kind of sandy sock. At the curb, we wiped our feet as best we could and continued on barefoot. The green apartment house had Mom and Bob's name on the mailbox, 3-B. We trudged up the outside staircase and knocked, feeling pleased with ourselves as we waited for the door to open. We were doing a good deed. It had preyed on our minds ever since the night Bob had tried to kill himself that we were somewhat responsible. Maybe he had suffered enough now and was humbled. We still didn't trust him, but for our mother's happiness we were being magnanimous and coming over to visit and make peace. Well, maybe not peace but some kind of cease-fire.

Now that we were here, we realized how hungry we were. The walk on the beach had increased our appetite. Our stomach walls had been shrinking for days from lack of real food and now started to grumble. On the second knock the door opened, and there was Bob in the already described blue silk pajama bottoms and undershirt.

"C'mon in!" said Bob, ushering us into the apartment. "Trudy, look who's here, your two girls!"

We stepped inside. The whole apartment was polished and scrubbed. Pastel walls and deep piled carpets enveloped us like thick rich cream. The bay window, cloaked in milky drapes, neat and evenly pleated, showed a patch of ocean between the houses if you looked at it at a certain angle. A model airplane was in the process of being built on the dinette table in front of the bay window—the skeleton of the fuselage standing upright like an oil rig against the sky. Mom came out of the compact kitchen. Behind her, the almost complete set of Blue Willow Ware dishes lined the shelves. "Have you eaten yet?" she asked, to our great joy. "I'll make something," and she disappeared into a creamy pink kitchen.

"Yep, you two girls look purtier than a jar of June bugs," Bob said, changing his line a little this time. "Walked all the way did ja?" he commented, as we thankfully sank a half-foot into the soft foam rubber of the tweedy couch.

"Yep, you're quite a crew," he added, and winked as if it was a secret joke between us. My sister and I winced at the hokey Andy Griffith impersonation, but smiled benignly. Mom emerged from the kitchen with two steaming mugs. The coffee tasted wonderful and when the thick tuna sandwiches finally came, we could hardly control our lunging hands.

While Arlene and I rested our tar-stained feet on the pristine carpet, our mother quietly puttered around, making more coffee and sandwiches and straightening things up. The clinking and clanking sounds from the pastel kitchen were like dim cowbells in a far-off pasture. In due course, Mom joined us in the living room as we were finishing the last crumbs on our plates and licking the mayonnaise off our lips and fingers. She selected a straight chair, leaving us to stay on the soft couch. I watched as the expression in her eyes changed from tension then to relief as she observed the seemingly easy conversation between Bob and her difficult children. Did I see her sigh? I hoped she was happy that we were being charming to her Bob. At least, she looked calm and contented, her rounded form comfortable in the chair yet ready to jump up and serve if anything was needed. "I'm making stuffed peppers. That's your favorite, isn't it, Lorraine? You'll both stay for dinner, won't you?" Mom's eyes were not anxious now, and the corners crinkled into a smile when we agreed to stay.

After making some arrangements in the kitchen, Mom again joined us in the living room. The TV was on a sports station, but the sound was low. Even watching television, our mother kept busy mending. Her hands that had once been calloused and red were being smoothed out by lotions and lack of harsh detergents. Eventually, there was an embarrassing lull in the conversation. Always the impulsive one, Arlene jumped up and gave Mom a hug and kissed her on the cheek with a big smacking sound. Mom giggled a little in embarrassment. I felt I had to follow suit and dutifully kissed her on the other cheek. It felt so soft.

This Mom was like another person. She had become affectionate. It was embarrassing. She had not been the huggy-kissy type of mother except when we were very little, and after we moved to "Cow Town," as Arlene referred to Riverside, there was not much time for that kind of thing, and besides, we were teenagers. Did we stop being affectionate to her, or had she stopped first? Even so, it was hard now to respond to this new personality since she met Bob. Before the Bob era, Mom had lived a nun's life of work and little pleasure. She never dated.

It had been a big jolt to all of us when she moved into this apartment building and within a few months fell in love. Maybe she finally gave up on our father. Maybe she was afraid to be alone. Whatever it was, it turned my Mom into a fluttery teenager with adoring eyes.

*She kept busy mending. Her hands that had
once been calloused and red were being
smoothed out by lotions and lack of hard work.*

MOM AND ME

As I sat on the couch, while Mom got back to her mending, I thought again about when I first heard about Bob. I had been living in Hollywood for several months when Arlene decided to visit me in my funny attic apartment. So much had changed, she said, since I had made my big move to the city. Arlene's face looked like she was about to burst with some news.

"Guess what?" She didn't even wait for my answer. "Mom's got a boyfriend! His name is Bob."

"What?" I was stunned. It was hard to believe that after all those years of being alone, my mother was not just dating but actually had a boyfriend.

"Remember when I called and told you that Mom had moved out?" Arlene reminded me.

I nodded.

"I didn't blame her," Arlene looked thoughtful for a moment, "with me and the kids plus Jeff and his saxophone. Well, it was finally just too much for her, and she moved into that apartment house with a roommate and . . . Well, it seems that Bob was the next-door neighbor. He's kind of funny in an old cornball way with his good old boy shtick. He looks and sounds a lot like that actor Andy Griffith who plays all those hillbilly types. Bob is a used car salesman, and I guess he just sold himself to our mother."

"He sounds like someone our father would describe as a 'square,'" I said. According to Harry, the worst thing you could be was "a square."

"Yeah, he sure looks like it, but get this," Arlene paused for emphasis. "He is an avid jazz fan! He has every Count Basie album, and they go to jazz concerts together."

When Arlene left, I began to warm up to the idea of my mother having a boyfriend. Why shouldn't she? She was only in her forties and still pretty.

REVELATIONS

Not too long after that, Mom made her own visit. There was a shine in her eyes that I had never seen before. I felt my own spirits lift too. Back when we were living in Riverside, I always felt a deep sense of sadness for her. She had been betrayed and abandoned by our father, yet she had hung on to him until the end, and what good did it do? Now things had changed. As I faced her, across the table at the Greek restaurant, I realized that, for the first time, I didn't have that old sinking feeling. She had her own life now and a boyfriend too. During our meal, we were like two girlfriends enjoying ourselves and laughing at how we had to use pita bread to eat our Greek dinner. I knew my Mom had a lot to say to me. She was fairly bursting with it and couldn't stop smiling.

"I'm in love again!" she blurted out finally. "I never thought it would happen, but I'm in love with Bob Porth." My mother had at last broken out of her chrysalis and reached out for happiness. Finally, she would get what she deserved.

"Well, then, when will the wedding be?" I teased, expecting my mother to blush and gush out with some sort of plans.

There was a pause. "We are not getting married," she said in a more quiet voice. "I'm moving into his apartment next week."

"Is that what *you* want?" I asked pointedly, all the good feelings ebbing away. "Don't you want to get married?"

"Well, yes, but . . . well, Bob . . . can't . . . and—"

"Why can't Bob?" I cut in. "Is he already married?"

"He says he can't."

"He won't even tell you?"

"He says he can't." Mom looked sheepishly down at her pita bread. "It doesn't matter so much, does it? He says he loves me."

I was trying to hold down the anger. Here it was all over again, my mother not willing to call the shots, not standing up for what she wanted. Of course, she wanted to get married! All my old feelings came flooding back. "And you are still going to move in with him?" It was almost a taunt.

"Well, yes I am," Mom said softly. She sounded defeated to my ears. There it was again—her willingness to settle for less than what she wanted as if she wasn't worth it. I don't remember the rest of the evening. I only knew that for a brief time I had hope for my mother, and too soon it was gone.

ACCEPTANCE

I was jolted back to the present and Mom and Bob's creamy apartment again, when Bob called out suddenly, "Trudy! Get me some more coffee—Trudy!" Mom rose and smiled in a motherly way back at him as she sailed into the kitchen. "Yep, that's a good girl," Bob winked a pink eyelid at Arlene and me as if we were sharing in a special secret. "You know, girls, your mother takes real good care of this boy, yep."

Bob made a snapping sound on the letter P in yep. "You know, she's older than I am?" he continued and winked again. "Yep, yep, real good," he repeated. "She's a Jim Dandy!"

How I wished he'd stop saying "yep" and calling my mother "Trudy." Her name is Florence Gertrude. The freckled frame leaned back in his chair and stretched his legs out full length, then took a long drag on his cigarette. *He looks older than his thirty-five years*, I thought. His pale face was crisscrossed with lines like a much-folded road map, I concluded with satisfaction. A few minutes later, my mother returned from the kitchen with his hot coffee. She smiled protectively as she handed him the cup.

It was 11:00 p.m. when Mom and Bob dropped us off at the red house. We kissed our mother's soft cheek again, then, hurried away. As we walked inside together, I shrugged at my sister then as if to say, "If she is happy, let's not gum up the works."

CHAPTER 25
SARA LEE (SARI)

INGER

I had my book ready to take to my spot on the back deck. It was only June, but all morning the sun had been beating down. It was hot and even hotter in the vacant landfill where the kids were playing. I could already hear them yelling back and forth to each other. Yet, before I could open the door to the back landing, Arlene plunged through it into the dining room, almost colliding with me.

"Lorraine, you are just the one I need." She was out of breath and seemed relieved to see me. "Go out there and see what you can do for Inger!"

"Inger?" I repeated, a little lost.

"Yes, Sara Lee left Inger and Neisha off here this morning. We are taking care of them so she can meet with someone who buys her drawings. And, by the way, where have you been all morning?" Her voice had an accusatory edge to it.

For a moment, I felt guilty. I had been up in the loft, trying to write. I was thinking back to when Harry moved us all to San Francisco, and Arlene and Bill had gone to that rough junior high school across the park and how Arlene's new best friend taught her how to fit in there. Claudette Sung was quite a character. Would that make an interesting story? I had made a start on it until hunger got the best of me and I came down to hunt up some breakfast.

"What about Inger?" I asked vaguely. Arlene was giving me the exasperated expression she gave me when I wasn't paying enough attention, then continued her story. "Everything was going fine. The kids were playing 'dig up the dinosaurs in the dump' when . . . I don't know what happened, but Inger is bawling her eyes out. I tried to help but she just cries harder. I can't do a thing with her. You go out there!" Arlene took my book and coffee and put them on the dining room table. "You were always good with little kids and animals," she said, giving me a modest push toward the door along with her offhand compliment. It was true, whenever we got a pet, it usually turned out to be mine, and I did have a way with children, maybe because I still remembered how it felt to be a kid.

Leaving my coffee and book behind, I stepped out onto the deck. I could see Lindee, Donnie, Laurie J., and Neisha, Sara Lee's younger daughter, playing in the landfill but no Inger. I looked around on the cement slab that made up our patio. Inger was standing in a far corner near a stack of orange crates Jeff had erected so he had someplace to sit while he practiced outside.

Inger was about five years old. She was a serious child with a narrow face. Now she stood locked in place, her slight body quivering, her shoulders heaving with every sob she took. I approached quietly, squatting down on my heels in front of her. "What's wrong?" I asked in my calmest voice. It was a hot day, and Inger's plaid shirt was knotted around her waist. Standing there in her ribbed undershirt with her rust-colored hair wisping down in delicate tendrils around her pale shoulders, she looked lost and vulnerable.

"You're all right now," I tried to convince her.

Loud sobs and more shaking followed. "I want . . ." she choked out. "I want . . . my mommy!"

I looked out into the dump at the other kids jumping and yelling and wondered what had happened. What had they done to reduce Inger to this trembling state? Yet, maybe they hadn't done anything. Maybe the hot sun, new surroundings, and the rough play had been enough in itself. Did her sister know what was wrong? As if on cue, Neisha tromped up the three cement steps from the dump and ran across the patio toward the house. "Neisha, do you know what happened here?" I called as she bounded past me and up the stairs.

Neisha stopped for a second. Jumping up and down in seeming agony, she grabbed the crotch of her shorts and grunted, "Can't stop. Gotta go to the bathroom," and rushed up the rest of the staircase, disappearing through the back door. I turned back to Inger and rubbed her quivering arms. She seemed to be calming down. A few minutes later, the back door banged and Neisha tore down the stairs at breakneck speed. She jumped the three steps into the dump and disappeared behind a rather large hillock. Inger and Neisha were so different, Inger, thin and delicate, Neisha, round and compact like the tough brown nut of a chestnut tree.

Inger wasn't sobbing quite so much now that I had both my arms around her pointy shoulders. There was only the occasional shudder and gasp of air.

On the deck above, I heard the click of the back door opening. A moment later, Sara Lee appeared. She paused, surveyed the backyard, and seeing me and Inger, gave a little wave and walked serenely down the staircase. I was always a little amazed at Sara Lee. Nothing seemed to faze her. She never looked rushed or rattled, and that was surprising because her life must be very hectic indeed. She was for the most part the sole support of her growing family, and now there would be another child to provide for soon.

Sari's husband, Chris, had been the darling boy of the El Camino's Design Department, but somehow all this failed to get him very many jobs in his field. His ideas were usually too grandiose to be practical, and clients moved on to more reasonable designs or artists.

I watched Sari's tall, straight figure glide languidly down the stairs, her long hair cascading over her right shoulder like a modern-day Brunhilde. Sara Lee's pregnancy was evident now, but it only added to her full-bodied beauty, the kind that harkened back to the Renaissance. A Titian or Tintoretto would have loved to paint her waist-length russet-brown hair and full white body. A Botticelli would have posed her as Venus rising from the sea. In her beige shirt, tan capri pants, and, although the day was hot, her orange cable-knit cardigan, my friend moved down the stairs like a festival of fall colors. Following my gaze, Inger turned to see her mother coming down the staircase. "Mommy!" she burst out, tearing herself from me and flinging herself at her mother who had reached the bottom step. "Mommy!" Inger continued, clinging to Sari and mashing her face into her mother's knees.

Still serene, Sara Lee leaned down and patted Inger's shoulder. "There, there, I'm here now." She sat down on the last step of the stairs and put her arms around her oldest child. Inger stopped crying immediately and all was quiet except the far away calls of the kids playing.

NEISHA

The newfound quiet was shattered abruptly when my sister burst onto the back porch.

"Jeff!" she shouted down, leaning over the railing. There was a bit of hysterics in her voice. Then more forcefully, "Jeff, I need you now!"

When there was no answer from his room, I pulled back the rug that functioned as a door flap. The room was empty. No wonder he hadn't come out when all the hysteria had first started. I guess he had met up with Tad after the Lighthouse closed and stayed at his house. Or maybe he had gotten up early for some reason and gone off in his van. You just couldn't predict what Jeff was up to these days. "He isn't here," I called up to Arlene.

"What?" She squawked back, "I have an emergency up here! The toilet is backed up. There is water all over the floor!"

Slipping by Sara Lee, I bounded up the stairs to find Arlene taking care of the flood by throwing all the towels, the bathmat, and a few tee shirts onto the bathroom floor.

"Where is that Neisha? She was the last person to go into the bathroom!" Arlene yelped, throwing some white socks on top of the tee shirts. Looking at the mountain of wet fabric sopping up the pool of water in the bathroom, I made a mental note that washday would be coming sooner this week. Ever since Mom's old washing machine had broken down, we'd had to pile our dirty clothes into the beat-up wagon and bump down the four blocks to the Laundromat on Hermosa Avenue.

Back outside, Sara Lee had found a shady spot by the staircase. Inger sat happily on her mother's lap. Sari smiled as I approached. "Is the emergency fixed?" she asked with a tranquil smile then, not waiting for an answer, said musingly, "Now I wonder where Neisha is? I see your kids playing out there," she gestured toward the landfill, "but I don't see Neisha." I looked out at the dump. Sara Lee was right; there was no Neisha in view.

"Well," Arlene called down from her perch on the deck, "she was the one responsible for the flood in the toilet."

"Oh dear," Sari gave a little sigh. "She's probably hiding. She does that when she thinks she is in trouble. We better go look for her. Come, Inger," she said. "Now, where do you think she would be this time?"

"The kids can help too," I added, stepping down with them into the landfill. We found Lindee, Donnie, and Laurie J. at a nearby mound of dirt. They had unearthed a pile of small rocks, several rusty bottle caps, and a bundle of sticks and twigs and were trying to assemble them into a brontosaurus. I asked if they had seen Neisha.

"Yeah, she's around somewhere." Lindee gestured at the several acres of landfill that ran all the way down to the railroad tracks and over to Second Street.

"She may be hiding," I said.

Dropping the small pebble he had intended to place as the dinosaur's head, Donnie jumped up at this new game and raced away hollering, "Come out, come out wherever you are!" Lindee and Laurie J. veered off in the opposite direction calling the same chant.

Sari, Inger, and I set off toward the far railroad tracks. "Maybe we can systematically work out a search," I said optimistically.

Sari strolled along with me calling out the occasional "Neisha!"

While I added, "Nobody is angry at you. It's OK."

Back and forth we walked, calling. At last there came a soft, "Woof, woof!" Then a few seconds later, another questioning little "Woof?"

Against all odds, there was a tree growing in the middle of the lot. It was small but bushy. As Sari and I neared it, the tree or shrub rustled and gave off another almost pleading, "Woof, woof?"

Sara Lee looked at me, then sang out, "I think a little puppy is calling us."

And with that, Neisha scrambled out of the foliage. "Nope, it's just me," she said. "Am I in trouble with Arlene?"

"Of course not," Sari crooned. "But what happened?"

"No one is mad at the little doggie anymore," I chipped in.

Neisha looked down at the ground and kicked a small stone. "Don't know what happened," she said. "There wasn't any toilet paper so I used some other paper that was there and then when I flushed the water, it just started going up and up and I got out of there."

I thought I remembered seeing some lined paper in the bathroom, probably something Arlene had scribbled on then forgot.

"Well, your mommy is here to take you home," I said.

Neisha gave a grin, then shot forward like a diminutive cannonball, leaving the rest of us to trudge back alone to the patio landing. Unhurriedly, Sara Lee collected her children, their stuff and corralled them up the stairs. Following behind, I thought again how easygoing she always seemed to be no matter what was happening. When we reached the top of the staircase, Sari stopped and turned to me.

AN INTERESTING INVITATION

"Lorraine, I almost forgot to tell you about the art show."

"Art show?"

"Yes, let's go inside, and I'll tell you about it."

Inside, Sara Lee shrugged off an offer of coffee. "Sorry, my mother is coming over this afternoon; she wants to show me how to make her special taco and bean dish. She says the secret is fresh cilantro, so if I stay I won't have time to straighten up the kitchen. I left it in a bit of a mess this morning."

"How is your mother?" I asked. Sari's mother was quite the character—always doing something new and unusual. She was a real "kick in the pants," Arlene always said. Leahdell had been trained in ballet, music, drama, and literature, but those things hadn't worked out. So after jumping from one job to another, even becoming a fortune teller and handwriting analyst, she went back to school and was now teaching third and fourth graders at the Redondo Beach public school.

"She's swell," Sara Lee smiled ruefully. "In fact, she just came back from a health retreat in Mexico, and she says she feels completely purged of all toxins. She learned yoga there too, and is now an enthusiastic advocate. But about the art show, sit down and I'll tell you all about it. Inger, Neisha, go play in the living room for a minute. Now where was I? Oh yes, after I dropped off my artwork with the man who buys my work for a measly twenty-five dollars apiece, I thought I would just drop by to see our old design teacher Mr. Bluske."

"Good old Mr. Bluske," I said. "Is he still ranting and raving at his students?"

"Well, of course he is, but not at me. Since I married his favorite design student, the fabulously talented Chris Staggs, Mr. Bluske has become a kind of mentor, father figure in our lives or maybe I should say Godfather figure." Sari gave a little laugh.

It was no joke. When I was in his class, I often remembered Mr. Bluske striding up and down in his green smock scowling over the assignments that were propped up on the ledge of the blackboard. If he really disliked a design, he would throw it on the floor. He could be scary, but I did learn a lot about color and esthetics.

"Soooo . . ." Sari continued, "there is going to be the Annual El Camino College Student Art Show Exhibition in a few months, and the art department is adding a special exhibit of former students. Mr. Bluske wanted Chris and me to enter something for the design department. He asked me to contact other former students that I knew."

"But I'm not doing any paintings now," I lamented.

"Don't worry. We are just supposed to inspire the younger students with what we have achieved."

It dawned on me that I hadn't exactly achieved anything yet. Sara Lee, seeing my face said, "Oh, just look around. I'm sure you will find something. It will be fun to go to the art show again! Remember when you won third prize for that anti-war poster? I thought it was very good."

I smiled to myself. It wasn't supposed to be an anti-war poster. It was supposed to say, "Live Free or Die," but I guess I forgot that and put "Wake Up or Die." My poster had a little girl huddling with her rag doll while a city burns in the background. Mr. Bluske was surprised and not too happy when I turned it in. Everyone else in the class had American flags waving and jet planes flying. I didn't know Sara Lee then but later found out that she had seen my poster and had persuaded Mr. Bluske that it should win a prize.

I was still smiling when I said, "OK, I'll look around. It just might be fun after all."

After Sara Lee and her brood were safely packed in her old Chevy and had rumbled away, I was glad to see that the car's passenger seat door was firmly tied closed with a rope. There had been that incident not long ago when the door unlocked and Laurie J., who was spending the day with Sari's kids, had swung out over the street. Luckily, she had hung on, and a few moments later, the door had swung closed again with Laurie J. still intact. With that thought and a sigh of relief, I walked back to the dining room. My book was face down where I had left it but, as for my coffee, Arlene was just finishing it off. "Well, it was just going to get cold," she said defiantly in response to my questioning look.

CHAPTER 26
WHO AM I?

MORNING

When I woke up it was already late. I stretched, and my arm automatically felt around on the floor for the gray notebook. It wasn't there! My hand grubbed around some more—still, nothing. Where was it? Thinking helped me wake up, and I slowly came to the conclusion that I must have left it downstairs.

By now, I was an expert at scampering down the ladder, hesitating at the bottom rung to feel around for my sandals. As my feet searched for my shoes, my mind tried to search back to when I was last writing. I wandered into the music room—nope—notebook not there. I took a sweeping glance around the other rooms—again nothing. Finally, sitting down in the dining room, I recalled just finishing *Roses for Tomorrow* right here last night. *It should be here on this table*, I told myself.

A moment later, the door to my sister's bedroom cracked open, and she crept out in her usual style, only more so this morning. One hand was to her head while the other reached out in the air as if to feel along a wall. Finding none, she dropped her arm and started moving slowly toward the kitchen.

Arlene and Sid had been out at the Zanzibar again. I figured they must have had a very late night indeed or too many Coco Loco drinks. Coco Loco, the specialty of the house, was rum, cream, and coconut juice whipped up like a milkshake and served in a genuine coconut shell with a straw and a paper umbrella.

Arlene finally reached the kitchen. Zombie-like, she started the ritual of lighting the stove. It took three tries before it lit and the gas caught fire. I was glad I had thought to buy matches back that day when I went looking for a job on Pier Avenue . . . then, not letting my thoughts linger on that fateful moment when I saw my ex-boyfriend on the beach with the redhead, I quickly turned my attention back to practical matters, noting that a new supply of matches would soon be needed. Meanwhile, Arlene had managed to fill a pot with water and put it on the flame to boil. She opened the cabinet and took out a jar of Yuban, then sleepwalked her way to the table and plopped down to wait for water to boil. At last, aware of me but still too groggy to look up, she murmured, "Want some?" indicating the jar still in her hand. I knew that until she had coffee it was useless to ask her anything, and besides, what she had worn to bed put the search for my missing notebook out of my head for the moment.

SLEEPWALKING IN STYLE

At this point, I have to stop and describe my sister's nightgown, but first I have to turn myself into one of those women who stand behind a lectern with a handheld microphone commentating at fashion shows.

Commentator: *And here is our next model, lovely Arlene, dressed in the latest sleepwear fashion.*

Imaginary Arlene moves down the runway, stops, turns, smiles a toothy smile, then moves on.

Commentator: *This pink satin negligee creation was designed by the famous Couturier House of ARLENA. Arlene, won't you show the audience the fanciful black taffeta ruffle at the hemline?*

Arlene twirls and lifts her skirt.

Commentator: *See how it sweeps to the floor? The combination of pink and black is very* Carmen *inspired, don't you think?*

Arlene goes into a quick Spanish flamenco step to illustrate this point.

Commentator: *Notice the whimsical decoration on the bodice.*

Arlene puts her hand to her bosom before she spins again and walks to the back and exits.

What Arlene had actually done to make her latest sleepwear was to take an ordinary pink satin slip and attach a huge, floor-length black taffeta ruffle to the hem. Another smaller dark ruffling was attached to the bodice and, running up one strap, was then topped off by a large artificial black velvet rose at the shoulder, which was a little crushed now having been slept on. The effect was a kind of Frederick's of Hollywood meets Blanche Dubois.

My sister always longed for glamour and romance in her life. It showed in the clothes she designed and even spilled over into her bedroom, which I could see into now through the open door. Above her headboard, she had festooned a canopy of sheer curtains and netting material, trying, I think, for a Scheherazade effect.

The water for the coffee was boiling, so I took the coffee jar from my sister's hand and made us both a cup, putting a little more instant Yuban into her mug. Then, sitting down again at the table, I asked, "Haven't seen my gray notebook around, have you?"

Arlene raised her head slowly from her coffee, then started chuckling softly. Finally, she blurted out, "Last night Sid and I came back and saw your notebook on the table, so we took it into the bedroom and started to read it out loud to each other." She chortled some more. "We were laughing hysterically. Oh my God! Sweating chicken soup, and there you were with a rolling pin for a weapon." Arlene continued to laugh, finally, gasping out, "Lorraine, *you* are so funny!"

Me funny—really? I momentarily hugged this new fact to myself. All my life, whenever I attempted to say something whimsical, no one ever laughed. My sister would even stop me sometimes and say, "Lorraine you are just *not* funny!" And now here she was telling me she couldn't stop laughing. I felt somehow justified.

Maybe I *could* be funny after all. Maybe I could be a lot of things I never thought I could be and maybe, just maybe, I let too many people for too long tell me who I was and what I should, could, and couldn't be. When did it all start?

WHEN DO YOU KNOW WHO YOU ARE?

Graduating from Abraham Lincoln Elementary School into Jordan Junior High felt like stepping from childhood straight into the adult world. One day I was a twelve-year-old kid, wearing short dresses with sashes that tied in the back and sensible shoes with little white socks to school. At home I wore jeans and went barefoot to play outside with my brothers and the kids on the block until our mothers called us in for dinner.

The next year, at Jordan Junior High, gone were the little dresses with sashes. The standard dress code for junior high was wool skirts and soft sweater sets with saddle shoes or full-skirted cotton dresses with ballerina slippers (little white socks were definitely out) and, unless I wanted to be pegged as a "weirdo," lipstick and a purse filled with girl stuff was mandatory. Of course, there were to be no more tomboy antics after school either. It just wasn't done now that I was a teenager, or so everyone said. I must fit in and find my group; I must flirt and giggle and gossip. I just wasn't good at it.

Teachers liked me because I was a solid student and well-behaved. I was the "nice, quiet, good girl." That's who they said I was in that oh-so-grown-up, thirteen-year-old world.

Other people reinforced this image. My mother was happy she didn't have to worry about me getting caught smoking in school or shoplifting in a store like Arlene did. She didn't have to be troubled about me being so shy I could barely talk to people or having trouble learning in school like Jeff, and she didn't fret about me constantly getting injured with broken bones and knocked out teeth like adventurous Bill. To add emphasis to this theme, when people learned my name was Lorraine, they would say, "Oh, so you must be '*Sweet* Lorraine' like the Nat King Cole song." Even my boyfriend added to it. He would sigh in pleasure and say, "Ah, you are so passive!" At the time, I was glad he liked my quietness. Yes, I was the "nice, quiet, good girl," everybody agreed, and I believed it, but things were a little different now—now that I was living here with Arlene and Jeff. I was learning new things every day and maybe I was not locked into being that "good, little, quiet girl" all the time.

DISCOVERY

"So where is the notebook now?" I said to Arlene, briskly. I was itching to get it back and reread what I had written, and until it was in my hands, I was nervous about its safety. My sister had a way of losing, destroying, or maiming the things she touched— her stuff, my stuff, it didn't matter. It was an inevitable action of her personality. "But the notebook, where is it?" I was getting nervous now.

Sensing my unease, Arlene responded impatiently, "All right, all right, don't have a hissy fit, jeez! Back there," she said finally, waving one bare arm toward her bedroom. "It must be in there somewhere." Then she moved into the tiny kitchen intent on her breakfast of fried eggs in bacon fat.

After searching through the linen drapery and the rumpled bedclothes with no luck, I finally found my notebook on the floor stashed under the bed. *I will have to be more careful from now on,* I thought, as I dusted it off and took it back up to my loft. What if Arlene had read something personal? Well, at least she thought my writing was funny, and that was some consolation for the invasion of privacy.

CHAPTER 27
A FINE SUMMER'S DAY

LATER THAT AFTERNOON

We decided it was a perfect day for the beach. I might get in some sun, even some writing, and Jeff had his music books to study. Lindee and Laurie J. caught the beach day bug and went scurrying off to look for things that would serve as pails and shovels. Arlene already had plans. She and Howard were rehearsing a new song but promised to meet up with us later. "Just tell me where you'll be," she said.

"What about by the pier?" I answered, after a minute's thought.

"What side of it?"

"Between the pier and the old Biltmore Hotel should be good."

Both the Hermosa Pier and the Biltmore Hotel were long past their glory days. The pier had been condemned and boarded up at the entrance for years, and the Biltmore, seven stories high and taking up an entire block, might as well have been condemned. In the '20s and '30s, it had been both an exclusive hotel and a private beach club. Someone told me it even had an Olympic-sized swimming pool in the basement. Now, sadly, it was mostly empty, just a huge gray building casting a large shadow on the beach, but as a landmark it would be hard to miss.

"OK," repeated Arlene. "Between the pier and the Biltmore it is." Then, raising her voice and pinching her nose, called out like someone on a public address system, "Now hear this! Now hear this! All the children residing in the red house must be ready to set out for the beach because the bus is leaving the station in ten minutes!" While the kids were gathering everything together, Arlene continued in the same vein for my benefit. "Aaaand," she was still using her bored dispatcher voice, "passengers should be aware that the next bus will soon be leaving for San Ber-na-dino, San Ja-cin-to, San Cle-ment-e, San Lu-is O-bis-po . . . annnnd CU-CA-MON-Ga!" Arlene loudly called out each syllable of Cucamonga, emphasizing the last one which was long and drawn out.

After this announcement, everyone completed final preparations—gathering up towels, and last-minute beach stuff, everyone, that is, except Donnie. Donnie, oblivious to everything, sat on the floor of the dining room engrossed in taking apart an old alarm clock he had found in the dump. Arlene, not wanting to quash a possible boy wonder inventor in the making, motioned us out the door. She would bring him later, after the rehearsal, she said. When we finally left, Donnie was still happily pulling parts out of the alarm clock.

Things like babysitting seemed to sort themselves out naturally with us. Often we left it up to them to decide who they wanted to hang out with. Today, it was Lindee and Laurie J. who trouped with me and Jeff to the old pier. No one thought they had any caretaking burden to perform. We all genuinely liked to have the kids around. They were usually cheerful, fun, never whiney or demanding. So today it was Donnie who wanted to stay at home and that was fine.

A half hour later, we were setting up camp at the appointed spot between the old pier and the obsolete hotel. Jeff and I relaxed on the sand near the shore, close enough to watch Lindee and Laurie J. play by the water. Lying on a white towel that said "Grant Hotel," Jeff was engrossed in his book on jazz, and I looked at the scene around me. It was a weekend in late June, and the beach was filled with day-trippers. I found it fascinating watching the people at the beach, especially when it was crowded on a day like this.

A few feet from me, the wearer of a two-piece check bathing suit stood up and deftly pulled down the seat of her swimsuit before parading to the ocean with the confidence of knowing she had a good figure. Three boys on a nearby towel rose up on their elbows and twisted their heads for a better look.

"Hey, yeah!" said the crew cut.

"Too thin," replied the black trunks.

There was only a smile from the other.

I watched as the check bathing suit carefully waded into the foamy ocean, careful not to get her hair wet. I looked with envy at her long, lean legs.

On the other side of our encampment, a four- or five-year-old sat with his mother on a large striped beach towel, sucking on a slender Popsicle that ran like orange tears down his stomach. It was getting hot, and I knew at some point I would have to go into the cold ocean. I looked over at Jeff, who was completely involved in his book. How could he take this heat? At least he had taken off his clumpy boots and unbuttoned his shirt.

I surveyed the beach again, knowing that by the end of the day, I would witness the usual fight between a little boy erecting a sandcastle and a bully demolishing it. I would see the proverbial father throwing his young son into the ocean for his first swim lesson, walking to the surf with the kid squirming and yelping under his father's beefy arm, ignoring the wailing, terrified protests. Sometime later, after being violently dunked by his father, the boy, in his turn, would throw his dog or his little sister into the sea and the cycle would end there.

It was getting too hot to loll on the sand. It was time to take the plunge. Conscious of exposing a few varicose veins on the back of my legs, I got up and walked down the little hill of wet sand. At the edge of the water, I stopped to admire the sandcastle Lindee and Laurie J. were making. I felt a bit of pride. I had taught them how to dribble the wet sand to make the fancy stalagmite turrets they had created. Their palatial manor was precise and beautiful. Laurie J. was working away at the moat now and her sister was dutifully filling it with water. After a thorough inspection and praise, I couldn't prolong it any longer and moved forward slowly toward the sea.

I always hated that first submersion. How could California be so hot and yet, have such cold water? In Florida the ocean was warm like a bathtub. Sometimes I missed living in Miami, with its temperate seas, brilliant flowers, and coconut trees growing right out of the white sand. With a sigh, I moved on. No stalling now. I would love it once I got in. I moved forward, the outgoing wave just touching my ankles. Steadily, I continued out to where the water hit my knees. Unexpectedly, an incoming wave splashed up to my waist. Impulsively, I dived head first into a large breaker that completely engulfed me. Now I could enjoy jumping the waves.

In Florida, one could sometimes walk out in the water for yards and yards and still be only knee deep, but in California a sharp drop-off is only a few feet from the shore, and right now I was teetering on the edge of it waiting for my first wave. Vigilantly, I watched a small swell far out start to gather and grow. Placing myself in just the right spot, I waited. Then, when the crest was poised at the perfect height, I jumped, and the wave buoyed me up high then crashed down safely behind me to spread its foam out onto the wet sand. Another wave crested and lifted me off my feet again. Why had I ever hesitated getting in?

SISTERS

While another wave gathered, I turned toward the shore to check on Lindee and Laurie J. Lindee was gathering pails of water for the castle. She would run into the surf and scoop up some sea-water then drag her full pail over to the moat and pour it in. Off she would go a moment later for another pailful. Sometimes, a wave would pitch her over and tumble her in the breaking surf. Undaunted, she would pop up drenched and grinning, then just scoop up another pailful of water for her sister.

Laurie J's full name was Laurie Janis, but it soon got shortened to Laurie J. She was named, or so Arlene said, after me, her only sister, and Janice, Don's younger sister. Right now, Laurie J. was out of harm's way on dry land. She had no desire to get into the water, so she just didn't. Lindee had been the daring one, always ready for a new adventure. She would go off with Jeff in his truck on his foraging treks to find treasure.

Laurie J., on the other hand, wanted to be in control—safe. Even as babies, the two girls were different. Lindee, always push-ing for the next thing, one day just got up and walked in her tenth month, yet Laurie J.'s first birthday came and went and she showed no desire to take her first step. It was as if she didn't want to do a halfway job and stumble around, so she waited until she was sure she could handle it. She had a strong will that you might even call stubborn. When Donnie was a baby learning to crawl, he just kept going until he fell off the bed. Laurie J. never did that. She would crawl to the end, then, reaching with her feet, care-fully work her way down to the floor.

I watched the two sisters now, so alike with their blonde hair and blue eyes and yet so different. Lindee was going to be beauti-ful with silver hair and light green flecks in her eyes. Laurie J. was going to be maybe something even better. She would be adorable. With her dimples, stark white hair and sprinkling of freckles, she was already everyone's favorite, like a beloved rag doll.

Back on the sand, I could see Jeff, still lying on his stomach reading the *History of Jazz*. He was wearing ragged, cutoff jeans and a plaid shirt with the sleeves rolled up as far as they would go. Every so often he adjusted his thick tortoise-rimmed sunglasses and turned another page. Arlene had said she would meet us, but I couldn't see how she was going to find us in this horde of people. It was more crowded than I thought it would be. Would she remember that we said we would be between the old Biltmore Hotel and the pier?

When it was first built in 1914, the Hermosa Pier had been the crème de la crème of piers, a fashionable and elegant place where all the populace would meet and promenade in their Sunday best. Along the walkways there had even been shaded pagodas where people could sit sheltered from the sun, but in 1957, after a severe storm, it was condemned and the grand entrance boarded up. The pilings were covered with clumps of clinging dark blue shells. Nailed to the end of the pier was a sign that said, "Don't Eat the Mussels." I always wondered why. Why not eat the mussels? Did someone have dibs on them? But the sign didn't explain.

A large wave broke and before I knew it, a wave crashed over my head, tumbling me over and churning me around like clothes in the washer. *OK, I deserved that for not watching out*, I thought, and caught the next one perfectly. Jumping in the water was fun, but it couldn't compare to being on a surfboard.

When I first moved to the beach, I was excited about learning to surf. Surely I could ride on one of those fiberglass boards! I had been a tomboy and had perfected my balancing skills on the backyard fences. At first, I hobnobbed with the surfers, who gave me rides on their boards. Then I bought a small used surfboard for sixty dollars. I was on my way. I would lean my board against the gray wall just like the other surfers. They showed me how to wax it so that I could have more traction and not slip when the surfboard got wet. The surfers treated me like a little sister and called me Gidget. I was making real progress but my newly acquired boyfriend didn't like surfers. *He* disapproved of my hanging out with them, so slowly I stopped surfing. Finally, I sold my board to "Bing's Surfboard Shop" on the Strand.

Just then, another wave swamped me. Coming up again for air, I realized that if I only had my board back now, there would be no one to stop me from doing what I wanted to do this time.

CHAPTER 28
THE MEET UP

ARLENE AND ME

At first it had been difficult to get into the water, but now I gave myself over to the comforting waves that buoyed me up, happily bobbing like a popped cork in a great sea of weightlessness. I was reluctant to leave but Arlene's rehearsal with Howard must be long over. Turning toward the shore, I scanned the wide expanse of sand filled with so many people now and started to look for my sister. There, miraculously, zigzagging her way through the beach towels and umbrellas, was Arlene hauling Donnie by the hand. I couldn't believe she had really found us.

I rode a last wave in, feeling the heaviness of the earth's gravity on land once more. Arlene and I reached Jeff on the towel at the same time. Donnie was already pulling his hand away from his mother to get to the water and soon plopped himself down next to Lindee and Laurie J.'s castle.

"Arlene," I said in amazement, "how did you find us in this huge crowd?"

"It was simple," she said, "I saw you in the water."

"But how? You could only have seen my head. I was just a tiny dot bobbing up and down along with all the other tiny dots!"

"Yes, but the tiny dot was bobbing just like you."

Did we know each other that well? Still wondering, I settled down on the towel. Lying next to my sister, it slowly came to my notice that she had been up in the loft digging into my clothing box again because she was wearing my turquoise Bermuda shorts and a ruffled white blouse that was also mine, although I had given up looking for it weeks ago. Annoyed as I was, I had to admit she did look fetching.

When the 1957 summer edition of *Seventeen Magazine* came out, the cover immediately caught my attention. Three girls were frolicking on a beach. Each wore the same playful pair of Bermuda shorts in different colors. The shorts came up high in the waist and had cunning straps going over the shoulders, crossing in the back. I fell in love with the pink one. My babysitting money was just enough to buy two yards of sturdy cotton, and using a Butterick pattern, my mother easily made an exact copy of the beloved pink one. Then, digging into her sewing box, she came up with enough material to make another pair in turquoise.

Now here was Arlene on the beach in *my* turquoise shorts, looking exactly like one of the models on the *Seventeen* cover. I didn't even say anything. I was just glad she hadn't found the pink ones. Arlene was also carrying a small stack of papers. "Look," she said, showing them to me, "Howard wants us to write some lyrics to his songs. See, here is the 'Sixty Foot Swing,' 'Wiggledy Waggledy Woo,' and 'Lost at the Fair.'"

"'Lost at the Fair'?" I said. "That already has words."

"I know, but Howard wanted to see what we could do with it."

My interest was piqued. I knew all the melodies to Howard's tunes (as he called his songs) from playing them on the piano. I was still diligently working at my music and had a good grasp of all the chord changes and inversions now.

"Which shall we start with first?" Arlene said, starting to hunker down on the beach towel.

"Mommy, Mommy," cried Lindee and Laurie J. down by the ocean, "come see our sandcastle!"

At their call, Arlene dropped the music manuscripts into my lap and trotted down to her children. "Hey, what you got there," she trilled, and plopped down on the wet sand to examine the structure, tower by tower. It was the second time I was glad she had chosen the turquoise shorts instead of the pink ones. I couldn't hear exactly what they were saying, but I could see Lindee and Laurie J. pointing and grinning, their spirits and excitement rising as they showed their mother all the features of the castle. That was Arlene: when she entered a room, the energy level rose. Soon my sister was digging in the sand with the kids, adding more towers and instructing Donnie to dig a pathway from the water to the castle moat so that when a wave came in, water filled the moat. I heard laughter and giggling. Arlene crouched on her knees now, unaware that her backside was completely covered with wet sand.

JEFF'S DISCOVERY

Sometime later, Arlene trotted back to the towel and plopped down near me. Jeff was still engrossed in his book and only looked up for a second, grunting again before he put his head back down.

"Ah, now about these songs." Arlene spread the pages out on the towel and pulled out a pencil from her straw beach bag. "So which one do you want to start on? How about—"

Just then, Jeff gave off a sound, something between his usual grunt and a guffaw.

"Just listen to this!" He had his hand on a page and his finger holding the place. "Just listen to what they say about our father!" Arlene and I stopped what we were doing and became quiet. We didn't expect to have Harry's name listed in a history book of great jazz musicians.

Jeff read aloud.

"'Harry (The Hipster) Gibson born Harry Raab, June 27, 1915.'"

"That's funny," I said, "I never knew the year my own father was born or his actual birthday either. I guess he was not ever home on that day. At least, I don't remember celebrating it, but then I don't remember his ever being there for our birthdays either," I added a bit sulkily.

But Arlene wasn't listening. "You know," she said in wonder, "I didn't realize it, but Harry and I are both born under the same sign—Cancer. Almost on the same day," she said, and sat back on her knees and looked thoughtful.

"Yeah," I quipped, using one of Harry's expressions, "you're just a chip off the old pill" (pill meaning some sort of upper or downer like Benzedrine). Arlene looked even more thoughtful.

"Hey, I'm reading here! Do you want to hear this or not?" After a short pause, Jeff cleared his voice loudly then continued.

In the early forties, a young Harry Raab was discovered by the popular pianist and singer Fats Waller. Fats had Harry booked as his intermission piano player at the Yacht Club. At the time, Harry was a graduate student studying at Julliard on a musical fellowship. At night, he played at clubs on Fifty-Second Street.

After giving three lightly attended concerts at Town Hall, Harry burst into popularity and fame in 1944 when he added "The Hipster Gibson" to his name and came out with an act featuring original songs, jive talk, and frantic barrelhouse boogie-woogie. His songs (many about drugs) and his wild antics at the piano brought in the crowds, and soon he was headlining at clubs such as the Three Deuces, Hickory House, and Spotlight.

Soon after, he was recording several of his frantic novelty songs such as "Stop That Dancing Up There," "4F Ferdinand the Frantic Freak," and "Who Put the Benzedrine in Mrs. Murphy's Ovaltine?" The records sold out and his songs became popular hits on the radio. Soon after, Harry recorded a boogie-woogie album that also hit the top of the charts.

Before long, The Hipster was enticed to Hollywood, where he made several star appearances in musicals while headlining at Billy Burgs nightclub in Los Angeles. In 1947 Harry made the cover of *DownBeat Magazine*.

After serving a year in prison on drug-related charges in the early fifties, Harry the Hipster slipped from the public eye.

There was a silence for a few moments. I spoke up first. "Gee, it's like he died in his sleep or something," I quoted the last line. "He just 'slipped from the public eye.'"

"Well, we know he is alive," Arlene said through her teeth. "He's probably somewhere playing in some sleazy dive bar and no doubt sponging off of some fan. I know what I would say to him if he popped up here and expected us to take him in. I would tell him where to go and—"

"But that part about him being a serious pianist," I broke in. "Wow, Julliard and the concerts at Town Hall and everything. I guess he really cared about music then."

"I wonder where he really is right now?" Jeff said in a muffled voice. Suddenly, he jumped up and rushed into the surf with a yell and a great splash. He didn't even take off his shirt.

Arlene turned to me. "Is it something I said?"

"Oh, you know Jeff always idolized Harry, and since he was the youngest, he had a father for the shortest time."

"Ha!" Arlene snorted. "Some father he turned out to be. It was all because of him we had no money and got stuck in that cow town Riverside. Yes sir, he really did 'silently slip away.'" Arlene was relishing her anger now. "And after he got out of jail," she continued, "he never sent us a cent, not a word from him either." Arlene was shaking her head slowly in disgust. "Well," she said, brushing some sand off the sheet music, "shall we continue with our assignment? Let's Do 'Sixty Foot Swing.' I think it will lighten the mood."

SONGWRITING IN THE SAND

I had never written lyrics before, but it sounded intriguing. Bending over the sheet music, Arlene and I hummed a line of the song, then tried to think up words to fit the beats in the bar.

After throwing out a few ideas, we got:

The sixty-foot swing has never been made.
When you're at the top you're never afraid.

After that, the words came faster. *This is fun*, I thought as Arlene and I faced each other, our heads together, the wind blowing Arlene's hair into her face and mouth. I thought again that some of the best times I ever had were the ones I spent with my sister. Today was one of those times. With the sun warming our backs, we lay on our stomachs laughing—the ocean's tangy smell in our nostrils. The lyrics came spontaneously, and we easily finished the first song.

"What is this 'Wiggledy Waggledy Woo' song?" I asked. "What could it mean? Maybe it's about a rabbit like Uncle Wiggily."

"Or a belly dancer wiggling her stuff," put in Arlene with a laugh.

My thoughts went back to "Vera" the stripper at the Zanzibar. "It seems more like a kind of children's song than a hoochy, coochy dancer," I said. We couldn't come to a decision, so we put the tune away for another time.

"I'm sure the idea for the song will just come to us one day out of the blue," Arlene joked. Little did she know then, but her words were prophetic. We saved "Lost at the Fair" for last. I wondered what we could do with it. There was a short verse at the beginning before the chorus. I liked verses and wondered why more songwriters didn't include them when they composed.

Maybe it fell out of use because singers had to leave them out when they recorded those early 78 RPM records. They were only about three minutes long, weren't they?

Arlene got my attention by tugging, not so gently, on my bathing suit strap and we soon got down to the business at hand. We hummed the verse together then, started with . . .

> *Hand and hand we walked to the fair grounds*
> *To the music of merry-go-rounds*

Then:

> *To those pop-corn sounds . . . oh*

The chorus was in ¾ time. "I love waltzes," I said dreamily, moving my hand rhythmically in the air.

> *Lit-tle girl at the fair*
> *Faces laugh-ing up there*

And finally:

> *While I search for the hand that I once held*
> *tight*
> *Why did I chase red bal-loons til out of sight?*

Next came the bridge to the song. It was tricky but we made our way through it.

> *Faces all above are gay strangers to me*
> *So I run and I stumble*
> *Tell me where are you? Where are you? Can't*
> *you see?*

Again, came the chorus. Arlene said, "Now we have to wrap up the story of the lost girl."

I wanted a happy ending, unlike Howard's version, which left the girl lost. "That poor girl in the song is almost hysterical look-ing for her lost love!" I said. "I want a happy ending." We came up with the last chorus, and it was perfect.

> *I'm so lost at the fair*
> *Crowds can't see my lost stare*
> *Then in car-ousel mi-rrors your sweet face ap-*
> *pears*
> *And I find your hand a-gain and hold it near.*

We were finished, and I felt a great sense of accomplishment. I couldn't wait to see the new version when Howard would write it out on onionskin paper and add our names as the lyricists. We ran through the song again singing the words, and when we were finished smiled into each other's faces. We had a good song.

Jeff, too, looked contented. He had been back for a long time by now and his shirt was almost dry. Down by the shoreline, Lindee, Donnie, and Laurie J. were trying to save their beautiful castle from the incoming tide, but it looked like a losing battle.

Arlene stood up and yelled out, "I'm going home now, kids! Say goodbye to your crumbling castle."

The girls reluctantly picked up the sand buckets and shovels and scrambled up to their mother, but Donnie lagged behind. "I just got here! Can't I stay?" he called to his mother and sisters, who were putting on their flip-flops to walk through the hot sand. "I'll save the castle to the very end," he promised.

Arlene was in a hurry now. "OK, OK, you can hang out with Lorraine and Jeff," she said with a wave of her hand as if she were granting a royal favor to one of her minions. Gathering up her straw bag, she stuffed the sheet music into it and turned to

Lindee and Laurie J. "Come, my little munchkins," she chirped, grabbing up her two daughters and trundling them through the sand, the umbrellas, and the many beachgoers. Finally, on the solid ground of the Strand again, she waved, then turning toward home, skipped away down the promenade. I could see the top half of her bobbing up and down behind the wall, but I could only see the tops of Lindee and Laurie J.'s heads as they hopped along trying to keep up with their mother. Arlene was, of course, totally oblivious to the curious stares of the beach crowd as she and the children pranced by.

I bet they are singing "We're Off to See the Wizard," I thought. That would account for the extra attention they were getting. *It does seem fitting*, I concluded. Arlene was the perfect Dorothy Gale, who had taken herself from dreary Kansas (Riverside) to the Land of Oz, to find her way to the Emerald City. *Is Hermosa Beach Oz?* I wondered. Sometimes it did seem to have magical qualities, at least for us.

I took the thought a bit further: *If Arlene is Dorothy, who is the Scarecrow?* It didn't take a moment to decide. *Of course, Jeff has to be the Scarecrow. He is so raggedy and floppy, and always studying books.* Warming to this parallel universe, I thought, *Now, who is next? In the movie it is the Tin Woodman, who is found rusted in the forest. He wanted a heart, didn't he? Now, who needs a heart?* It was coming to me slowly this time. *Without a heart . . . it could be . . . it sorta sounds like . . . our brother Bill.* Yes, Bill, who was so far away from us now in Hawaii but was still part of us. Our Bill, who, after that trip across the country with Harry just sort of closed up like he was alone against the world and it was every man for himself. Sadly, he could seem coldhearted. Yet, as a kid, he used to work at being the perfect boy. He actually tried to do a good deed daily. *Yes*, I concluded, *Bill needs to find his heart again.*

What next? Ah, the Cowardly Lion—hands down, it's got to be Howard K. Small. He even looks like a lion with his big shaggy head. He tries to act stern sometimes but is a complete pushover, and of course no one else could be Glinda, the Good Witch, but Rita—perfect casting there. I was on a roll now. *And Bill Connelly is the ideal Wizard of Oz. Oz, of the scary green head, who just turns out to be an ordinary man masquerading as the 'Great and Powerful,' just like Bill Connelly pretends to be Clark Kent and Superman. I suppose Mom and Bob must be Aunt Em and Uncle Henry, and of course, like Arlene said, the kids are the Munchkins—all of the kids including Rita's, Sara Lee's, and ours.*

The Wicked Witch made me wonder for a while until I came to the conclusion that even though Arlene was Dorothy, she was also the Wicked Witch, who could pop out at any time and mess things up. *My, my, I didn't know I was going to get so psychological when I started this game.* Rita also had her Wicked Witch side too, I had to admit. Just as she could make you feel wonderful, she could also make you feel lame and terribly embarrassed. *But wait! Who am I? Where do I fit in? I mean, who is left? Scarecrow, Tin Man, Cowardly Lion . . . Oh, no, that only leaves . . . Toto, the faithful little terrier.* The truth was a little slow to dawn on me, but when faced with it, I had to admit the character of Toto fit. If you watch the movie, the little dog is always there to follow and comfort Dorothy, even to fight when circumstances call for it. I was Toto and knew that as long as I lived with Arlene, the kids, and Jeff, I would always be Toto—ever in my sister's orbit, ready to calm her down when she got sad or angry. Yes, as long as I stayed at Culper Court, Toto would be my role.

CHAPTER 29
DONNIE

AND

FROM THE GRAY NOTEBOOK
OBSERVATIONS OF LIFE AT THE SEASIDE

LATER THAT DAY

The sun was getting lower in the sky. It was time to get some work done. I reached inside my straw beach bag with the small Mexican sombrero embroidered on it and pulled out the gray notebook. It was heavy to lug around, but if I got some inspiration at the beach, I wanted to be ready to jot it down.

Just then, Donnie made a great splashing noise and plunged about in the oncoming tide. I closed the notebook. I had better watch him, I decided, remembering that Donnie was the baby who always fell off the bed. Even now, he could be a hazard to himself.

Donnie had a way of getting into trouble. Once, under my care, he fell down a cement stairway. We were waiting there for some reason, so I let him play while I read my book and completely forgot about him until sometime later he tapped me on the shoulder. There was Donnie, all dusty and bruised. He told me he had tripped and tumbled halfway down the stairs. After an examination, he seemed OK, but the incident taught me to be a little more watchful.

You could conclude from this story that I was not always the greatest of babysitters, but I had grown up at a time when kids took care of themselves. When I was Donnie's age, I was already hanging out with my brothers, far away from any parental watchers.

OUR UPBRINGING

My mother and father decided early on to raise their children in a rather laissez-faire manner. It was Harry's idea, really. "They are not going to be squares and sissies, or highfalutin' snobs. I want them to be free, not hampered with a lot of rules like the way you and I grew up, Flossie." Mom's father was a stern, serious man. Rules were strict and you got a licking if you broke them. On the other hand, Harry's mother warned him a lot about sin and made him become an altar boy in the Catholic Church. "I don't want that for my kids," he vowed. "I'm going to be a fun father and their friend. They can call me Harry. No *Daddy*, *Papa* for me and I want them to go out and do what they want—to have adventures, create, and play in the mud if they want to. I don't mind if they look like ragamuffins when they come back!" That's what my father would say.

Hence, as kids we looked out for ourselves. We didn't ask permission to rove the neighborhood or to turn the backyard into a circus or a warren of forts and tree houses. On Saturdays, we took our bikes miles away to parks, horse trails, swimming holes, and mountain peaks. It would be dusk sometimes before we returned home and as long as we got back for supper, Mom didn't worry. At least she didn't say so.

As I sat on my towel watching Donnie at the shoreline, the lovely palace of sand Lindee and Laurie J. had made was already gone, and Donnie was building his own fort higher up on the beach. I watched for a while then turned to my notebook. I looked around at the crowd around me and started.

FROM THE GRAY NOTEBOOK
OBSERVATIONS OF LIFE AT THE SEASIDE

It was peak time at the beach. I always found it fascinating to watch people.

I paused. *Move the second sentence somewhere else, or lose it. And I should write it in the present tense. I started again.*

It is peak time at the beach, and the seashore is filled with "Day-Trippers" from the outlying suburbs. From my towel, I view the scene, and it is quite fascinating watching the people, especially when the beach is crowded on a day like this. Every variety of the human body can be found parading by, no one ever quite the same, no two figures repeated, yet somehow they are alike. These groups that come and go at the shore also repeat the same motions. Still, somehow, each one remains unique.

Does that even make sense? Maybe not, but it does sound kind of deep. I can always fix it later. If it is any good, I might even type it up on my next trip to Hollywood with Lenny.

To make things clear, people at the beach can be classified into categories of "The Wet," "The Sunny," and "The Shaded."

Hey, that is pretty clever. I should keep it in.

"The wet" ones are the children and the surfers. A few muscled young men are braving the icy roll of the surf for the benefit of being eyed by the females on the dry home-land, but it is the children who really populate most of the sea. They are everywhere, jumping and diving and dunking each other.

Mothers and babies skirt the water's edge like fluttering ruffles. Every so often, a mother dips her child's legs into the foam as a wave subsides. Only a few feet in, two little girls stand giggling, thigh deep, letting the water graze the top of their bathing suits.

I see far out, a lone bathing cap skimming along belong-ing to a serious swimmer. I wonder if it could be the same swimmer that I have seen a few times before. I pretend he or she is an ex-champion, an English Channel crosser or Olympic winner of long ago who is still active in their reclin-ing years.

The part about the lone swimmer is good. OK, so much for the "wet ones," and now on to describe the "sunny ones."

On land, some of "the sunny" and dry ones are still close to the sea. They are the little children like Lindee and Laurie J. and Donnie building sandcastles and forts, drawing in the sand with sticks or just picking up the rare sand dollar. Also near the shore are the protective parents of the bigger chil-dren who are splashing way out by the plunging waves.

Of the "sun" people, there are the brown-skinned locals, and of them there are the serious "tanners" usually lon-ers who carry on a love affair with the sun. Every day they appear when the sun has hardly a chance to get up into the sky. With backrest, novel, and towel in hand, their well-kept bodies bake all day marinating in Coppertone. Many older ones, their bodies tough and gnarled, have been charring in their favorite spot on the beach for years. They look like antique mahogany furniture—dark, polished, and gleaming.

The younger ones are not as interesting. When you see them sunning on a towel, carefully lying on their backs slathered in baby oil, bright-colored plastic protectors shaped like glasses covering their eyes, you have an impulse to throw sand on their shiny brown skin to see if it will stick like salt on a baked pretzel.

And now, I have to describe the "shade" people and who they are.

The last group is called "the shade" people. One subdivision are the teenage couples necking furiously under their blankets. Another group is easy to spot, loaded down as they usually are with a mountainous morass of thermos jars, pillows, blankets, mystery novels, playing cards, and copious baskets of food.

These families have come with all their generations, from great-uncles to tiny grandchildren. They usually arrive early with enough paraphernalia to start a new world. Fat old aunt Lizzy sits knitting and gossiping all day with the other older women under the protection of a large red umbrella, while the men, under another canopy, play cards and sweat nearby. The younger ones (being the wet ones) have left the protection of the umbrellas and tents for the cooler refreshment of the ocean. They return later shining wet only to grab a mouthful of food then run off again.

Many of these families are of the white and pink hue so they huddle under their umbrellas and sunshades all day. The tan locals look down on these outsiders and call them typical pale-faced "day-trippers."

I paused from my writing. *It's not very nice to look down on the people who don't live at the beach, but I have to admit I do feel that way sometimes too. I selfishly want the beach to be just mine.*

Well, I guess that is all I have to say. I closed the notebook firmly and put it into the straw bag. I would read it over again when I got home. The sun was not overhead anymore but moving west to get in the right position to be able to sink into the water. Soon it would be time to go.

CHAPTER 30
INVASION

SLEEPLESS

I woke up and didn't know why. Maybe it was the rain tapping on the roof, a dream I couldn't remember, or the heat of the blankets. Odd that I should feel warm when outside was wet and rainy. My face was hot and my eyelids itchy. How could I go back to sleep? Tossing off the covers, I tried not to wake up too much as I scurried down the ladder in the dark, feeling my way into the bathroom where I dabbed water on my face and smoothed Vaseline on my eyelids (at least, I hoped it was Vaseline). I did feel better.

Slowly, I crept back up to bed again but sleep wouldn't come. I wondered how long it would be until morning. It seemed like the middle of the night. All was quiet now that the rain had stopped except for the drops that still fell from the ceiling. I could hear it over by the wall. I thought about my box of drawings getting wet but I didn't get up. I hoped the dripping would stop soon.

A gurgle bubbled in my stomach. I was hungry. Sleep might come if I thought of nothing but instead of nothing, I pictured peanut butter sandwiches; I could make that in the kitchen if I got up. I wondered if lack of food could make someone weak enough to fall asleep? If I couldn't go back to sleep, I might as well get up and eat something and save my drawings too. Minutes passed and at some point my eyes closed.

I was in the kitchen. All over the tile counter were cookies. Each time my hand closed over one, it oozed water. As I tried to wring out the wetness, the cookies got even soggier and dissolved before I could eat them—and I was so hungry! I opened my eyes. It was still dark. I had fallen asleep but this time hunger woke me up. *That does it! I might as well get up and get something to eat.*

A SOCIAL GATHERING

I got a dreadful surprise in the kitchen. The sudden bright light illuminated hundreds of shiny dark brown bugs, one to two inches long. Caught off guard, they froze for a second, then, as if on cue, the entire horde streaked off in different directions—scurrying, scrimmaging, and scuttling all over our kitchen. Some ran into drawers, some into cupboards, some headed for the nearest crack. "Arggggh, cockroaches," I gasped, grabbing a magazine from the dining room table and lunging back into the kitchen. Blindly, I swung and slapped away at the retreating battalions of insects until they were gone.

I had seen a few of these repulsive creatures before, but if one of them ventured out in the daytime and saw me, they quickly darted into the nearest dark space again. I had seen more of them lately but . . . I had no idea . . . I had never . . . I had never seen anything like this before! Apparently, they all came out at night and I had interrupted a wild madcap party but how could there be so many? How did we not know about this?

I sat down on a dining room chair, dazed, the magazine limp in my hand. The awful picture was seared into my brain, first the bright light illuminating the kitchen, freezing the scene of the cockroach orgy, then, the horrible scurrying, scuttling, and scampering of thousands of legs crawling all over everything—over the white tiles on the counter, over the cupboards, walls, and ceiling, over the checkerboard black-and-white floor, and worst of all, those spindly legs had crawled over our dishes.

A story told by my mother came back to me. "It was when we lived in New York City," my mother would start. "We lived in Brooklyn. It was 1940. You were just born, Lorraine, and Harry was playing on Fifty-Second Street at the Three Deuces. Our landlady, Mrs. Murphy, just loved you and would take care of you for free. There was even a little patio with a garden in the back. Billy loved the flowers and kept picking them, but Mrs. Murphy didn't mind. She loved us all so much, but we couldn't stay—the cockroaches were everywhere. We couldn't get rid of them, so after six months, we moved to Edgewater Park, and it just broke Mrs. Murphy's heart."

Only now did I fully understand what my mother must have gone through. No wonder she fled from the nice landlady and perfect ground-floor apartment. I sat exhausted on the dining room chair. The cockroaches had all disappeared except for the ones I had killed.

"You can never get rid of them!" Mom's words echoed in my brain as I cleaned up as best I could. I tore off the front cover of the magazine that had the dark stain of the battle on it and crumpled it into the garbage. I swept up the dead bugs from the floor and washed off the counter. Tomorrow I would rewash all the dishes. Now, I needed a cup of coffee. I would not be going back to sleep any time soon. Later, sipping my coffee and taking bites out of my peanut butter sandwich, I watched out the back windows as a pink dawn rose over the hilly landfill. I would have to tell Arlene about the roaches and get some bug spray. Maybe Betsy had some at her house to start us off.

BRUSH UP YOUR SHAKESPEARE

A few days later, Arlene and I were sitting around the dining room table nursing our second cup of coffee. Jeff was in the music room fiddling around on the piano, trying to work out the chord changes to Thelonious Monk's song "'Round Midnight." He would play a little of the record; then stop it and try to find a chord on the piano that went along with the melody. It was slow and painstaking. Monk's tune, Jeff had already figured out, was written in a key that had six flats. He had so far worked out the opening eight bars. Now he hummed the melody while playing the chord changes on the piano as far as he had gotten. Laurie J. sat quietly and listened nearby in the Indonesian apple-green wicker chair with the curly scrollwork on top.

Lindee and Donnie were in the front yard playing in the dirt, making a miniature town they said, digging tunnels, making mountains and roadways, and using the hose to make the mud houses and to fill up the rivers and dams. We could see and hear them from the open front door. Donnie on his knees surveyed the terrain. He scratched his head slowly. "We are going to need more dirt for the mountains," he remarked authoritatively. Lindee reminded him that there was plenty of it in the dump.

A moment later, we heard the roar of an engine and Lenny Glassman's MG pulled up in front of the cottage. Lenny bounded out and strode briskly up the brick walk. Leaping gracefully onto the porch, he turned briefly toward the kids who looked up questioningly from their digging. "Carry on as you were, my good yeomen," he boomed, then, with a flourish of his arm, proceeded into the house. Discovering us in the dining room, his act continued. "And how are the fair maidens of the castle this morning?" he said, bowing low, then, not getting an answer, he flopped into the nearest chair.

Arlene and I were in no mood to play games today. We had been talking about the insect menace in the kitchen. I was still in my pajamas, and Arlene wore a faded, much-washed flannel nightgown with no style or flourishes this time.

"Oh, Lenny," Arlene moaned. "OK, I give up! What's with the funny talk?"

Mr. Richardson, alias Glassman, was taking great delight in his entrance. "I signed up for some summer courses at our local El Camino City College. I'm taking Music Theory and Drama!" When he got no reaction, he continued talking. "We just started reading *King Lear*. I, naturally, got a part. I play the Fool."

"Of course, you do—typecasting there!" Arlene muttered with a smirk.

"I heard that," Lenny said. "Actually, the Fool is very smart and clever. Hey, and guess who is in the class too?"

My body tensed, and I geared up to hear the name I had been training myself not to think about, but it was not my ex-boyfriend Lenny was alluding to. It was Rita's ex.

"Yeah, ol' Steven D. is in the class too." He rubbed his hands together. "Wait till I tell ol' Rita that—" He didn't have a chance to finish before Arlene jumped in.

"Now, you just leave Rita alone. She doesn't want to hear about her nasty ex-boyfriend anymore than Lorraine does about hers."

Now how did she . . . ? I had not bared my soul to anyone, especially not my sister. I hated the idea of anyone analyzing my broken heart.

Lenny was still going on about Steven D. "Of course, the title role of Lear went to ol' Steve-a-reno. He gets everything. He was Mercutio in *Romeo and Juliet* and Petruchio in *The Taming of the Shrew*." An image of Rita and Steve again battling it out on stage flashed across my mind.

"OK, I admit he is good," Lenny rattled on, "but such a ham you won't believe!"

Arlene and I gave each other sardonic glances as if to say, *look who is talking about ham.*

"You should hear him spout his lines in the part where Lear goes insane in the storm." With this, Lenny started loudly spout-ing himself, "Oh, blow winds and crack your cheeks. Blow and rage, you cataracts of hurricanes." Here, Lenny looked up and shook a fist at our ceiling. "Now, if ever we do *The Merchant of Venice*, then watch out! The part of Shylock will be mine! Or my name isn't Glassman." Then, right on cue, Lenny started the Shylock soliloquy. "Hath not a Jew eyes? Hath not a Jew hands? If you prick us, do we not bleed? If you tickle us, do we not laugh—" Midway, he stopped. "Arlene, you should take the class too, as you are naturally very dramatic. There is a new semester starting in September, and there is still time to enroll. It's at night, but we could go together, I could take you in the MG."

Arlene was about to bridle at the word "dramatic," but then actually perked up at this new thought of the theater. I looked at her. She must be remembering her high school drama classes. "You know, I just might take you up on that offer and the music theory class too," Arlene retorted, throwing Lenny a "got you there" look.

"Great! And you know it's practically free. Registration is only eight dollars."

"It was only five," I interjected, "when Sara Lee and I took our art classes there with Mr. Bluske."

Ignoring me, Lenny continued, "But as I was saying, I am stopping by because I'm going to Hollywood and I could use some company. Lorraine, Arlene? Are either of you up for a spin in the old MG?"

"I'm not in the mood today," I said. "We have a problem to figure out." In the music room, the halting sounds of "'Round Midnight" came to an abrupt halt, and after a moment of silence, the melodic tooting of Jeff's flute started up. Ever since my discovery of the unwelcome guests in the kitchen with their nightly revelries, Jeff had been playing his original composition "The March of the Cockroaches." By performing this musical ritual several times a day, my brother thought he was doing his part to rid us of the infestation. There was a creak from the apple-green Indonesian wicker chair with the curly scrollwork on the top as Laurie J. jumped up to follow Jeff as he marched out of the music room.

Outside, Lindee and Donnie, hearing the now-familiar melody, brushed the dirt off their hands and joined in behind Laurie J. and Jeff. Soon the group, marching in perfect lockstep, entered the dining room. Lindee carried a large serving spoon and a rusted and dented cookie tin which she was banging on in march-time. Donnie took up the rear, lifting his legs as high as he could get them while still holding his hand to his head in a kind of salute. They circled the table a few times before heading into the kitchen.

Arlene and I were used to this pageant, but Lenny gaped and looked mesmerized as the strange troop moved by him into the kitchen where they marched in place for a few more bars. Then, in an abrupt about face, Jeff started moving again. At the doorway he paused and out of the side of his mouth hissed back at the kids, "Are they following us yet?"

"Not yet," Donnie hissed back, still marching in place.

"OK," Jeff said. "We'll try to get them again tomorrow." He was soon back in the music room again. A short time later, we heard the strains of "'Round Midnight" start up again.

In the dining room, Lenny was shaking his head laughing. "Oh boy, you guys are too much! You know, a while ago, I accused you of re-creating A Christmas Carol—you even had a Tiny Tim—but now I see that you have switched the theme to a fairy tale because I just saw the Pied Piper followed by a bunch of kids go by."

"That's not far from the truth," Arlene said. "I have to tell Jeff to be careful playing his flute outside because it *does* collect kids. They love to follow him. I told him we have enough trouble here without irate mothers of the neighborhood demanding their children back."

Lenny rolled his eyes. "Anyway, I think we have lost the thread of the conversation here. Let's start over. I said something like 'Does anyone here, want to go to Hollywood with me?' And Lorraine said there was a problem, and did that marching spectacle I just witnessed have anything to do with the little problem you have?"

"Yeah, but it's a big problem," Arlene corrected. "We have been invaded by aliens!"

"This sounds interesting. Aliens, you say?" Lenny was alert now.

"It's an invasion of cockroaches," I explained mournfully. "We don't know what to do. Every night they converge on our kitchen. It's just awful. We spray and spray! There are hundreds . . . thousands . . ." My voice trailed off.

"Thousands? Oh, I gotta come back and see this. It's at night, you say?" Lenny rubbed his hands together in glee and cackled. I wondered if he was still in the character of Lear's Fool, or was it Shylock?

"Well, I hate to leave you poor people in your dire need, but I gotta go. See you all later." Lenny unfolded himself from his chair. Then as he turned to go, he came back.

"I almost forgot the real reason I am here—it's an important commemoration for you," he said, bowing to my sister. "I was told it was your birthday, and I got you a present. Look!" Arlene looked up with vague curiosity as Lenny fumbled in his jacket pocket and pulled out a small white cardboard box, the kind you would put jewelry in.

"You're a bit late," Arlene said, but smiled in spite of herself. "My birthday was last month." My sister was looking at the box in Lenny's hand with real interest now.

"Well, then, this is a belated birthday gift," Lenny said, handing his gift to Arlene. "I wanted to give you something really personal." Arlene, still smiling, opened the box and stared curiously at the bit of light brown fluff in it.

"I know how you admire my manly hair," Lenny explained, "so I thought I would give you some of it."

Bemused, Arlene said, "You gave me a lock of your hair . . . off your head?"

Lenny said, "Well no, not from my head."

"Your chest hair then?" Arlene moved the small container away from her a little.

"Well, actually, I didn't think I could spare any there either, so I took it from a different place." Lenny smiled a secret smile.

Arlene was looking down at the little box in confusion, then exploded, "You . . . your . . . pubic hair?" she yelled. "You gave me your pubic hair! You, you pervert!" Arlene threw the little white box, lid and all into Lenny's chest where it bounced off and onto the floor. Lenny was snickering wickedly. He had gotten the reaction he wanted.

But Arlene was not through. "Get out! Get out of here, you depraved, decadent, degenerate—" Arlene ran out of D words so she rushed at him waving her hands as if she were sweeping him out the door. "Take your hairiness and go!"

Lenny was still chuckling as he swept up the little container (luckily the fuzzy contents had not fallen out) put the lid firmly on again, then secured it in the pocket of his jacket.

"Well, goodbye, fair damsels, sweet ladies." Then, aside to Arlene, he said, "I'll be seeing you in class, Miss 'Can't Take a Joke' Gibson." Then he turned and walked out the still-open door, past the kids and their mud town. With a hop, he jumped into the MG and roared away.

Arlene was still sputtering, "The nerve of him, the nerve!" Then she stopped to take a breath and burst into laughter. A moment later she stopped short. "Lorraine, do you really think it was his pubic hair?"

CHAPTER 31
WAR

THE BATTLE CONTINUES

As the days and weeks progressed, it seemed everyone got to know about the cockroaches. They all had comments and advice. Mom shook her head and said that she was not surprised by the influx of the creepy crawlers. "I'm sure we never had them when Lorraine, Jeff, and I lived here," she said. Mom tried to look at Arlene severely and tried to assume an authoritative tone, but it was out of character, so she gave up and just gave a tiny sigh and said, "It's the way you let Jeff drag in all that trash he finds. I'm convinced the infestation came in with that stove." Here our mother pointed into the kitchen at her suspect. We all had loved the cute little stove Jeff found but now we looked on it as a kind of Trojan horse. Had the bugs really been there in the oven all along and then crept out and found cover in our kitchen?

It was embarrassing that everyone knew about our plague, but it was also sweet how they tried to help in their own way. Whenever Bill Connelly came over, he politely never mentioned our problem, but we would find a few cans of bug spray on the kitchen counter after he left. Rita and Sara Lee were against poisons and were all for natural cures. Rita suggested we use boric acid. "They eat it, and their little tummies explode," she said gaily. Jim Bishop advised us to seal up all cracks and crevices, and the Bird Lady advised prayer.

Tad looked genuinely concerned when he came over one night to see for himself. "This is crazy, man, crazy," he said, shaking his head at the scattering insects when he turned on the light.

Lenny liked to come over at any time. He would take the bug spray and shoot away into cupboards and cracks in the walls and then watch all the bugs run out drunkenly from the safety of their lairs. Caught in the open, they were no match for Lenny. He would blast away at them directly. Others, he would crush under foot, which made a sickening, popping noise as their shell-like bodies collapsed under the weight of his shoe. Lenny took many casualties on these annihilation expeditions, but still, hordes of bugs were left to continue their dominance the very next night. The invading troops seemed as strong as ever.

"Maybe they call in for reinforcements or replicate themselves, like aliens." Lenny concluded one night. "Remember that movie about the pods?"

Arlene shuddered. "Yes, I'm sure they do replicate, and they have hundreds of little babies at a time, no bigger than a dot at the end of a sentence and I've seen that some of the bigger bugs have egg sacs attached to them too!"

The kids assured us that this was true. "Yeah," Donnie said. "They have little yellowish sacks almost as big as they are, and they carry it around under their bellies."

Lindee piped up. "And did you know that they don't have bones like us? The skeletons are on the outside not the inside. That's why they have a hard shell. It's their bones." She stopped here suddenly and smiled at her own knowledge. "Mommy," Lindee continued, "did you ever see a bug that was striped like a bumblebee, but it didn't have any wings and its head is very big with jaws too? I dug up one in the dump yesterday.

Then one night we all sat down to a spaghetti dinner.
We were not prepared for what happened next.

Arlene looked distracted, "What, no, and it sounds totally disgusting." Lindee sat back and said no more.

Day after day, the battle continued. Arlene said the cockroaches were spreading "like acne on a teenager's back," and nothing could stop them. Sometimes I tried to get along and just brush them aside, but other times my anger would flare, and I would blast them with the spray can.

Lenny had the idea of calling a mass meeting—inviting all the bugs in the kitchen to come in for a conference, a kind of détente or cease-fire, he said. "Can't you imagine them all sitting there on little chairs, their dark heads nodding," he said. "You could say to them, 'OK, look, you guys are not wanted here. Can't we come to an agreement or something? Just take your egg sacs and leave, or else it's all-out war!'" Lenny's comic bit of reasoning almost seemed sensible by then because, at times, we were willing to try almost anything to get rid of the bugs.

TAD'S SURPRISE

One night when we were finishing one of my sister's spaghetti dinners, something unexpected happened. Arlene had invited Howard to stay for supper. We all cheered when the great fry pan filled with spaghetti and meatballs arrived at the table. Later, after dinner, as we leaned back in our seats, our empty plates in front of us and a comfortable quiet settling around the table, we heard a gentle tapping at the door.

"Come in!" we called. "Door is working!" Jeff added.

A moment later, Tad slithered through the front room and appeared at the arched doorway of the dining room. "What's happening, man?" he said as he stood there, his sleepy eyes half closed and his elfin grin beginning to spread.

Howard took this moment to pop out of his seat. "Well, thanks for dinner folks—gotta go and get my car out of the garage. The battery must be all charged up by now, and Gillian must be wondering where I am. I told her I was just going to drop off the new rendition of 'Lost at the Fair' to you guys. She will never believe I had car trouble." It didn't matter whether Howard really had car trouble or not—Gillian would be angry with him for something.

Earlier, Arlene and I were so excited to get our own copy of "Lost at the Fair" with our own names on it—"Lyrics by Arlene and Lorraine Gibson" right there on the top right-hand corner. Tad, still smiling his secret smile, eased back in the doorway as Howard squeezed by, still continuing his never-ending monologue about car and Gillian troubles.

"Hey, Tad," Jeff said, "we still have some meatballs left." He indicated the large frying pan and three meatballs at rest in the middle of it.

Tad, still standing in the archway, like an actor waiting for his entrance, grinned even more. Putting up his hand, he said, "No thanks, man, I'm good. I had dinner with my boss." Tad was wearing his usual white shirt, smart suit, and thin black tie. His shoes had the usual high sheen. He would have fit in easily at a fancy restaurant and conversely, always looked a little out of place in our red cottage. "I just came by," he continued mysteriously, "to save the day!" and lifted up a brown paper sack neatly rolled several times at the top. "The store was just closing, but I managed to get this for you guys. This," he paused for emphasis, "will solve all your problems." We stopped what we were doing then and looked at the seemingly innocuous paper sack. Tad was now moving into the kitchen. "I think we need more light," he said. By this time, we were all up and gathered around Thomas A. Duke peering at the mysterious bag in his hands.

Slowly, Tad unrolled the top of it. Carefully, he dipped his hand in and surprised us all by pulling out a large green lizard.

"What is it?" we gasped almost in unison.

"It's a gecko," he said with pride, holding the animal gingerly with two fingers around its body. The gecko was bright green and about a foot and a half long, if you counted the tail. It had delicate looking feet and on each delicate toe there was an even more delicate little round pad. The gecko at first just stared ahead with its beady, unblinking round eyes, then a tongue whipped out and licked one of the pupils. Disgusted, we all cried out, "Eeeyoooo," this time, in perfect unison. Suddenly, the body of the gecko in Tad's hand arched. The smooth green head whipped around and bit its new owner right on the thumb. Tad howled and dropped the lizard, which hit the floor running. Simultaneously, every one, except Tad and

*Tad reached gently into the paper bag and
pulled out a large lizard. "It's a gecko!" he said.*

Jeff, broke for cover, screaming and runningfor higher ground. A moment later, the gecko scurried under the refrigerator.

"Get it out! Get it out!" Arlene bawled at Tad from atop a dining room chair.

Tad held his bitten finger and watched, fascinated, as two drops of blood plopped onto the paper bag still in his left hand. "No, it's all right. I was just about to tell you that geckos eat roaches. You just leave him where he is and tonight he will come out and have a feast. Just think of him as a kind of guard dog."

"Will he really be able to catch the roaches?" I wanted to know. I had stationed myself on another dining room chair.

"Yeah, sure, you saw how fast he was going under the refrigerator. Did you notice the little suction cups on his feet?" Tad said, "Well, this gecko can chase the bugs right up the wall and across the ceiling too."

I really didn't want to know this fact. I soon pictured myself in bed and the gecko climbing up into my garret. Donnie and Laurie J. were in a corner, still clinging to each other, but Lindee was leaning down trying to see "Mr. Gecko" under the refrigerator. Arlene had gotten down from the chair and picked up the broom that was leaning against the wall for protection. I was right behind her. Only Jeff stood still. He was just smiling and looking amused at all the commotion. Tad's finger had stopped bleeding but looked pink and painful. He was still holding on to it. Finally, he said, "Just give him a chance. The man at the store said geckos are harmless."

We decided to leave Mr. Gecko where he was. Maybe he could help. Maybe he would just slip out the door and live in the dump. Or maybe we would get used to a green reptile living in our kitchen. It was a tiring evening, and after the dishes were done, we all went to bed. My sleep was not peaceful. Sometime in the night, I dreamed that somehow I was in Tokyo with the actor Raymond Burr, who was telling me that he needed my help because Godzilla was attacking refrigerators.

We never saw the gecko again until several weeks later when we got Jim Bishop to move the refrigerator. There was Mr. Gecko, only he wasn't green anymore; he was a dull grayish color, and his stomach was all shrunken. He was dead. We felt defeated— even a full-fledged gecko didn't want to eat our cockroaches. The kids, though, were sad and gave Mr. Gecko a nice burial in the dump.

CHAPTER 32
WIGGLEDY WAGGLEDY WOO

AND
LYRICS TO HOWARD'S SONG

EXTERMINATION

It was several days after Mr. Gecko's funeral. The night was cool, and I found myself in the living room comfortably reading a new book. I could hear my sister taking a shower in the next room. The water made splish-sploshing sounds, then dribbled to a stop.

"Hey, there're no towels in here!" my sister screeched from the misty room. This was not an unusual occurrence. We were always running out of towels or toilet paper, or, for that matter, soap, toothpaste, and razor blades. Somehow these essentials seemed to disappear almost as fast as we purchased them.

"The kids probably left them at the beach," I yelled. "I'll look in the wash for some."

Out on the back deck, I dug into the mountain of damp clothes waiting to be taken to the Laundromat. Somewhere in the middle of the pile, I pulled out a dry towel. It was small, but it would have to do. "Here it is," I said, as I opened the door a crack and shoved it in.

"Thanks," Arlene's wet hand grabbed it and closed the door before any cold air could come in.

I was just finding the place in my book again when I heard a scream and a second later Arlene's dripping figure barely covered in a tiny towel, raced out and pointed speechlessly back at the foggy bathroom. Finally, Arlene choked out, "Do you know what I found in there? I have had it! I can't stand it anymore, I mean it. Not another night!"

"What? What?" I kept asking.

Arlene finally sputtered, "I was drying off, and then I saw the bongo drums and . . ."

"What were bongo drums doing in the bathroom?" I asked, confused, as I watched the water drip down my sister's legs and make a small pool at her feet.

"That's just what I thought, what are these bongos doing in here?" Arlene gestured with one hand and held the towel with the other. "So, I picked it up and . . . Those kids! They must have stuffed bugs into it because all these fuzzy disgusting things fell out. Uggg!" Arlene shivered. "Stop laughing, Lorraine, these damn insects in the house are driving me insane!" Her voice was getting higher and higher.

"So, call an exterminator," I responded sarcastically. "They probably *only* cost about a hundred dollars." I was being facetious because where would *we* get a hundred dollars, but Arlene's face looked determined.

"Well, that's just what I'm going to do. I don't care how much it is. I'm going to Betsy's right now to call. We'll worry about the money later." Arlene made a move toward the door.

"Um, don't you think you'd better get more covered up first?" I motioned toward my sister's backside, which protruded from the small terrycloth towel clinging around her still damp body.

Arlene rushed out of the bathroom shrieking.

THE EXTERMINATOR COMETH

The next day, everyone got up early for a change, even Jeff. The man to end all our problems was coming at noon. We had gotten a special deal somehow at Bug's R Us Co. It would only cost thirty-five dollars, but he wanted to be paid up front in cash. We would have to leave the house for three hours, but first we had to clear everything away. All that was not nailed down, we took out of the kitchen and put outside. Boxes stuffed with dishes, utensils, and food lined the front porch like rejected CARE packages. We scoured out the kitchen in readiness for the operation.

"Look, Lorraine," Arlene said, wiping out a shelf with what looked like someone's tee shirt. "You go down to the bank and take out thirty-five dollars. I'll pay you later." The tee shirt was getting grayer and grayer with the wiping. "I'll send all the kids to Rita's for the night and wait for this extermination guy," she continued. "He wants his money right away, so hurry!"

THE BANK

The lines were already twenty people long at each window when I hurried inside the bank. I groaned as I got into one of the lines. It took fifteen minutes before I reached the teller window.

"I'm sorry," the teller's trained voice singsonged. "This is an outer branch bank book you have. You will have to get it verified at window number two." My heart sank as I dashed over to window number two. Luckily, it took only ten minutes to get my account verified, but by then, the regular windows had queues up to twenty people long again. There was nothing I could do but choose a line and wait. I kept glancing at the clock on the wall as if I could will it to hold back the time. It was already 12:14 p.m.! *He must be there by now*, I thought, *but what can I do?* Arlene would have pushed to the front of the line with some story, but I was not my sister. *Hurry, hurry*, I cried inwardly, hopping up and down with impatience. What is holding up the line?

The man in the red striped shirt had been at the teller window at least ten minutes already, only four more people to go. *Hurry . . . hurry*, I breathed, *please hurry!* Other lines moved and rotated while mine stood motionless. My arms swung back and forth. My big toe tapped furiously. Looking down, I noticed the pink nail polish on it was chipping. People walked into the building, stood in other lines, and a few minutes later, walked out finished with their business, but the man in red was still clinging to window number one. *Come on, come on*, my brain screamed.

Twenty minutes later, I panted up to the porch fearing the worst. Arlene was standing at the door quivering in her cutoff jeans and sweatshirt. Her eyes were wild. "Where were you!" she demanded. Her hair was standing on end as if she had been pulling at it.

"Why are *you* so hysterical? *I'm* the one who had to do all the waiting. Here's the money," I said, stretching out the bills toward her.

But Arlene just stood there, not looking at me but far into the distance. Then she started gritting her teeth (a bad sign). Finally, she choked out, "You would think . . . you would think . . . a simple thing," her voice was low, but gathering angry steam, ". . . that we could have a simple thing done . . . without complications." The word complications came out of her mouth strange and strangled. She was twisting her hands. Suddenly, she tore at her face. "Nothing ever goes right with us without a lot of SHIT, SHIT, SHIT!"

On the last SHIT, she turned to the front door and smashed her fist into one of the remaining small glass windows surrounding the door (scratch, one more window). A pie-like hole appeared on it.

What had happened was so fast. Arlene didn't even notice she was bleeding while I stood frozen as the ruby-colored blood dropped onto the porch from her hand. Finally aware of her injury, my sister clutched her hand as more blood oozed between her fingers. Strangely enough, she was now totally calm, her face relaxed. That's when the story came bubbling from her lips.

"The exterminator, he came and sprayed the kitchen, but he wouldn't do the rest of the house because we didn't have the money. He just left. Go look . . . And there are dead bugs all over the kitchen, all over the kitchen," she repeated. "It's just awful. Just go and look," she repeated again weakly, now holding a tight fist around her injured hand.

Inside the kitchen, harsh vapors of insecticide tried to force their way into my nostrils. Thousands of wiry legs waved in defeat as the roaches died slowly on their backs. A few were running in circles, crazy-mad from the poisoning fumes. Many were coming out of crevices gasping for air, groping for life. I almost felt sorry for them—poor suffering scavengers. Then I remembered that the rest of the house hadn't been fumigated and some of the bugs in the kitchen were escaping into the other rooms. If the man didn't return, they would quickly multiply again and my sympathy vanished. My breath too was almost gone so I stormed out of the kitchen and raced back outside.

The porch was empty. Arlene had gone to Betsy's to call up the exterminator man again. When she returned, she was bandaged and all smiles. Arlene said it took arguing and pleading, but the exterminator finally agreed to finish the job. He was coming the very next day. We could breathe a sigh of relief. Tomorrow our long trial would finally be over.

That night, we slept with all the windows and doors open in a half-fumigated house. My thoughts were on the tiny dead bodies still lying out in the kitchen, and I wondered what else there would be to plague us after they were gone.

Some good did result from our terrible encounter with the bugs, which we started calling "Our Battle with the Great Creepy-Crawlies." For us the experience had resulted in an inspiration for a song which just proves that sometimes chaos can result in creativity.

For weeks, Arlene and I had been trying to set lyrics to the last tune Howard had given us back on that fine summer day. After our battle with the bugs, we were finally able to write the lyrics for "Wiggledy Waggledy Woo." Arlene and I composed it at the beach the next day while the exterminator was eliminating the last pockets of resistance.

WIGGLEDY WAGGLEDY WOO
   FIRST CHORUS
   Jars of red ants
   Lizards that dance
   Snakes in a box
   Snails under rocks
   These are things that children bring
   home as presents every spring
   Oh, how they wiggledy waggledy woo

   SECOND CHORUS
   Miss ladybug
   Under your rug
   Frogs in the sink
   You'd never think - that
   They could like those crawly things
   Oh, but how their laughter rings
   Look at them wiggledy waggledy woo

   BRIDGE
   Then in the nighttime, a chorus of crickets
   Children join in
   with harmony
   Spiders are spinning their webs . . .

THIRD CHORUS
Old winter's hand
breaks up the band
They hibernate
but as of late - I
Still don't like those slimy things
Oh, but how kids' laughter rings
watching those wiggledy waggledy woos.

~~~AUTUMN~~~

CHAPTER 33
'TIS AUTUMN

THE DAYS DWINDLE DOWN TO A PRECIOUS FEW

I read once, that for those living on the coastline of California, the temperature is markedly cooler in the summer and warmer in the winter than just a few miles inland. This explained why living at the beach sometimes gave one a sense of timelessness. Here at the edge, we are lulled into a kind of Never-Never Land.

At the red cottage, there were few clues to prepare us for the grayer times ahead when days got shorter and cooler, making us pull on our heavy sweaters. Sunny beach days had lasted deep into October, but finally, fog blew in from the ocean and the mornings got chilly. Without our noticing, summer quietly moved into fall with hardly a murmur.

Our beach house had little insulation especially since Arlene pulled the ceiling down. Except for the fireplace, the gas heater in the dining room, a big square metal thing sitting on short legs, was our only source of heat. In the mornings, we huddled around it waiting for the bread we put on the top to toast. After that, we warmed our clothes before putting them on. Earlier in September, the kids had gone back to school, even Laurie J. Arlene had to make a special trip to take her on the first day.

As planned, my sister registered herself at El Camino City College for the night courses in music theory and drama, three nights a week. That meant she had less time for Sid, Howard, and the Zanzibar, but the thrill of new beginnings tempered her feelings of loss, she said. True to his word, Lenny picked my sister up each school night and delivered her, three hours later, back at the cottage. We soon got used to this new schedule. Arlene made dinner, and I cleaned up and put the kids to bed. Actually, all I had to do was say "go to bed."

Halloween and Thanksgiving were coming soon and the kids brought home pumpkins made from orange construction paper with cutout triangular eyes and mouths grinning with jagged teeth.

While the kids brought home holiday artwork, Arlene brought home a new jargon of words inspired by her music and drama courses, which she sprinkled into her conversations. Every so often she would throw into a sentence terms like *Aeolian*, *diatonic*, and *chromatic scales*. She liked to tell you the difference between a gavotte and a cadenza. At odd times of the day, she would go to the piano and strike chords dramatically, moving from major to minor-flatting, augmenting the fifths and even taking on a string of seventh, ninths, elevenths, and a thirteenth or two.

As for drama, she expressed a preference for the Method technique developed by Stanislavski and brought to perfection, she added, by Marlon Brando. She was excited about starting to do improvisations with the other students. At the end of the term, they were all to pick out and perform a scene from a famous play, but for now, they just did funny exercises that stretched their imagination. Arlene demonstrated one that the class had been doing that week. They were supposed to imagine themselves as mechanical objects. Arlene showed us hers, which was a hilarious manifestation of a vacuum cleaner that buzzed around, then got stuck, and instead of picking up dirt, spewed it out all over the room. She proudly reported she got an A for imagination. That was so like Arlene—always going for the striking effect. I probably would have chosen to be a washing machine, the old-fashioned kind that had a hand wringer attached to it like the one our mother had used for years until it broke. It was still sitting on our back patio. If I had been in my sister's class, my washing machine would have churned out spanking clean clothes, wrung dry, then folded into neat piles.

I had recently lined up a temporary job. It was to start soon at Marches Department Store, selling toys in the basement for the Christmas season. Luckily, I could catch a bus that went directly to the shopping mall.

THE INSOMNIAC

When Jeff was not working nights, sweating it out at the Lighthouse kitchen under the rule of Chef Wong, Arlene and I worked at the Insomniac Coffee House. Rita had really come through for us when she convinced the manager she knew of two experienced waitresses who could work the odd weekend or two. I always felt a little dishonest working there. The artwork was knock-off impressionism, Arlene and I weren't beatniks, there were no writers or poets hanging out at the little round tables, and we didn't even have an espresso machine.

BETSY

Halloween came and went. It was pretty low-key. Most of the kids bypassed our out-of-the-way alley. Today, Arlene and I were over at Betsy's house, sitting around her Formica kitchen table drinking coffee. The TV in the next room was on.

As Betsy and my sister talked, I thought vaguely that the world could be divided into the people who always had the TV on and the people who didn't. At the moment, Betsy was talking. She sat solidly on her chrome kitchen chair, her sturdy body rock-hard since she started working out at the local gym. She was telling us in her slightly gravelly voice about her ex-husband. We used to wonder why Betsy remarried an older man. He must be almost forty, we thought, and worked at Douglas Aircraft in Long Beach. Every evening when he came home, Betsy's two little girls would run out to greet him, and he would swing them up into his arms and carry them into the house. They were a stay-at-home (play bridge on the weekends with the relatives) type of couple, Betsy said.

Now, she was telling us how her first husband had walked out on her when their two little girls were only three and four years old. "The bastard," she growled, screwing up her face and throwing back her head, making her short curly hair bounce. "God, we were so young, only seventeen when we got married." Arlene and I had seen Betsy's ex-husband one morning when we were sunning ourselves on the front porch.

There was a roar of a car engine, and a red convertible pulled into Culper Court. A blonde Adonis got out and strolled leisurely up to Betsy's house. He had come on one of his rare appearances to visit his kids. He still looked seventeen with his impish grin and sun-bleached hair, waiting there on Betsy's front stoop for the door to open. He turned and gave Arlene and I a little wave and wink before he ducked into the house.

Now, sitting with Betsy over coffee and hearing her ruminate about her early marriage, we knew why she had married an older man. The blonde Adonis had never been faithful and rarely supported her and their children. The TV was making soft background noises to Betsy's story. It had a thrumming-drumming sound. I glanced at some sort of parade.

Yes, I could easily believe the unfaithful part of Mr. Adonis, the way he had leered at my sister and me that morning. Why were some men like this? I wondered, thinking about my own father and his infidelities. It didn't matter how wonderful the girl they had was, they always wanted more. Was it ego or insecurity that drove them? I didn't know.

Anyway, now Betsy had Frank—Frank, with his large teeth and receding chin was no physical match to the blonde god, but he loved Betsy and her children. He had saved her when she was left all alone, and now she was smart enough to cherish him—no chin, and all. On the TV, the parade was still rolling along going someplace. Every so often, there was a voice-over as the cars slowly cruised by.

My attention moved back to Arlene and Betsy as they compared rotten husbands. Arlene was starting to trash *her* ex, Don. I had heard this story before. Heck, I had lived through it often enough with my sister and the kids. At least Betsy's ex-husband had stuck around to get divorced and then stayed to visit and give the occasional birthday present, not like Don, who disappeared completely.

SHOCK AND AWE

As my sister delved into the nitty-gritty of her narrative with Betsy, I zoned out and paid more attention to the parade. Was it the Thanksgiving Parade in front of Macy's department store? I didn't see any of those big balloons or brass bands, just cars going by. Slowly I began to comprehend what the voice-over was saying.

"President Kennedy has been shot!"

I heard the words but didn't at first make sense of it. Shot? How could that be? As if in answer, the announcer spoke again, "The president has been shot by an unknown assailant while riding in a motorcade in Dallas, Texas." A moment later, the man was saying the president had been taken to the hospital. The broadcaster started each sentence with the words *the president.*

I was beginning to grasp the reality but several more beats of the motorcade went by before I fully understood. Finally, the announcer went on to report that the governor of Texas had also been shot and was at the same hospital as the president. Then he repeated himself all over again, almost as if he didn't believe any of it either.

"President Kennedy has been shot by an unknown assailant while riding in a motorcade in Dallas, Texas. President Kennedy has been taken to the nearest hospital, and we are awaiting news. We don't know the president's condition at this time. We are not receiving information. It is feared the president is in critical condition."

"Arlene, Betsy! Someone just shot President Kennedy!" I said, breaking into their conversation. "He may be dead!"

"Dead!" The talk around the kitchen table stopped, and we listened to the announcer repeat the exact same message over and over, while on-screen, the motorcade rolled on and on.

Later it was confirmed that President John F. Kennedy was dead—shot by an unknown gunman. On the TV, newsmen were crying and like a broken and scratched record, kept repeating the same words over again like a musical phrase. The film clip of the shooting in black and white also kept playing on the screen. We left Betsy still watching the TV.

Although our family had never been involved or interested at all in politics, everyone had agreed that it was great to have such a young, vibrant, good-looking president and first lady in the White House even if they did talk funny. Now, we were horrified and subdued. To be honest, I was more shocked that a president of *our* United States had been assassinated than who it was. This was America, I reasoned. We were not some third world Banana Republic erupting in assassinations, civil war, and military coups every few years. Yes, there was the assassination of Abraham Lincoln, but that was a hundred years ago.

FROM THE GRAY NOTEBOOK

Correction: I am completely forgetting about President Garfield and McKinley, but who can remember them, anyway.

Things got even more confusing when Kennedy's shooter was found and then killed before there could even be a trial. The weeks that followed went by in a muted haze. On our tiny black-and-white TV, we caught bits and pieces of what was happening—a heavily veiled Jacqueline Kennedy, a casket on an old iron-wheeled wagon pulled by white horses, an eternal flame by the side of a grave.

CHAPTER 34
ENTER PAUL

THE SOUND OF MUSIC

There was always music at 230 Culper Court, either someone was singing or playing an instrument or listening to the radio or phonograph. The kids especially loved dancing along to jazz or classical records like *The Rite of Spring.* More often, it was the radio turned permanently to the jazz station KNOB that played mostly nonstop throughout the day.

Growing up with Mom and Harry, our house in Burbank was also filled with music. Mom always had the radio on in the kitchen as she cleaned and cooked or ironed a ton of cotton clothing. Often at night, when all the work was done, she played records in the living room for us. She called these events her "Roseland Ballroom Nights." Her favorite entertainers were Fats Waller and Ella Fitzgerald. She would put on a record then pick up one of the littlest of us and dance around the room. Arlene and Bill danced together, sawing their arms up and down and rocking back and forth like they had seen people do in old movies. Then we would ask for some of our favorite records to be played like *Air Mail Special* by the Benny Goodman Trio or some of our father's boogie-woogie songs so we could dance very fast.

By the time the evening ended, Mom would have taught us how to do some cool dancing steps from the Foxtrot, Lindy Hop, and various versions of the Swing. Growing up in the Bronx in her large, tight-knit family, Mom, her sister, and five girl-cousins, as teenagers, would all dress up on a Friday or Saturday night to go out dancing in clubs. Boys, she said, had to pay, but girls got in for free. Later, when she and Harry were dating, they hung out at Roseland Ballroom on Fifty-First Street in Manhattan. "There were two bandstands," she recalled, "one on either side of the room so you could start out dancing to Count Basie, then, almost without pause, switch to Fletcher Henderson or Glenn Miller. Back then they called it the 'battle of the bands.'"

When Harry came back from one of his tours, we got to go into the living room again. My father would sit at the piano and play for us. There were popular songs like "Chattanooga Choo Choo" and his own comical songs. We liked to dare him to make one up on the spot, which always amazed us. He usually finished the entertainment by picking up his high school fife that always sat on top of the piano, and, piping out the melody to the "Mexican Hat Dance," left the piano and marched around the room with us following close behind.

After a few turns around the parlor, he marched right out the front door and down the middle of the street with us still trailing him. Kids playing on the block ran over to join us as my father took the parade around the whole block, gathering as many kids as he could. As you can guess, Harry was very popular with children, mainly because he was so much of a child himself. When he came home from one of his trips, the neighborhood kids would start calling out, "Hey! Harry's back, Harry's back!" By the time he got out of his car, there would be a crowd around him. He was our very own celebrity.

THE DIVA

One afternoon I was sitting in my favorite spot on the top step of the back porch reading *Sweet Thursday*. Arlene had read it first and given it to me with the words, "After you read this you, will want to become a prostitute and work in a bawdy house." And, yes, I was having a good time with the funny characters that lived in John Steinbeck's novels. This was certainly easier going than *The Grapes of Wrath* or *East of Eden*.

Suddenly, I heard Arlene call from inside, "Lorraine, come here in the living room, you just gotta see this." Her voice had a giggle in it. "Hurry!"

"OK, I'm here," I said moments later, trotting into the front room where my sister waited. Arlene had a gleeful look on her face as she stood poised over the phonograph holding the arm of it a few inches in the air above a record that was already spinning. "Are you ready for this?" she asked, making sure she had my full attention.

I looked around. Lindee and Donnie were standing nearby, but Laurie J. was next to her mother in front of the record player, her hands clasped in front of her with a smile on her face, the kind kids get when they are the center of attention.

"Ready?" Arlene positioned the arm on the record. There was a crackle as the needle touched the spiraling disc. A woman's operatic voice rang out a heartrending aria in Italian. Laurie J. opened her lips and silently mouthed along to the sad lament— swaying to the music, wringing her hands, and quivering with passion. The singing voice really did seem to be welling out of Laurie J.'s three-foot frame. I was about to say something, but Arlene shushed me.

"Wait for it," she warned. Just then, the singer ended her song on a high, sustained note, hitting a strange mutual vibration in my own body. At this point, Laurie J. thrust her arms into the air and threw back her head, her body trembling along with the vibrato of the singer. My sister took the arm of the record player off the disc. "Well?" she said expectantly, but I was laughing and couldn't speak. Lindee and Donnie, joining in the general enthusiasm, were giggling too.

"It's Maria Callas," Arlene explained with a touch of importance in her voice. "Rita loaned it to us for a while. Isn't it too much? Rita said we needed a shot of Maria Callas so we wouldn't be just jazz snobs."

"Let's hear that high note again, Laurie J.," Arlene chortled, putting the needle back on the record near the great finale. Laurie J. obliged again and again, and each time she came to the high ending note, we roared our approval.

"OK, OK, enough of that." Arlene was holding her sides. "Hey, kids, what do you want next, how about *Gypsy?*"

"Yeah, yeah!" The kids clapped their hands. "Put it on," they chanted.

Arlene shifted some LPs around until she found the right album cover, *Ethel Merman in Gypsy*, then took Maria Callas off the turntable and tossed it on top of the records stacked on the window seat. I cringed thinking of the scratches that were collecting and wondered if Rita would loan us records if she could see how they were treated, and what about the four dimes that were taped to the end of the arm of our record player to make it heavier (it had a tendency to skip). Surely the extra weight was gouging the grooves deeper.

Now *Gypsy* was spinning around on the player and Arlene skipped the weighted needle past the slow songs until she found a lively one like "You Gotta Have a Gimmick" and "Together Wherever We Go."

We knew all about the story of the Broadway show which was based on the early life of Gypsy Rose Lee, a striptease artist back in the '30s and '40s. Her mother had gotten her children into vaudeville. There was something just a little familiar to me about the forceful personality of Mama Rose and her relationship to her kids and my irrepressible sister and her children. Seeing Arlene and the kids singing and dancing I thought must be almost like watching the play or the movie that now starred Natalie Wood and Rosalind Russell.

After a rousing pantomime of "Let Me Entertain You" by Lindee, Laurie J. took center stage again as a totally believable pint-size Ethel Merman lip-syncing perfectly as Merman belted out "Everything's Coming Up Roses." Again, Laurie J. threw back her head to simulate the delivery of the wobbly vibrato of Miss Merman as she yells out "For me! For me! For MEEEE!"

Finally, the kids wanted to hear "Have an Eggroll, Mr. Goldstone." They loved the song that got faster and faster. By this time, I was up, singing and dancing along with everyone else. Soon we were running crazily in fast motion and almost didn't hear the tapping at the door. Finally, Arlene rushed over to it— the rest of us following, just as the song came to its conclusion. When the door was finally flung open, we all cried out the last line of the song, which was "Mr. Goldstone, WE LOVE YOU!"

AN OLD FRIEND

Standing there looking a little bewildered was Paul Milner holding a thin portfolio. He became even more flustered as we dragged him inside. The needle of the LP, having played out its one side, moved back and forth, back and forth, making swishy, slurry sounds.

I had met Paul a few times before, when Arlene lived on Harbor Drive. He was a rather shy young man somewhere in his twenties with tightly curled red hair. Like a lot of Arlene's friends, he showed no signs of living near the beach—his complexion, pale; his build, slight with slender hands. "Where have you been all this time?" Arlene said, pushing Paul down on the couch and throwing a pillow at him. "You disappeared. Have you been designing sets all this time and you didn't have time for me?"

I think Arlene was still feeling like Ethel Merman and under the spell of the exuberant Rose character, because she was pushing and pulling at Paul as if he really was Mr. Goldstone about to do wonderful things for her children. "Hey, wait," said our new visitor with a grin, defending himself from the pillow. "You were listening to *Gypsy* just now, weren't you? What a coincidence! I happened to see the movie just last week. It was great and I saw *West Side Story* the week before that."

Paul still had a smile on his face at the unexpected attention he was getting. A moment later, he jumped up. "My favorite number in *Gypsy* is the one where the guy in the troop is telling Louise, that's Natalie Wood's character, how he is going to go out on his own to become a dancing star, and he describes to her what his act will be like."

"I think we jumped over that one!" Arlene said, going to the turntable and skipping around on it until she came to "All I Need Is the Girl." While it played, Paul threw aside his shyness, explaining to us how the scene went in the movie. "You see, at first he just talks to Natalie Wood how the song will be set up, and then he starts to slowly sing and dance." Paul must have seen the movie more than once because he jumped up and mimicked the words perfectly, adding all the appropriate gestures of looking into a mirror, straightening his tie, then taking out an imaginary comb and raking it through his hair just like the lyrics on the record sang. After putting an imaginary flower into his lapel, Paul broke into a soft shoe and glided around the living room adroitly avoiding any collision into the kids or the coffee table. By the end of the song, Paul was singing out loud with the record and leaping into the big finish. He ended by collapsing into the bathtub love seat—the very one he had made himself for the *Breakfast at Tiffany's* play.

Everyone cheered while Paul, a little out of breath, became shy and quite himself again. "Hey," he said abruptly, now looking at his creation with a critical eye, "what happened to the colored-glass lantern that was attached to this couch? It was my own special touch for *Tiffany's*."

Arlene looked embarrassed. "You know, one of the kids must have knocked it over." The children looked at each other blankly. They all knew their mother had more likely broken it herself when she and Howard had gotten into one of their blowups. Paul was still looking sad at the destruction, and my sister quickly changed the subject. "Well, and where have you been for so long that you didn't come to see us?" She put a touch of accusation along with a tinge of sadness into her voice.

Forgetting his broken creation, Paul brightened. "Oh, let me show you!" he said, moving over to the other side of the room where Arlene had tossed his portfolio. He picked it up and held it close for a few seconds in his arms. "I think I should explain that for the last several months I have been taking . . . dancing lessons!" When there was no comment from us, Paul hurried to explain. "I always wanted to do it, but now I am and that's why you haven't seen me. I even cut down on my theater work." His fingers were fumbling with the zipper of the case.

"Well, that explains your sudden rush to see musicals like *Gypsy* and *West Side Story*. Didn't Rita Moreno get an Oscar for her role as Anita?" Arlene remarked.

"Ah, yes she did," Paul assented, then paused and looked serious. "But you know I was quite upset when she did the dancing number on the roof with her girlfriends. None of them pointed their toes when they did their high kicks."

"My, my, aren't you the great critic now that you have put on your own dancing shoes!" Arlene teased.

"No, you don't understand. I'm upset about that because I'm not just taking dancing lessons, I'm taking classical ballet." He paused for a moment, then unzipped his portfolio and carefully took out a black-and-white 8 x 10 photograph. "See," he said, holding it up for us to see. It was in a white cardboard frame. I could see a background of clouds and that the lighting was dramatic. It was clear that he had a professional photographer take it.

In the photo, Paul was in full ballet gear—a thin light top with skintight white tights. Silky ballet slippers graced his feet, and he was carefully posed with his left arm up in the air and right arm extended gracefully behind. His weight was on one leg while the other was thrown back dramatically with the toe of the silky slipper carefully pointed. Paul's head in profile, gazed upward like someone in an otherworldly dream.

Faced with the photo, Arlene, for once, was speechless. "Uh . . . uh . . ." she choked out, not knowing how to respond to Paul's fanciful pose and revealing costume.

Donnie piped up. "Do they always let you dance in your underwear?"

As for me, I tried not to focus on the alarming bulge under Paul's tights in the picture. I knew Arlene was doing the same thing. I felt my face getting hot and turned away so Paul couldn't see. *Oh darn! Aren't I ever going to get over being embarrassed for other people?*

THE RELUCTANT CRITIC

Feeling the familiar warmth and mortification creep over me, I remembered all the awful talent shows of my youth in school. How was it that so many kids didn't realize that they couldn't sing or dance or play an instrument? The worst was in my senior year when Erin McKenzie and her ballet teacher presented a pas de deux. There were snickers and tittering laughter running through the teenage audience when the curtain opened to reveal Erin and her teacher frozen in a classic ballet pose. The teacher was at least thirty and his hair was receding, but most unfortunate was the bright spotlight hitting the great bulge in his tights, or so it seemed to me. I distinctly remembered my eyes burning.

WONG THE TERRIBLE

At least this time there wasn't a giant spotlight in Paul's picture, but before any of us could think of something to say, we heard the sound of stomping boots coming up the back deck stairs, and Jeff appeared in the living room doorway, holding my book still open to the page where I had left it. "Hey," he drawled, "anyone up for some ko-ffee?" Then seeing Paul, drawled out, "Hey Paulie-boy, long time, no see! Want some ko-ffee?"

Later, sitting around the dining room, hot cups warming our hands, I realized something was a little off about Jeff. "Hey, don't you usually sleep about now?" I asked. "Should you be having coffee? You need to rest before your shift at the Lighthouse." Jeff looked sheepish but that was not unusual for him.

"Well, ya see. I don't work there anymore. I sorta quit."

"What do you mean sorta quit?" Arlene blurted out.

"I guess you could chalk it up to a lack of communication," my brother mused, rubbing his finger around in a bit of spilled coffee on the table.

"But you loved the music," I said.

"Yeah, I loved the music," Jeff repeated, "and I loved the food, but it was Wong. He just didn't love me. It was hard to tell at first because of his English." Once started, Jeff blurted out the rest. "Ya see, one day, I swear I don't know what I did, but Wong was swearing more than ever before. First, he just muttered and rattled his pots and pans around but then . . . then he picked up his cleaver and started moving toward me, still swearing under his breath. That's when I took off outa there, out the back door and didn't come back. I had just started my shift, so I wasn't out any money since he was paying me by the day, I mean night."

"But you can't think he would really hurt you, do you?" I asked.

"Sad," said Paul. "I guess all true artists are excitable and a chef is no exception."

"But now no more free jazz," Arlene lamented.

"But that's OK," Jeff continued. "I made a lot of contacts there, especially with the younger guys. I found there are skads of late-night clubs that cater to young musicians." Jeff took another sip of coffee. "They all dig the new music—free jazz. I've been going to a place called the Blue Horn in Venice Beach out near Santa Monica. These guys really like the way I play."

"So, all is well?" Arlene asked. "Actually, it works out for me too. Now that you have so much free time, I'm going to expect you to start pulling your weight again in this house. We are getting low on firewood for the fireplace. You may not realize it, but Christmas is coming soon and I've got nothing. I'm going to need help there too. I'm counting on you, Jeff, to find me some toys we can fix up and make over. Maybe you'll even find enough parts to complete that bike out on the front porch. Lorraine is working, so she will be mostly busy until after Christmas. So, it looks like it's just you and me, Jeff." She ended this on a sad note, then her eyes swept plaintively over to Paul.

Immediately, Paul piped up. "Oh, I can help too. I'm perfectly free until my dance class starts a new semester."

"What do you mean? Aren't you working on some *Christmas Carol* or *Miracle on '52nd' Street* production or anything?"

Paul shook his head. "I'm all yours for the taking."

"Well, that's wonderful, that's great! I can really use your talent as an artist." Arlene clapped her hands, happy to know that Christmas and Paul were shaping up just as she had planned. Suddenly alarmed that her voice had gotten too loud, my sister hushed herself and quickly tiptoed to the living room doorway to make sure the kids hadn't overheard any of her plans but all was well; they had long ago wandered away from the adult conversation and were engrossed in a Deputy Dawg cartoon. They hadn't heard a thing about Christmas.

WINTER

CHAPTER 35
CHRISTMAS AT CULPER COURT
PART I, II & III

AND

FROM THE GRAY NOTEBOOK
JEFF'S VAN

PART I
TRANSFORMATIONS

There was a star on top, and blinking colored lights wove in and out of the steel girders and ladders. From a distance, the Southern Edison Electric Company on Hermosa Avenue in its way was trying to be festive in its holiday garb but within the glitter of lights, five chimneystacks still shot columns of smoke high into the air.

It was already dark as the bus pulled up and let me off on the corner of Second Street. I gave the twinkling lights another look before crossing Hermosa Avenue and continuing home. It was only four blocks but uphill, and since I was wearing heels and had to take tiny steps in my slim sheath dress, I was slowed down considerably.

During the three-day training period at Marches Department Store, the Christmas apprentices were taught the dos and don'ts of being proper temporary workers. We learned how to ring up sales on the cash register and properly count back the change; we learned how to properly treat our customers (no matter what, the customer is always right); and we were also coached in the proper attire. Hair must be neat—if long, pulled back from the face. A plain black dress is ideal, but one can also get away with a subdued pattern in a neutral color. I was puffing and a bit out of breath as I finally chugged up the brick path and stepped onto the porch.

The house was dark, and of course, the door had accidentally locked itself again. *At times, it seems to have a will of its own,* I thought gloomily, as I jiggled the doorknob, then knocked and knocked. Where was everyone? Eventually I decided they must all be at Rita's. Giving up on the door, I went over to the music room window and, stepping up, pushed against the two windows. The French doors flew open immediately, and I plunged into a black abyss almost falling to my knees in my tight dress and heels and almost ruining my only stockings. Luckily, I recovered my balance and moved on. Instinctively, I stepped up into the living room. Feeling bolder, I took a couple of paces forward toward what I thought must be a lamp and promptly tripped over the coffee table. I had no time for this now. I was tired from working. I was tired of the toy department. I was tired of trying to talk parents out of buying cap pistols and nudging them toward toy drums. I just wanted to take off my proper clothes and relax.

Finally, I found the lamp. I assumed the light would reveal the usual every day disorder but instead, the room was neat and—"Fairy lands of the Noel Season!" I breathed in awe, gazing around me. "It looks like the magic elves have been here!" All had been transformed.

Gold was everywhere—on tables, on shelves, on every available space. Several golden bulbs clustered together in a large wooden bowl on the coffee table I had just tripped over, and next to it, a jar of cookie gingerbread men grinned up at me. The mantel, too, was garnished with a gilded tree branch and two gold-painted candles stuck in empty basket wine bottles (also painted gold). They stood guard on either side of the festooned branch like soldiers protecting a king's treasure. Chains of garlands wreathed the doorframes and windows. Arlene must have found our family's old decorations. I didn't even know any had survived the many moves we had made as children. All in all, I felt I had broken into Santa's cottage and I was a Christmas Goldilocks.

As I looked around, I could see Arlene must have bought more than just one bottle of gold paint and, just like Arlene, she had gone to town with it. Along with the golden tree branch, I could see gold touches everywhere. In the living room, another gilded branch was squeezed in with the TV, radio, and record player. The bathtub love seat that Paul had made was already painted gold inside, so now its radiance was echoed in other objects—rocks the kids had brought in from the dump were painted, seashells from many beach trips. I found touches of gold paint in the kitchen and dining room. It looked like the bottles of gilt had at last run out, but not before all the handles to cabinets, knobs on drawers, and doorknobs had received my sister's Midas touch.

THE ENCHANTMENT OF CHRISTMAS

After the first surprise transformation at the cottage, I would discover new additions to the Christmas theme whenever I came home from work. One day a fat fir tree appeared. It was propped against the wall in a bucket of water in the far corner of the living room. Arlene said Tad had dropped it off along with some candy canes.

The next day, the tree was decorated with the red and white canes and a few strings of popcorn. In the dining room, the children were sitting around the table, each with a needle and a long piece of thread attached to it. White fluffy popcorn overflowed a big bowl in the middle of the table. As the oldest and most dexterous with her fingers, Lindee's string was halfway filled already, while Donnie and Laurie J. only had four or five pieces on their threads. I sat down at the table to help things along. That's when I noticed Laurie J. She had gotten into her mother's cosmetics again, and her mouth, cheeks, and even her nose were smeared with my sister's bright pink lipstick, Passion Fuchsia. Ever since she had gotten so much attention with her Maria Callas and Ethel Merman impersonations, she had started looking for more ways to impress us and make us laugh, so I was not surprised to see Laurie J. in clown face. Another trick she had devised that diverted us was her impersonation of a dandelion. Standing very straight with her arms to her sides, she vigorously shook her head back and forth until her white, chin-length hair stood out straight from her head in a cloudy blur. Lindee and Donnie started to nickname their sister "The Clown."

After an hour of laborious popcorn stringing and trips to the bathroom for toilet paper to wrap around pricked fingers, we tied all the ends of the strings together and added it to the tree. It took several days to complete the job, but the white popcorn playing off the deep green of the fir tree was endearing and effective. During the next few days, other ornaments appeared—a silver bird with a long, white tail made of the softest bristles, a small number of fragile colored-glass bulbs in various colors and sizes, and a few bunches of very wrinkled tinsel leftover from our mother's old box of Christmas stuff.

THE GHOSTS OF CHRISTMAS PAST

Christmas in Riverside had always been low-key. Gone were the glorious Christmases we had back in Burbank when we were little kids, days I always remember as magical. On Christmas mornings we awoke before dawn, and with only the glow of Christmas tree lights, would run into the living room to see our presents. One year, two shiny bikes appeared for my older sister and brother. Arlene had a red one with many extra features—a bell, headlights, and a metal basket gracing the handlebars. On the back fender, a metal seat could carry an extra passenger. Even the tires had fancy mudguards.

Bill's blue bike was similarly equipped, although it wasn't long before he stripped it down and made it his own. Just a few weeks later, all the fancy stuff like baskets and racks were discarded along with the fenders, even the chain guard disappeared. When he was done, only the bell and light on the handlebars remained. My big brother had turned his practical bicycle into a sleek maneuverable racer, even if it still did have balloon tires. In time, he would fix that too. Bill tightened the handlebars so he could ride with no hands if he wanted, but mostly he liked to tear up and down the street jumping curbs. He became adept at all sorts of wheelies and tricks, like riding his bike while facing backward. It was probably one of these times that he smashed into a pile of rubbish where somehow a small pipe got lodged into his lower lip, leaving him with a small circular scar.

A few years later, two shiny bikes again were reflected in the Christmas lights. This time, they were for Jeff and me. Another memorable Christmas was when Bill got his mother-of-pearl drum set complete with snare, tom-tom, bass drum, and sock cymbal or, as Bill called it, the high hat. It even had a cowbell attached to the top of the bass drum to clang. One slight drawback was the large black initials of RK painted on the front of the bass drum where it should have been, if anything, the initials BG for Bill Gibson or even WG for William. It turned out Harry had gotten the set cheap from another musician who worked in a band and owed him a favor. We never did find out who RK was.

Harry was hardly ever there for Christmas. If he was, he was certainly never up at dawn to open presents with us. He would continue to sleep until past noon when he got up to have breakfast. The one time I definitely know he was with us was when he showed up unexpectedly late on Christmas Eve with a lumpy sack of toys. We called it "the Grab-Bag Christmas," because Harry had us reach into a pillowcase and what we pulled out became our present. He didn't get up that morning either.

A most special Christmas was when I got my dollhouse. It was made of wood and painted white with a peaked gray roof just like our own house. Upstairs were two bedrooms with a tiny bathroom in between. A cunning staircase went down to the living room and kitchen. Even in the dim Christmas tree lights, I could see that the dollhouse already had a family occupying it. There was a mother, father, sister, and brother, all made of lead or some heavy kind of metal.

The dollhouse moved permanently into our back porch where I played with it, rearranging furniture and moving the little metal doll family from room to room. They had articulated arms and legs so I could sit them properly on the toilet in the bathroom or on the couch in the living room. I could get the whole family sitting around on the chairs in the kitchen for breakfast or straighten them out and put them to bed at night. I particularly liked making the metal family walk up and down the stairs, moving stiffly like soldiers.

Arlene had been responsible for getting me my dollhouse. She had spotted it at one of her friends' homes—unused and unwanted—and persuaded her pal to give up her outgrown toy. Then, in great secrecy, spirited it home where she and Mom repainted, re-wallpapered and fixed it up for me that Christmas.

PREPARATIONS

With that history in mind, it was not surprising Arlene was determined her children's Christmas would be a magical time too. Arlene was the perfect holiday elf. Her spirits and enthusiasm for the season knew no bounds. She drank eggnog, warbled Christmas carols, and stealthily brought mysterious objects into her bedroom. The hum of the sewing machine was another constant.

Sometimes, the smell of paint escaped from under the bedroom door. I should have called my sister the head elf, with Jeff, Paul, and even Tad and Bill Connelly her elfin underlings. She would order them about, asking them to find different materials for her to turn into Christmas treasures. Paul hinted he was working on a special toy of his own. He wanted it to be a surprise for Arlene too, because even with teasing and prodding (and no one could tease and prod like my sister), he didn't break down and tell her what it was. The kids were told never to enter Mama's bedroom because, as Arlene said in a conspiratorial and hushed whisper to the children, her bedroom was an offshoot of Santa's workshop!

Jeff labored faithfully too, roaming the streets for interesting remnants, which he grabbed up and stashed in his van. Along with the back streets, Jeff was also told to scour thrift stores and junk shops for anything that could be turned into a plaything. Jim Bishop said he would save any toys for us at Sandow's Swap Shop where he worked.

FROM THE GRAY NOTEBOOK
JEFF'S VAN

I don't believe I ever described Jeff's truck before. He is very proud of it. The original color might have been white or light blue, but to cover all the dings and rusty spots, gray primer is the outstanding color now. Later, when Jeff found some dark blue paint, he drew a large treble clef on one side of the van followed by several wiggly musical notes. He says it is the melody to "'Round Midnight," the Thelonious Monk tune he is working on. On the other side, the musical staff is a bass clef and the corresponding chords to the song. The remainder of the blue paint has been randomly dripped and drabbed over the rest of the vehicle like a Jackson Pollock canvas.

The inside of Jeff's van is perhaps even stranger than the outside. For some reason, he has stripped away every soft covering—all the padding on doors and dashboard, all the carpeting too is removed, bringing everything back to its metallic beginnings. The back of the van is very dark; if someone has to ride there, they will have to sit on bare floor and bump along, sharing the space with spare tires and tools that clink and clank and shift back. The front seat is not much better. All that separates you from the street is metal. You can even see a piece of the road racing below through the cracks in it as you drive along and sometimes smell fumes coming up. It's always a good idea to keep the windows open.

Riding with Jeff is always an experience. This is the way he starts his truck. Before getting in, he unlocks the brake and puts the gear shift stick in neutral, then with the door still open, gives his truck a good push and runs along beside it as it slowly picks up speed as it rolls down the hill toward Second Street. And just at the right moment, when it is going fast enough, Jeff jumps back in and madly starts yanking at the gearshift and stomping on the peddles on the floorboard until the motor kicks in which makes a great roar. When this finally happens, there is more gear shifting, and the truck surges forward abruptly, causing the front seat to slide back as if on skis. The next sudden gear shift however, makes it slide forward again into its original position. After this last spasm, the truck finally rumbles contentedly away down the street.

It may be hard to believe, but Jeff is happy as a lark in this truck, and as he drives, he hums the melodies of famous saxophone solos. Sometimes when he hears an interesting traffic sound—the beep of a car, the clang of a railroad crossing, or the wail of a fire or police siren—he immediately mimics the sound, then reaches over to a strange-looking metal wire that is sticking out of the bare dashboard and gives it a twang. He knows the vibration of the wire sounds the note for G so by humming the interval between the interesting sound and the wire's boink, Jeff can pinpoint the musical note. He always smiles when this happens. I used to worry about that rusty, twisted piece of wire jutting out from the dashboard, wondering if someday the car seat will catapult Jeff's forehead into it. Luckily, this hasn't happened, and my brother so far remains unhurt and free to scour the back alleys for his treasures. After a successful haul, he will rumble home and cram the street finds into his bedroom under the back porch stairs. Later, we will hear the sounds of hammering come up from below the staircase.

COUNTDOWN TO CHRISTMAS
As winter progressed, Jeff swore he was getting rheumatism from the damp and cold in his haunt under the stairs. Moss was growing on the cement walls, he said, and a colony of snails was making it their permanent residence. It was true. He was really suffering. We could hear him in the mornings hacking and coughing when he woke up. He would walk to the end of the cement patio and hack and cough and spit gooey things out into the dump.

My little brother had probably always been affected by allergies, and the mold now was aggravating them. As a child, he was constantly sniffling and rubbing his nose. His huge sad eyes always had dark circles under them. It's also very likely that Jeff had suffered from dyslexia too. I remember one particular Christmas when he had labored long and hard writing our annual thank you letter to our grandparents for the presents they sent. When it was finally finished, I saw it was only two sentences, but his scrawled, huge, awkward letters covered the entire page.

Poor Jeff, he struggled so in school. He needed help but nobody did that sort of thing back then, so he just limped along through elementary school also with the added disability of being severely shy. In junior high, he enrolled in band and learned to read music, but by high school, he had had enough and quit. From then on, he was his own teacher. He read avidly, yet his handwriting remained much the same.

Now he was suffering again, and along with the cold, his room had also gotten very crowded with the things he dragged in. As the nights got worse, he finally admitted defeat and moved his bedding upstairs for the winter. Paul's bathtub love seat was pushed against the living room wall and the larger couch stationed in front of the fireplace for added warmth.

Meanwhile, Santa's Workshop in Arlene's bedroom continued to be endlessly busy throughout the day and sometimes into the night, stopping only now and then for a bite of food or a cup of coffee. Christmas got nearer and nearer, and Arlene got more and more into a frenzy of sewing outfits and reconstituting old dollies and toys.

As each day passed, more bric-a-brac collected on the tree. Paul came over almost every day to add another stained-glass ornament or a string of stained-glass lights, which were spectacular. With all her friends working for her, my sister knew this Christmas was going to be the biggest success of them all.

PART II
NATIVITY SCENE

Christmas break at El Camino had ended the music and drama courses for a while for Arlene and Lenny, which was OK because Arlene was busy with her Enchanting Christmas, and Lenny, her faithful chauffeur during that time, had gotten a job singing with a small combo in Hollywood for the season and was too busy now to hang around our house. There were no more trips to the office of Goliath Records for me to type out my latest stories, but I had no time anyway now that I was selling toys five days a week at the department store and working the Insomniac on weekends.

It was Sunday afternoon. Arlene and I had been up late the previous night working at the Insomniac, and now I had been dragging myself around the house for the last hour trying to do a little clearing up. Even the cup of coffee sprinkled with cinnamon and nutmeg had not perked me up. In the living room, the old couch facing the fireplace seemed to invite me to sit down for a bit. The couch still had Jeff's rumpled pillow and blanket on it. I started to reach down to fold up the blanket but stopped; the couch really did look warm and comfy!

On the other side of the room, the kids were quietly drawing Christmas pictures on brown paper bags from the supermarket. Lying on the floor, an old cookie tin full of crayon nubs between them, they looked happily occupied. I told myself that I would just rest for a little while before I finished cleaning up, and plopping down on the couch, pulled the flannel blanket over me. It smelled vaguely like tobacco and Jeff. As I lay there, I listened to the children's voices talking about what they were drawing and heard the pang and pong sounds of rejected crayons being discarded into the tin container as the children searched for that certain shade of green, red, or purple they were looking for.

The murmur of the kids soothed my tired mind and body. Very soon, their words slurred together and lost meaning. Before I knew it, I had drifted off. I don't know how long I was in that delicious state, but eventually the talking sounds again turned back into words and I slowly became aware that along with the voices of the children, an adult voice had been added. As I caught the meaning of the last sentence, I realized that it was Miss Wilhelmina Beek, the Bird Lady. Apparently, she had not seen me on the other side of the couch taking a nap and had silently slipped in to give the children another shot at religion. She was just finishing up her story.

"And so," she said in a hushed voice, "it came to pass that Mary brought forth her firstborn son and wrapped him in swaddling clothes and laid him in a manger because there was no room at the inn."

After a beat, Donnie piped up, "Yeah, but what's a manger?"

"It's kind of a stable or barn," murmured the Bird Lady, still wrapped up in the glory of her story, hardly aware of the momentary pause.

"Like a real barn? Did it have any animals living in it?" inquired Lindee politely.

"But of course, you remember I told you that Joseph and Mary rode to Bethlehem on a donkey? It must have been in the manger too." Becoming more aware now, she sounded pleased that she could pull in this fact and engage the children a little more into the story of the birth of Jesus.

"And what else?" burbled Laurie J. with rising excitement.

"Yeah! What else was in the manger?" echoed Donnie.

The Bird Lady was probably not expecting this sudden interest in animals but sounded happy enough to see they were at least interested in the story.

"Now let me see. Yes, there must have been sheep too, because remember the angels told the shepherds abiding in the fields minding their flocks and said unto them, 'I bring you tidings of great joy for unto you is born a savior, Christ the Lord.' And the shepherds said, 'Let us go and see the Christ child.'"

"—and they brought the sheep," Donnie butted in gleefully.

"How many sheep?" he wanted to know. "A hundred? How could they all fit in the manger?"

Lindee thoughtfully supplied the answer that some of them must have remained outside or maybe the sheep took turns looking at Jesus and then moved on.

"Now, now, children, we are forgetting the most important thing was that the Christ child was born to mankind to save us from sin."

"But what other animals were in the barn with Jesus?" Donnie was not giving up on this train of thought.

"Oh, very well, I guess there must have been a cow or two."

"And chickens," Laurie J. whispered joyfully.

"And ducks," Lindee added. "And geese better scurry," she sang as an afterthought.

"And bears!" Donnie almost yelled.

"No, silly." Lindee was adamant. "This is not The Wizard of Oz. There are no lions or tigers or—"

"—bears!" Donnie yelled again.

"Oh my!" Laurie J. giggled out on cue.

Now the Bird Lady must have thought that things were getting just a little out of hand and wanted to take control of her story again. "Well, actually, Lindee," she said in a serious voice, "they did have lions back then. Remember the story of Samson 'and he slew a lion with his bare hands and a thousand Philistines with the jawbone of an ass.'"

"An ass?" The children giggled.

"Now let's not get silly. That's what they are called," the Bird Lady reprimanded gently.

"So, if there were lions, there could still be bears, so hah, Lindee." Donnie's voice was triumphant. Donnie was a true animal lover, it turned out. His favorite Bible story so far had been Noah and the Ark.

"Now, now, let us get back to the birth of Jesus, shall we?" The

Bird Lady moved on with her story dauntingly. "Now, when Jesus was born in Bethlehem of Judea in the days of King Herod, there came three wise men from the East. They came on their camels asking, 'Where is He that is born King of the Jews, for we have followed his star and have come to worship him?'"

"Hey, wait, wait. How did they follow a star?" Donnie let out a guffaw. "Gee, if you did that you would wind up on the moon!"

I heard the Bird Lady heave a little sigh. "This was a special star, Donnie, and the light from it was so bright that it shone down right onto the manger."

"So now we have more animals in the manger because you forgot to say camels before," admonished Lindee.

Poor Miss Beek, I thought from my warm hideaway on the couch.

Donnie spoke up again. "Those camels are too big to go in the manger. They better stay outta that manger, I think."

"Now children, we are forgetting about the birth of our lord Jesus again, I am afraid," and here she tried for a little laugh.

"Did Jesus get any presents on his birthday?" Laurie J. sounded concerned.

"Why yes," said the Bird Lady, happy to segue into the next part of the story. "The Wise Men brought baby Jesus three gifts."

Laurie J. clapped her hands "Hooray!"

"They brought gold . . ."

"Ahhhhhh gold," breathed the kids in unison.

"And they brought frankincense and myrrh."

"Frankfurters and what?" questioned Lindee.

"Not a puppy?" Donnie broke in sadly.

I could tell by the tone of her voice that the Bird Lady was eager to wrap up the story before she fell into another trap of having to explain what frankincense and myrrh actually were. I'm sure she thought these children were much too curious for their own good, so she diverted them by saying, "Why don't we sing a song about the story I was just telling you about? Shall we sing 'Away in a Manger'?" And before another question could be asked, she started singing in her wobbly contralto. Soon the children joined in.

I had not moved from my position on the couch, so it was not until I heard the end of the song and the Bird Lady tiptoe out of the room closing the door after her, that I lifted up my head and peeped over the back of the couch.

The children had gone back to their drawing. Donnie was now trying to draw a camel. It was then I noticed that Laurie J. was in clown face again.

THE GIFT OF GIVING

Days went by, and now that the tree trimming was done, presents started to appear under the fat fir. Grandma Pauline stopped by all the way from Riverside to drop off her gifts—neat boxes wrapped perfectly in gay paper topped with immaculate bows. Judging from the shape of the boxes, we knew they must all be clothes. I wondered if Pauline ironed her wrapping paper like she did almost everything else. But then again, she didn't have to because everything from her was brand new—unlike our mother's presents that always showed up looking familiar because they would be wrapped in last year's Christmas paper and tied with last year's bows. Her packages always looked a little wrinkled, the ribbons a bit stringy, and there was always that telltale sign of last year's scotch tape yellowing and clinging to the wrapping paper. Mom didn't have to scrounge and save anymore, but the habit was too great for her to change.

Arlene added to this growing horde under the evergreen with her own wrapped gifts. She loved the look of abundance, as if the tree was a cornucopia spilling out presents. In keeping with her personality, my sister's presents were wrapped in a slapdash manner and tied ad hoc, with anything that would do. The so-called ribbons were often strips of material from her sewing box—a bit of rickrack, a piece of velveteen, or a remnant of silk or lace. And sometimes, if you looked closely, you might even recognize that one of those bows on a present was really the sash from Lindee's bathrobe.

One night, about a week before Christmas and just after dinner, all was calm, all was bright. The children, after changing into their pajamas, were playing a game of Chutes and Ladders at the dining room table. Jeff was in the music room practicing one of his Ornette Coleman solos. I was just sitting on the couch after starting a fire in the fireplace, and Arlene was doing the dishes in the kitchen.

Every time Jeff stopped playing, I could hear the murmurs and exclamations of the kids as their pieces rose and sank in the game. Beyond that, I could hear water running in the sink and the gentle clinking of dishes and silverware as Arlene set them out to drain. Actually, they didn't drain as there was no draining rack, and Arlene, for some reason, invariably placed the dishes right side up so that when you picked up a cup or plate the next morning, there was often a little puddle of water in it.

I had just gotten comfortable back on the couch, when there was the familiar light tap of the Bird Lady at the door. It was strange, I thought, reluctantly getting up, for her to visit at night. When I opened the door, I was surprised to see she was not alone. Standing next to her was a middle-aged man and woman. They stood dwarfing her with their stolid bulk. They had with them a young boy of about ten or eleven years old. The man held an open cardboard box in his arms. The woman clutched her purse tightly before her, and the little boy held onto an undernourished two-foot Christmas tree.

They stood there for a few seconds looking uncomfortable with the darkness behind them before the Bird Lady finally spoke up. "Hello, dear," she said to me as she stepped gingerly into the living room. "Is your sister and the children at home?" The silent family followed closely behind Miss Beek and immediately started to peer surreptitiously around the room. The mother and father soon had a look of distaste on their faces. The boy just looked.

About then, Arlene came to the living room doorway, drying her hands on her capri pants. There was a questioning look on her face. She was used to people dropping in at all hours, but she sensed that this time something was different. I was easing backward away from the cold stare of these people as Arlene, still a little confused, moved into the living room. As I continued to step back, the Bird Lady smiled at my sister and introduced the formidable group still behind her.

"This is the Robinson family," she burbled out gaily. The Robinson family mumbled their hellos. "They belong to my church. We are all members of The Sacred Heart of Our Lady of the Apple, and I have told them all about the unfortunate circumstances that have come into your life."

At this point, the man with the box thrust it out toward Arlene, who was standing stock-still as if in shock. "Here," he said a bit gruffly, "some food." When Arlene didn't respond, he put it down at his feet, annoyed.

"Well, we thought it could help," the woman said stiffly.
By this time, the kids were peeking around the dining room door. Slowly, they inched into the room and clutched the waistband of their mother's capri pants, which were still damp from the dishwashing. For my part, I continued my retreat, slowly backing up and almost bumping into Jeff, who had stopped playing when the door opened. Now, he was peering around the fireplace from the music room. He still had his sax strapped to his neck.

Back in the living room, I could see Arlene's hands begin to clench—opening and closing, opening and closing. I hoped she wouldn't get too angry. The Bird Lady was only trying to help, but the whole thing was humiliating. Finally, Arlene choked out some sort of greeting. The funny thing was that the only one who wasn't ill at ease was our Bird Lady. She warbled on and on about "Christmas is the season for love and giving." The Robinson family remained almost mute and seemed to be stuck to the floor, unable to move their arms and legs except in a rigid way. They reminded me of the tin family from my old dollhouse.

At last, Mother Robinson nudged her little boy, who was still looking around at the house.

"Stewart," she hissed. "Remember what you are supposed to do."

Stewart eyed the fat, decorated tree and the buxom pile of presents underneath and in a stilted voice, as if reciting in front of his class a rehearsed poem said, "Here is a Christmas tree to give good cheer for you and your family." He took another look around the warm living room at the cozy fire in the fireplace, at the room flickering and glowing with golden accents and at the tree again decked out with its cornucopia of presents underneath, then blurted out. "They don't look so poor to me. You said they were poor!" He glared at his parents because they of course probably had to wheedle and drag him here with a big sob story.

With this blast of refreshing honesty, Arlene stepped forward and received the spindly little fir with a grim smile and wedged the pathetic object next to our luxuriously plump evergreen as if to say. "Wah-da you tink of dat, Mr. and Mrs. Robinson?"

The Bird Lady, sensing the tension at last, clapped her hands together. "Well, isn't this just lovely," she said gesturing at the cardboard box and runty little tree. I think we should all sing a hymn, don't you?"

For my part, I found the whole thing embarrassing, and continued to ease myself out of the room just as the Bird Lady started to warble out the beginning of "Oh Come, All Ye Faithful" in her flutelike voice. I made my way backward silently, remembering to step down just in time into the music room where I hid behind the fireplace, hoping I wouldn't be spotted and called in to join them in song.

Before ducking behind the fireplace, I got a good look at my sister who now had an amused look on her face because the Robinson mother and father were clearly more uncomfortable than she was as they stumbled into the choral piece in low, muted voices. Music was Arlene's territory, and to show she could not in the least be intimidated, she started singing out in a clear strong voice the way she used to do when she was in The Girls Chorus at Jordan Junior High School. She even added a second soprano harmony part to the carol.

Soon, the children joined in the song, and a few seconds later, I heard Jeff shuffle over and add, with his saxophone, a jazzy riff behind the melody. I peeked around the corner. The light from the fireplace flickered on the little group and made them stand out in the dim living room. They were now gently swaying to the music. When the song ended, the Bird Lady, all aglow, and the Robinsons, looking tired, took their leave. It was sometime later that we remembered to look into the cardboard box.

There were only five or six items in the carton. We picked them up one by one to marvel at them. It was obvious the Robinsons had gone through their cupboard and discarded all the things they were never going to eat. "Look at this! No home should be without these items," Arlene remarked glibly as she pulled out first a small skinny bottle of horseradish. "That must have been in the back of their refrigerator for at least eight years," I added tartly.

Next were two cans of peas and carrots. I couldn't see the expiration date, but the rims of the cans were beginning to rust. After that was an equally rusted and dented can of Campbell's Spaghetti-O's, then, nestled between the cans, we retrieved a squatty jar of cocktail sausages looking to my mind like pink cutoff thumbs sitting in a glutinous, jelly-like substance. Almost as awful was a larger jar of pickled cauliflower and almost as an afterthought, the family had stuck into the carton, a box of number #8 spaghetti—already opened. "Ah," said Arlene in her most sarcastic voice, "we feast tonight!"

PART III
CHRISTMAS DAY
SANTA CLAUS HAS COME TO TOWN

The big day finally arrived. We had stayed up late the night before, first to outwait the children until they finally settled down and went to sleep, and second, to arrange all the unwrapped presents so they would be there when the children first woke up. At last, Arlene came tiptoeing back from their room and heaved a sigh. "They are finally dead to the world. We can start the magic now!" Out came the hidden treasures everyone had been secretly working on. This was Arlene's favorite part, to put everything on display so it would make a big impression as the morning light hit the tinsel. Finally, all was arranged and we crept off to bed.

The next morning, I heard the scramble of small feet running into the living room and the giggles and shrieks of joy as the children saw all the toys. They were still oh-ing and ahh-ing as I climbed down from the loft and Jeff unraveled himself from the blankets on the couch. Even Arlene, sleep tousled as ever, crept out of bed when she heard the children. Tottering out of her room and clinging drowsily to the doorway of the living room for support, she smiled at the happy scene before she made her way into the kitchen to start the oatmeal and coffee.

There were so many things crowding the living room. Everyone had come through for the kids. The largest present was from Jeff. He had put together a bike. There had been many different sources for the parts used to make this vehicle, and each one was a different color. There were no fancy trimmings—no lights, bells, or even handlebar grips, and the tires were made from a strange rock-hard substance; even so, the children were ecstatic.

There was a cunning dollhouse from Paul made from cardboard boxes. The outside, a replica of Culper Court with painted red shingles and windows and doors trimmed in white. It also had a pitched roof but instead of shingles, it was covered with Christmas candy stuck firmly in place. The interior was decorated with remnants of wallpaper, while an assortment of matchboxes, toothpicks, hairpins, and empty wooden spools of thread were transformed into furniture for each room. As a bonus, a whole pipe cleaner family—mom, dad, and two children—were cleverly fashioned and smartly dressed in scraps of fabric. Some were sitting around the kitchen table on the wooden spool chairs, and while others relaxed on the milk carton couch in the living room, another was to be found asleep in its matchbox bed.

Next to the dollhouse, two newly painted Tonka Trucks—a yellow cement mixer and a green dump truck—stood side by side for Donnie to find, along with a set of timpani drums made from several different sizes of coffee cans. There were new dresses for the resident dolls of the house and new blankets and pillows for their cradles and beds that Arlene had produced.

Yet, out of all the presents, the two pint-sized perambulators for Lindee and Laurie J. were the most impressive. They were sparkling white and decorated with a regal gold emblem on each side making it look as if they were baby carriages for royalty. Tucked inside each buggy was an old-fashioned Kewpie Doll with a single curl gracing the top of its head and a pair of permanently pursed lips ready for a bottle. The previous night, when Arlene proudly brought the carriages out, I gasped and asked where she could possibly have found such wonderful things? She shook her head and said she couldn't tell me. She had taken a vow of secrecy, then, grabbing my hand and squeezing it, told me in an awestruck voice. "They are from an honest to God antique shop." It was then I realized I knew who had brought them. It was the "secret" part that gave it away. It had to be from Bill Connelly. Bill Connelly, who never wanted to be thanked for all the nice things he did for us. The Bill Connelly who would never have come to someone's house with a mangy Christmas tree and a few rusty canned goods, embarrassing everyone by making them feel poor. Bill Connelly, like Father Christmas, knew just how to give.

After all the big stuff was properly admired, the kids tore into the wrapped gifts. Arlene had outdone herself with her latest designs for the girls, using brocades, velveteen, or taffeta fabrics for their dresses, further adorning them with pearl buttons and lace appliqué collars. I had fallen back on my art skills to make the children small replicas of themselves in the form of cardboard paper dolls. Each doll had its own line of clothing, designed and drawn on paper all ready to be cut out. Being practical, I also purchased three children's-size scissors. Laurie J.'s paper replica had a sturdy cardboard body, chin-length white blonde hair, and freckles across her nose. Lindee's double was taller and her blonde hair longer. She was posed like a dancer. I gave Donnie's cutout light brown hair, a little potbelly, and, for good measure, added a cardboard puppy to keep Cardboard-Donnie company.

From their "Mema" (as Arlene had dubbed our mother when Lindee was first born), the children received some much-needed outfits for school. Mom had made them on her still-trusty portable and beloved Singer sewing machine, which I remembered being with us through every move and new home. From gay summer shorts to Halloween costumes, I lost count of all the clothes and bedroom do-overs she had fashioned for us over the years on that very same machine.

From Grandma Pauline, there were practical socks and underwear, plus three matching outfits handmade by Pauline herself. Arlene tried not to laugh when she saw that her mother-in-law had chosen a fabric covered in large red geraniums in flowerpots for the three matching outfits. "Did you ever see such a god-awful pattern than that?" my sister whispered to me out of the side of her mouth.

FLAUNTING THE RICHES

As soon as breakfast was finished, the kids were out the door: Donnie to dig in the dump with his trucks and Lindee and Laurie J. to parade with their grand perambulators and their "Siamese twin dolls," as they called them. It was Lindee's idea to pretend to be snooty, stuck-up rich ladies with their babies, so Lindee and Laurie J. put their noses in the air and strutted up and down the alley drawing comments from the neighbor kids who were out with their new toys.

When the Christmas bike came out, everyone on the block wanted a turn to ride it. None of the children were even big enough to sit on the seat, but that didn't stop them from coasting down the hill. All went well until one kid refused to wait his turn and a tug of war broke out between the boy and Lindee. After a scuffle, Lindee's eyebrow received a gash from one of the bare handlebars, a scar she would carry through her life. Yet, even that calamity didn't take the glow off of this very special Christmas.

Later, I was told that they were the envy of all the kids on the block and, strangely enough, not because of the fancy perambulators with their antique dolls and not the exciting bicycle; no, Lindee said the other kids were the most amazed and impressed by the paper dolls I had made that looked just like them.

PART II

A man works for the circus. It is his job to clean up after the animals. All day he picks up manure from the horses, camels, elephants, even lions and tigers. After several months, he notices a rash. He tries every kind of ointment and salve, but the rash doesn't go away. At last, the man goes to a doctor who puts him through all kinds of tests. When the test results are in, the doctor tells the man that he is allergic to animal dung.

The man. But doctor, what shall I do?

Doctor: That's easy; you must quit your job.

The man: What? And give up show business?

A variation of a 1958 showbiz joke first printed in a column by Hedda Hopper.

CHAPTER 36
HEALTH KICK

AND

FROM THE GRAY NOTEBOOK
ARLENE

JANUARY

The New Year came quietly. I watched the crowd in Times Square on our small TV. Except for Arlene's children, everyone in our family had been born in New York City. *We might still be there if we hadn't come to California,* I thought a bit glumly. I might have been part of that crowd whooping it up, throwing confetti and blowing paper horns out there on the streets of the Big Apple if my father hadn't been tempted to become a movie star back in the 1940s. Maybe I would already have gotten a job in an art department and been living somewhere in Greenwich Village.

I had only vague memories of New York: riding on a subway with my mother and zooming out of a tunnel to suddenly find ourselves high up in the air looking down on a dark city. I remember icicles hanging from the eaves of roofs and bottles of milk left by the milkman frozen on doorsteps. I remember kids taking turns sledding down a hill. They told me I was too little to take a ride. When our family left for California, I was four and never did get to take that sled ride down the hill.

We still had relatives in New York: grandparents, aunts, uncles, and several cousins. Every few years they came to visit. We didn't know them very well. We were used to growing up without relatives, and it never occurred to me until now that my mother must have missed her family, that great plethora of aunts and uncles and cousins she had. When Harry brought us all out here to live, she must have been lonely sometimes, especially when Harry was away.

On the TV, the crowd was still reveling, but the New Year wouldn't arrive here for three more hours. There was really nothing to stay up for. There would be no ball dropping or fireworks. I turned the knob all the way to off and with a click, the screen shrunk down to a white dot, then disappeared. I sighed. *Shouldn't I be making a New Year's resolution?* Two days ago, I had my birthday. I was twenty-three and next year I would be twenty-four. That was only one year until twenty-five. I was pushing twenty-five. A person should *be* something by twenty-five, shouldn't they?

A scary feeling crept over me. How could I be anything here? In California, one needed a car to get to work, but to buy a car one needed a job to get that money to buy that car to get to work . . . It was a vicious circle and, well, I didn't even know how to drive. At some point, I realized, I would have to move to a city with good transportation like San Francisco or Chicago or New York. It was something to think about, but hadn't I seen snow on the ground in Times Square? The beginning of winter was not the right time to rush off to Chicago or New York and start a new life, I told myself, and then I got up to make a cup of coffee.

NEW YEAR'S RESOLUTIONS

"We are going on a health kick!" Arlene stood, almost defiantly, feet spaced apart on the dust-colored rug. "I am going to give up everything bad!" She listed on her fingers, "Late nights, coffee, cigarettes (now there's a bad habit and expensive too). This new year will be different. From now on, Lorraine, we are going to take a therapeutic run on the ocean every morning!"

"I'm glad you consulted me," I said a bit archly, sitting down at the table with a now-forbidden cup of coffee. "Look, I believe in health and all that but Arlene . . . running out in the cold . . . morning?" I couldn't imagine it. The first thing I ran for in the morning was the heater or the kitchen for a hot cup of coffee.

"Look at you!" continued Arlene, the health expert. "Your skin and eyes are yellow! You are out of shape. And me, look—a pot belly at twenty-six!"

"Twenty-seven," I corrected, then added, "Is my skin really yellow?"

Arlene nodded.

"OK, OK, let's exercise, but not out in the cold morning. And to start things off," I dared, "let's see *you* do a sit-up."

Arlene got down on the floor and lay on her back, arms folded behind her head, and started grunting. Several attempts at rising more than an inch failed. "Oh my God!" she panted out. "Every last muscle in my stomach is pooped. Oh well, I'll soon get it back." She scrambled to her feet. "Now we have to make a list for our new beginning. Quick," she snapped her fingers at me, "I need paper and pencil."

I purposely did not tell Arlene about the ballpoint pen and the gray notebook of blank pages I had up in my loft, which would have been to lose them forever, so after searching ten minutes, a stubby pencil turned up and, except for a small tear in one, a few presentable pieces of paper. It was starting again, I thought—big plans and good intentions that never materialized.

"Number one," Arlene said out loud, pencil poised. "Get rid of bad influences. That means Sid, Rita, and Howard." Arlene firmly wrote down their names on the paper, then rested her pencil on the table.

"Why are they bad influences?" I asked, a bit confused.

Arlene didn't answer. She was still thinking hard, then picked up the pencil again. "Number two," she called out. "Eat healthy diet." Then she was several minutes scribbling on the paper inventing her diet. She wrote in capital letters: ELIMINATION DIET. After that she wrote down a list of things. It wasn't that long because it was an elimination diet, after all. There was a lot of water and juices and salads and vegetable broth, also goat's milk and a coffee substitute.

Coffee substitute! Oh no! I thought, and also wondered where we would get the goat's milk. We didn't live in farm country anymore but Arlene kept writing.

"There, that should do it," Arlene said as she used the last bit of the stub of her pencil to draw a line under the title: ELIMINATION DIET.

After rereading what she had just written, Arlene finally answered my earlier question.

"Now about Rita, I like her, and yes she is a wonderful person." Here, Arlene paused for a moment and thought. "But she has bad hang-ups. She is sick and I get the brunt of it." Arlene looked at me seriously. "You know after that last fight, I'd had it! I'm finished being her friend! Now, don't look at me that way, Lorraine. Don't you remember what she did to you?" I didn't respond so Arlene refreshed my memory. "Remember that time when she first started as an artist model, when she wanted an all-over tan and started sunbathing in the buff?"

I nodded.

"Well don't you remember how Rita got you to join her one day? She even persuaded little modest you to take off your bathing suit, and then later she told everyone what you looked like naked!"

I winced at the memory. We had all been sitting around the table one night. Paul and Howard K. Small were there too, and when the conversation drifted into a lull, Rita blurted out gaily all the details of my anatomy. I wanted to disappear under the table, but I think poor Paul was even more embarrassed than I was.

"You see what I mean now, don't you?" Arlene gloated, reading my face.

"She just thinks she is being entertaining," I said in Rita's defense, and then added weakly, "I don't think she can help it!"

"Exactly, that is why we should stay away from her." Arlene rested her case.

It was useless to argue when my sister was in this kind of mood. I wondered about Howard and Sid being on the kick-out list too. What did Sid do? Did he go back to his old girlfriend? I decided not to ask.

As it turned out, Howard refused to be gotten rid of. Arlene tried to tell him he was sick, and it was upsetting to her—his tics, his weirdness, his nonstop monologues. He was driving her crazy, but he would hear none of it. He just kept returning to Culper Court, bearing gifts of firewood that he stole from houses under construction and, of course, he still wouldn't stop talking.

"My romantic situation . . . Man—Gil and I are nowhere . . . I don't know what to do . . . also my ex is bugging me for back alimony . . . this money scene is really ridiculous!" As usual, Howard explained in great detail all the actions of his day: "Got up, man . . . ate a peanut butter sandwich . . . Worked on tunes on the piano . . . put some of them down on onionskin sheet music . . . sent some tapes to recording companies, then went to Hollywood to record more tunes . . . stopped at the Laundromat . . . washed a few shirts . . . Hey, is there any coffee?" he would ask as the new kettle on the stove suddenly whistled shrilly. Anyway, Howard was here to stay.

In spite of this failure, Arlene stuck the finished (we did have to hunt up another pencil) Health Kick list on the outside of her bedroom door. It read:

HEALTH KICK
1. Get rid of bad influences
2. Eat only good food
3. Exercise every day
4. Practice singing
5. Learn to read music
6. Practice piano
7. Start sewing again
8. Get clothes in order
9. Get house in order

We never did go on that therapeutic morning run on the beach, for which I was very glad and after only a few days of the elimination diet, Arlene proclaimed us purged of all toxins and thereafter, fell back into her regular diet of coffee, cigarettes, and a morning breakfast of greasy bacon and eggs. As for the other demands on the list—there was a real effort for about a week with Arlene at the piano, painstakingly playing the chords from the sheet music of "'Round Midnight" while singing the melody. That took care of four, five, and six on the list. Then there was a flurry of cleaning house and straightening out cupboards and drawers one weekend, which was good because Arlene then uncovered the sewing machine that had been buried under a pile of her clothes and, inspired by the find, whipped up another one of her creations that she called her "Betty Grable lounging pajamas," made from an old chenille bedspread. All this effort seemed to satisfy Arlene, and a few days later, the list was gone from the door.

As for Arlene's Elimination Diet of cleansing herself of "certain people," well, that weakened too. Soon Rita was back at our house as vivacious as ever, giving out sage advice and telling bawdy stories of her flirtatious adventures, with the airline pilot from Brazil. The only one not to return was Sid. I guess he did go back to his old girlfriend after all.

My New Year's resolution was to get back to writing again. All the rush and bustle of Christmas and working had gotten me out of the habit. With no work to interfere now, I crawled up to my loft and scribbled away in the gray notebook with my still intact ballpoint pen. I was pleased enough with the results of my first attempt and put the finished piece onto the pile of writing that I would eventually take with me to type out in Hollywood now that Lenny had finished his stint with the singing group.

FROM THE GRAY NOTEBOOK
ARLENE

Arlene is my older sister, an incurable idealist who flutters hysterically through life. Her one marriage has been a series of short turbulent love affairs and long separations. Eight years of this has brought her three tow-headed children and one brother and one sister for babysitters. Her romantic spirit, however, still runs high and she returns time after time to the dream of the one perfect love.

Her day is a series of dramatic episodes in which she plays many roles. She is a scatterbrained dumb blonde doing everything backward, a sophisticated jazz singer, an innocent baby bursting with excitement, a hardened gun moll, brittle and cynical—talking crude, swaggering, hands on hips, cigarette dangling—or a neurotic old lady wilting in bed with a headache rag soaking her forehead, fingers curled in pain like twisted twigs.

In a group, she is the center of attention. Her animated face and dramatic gestures dominate the conversation, and people cluster to watch in amused fascination. Coming out at night, glittering and sparkling, Arlene is a firefly—never still.

Nothing is commonplace about her life when she tells you about it. A simple trip to the store turns into an adventure with all the drama of an Alfred Hitchcock thriller. Strange men stare ready to attack, or fall in love and follow her home.

Fierce family ties cause her to verbally demolish anyone who speaks out against her family. She expects the same loyalty in return. She is generous and giving and can't stand stinginess from others, especially her family.

She races around for her happiness like a kid who tears into the Christmas presents at once and ends up confused and disappointed, not knowing which toy to play with. She has no conception of what the "one big thing" to do with her life is, so she does them all.

"I should study and learn to be a technically good musical artist.

"No, I should go to school and learn a practical trade.

"I should go back to my husband and be the woman behind the man and a normal mother to my children.

"I should move away, start all over again."

Her standing joke is "I'm going to give up ridiculous ideals and marry a fat old millionaire who will love me and take care of us all."

But we know her romantic illusions would never let her do it.

She is the type of person who:

- Wants many things and tosses them away when she gets them,
- Can't be left alone at night because she is afraid of maniacs,

- Tells a bus driver who won't let her on for free, where to shove it,
- Skips down the street with the kids on each arm singing like Ethel Merman,
- Thinks the president's "New Frontier Policy" was a new western series on TV,
- Throws a plate of spaghetti in anger then ends up laughing,
- Thinks her soul will get lost if she is hypnotized.

Surprisingly enough, Arlene's children are fairly normal, not the thin emaciated souls with tortured eyes cringing in corners sucking their thumbs that you might think of, but three bubbles of pot-bellied energy bounding and crashing—dragging sand and bugs through the house.

Lindee, the oldest, is silver tinsel—a seven-year-old kicking slim legs in perfect rhythm as she dances through the house. Six-year-old Donnie is a miniature football player picking daisies in a field or softly crying over a Shirley Temple movie. Laurie J. is the shy one who silently creeps into your lap to kiss your hand. She is five.

They are quite used to moving in and out of the red house, having a grandmother living with them one day then an uncle or an aunt or all three the next week. The house and the people are part of their lives and they embrace it all.

BABIES

I think I should add a bit of a postscript here. Reading this character study over to myself, I was struck with how Arlene is known for being excitable, out of control, and, let's face it, sometimes angry at the drop of a hat, while I am thought of as passive and giving—no trouble at all. The surprising thing is that it wasn't always this way.

Some years ago, I was rummaging in a closet and found a Baby Book. There were some blank pages where Mom had written what we were all like as babies—our personalities. Jeff was a mama's boy—very shy and loved to be kissed and carried. Bill was loveable but hard to potty train. He liked to play with toy soldiers and open and close doors, which frequently ended with his fingers getting caught.

Since Arlene was first, Mom had more time to write about her, and what she says is a glowing report. "Baby Arlene is very sweet, and good. She is joyful and sunny and sings and plays happily all day long." Then later, "At three she can recite poems and nursery rhymes and performs patty cakes—a happy baby." That surprised me because it did not sound like the volatile sister I knew. What surprised me even more was what my mother said about me: "Lorraine is a happy baby and loves to dance to music but has a quick temper." And later she added, "Lorraine at three is very stubborn and will throw tantrums."

When I asked Mom about this, she said it was true. I was so bad that one day, when Harry came home, he had to give me a big spanking. I don't remember any of this, and it just goes to show that . . . actually I don't know what it goes to show. Just, I guess, that life is strange and maybe we don't know who we are until it is all over.

CHAPTER 37
BLOW ILL WIND

AND
FROM THE GRAY NOTEBOOK
THE RED COTTAGE

NEW YEAR, OLD MEMORIES

After Christmas, Marches Department Store called me back and kept me on for a while doing inventory of their stock. I was shifted to different departments with a clipboard and pen to count the merchandise. It had something to do with declaring taxes on leftover items.

The kids went back to school, and Arlene signed up for a more advanced drama class. Lenny had dropped out and was making another attempt at living in Hollywood, but by now Arlene had enough friends in the class to be able to get rides back and forth to El Camino. In a pinch, Jeff could be counted on to ferry her there too, if he wasn't hanging out with his new musician friends in Santa Monica. There were new things starting too. Sara Lee had had her baby. He was a boy, and they named him Valiant or Val for short. Now that he was a few months old, it was more important than ever to find a bigger place, she said.

Every so often, I remembered the thoughts I had on New Year's Eve, about making some sort of move in some sort of direction. One morning, in this mood, I sat down and tried to sort things out. The trouble was it was much easier to just keep going along as I was. I knew my sister would let me live with her and the kids forever. She always did want me around, even when she was a teenager and I was just the little sister she dragged along to the movies or to her friends' houses. From the beginning, I was her best audience and confidant. Even when she married and had her first baby, she still wanted me there with her.

Living with Arlene, all in all, was not a bad trade off. We balanced each other. She brought drama into my life, and I calmed her and kept her steady in hers. Even being poor was entertaining, while being poor with my mother had just been sad. Again, that old feeling of being ungrateful flooded over me. My mother had always worked hard to make things easier for us. With Mom, you would always be clean and well fed and you wouldn't constantly run out of tissue paper or continually experience large and small disasters but . . . but—and here was a new thought—hadn't Mom chosen Harry to marry because *he* made *her* life exciting? I had to admit that being with my father *was* always entertaining. Even when you were two hundred miles from home in a broken-down car with two flat tires, stuck on the side of a dark and busy highway in the middle of the night with no flares, my father could turn something like that into a thrilling escapade. Or when we finally limped home and a mile from our house, the car started pouring out black smoke from the engine and Harry yelled . . . "It's going to blow! Everybody run for cover!" and the whole family barreled out of the vehicle any way we could and ran for our lives. (We even had to save Harry's snarly new dog that kept trying to bite us as we ran.) And when we were finally safely away, waiting for the big explosion, and instead witnessed the car just give a little sigh, then die right there by the curb—that, we all agreed, was truly hilarious. Or the biggest adventure of all, when Harry took the family (except me and Mom) and drove across the entire United States in a new Cadillac hooked to an overloaded U-Haul trailer. Arlene, Bill, and Jeff talked about it for weeks afterward. I could go on telling Harry stories. With all his faults, Harry, like Arlene, made everything—no matter how dire—fun.

So, if Mom married Harry for an exciting life, what did Harry get from Mom? I was surprised that the answer came to me so easily now that I had taken the time to think about it. Mom and all the rest of us and the white house and the green lawn and the backyard with its vegetable garden and chicken coop and dogs and cats and even a horse once, was his safe harbor, his periodic dip into normalcy, his very own health farm. My father even had a car once, a station wagon, and on one side he painted in big white letters "Harry the Hipster's Health Farm."

When Harry came home between engagements, he left behind his wild nightlife and turned into a day person. He started getting up earlier and earlier until he was on our schedule. He sat in the sun and got tan. He put on comfortable corduroy pants and cowboy boots and went for long walks. He ate good homemade food. He relaxed and gained weight.

Harry loved to be pampered and served. He demanded a special diet unknown to the rest of the family. If he had breakfast, it was the works—fresh-squeezed orange juice, sausage, bacon, sunny-side up eggs—no oatmeal or cornflakes for him. On his toast was real butter not margarine. For dinner, he had a chop of the best quality meat—a tenderloin or a sirloin steak, a center cut of lamb with potatoes and fresh vegetables. At least we ate the same vegetables. We still had our regular dinner fare with Mom of meatloaves, pot roasts, soups, and stews. Whenever my father lived with us, our refrigerator and cupboards would suddenly be filled with exotic things like spicy Italian and German sausages, bagels, matzos, and pretzels. There were bottles of seltzer water, beer, and wild cherry soda. There was bread from a bakery, usually rye, with caraway seeds.

When Harry had his meals, he would sit at the formal dining room table that we used only on special holidays or birthdays. He would eat with great gusto, talking all the while about what happened on one of his tours, how the audience loved him and wouldn't let him stop playing.

I was amazed my mother said nothing at all about the food my father didn't eat. We could never leave the table unless our plates were absolutely cleared, but Harry could take a few lusty bites of his dinner and push his plate away with enough food leftover for a whole kid's meal. There would always be bits and pieces of his dinner scattered around the plate—hunks of bread sucking up gravy, the remnants of a chop with big chunks of meat still clinging to the bone (the gristle and fat untouched of course), the less chewy part of several spears of asparagus piled languidly over each other . . .

With the thoughts of my father's love of good food still resonating in my head, I slowly realized I had become very hungry. I still hadn't decided on any course of action for my life, but I had figured out some things, and I didn't have to be in any hurry about life changes yet, did I? Getting up from the couch, I wondered, *Do I have time for a peanut butter sandwich before dinner?*

STORMY WEATHER

There is a saying that "It never rains in sunny California," but that isn't true. January and February are the wettest months. When we had to sell our home in Burbank and move to Riverside, it was Valentine's Day. The moving van pulled up to the wooden two-bedroom bungalow perched on a sloping hill, and it had looked pretty. Everything was a deep verdant green, and our hilly lawn with the cement staircase going up to our small clapboard house looked almost picturesque. Across Mission Boulevard, which was really just a sleepy country road, was an emerald field with horses grazing.

We were out in the country, but we decided "This might not be so bad after all," as we pulled to a stop in front of the house and let the cat out of the car. By June, the green meadows had turned yellow and the cool breezes had given way to hot, arid ones. During the summer, a hot blast of air hit you in the face like a fired-up furnace whenever you opened the door to go outside. We discovered that Riverside was a semi-desert; ninety degrees was almost the norm throughout August.

In contrast, Hermosa Beach was cooler in the summer and warmer in the winter than just a few miles inland. Nevertheless, winter could get cold, especially if a storm came in from the ocean. This new year was bringing on some rainy days. Jeff was still sleeping on the couch, so he was unaffected, but I had to rearrange my boxes again in the loft so they wouldn't get dripped on. Arlene's room also got a bit damp, but it was the children's room that suffered the most. I could always hear Arlene swearing loudly after a downpour as she discovered the damage where again she had to drag the children's mattresses outside to dry.

One day, dark clouds rode in from the ocean and a true storm overcame our beach town.

Earlier that morning, Rita had come by hoping Arlene could fix her hair before she went to work. "Yoo-hoo!" she called, jumping out of her scarred-up station wagon that was still running. "Yoo-hoo!" Rita was wearing a black lace slip underneath a short car coat and using a shower curtain to protect her hair from the rain. The yoo-hooing continued as Rita jumped over the puddles to our porch. Left behind, the car engine idled in the rain, quivering and moaning like an impatient puppy in expectation of its mistress's speedy return. Arlene did her best with Rita's uncooperative hair, and soon she was off again rumbling down the hill in her grumpy car.

"Yoo-hoo," sang out Rita as she jumped out
of her scarred-up station wagon clad only
in a short car coat and a black lace slip.

We were glad later when Howard K. Small came by with some scraps of wood for the fireplace. He and Arlene ran over some tunes, then he said he had to get back to Gillian before she threw a jealous fit. By noon, the day had gotten even darker, and along with the rain a wind started swirling around the house, blowing into all the cracks and crevices and making mournful sounds. Every so often, a gust shook and rattled the windows and doors. On and on it continued throughout the day.

Arlene went to bed with one of her migraines. She blamed it on the weather. According to her, the storm had brought some sort of inversion in the air and it was crushing her brain, so the rest of us tiptoed around trying not to make loud noises. Except for the din outside, it was unusually quiet. The wind and a sick mother had subdued the kids. School had been canceled and they were at the dining room table playing a restrained game of Parcheesi with Jeff, who had been outside earlier. He had felt the wind blowing on the side of his truck, making it lean precariously whenever he turned corners, he said.

I thought it would be a good idea to make popcorn in the fireplace, but we soon realized it had all been used up for Christmas. There were no marshmallows either, so we settled on pieces of bread stuck onto straightened-out hangers. Every so often, a gust of wind howled down the chimney making the flames of the fire flare up.

Why was the wind so eerie? It made me remember a book I read about the life of Vincent van Gogh. When the painter was living in Arles, he wrote a letter to his brother about the wind. He called it a minstrel. It blew so often and so constantly that he felt it was driving him crazy, and soon he cut off his ear and was later sent to a sanatorium for the insane.

Now, I knew what he meant. The wind was creepy, mournful and desolate were apt words. Also, if I listened closely, I could hear the ocean just a few blocks away, adding its angry roar to the doleful wind. I huddled on the couch. *I better not think about this too much*, I cautioned myself, *or I might just wind up cutting off an ear or two.*

My minstrel increased in force. If you opened the back door, it flew open out of your control, if you tried the front door, a giant hand pushed it closed again. At times, it felt as if we were being mauled by the constant vibrations of the wind that whooshed and howled and threw gusting blasts of air.

I decided to take my mind off morbid thoughts, so up in my loft, I got out the gray notebook. I hadn't written in it since that piece about Arlene. I opened to a blank page and started to write. Later, what I wrote would be typed out on my next trip into Hollywood (whenever that would be).

THE RED HOUSE

I love and hate the red house. It is home, but sometimes I run away to Mom's to sleep on a bed with legs and have meals served to me. Then boredom comes, and I return to scrub and sweep, but the bathroom looks like throw up and the kids screech and fall under my feet. The roof leaks, making swampy bedrooms, and floors lie dingy and dull to taunt a scrub brush. The rug, too, a dust and jam incrusted mat that defies sweeping. It's clutter, clutter, peanut butter on the sofa.

Why does Arlene have to use my toothbrush?

Why can't the children shut the door or pick up wet towels?

"Kids, eat that squash, it's good for you!"

"Lindee, don't tattle!"

"Donnie, must you fall into everything?"

"Laurie J., stop talking baby talk!"

But sometimes a light falls on a wooden bowl filled with oranges near children absorbed in van Gogh-like images of their minds—fat fingers struggling with crayons. Or the phonograph plays "Fire Bird Suite" and everyone is up in an impromptu dance-drama—rolling, twisting on the floor, Lindee twirling, Donnie jumping, Laurie J. running in circles.

It's all alone at 1:00 a.m. practicing piano, reaching out for a "Howard K. Small Chord"—a dominant seventh with a flatted fifth and an extended ninth, while ginger cookies bake in the oven.

It's Rita, Tad, or someone dropping by to talk—coffee steaming into the evening and a fire to burn our backs while we keep warm.

It's a walk on the Strand singing *The Wizard of Oz* while the air is cool and the sky purple with boat lights in the harbor.

It's sun on the back porch in the morning watching the kids pick daisies in the dump by the oil wells that peck at the earth like great black crows or frosty mornings dressing by the heater, toasting bread on top, melting gob-drops of butter and cinnamon.

And then, the red house can be a magic house.

After I finished writing the short sketch or vignette, as I would now call them, I went back and reread it, making a few changes. It was pretty good, I thought. I could do one for Jeff or maybe Mom. Maybe I could just sprinkle them throughout the book I was writing like I was going to do with the illustrations and . . . I had almost forgotten the wind.

CHAPTER 38
A GOOD DEED

BILL CONNELLY

I stared at the walls of Bill Connelly's bathroom. I had never seen a purple bathroom before. It reminded me of that silly rhyme about a cow.

> *I never saw a purple cow,*
> *I never hope to see one.*
> *But I can tell you anyhow,*
> *I'd rather see than be one.*

Actually, it would be more accurate to describe the color in the bathroom as a radiant lavender. Lavender or purple, it was a striking color for a man's bathroom. I turned to Bill Connelly who was standing in the doorway with his Siamese cat, Fang, in his arms.

"Just what did you have in mind for me to do to this bathroom?" I asked. "Rita told me you wanted a mural so I brought my paint box."

Bill smiled shyly. "Well, Rita said you were a fine artist and then you did so well with the Superman emblem, I thought you might like another challenge. As you can see, I have already prepared a canvas for you." He motioned to the walls.

"Yes, it looks newly painted," I said.

"It is. Actually, I am really doing all this for Fang here. You see, whenever I come into the bathroom to do my business, Fang here goes right to his dreck box and does his. So, I thought, since we spend so much time here together, that a mural would be interesting and entertaining for us to look at."

After this somewhat curious speech, he put his cat down. Fang promptly started poking around looking for his dreck box—I mean his litter box—but it was now in the other room, so the cat wandered out in search of it. I heard the squeals of the children in the other room and figured that they had discovered Bill's cat.

This morning, Rita, with her newly acquired Volkswagen, had dropped us off at Bill Connelly's apartment house just a few minutes earlier. When she had approached me to do something for her good friend Bill, saying that he needed my artistic help again, that was enough for me. Bill Connelly had always been so good to our family, so of course I jumped at the chance to pay him back. It wasn't an easy thing to do either.

FRENCH COOKING

Not too long ago, Arlene and I decided to invite our good angel over for lunch just to let him know we appreciated him. It would be a quiet meal with just the three of us; the kids would be at school. We were all in a flutter about what to serve this unusual man. We knew he could afford to go to any expensive restaurant he chose, so we wanted the lunch to be special. I got a cookbook from the library, and we poured over each recipe. "How about something French," Arlene said at last. "They are the best cooks."

After much deliberation, we decided on beef Bourguignon. We didn't know what it was, but it called for a sauce using burgundy wine. Other exotic ingredients that caught our attention were pearl onions and half a pound of bacon cubed. We wrote down the ingredients and went to the market on Pier Avenue. Arlene made me buy the stew meat because she didn't want the butcher to recognize her. "Maybe he is still sore about embarrassing him into giving us free bones that time," she said. "He still might be holding a grudge." We found all the ingredients at the market, even a bottle of red cooking wine. At home, unlike our usual style, Arlene and I scrupulously followed the instructions in the cookbook. After browning the meat in the bacon fat, we combined the rest of the ingredients and set it on the stove to simmer for two hours. Soon, a wonderful aroma filled the kitchen. We took a sip of the sauce. It was heaven we both decided, and giggled over our expected triumph—an elegant meal for our friend. We set the table in excitement. This had to be just as good as anything in a fancy restaurant. Wouldn't Bill Connelly be surprised when he tasted it?

When the table was set, we heard our special guest's light tap at the door. He was smiling shyly like a bashful beau when we opened it and presented us with some yellow daisies. As I was putting his bouquet into the biggest jelly jar we had, Arlene clucked and fussed around Bill Connelly as she seated him at the table.

"So groovy of you girls to wine and dine me," he said in his most hip and whispery voice.

"The only wine here is in the sauce. We made you beef Bourguignon," I called out proudly as I brought out a steaming bowl and put it before him.

"This smells very aromatic," said Bill Connelly, with his usual deadpan delivery and a slight lisp I hadn't noticed before.

"Well, dig in!" Arlene and I said together, and we stared at him expectantly, forgetting to eat ourselves.

Bill took a tentative bite. "Ahh, very good!" He smiled at us, and we beamed back.

Arlene and I had no trouble finishing our bowls of the delicious stew but soon, we noticed that our guest had only taken a few small bites then just moved the food around on his plate.

"Isn't it good?" Arlene asked. "We thought it was the best thing we ever tasted."

"Yeah, those French sure can cook," I added.

"Oh, it's not that." He smiled sheepishly. "It's just that I'm never very peckish."

I thought this was odd because Bill wasn't thin at all. In fact, he had a pot belly and a general puffiness about him. Even though he didn't eat our lunch, Bill Connelly was the perfect guest and thanked us profusely when he left, moving out the door in his slow, deliberate way.

PICASSO

But today will be different, I thought. Painting a mural on the wall would be just the thing he wanted. "What do you have in mind?" I said, turning from my thoughts back to Bill Connelly. I felt ready to take up this new challenge and picked up my box of acrylic paints.

I had never done a mural before, but I was game. I remembered Sara Lee had done one for an ice cream parlor when she was only eighteen, and it was a great success. Her husband Chris had gotten the job first. His plan had included Greek columns encrusted with seashells, and a working fountain. On the walls, a painted swath of ocean would merge into a night sky that twinkled with electric lights. Sara Lee saved the day with a more feasible plan. The mural became a simple old-fashioned park scene dominated by a fountain and a giant pear tree. Certainly I could handle a small purple bathroom.

"Do you think you could copy some of these drawings onto the walls?" Bill Connelly showed me a small book called *Picasso's Artists and Models.*

I skimmed through the pages. It was mostly sketches of artists who were in the process of painting female models. They were sly, satirical, and rather bawdy. Some of Picasso's artists looked a lot like him and leered lasciviously at young voluptuous girls posing in the nude. "Do you think they are too naughty?" Bill asked.

"Well, yes," I said, looking at one particular sketch where the artist, in a much-excited state, is nude himself.

"Oh goody," Bill said in his softest Mr. Peepers voice. "That was just what I was going for."

I had to laugh at that and the whole idea of the mural. Bill Connelly was such a sweet and passive guy, a perfect gentleman— the complete opposite of the bombastic Picasso, who was well known for his many mistresses. I checked my paints to see if I had enough black for the job and was happy to see that I had a large tube.

"Do you need anything?" Bill asked.

I shook my head. "No, it will be fine. I'm all set."

"Well, er . . . then, I'll just get out of your way and don't mind Fang. He will probably just go and sleep in a closet. I already fed him and have taken his dreck box into the bedroom, so it won't get in your way. I believe I have some Coke in the refrigerator if you get thirsty. I'll just go out now to do some chores and let you have the run of the house. Oh, if there is a delivery, just let them in."

After I heard the click of the door as Bill Connelly went out, I wandered to the kitchen. I thought I would go over the drawings and decide which ones to put on the wall while I took Bill Connelly's offer of a Coke.

DEPOSIT ON RETURN

The kids were in the kitchen taking empty Coke bottles out of the cupboards. On the shelves, were rows and rows of the curvy glass containers. Donnie was standing on a chair handing them down to Lindee and Laurie J. who were filling a wooden box. The label stamped on the box said, "Marty's Liquor Store Eighteenth Street Manhattan Avenue."

I stared at the shelves. "Wow, what a lot of Coke bottles."

"Bill Connelly told us if we took them back to the store, we could keep the deposits," Donnie said, still handing bottles off to his sisters.

"Really, well you have your work cut out for you." I had never seen so many empty containers of soda before. "It's going to take a long time to bring all of them back," I said.

"I know," interjected Laurie J. "We will have to make nu-mer-ous tripths." Laurie J. smiled at the big word. "That's what Bill Connelly told us."

"Yeah, it's a good thing we won't have to cross any streets." Lindee spoke in a serious motherly kind of tone she assumed sometimes, being the oldest. "It's just around the corner."

Bill Connelly's apartment was right on Manhattan Avenue. He lived on the second floor of a white stucco apartment house. There was no yard and his window looked right down on the sidewalk of the busy street.

Lindee tugged my shirt to get my attention. "You know what?" she said in a whispering voice.

"What?" I whispered back in fun.

"Bill Connelly doesn't have any food! Just look."

I opened all the rest of the cabinets in the kitchen. Except for the empty Coke bottles and a few cans of cat food, the cupboards were as empty as Mother Hubbard's. It didn't even look like they had ever been stocked; they were so clean. I opened the refrigerator. There were a few six packs of Coke, but it too was bare of food. I didn't count the jars of cocktail onions and olives as food.

Then I remembered Bill telling us that he didn't eat much.

Well, here was the proof. "I guess he doesn't like to cook," I told the kids. He must eat out a lot," I added a little uneasily.

I helped the kids fill the box and assisted them down the steps that ended on the sidewalk and busy Manhattan Avenue.

WALL TO WALL

Going back to the bathroom, I surveyed the walls again. I had picked out seven sketches I thought would look good and decided on their best placement. Although each composition in the book had an artist at an easel painting a model, each individual artist and model were unique individuals and portrayed in various and diverse styles. Picasso, if anything, was versatile. Some sketches were realistic, while others were abstract and distorted, as if Picasso was going through his different styles for fun—from realism to abstract to cubism, then back to a comical kind of round fat person. What would pull the mural together was that all the figures would be in black paint with no shading or etching. I picked up my chalk and started.

After rendering the figures in chalk, I made some corrections, then squeezed out the Lamp Black into a cup, adding a bit of water, and started to paint. It felt good to have a brush in my hand again. I was missing art—the feel of the canvas bouncing gently back when touched with the brush, that feeling of pleasure when your eyes and hand and brain are all working confidently and smoothly together, getting that energized lift when a drawing or painting starts to really pull together.

I thought about my old art classes: drawing and painting classes with Miss Walker, Mr. Suzuki, and Mr. Bluske, the design teacher. I could never forget the way Mr. Bluske paced the floor and bellowed at us. Would he approve of this fanciful bawdy scene I was producing? He did not approve of most modern art, steering us more to admire Michelangelo rather than Matisse, Beethoven over Brubeck, and Frank Lloyd Wright's cantilevered buildings over Buckminster Fuller's geodesic domes.

Soon my mind wandered to different things. A while ago, Rita had suggested I go along with her on her modeling jobs. "I'm the class pet," she had said. "The teachers all say they get the best out of the class when I model, so I'm sure they wouldn't mind an extra artist coming along with me." Well, I just might take her up on that. I hadn't realized how much I missed art. Of late, Arlene and Rita were spatting. They were too much alike, and every so often there would be a blow up, and they wouldn't be speaking but that didn't mean I couldn't still be Rita's friend.

The mural was taking shape nicely, and I began to think that a bathroom was the best place to have one. You really did have the leisure and aloneness to contemplate. Well, there was going to be plenty here to contemplate. The doorbell rang, It must be the kids back for another load of deposit bottles.

When I opened the door though, it was a deliveryman carrying a now-familiar box. "Delivery for Bill Connelly from Marty's Liquor Store," the delivery man said. "It's the usual order." The man moved past me and into the kitchen. He seemed to be very familiar with the surroundings—opening a pantry door, taking out an empty liquor box, and depositing the new one in its place. As the man passed me going out the door, he put up his hand. "No tip needed. We will just include it in Mr. Connelly's bill." I was glad of that. I had no idea how much money to tip a delivery person, and I didn't have any money to tip him with anyway.

The deliveryman moved down the outside stairs just as the kids were coming up with their empty box. Each had a Popsicle in their mouth. Inside the apartment, they chatted happily about their newfound wealth as they sat around the kitchen table finishing their Popsicles. "I wonder how much we will get when we take all the bottles back." Donnie gave a big suck on his Popsicle which had dyed his mouth and tongue a deep purple.

Lindee answered that the box could fit twenty bottles. "So that means twenty bottles in a box at four-cent deposit, uh . . . each . . . makes . . ." There was a long pause as she calculated on her fingers, then finally, "Eighty cents—wow! That's almost a dollar!" Lindee smiled broadly, showing an orange tongue.

"Goody!" cried Laurie J., exposing her cherry colored one.

Donnie scratched his head. "I wonder how many trips we will have to make? There's an awful lot of bottles."

I went back to the bathroom, leaving the kids to work out the math problem and finish their pops. *We all have our work cut out,* I thought. As I walked through the living room, I noticed the cat, Fang, napping on the windowsill in a square of sun. He had not, in the least, been disturbed by the ring of the doorbell and the deliveryman.

A few hours later, the mural was finished except for a bit of space above the toilet. The kids had gone out on their last run with the Coke bottles. *Now what can I put in that space? It's too small for two figures.* Then I got an idea and sketched it in with my chalk: a cartoon of Fang in his litter box, hovering over the toilet as if on a magic carpet. When I was satisfied with the sketch, I quickly painted it in and stepped back to survey the effect. It was even better than I thought. The lavender color made the black lines stand out clearly. Crazy artists were cavorting all over the bathroom with voluptuous nude models while an image of Fang presided over it all in the magic dreck box.

The kids came back from their last run. They were tired out from all the climbing and carrying heavy boxes up and down the stairs, but they were elated too. "We made two dollars and forty-eight cents!" they chanted excitedly.

A HAPPY PATRON OF THE ARTS

A short time later, Bill Connelly returned. "Hi, Honey, I'm home," he warbled, like a husband coming home to his family. We all rushed out to meet him. He smiled and picked up Fang who was still sleeping on the windowsill and gazed at all of us fondly. It was then that it struck me that Bill Connelly didn't have anyone to come home to except Fang. I had once asked Rita if Bill Connelly had a girlfriend. She said he did have a friend who was a woman but that they were just friends except that every now and then, when they both got too lonely, they did sleep together. That had made me sad, but now he was smiling as he looked at his newly illustrated bathroom. "Well, I call this a really cool, way-out kind of pad," he said. "And look, Fang, you are immortal now." Bill moved his cat over to the toilet to show Fang his doppelganger.

"Do you really like it?" I asked, pleased that, for once, we could give our friend something he could really appreciate.

"I think it is truly, truly groovy," he said in his best nerdy Mr. Peppers voice, and he did look pleased and happy as he continued to pet Fang.

"Yoo-hoo!" It was Rita at the door, just in time to take us home. A moment later, she burst into the bathroom. "I must see how it all turned out!" Bill Connelly and I stepped aside so she could have an unimpeded view. A mischievous grin spread on Rita's face. "Oh, isn't this fantastic? Isn't Picasso a wicked, wicked man? Look how his artists leer at the nude models." Rita went on with her praise, the way she always did. "Lorraine you must do something for *my* house."

"Sure, Rita, I would be glad to."

"Sunflowers, I want huge yellow sunflowers all over my kitchen, one painted right on each cupboard!"

Big bright sunflowers suited Rita perfectly, I thought, and promised I would get to it soon unless a job popped up. After gathering up my paints and rounding up the kids, we left Bill Connelly and Fang still standing in the purple bathroom looking at the walls.

CHAPTER 39
BROTHER BILL

BEHOLD THE TIN MAN

At Culper Court, Rita stopped her Volkswagen in front of the house. An unfamiliar car was parked next to Jeff's truck. As the kids ran inside, I told Rita that I would paint her sunflowers very soon and was also interested in tagging along sometime on one of her modeling jobs.

Walking up to the porch (the door left open as usual), I heard the murmur of two adult voices. Inside, the children had stopped their chatter and were shyly standing around the living room looking in the direction of the fireplace. "Hey, Lorraine!" an almost forgotten but familiar voice rang out as I moved into the room. In the dim light, a tall figure stepped forward and loomed over me. A moment later, I was lifted up into the air close to the rafters by strong arms. "How's my little sister doing?" the tall figure chuckled as he dumped me back down on the floor with a jolt.

Suddenly, I was back in Riverside again. My older brother Bill regularly performed this maneuver almost every morning when we were teenagers. With four kids in the house and one tiny bathroom, we were always jockeying for control. If Bill found me primping at the mirror when he had to use the facilities, he just picked me up under the armpits and dumped me out of the room. "Bill!" I said, at last recovering. "What a surprise! But when did you get here? Have you seen Mom yet? You didn't tell us you were planning to come."

"Yeah, yeah, you know, I'm not much for writing letters." Bill sat down again, dwarfing the squat bathtub love seat, his knees and long legs jutting out into the living room. Arlene sat opposite from him on the couch (now back in its place against the wall), her arms crossed in front of her and one eyebrow sardonically raised. I wondered what they had been talking about before I came. There had always been competition between them as far back as I could remember.

Arlene called out in an overly dramatic voice, her eyebrow still raised, "Bill was just telling me about his *wonderful* life."

The kids were staring at their uncle trying to place him in their minds. He looked familiar, yet they probably had seen him only a few times briefly when he was home on leave from the Navy or later in their grandmother's apartment as one of the black-and-white photos she kept in her bedroom.

The picture of Bill was taken just after he had joined the Navy. It showed a good-looking young man in a uniform, his blonde hair parted and Brylcreem-ed into a tidy wave, a small smile playing on his lips. It is signed "To Mom, with all my love Bill." Next to the photo is a little Hawaiian figure of a hula girl in a real grass skirt with a plastic lei around her neck conveniently covering her breasts. "Kids," Arlene spoke with a forced gaiety, clapping her hands, "this is your Uncle Bill from Hawaii!"

Bill had joined the Navy a few months after graduating from high school. He was not going to college; the word had never been mentioned in our house, and we all knew there was no money anyway, so Bill enlisted. The recruitment letter had said, "Join the Navy and see the world!" Yet for the first few years, the only new part of the world Bill saw was the base in San Diego, about ninety miles away.

The kids were so young then; Laurie J. wasn't even born yet. Donnie moved in closer to study his strange male relative, and I wondered how long it would be before he would attempt to hang on his uncle's arm.

Bill wore a floppy Hawaiian shirt with brightly colored parrots roosting on it and, even though it wasn't summer yet, he was wearing shorts. His long legs, furred with blonde hair were still strung out across the floor as he squirmed uncomfortably in the low Holly Golightly love seat. He had finally filled out from his skinny teenage days and looked manly now. The only thing that was a little off was his voice. Looking at him, you would expect a deep baritone. Yet Bill still had the reedy voice of a teenager.

BILL, THE EARLY YEARS

Unlike the rest of us, who were small like our father, Bill was over six feet tall, taking after our Grandfather Holzkamp on our mother's side of the family. Tall Bill, with his bullet shaped head, white blonde hair, and blue eyes, looked the most German of us all.

He was not exactly the protective and concerned older brother—throwing me casually out of the bathroom every morning like so much dirty laundry. Of course, we were teenagers then and fought all the time. Yet even as a kid, Bill made sure he always got his fair share of things. As a consequence, he was very good at acquiring stuff and a genius at thinking up ways to make money—collecting Coke bottles, buying things cheap and selling for more with his Kool-Aid stands that started with a packet of three-cent Kool-Aid which he parlayed into several dollars by the end of a hot summer day. He would go out with a wagon full of comics or old toys to swap and always come back with better stuff than what he left with, and I will never forget the time he turned the garage into a gambling casino. That really raked in the dough. He kept his money and candy in a small metal safe with a real combination in his bedroom closet and even told me once that he was stacking up gold bricks in heaven too by performing good deeds. It was important for him to come out on top, which he did often, easily winning every card and board game, especially Monopoly, which could go on for days. Yet, there was more to Bill than that; he was musical, and clever and funny too. He liked to amuse us with his one-man mystery shows and comedic monologues. Before stand-up comedy was invented, Bill was doing his own routines.

The only real obstacle for Bill was Arlene. As the two oldest, they competed for dominance. Jeff and I vacillated between them. When I wanted adventure, Bill could provide endless escapades of mountain climbing, tunnel digging, and cave exploring. He could build tree houses, glider planes, row boats, and rockets propelled by firecrackers. When I wanted to grow up a little, Arlene supplied girly stuff. By the time I was thirteen, I had more or less joined Arlene's side.

As teenagers in Riverside, it was usually the girls against the boys. Bill had height and strength on his side, but Arlene had the rapier tongue and usually won out in the end because she could always get Bill to cry. "Give up," she would say when one of their put-down arguments got heated. "I already won 'cause I can see your bottom lip is trembling and you are about to cry." And, sure enough, Bill's lip did start to tremble. Then she would say that his eyes were starting to tear up, and Bill's eyes would get watery. Slowly, slowly, Arlene pushed and prodded until the final cut when she would say, "Just let it happen, you know you want to cry, and you can't hold it back anymore. C'mon, c'mon, I can see it coming." As Bill's face got redder and redder, he would start to quiver all over until—boom! Everything would blow. Tears streaming down his face, he would jump up and slam Arlene against a wall or a picket fence or a chair. Mom would punish him then and Arlene would have a double victory. Arlene couldn't make him cry anymore, but she still liked to throw a poison dart or two.

ANCHORS AWAY

I joined Arlene on the couch and studied grown-up Bill. He was not the skinny pigeon-chested kid anymore. He was full bodied, and his arms and legs were thick and weighty. When his shorts hiked up a little, I could see the end of a long scar on his upper thigh, one that he had gotten in a terrible car accident. It was just one of his many calamities but it was the worst.

When Bill was stationed in San Diego, he drove back and forth from the base to Riverside every weekend to see his girlfriend, Annie. One night, he fell asleep at the wheel and had a head-on collision that totally wrecked his car and landed him in the Navy hospital.

It was a ghastly sight that greeted us when Mom, Jeff, and I entered the sick bay on our first visit. Bill lay motionless in a full-body cast with one leg strung up on a hook above the bed like a piece of mutton in a butcher shop. His face, covered in scratches and black and blue marks, was now turning a dark purple and yellow. In our family, we had all had our share of broken bones and injuries, and Mom was used to Bill's regular disasters, but this one, by far, was the worst. Bill raised his head a little as we approached. In a cracked voice, he started to explain to us that he now had a metal pin in his upper leg. It was then I realized that Mom had turned away from the bed and was stumbling into the next room. A few moments later, we found her lying on the floor where she had quietly fainted.

Seeing the scar again, I shivered to think how close he had come to getting killed, no wonder Mom had fainted that day. Bill, unaware of my thoughts, was still searching for a comfortable position in the bathtub. He arched his back and stretched out his arms. There it was, the familiar bump on his right elbow where at seven years old he had broken it in two places trying to fly like Superman off the top of his bunk bed. Another broken arm (this time the left one) happened at fourteen when the rope swing broke during his Tarzan act. Almost as if he was reading my mind, Bill suddenly smiled at me, and I noticed his front tooth, that he had knocked out while building a tree house, was now capped and whole again.

SIBLING RIVALRY

I smiled back. "Do you want some coffee?" I asked.

"I'll have a beer or a Coke," he replied, stretching out his long arms again.

Arlene snapped out, "We can only offer coffee. You didn't let us know you were coming."

"Fine, then, I'll have coffee, sugar no cream."

I jumped up. "I'll have some too, how about you, Arlene?" I hoped the visit would not turn out to be a bumpy ride. Arlene was in one of her grumpy moods. When I came out later with three cups of coffee, I noticed that the kids had settled on the rug and were quietly watching and listening to the conversation between their mother and this unknown uncle. Bill was readjusting himself in the bathtub again. Had Arlene seated him there on purpose? Unconsciously, he jiggled his right leg up and down. Was he nervous or bored or impatient? I couldn't tell. He put his coffee on the floor next to his jiggly leg and took a sip now and then. There was an awkward silence.

Arlene turned to me. "Bill was just telling me about his *little* band in Hawaii." The arched eyebrow came back up again.

Bill bridled a bit at the word *little*, but chose to ignore it. "It's basically a rock and roll band," he said, "but we have to be flexible because mostly people want to dance and we have to be up on the latest dance crazes too."

"Like what?" I asked. I had stopped learning new dance steps in junior high school when the twist came in.

"Well, like the frug or the mashed potatoes or the Watusi for one." To illustrate, he jumped up and started to hum a tune and gyrate his whole body, making it quiver from his shoulders to his hips—his head and body making a steady back and forth movement while his long legs pranced like a high stepping pony. Every so often, he would leap into the air and fling his head around as if he had a great plume fashioned there. The kids were rolling around on the floor giggling with pleasure. I was impressed too. Even though Bill was big, he danced gracefully, if you could call the Watusi a graceful dance.

Bill sat back down and took a gulp of coffee. "Like that, but mostly, we do a lot of Ray Charles, Fats Domino, and Little Richard."

"And just where does your *little* band play?" Arlene's eyebrow had receded to its proper level, but her voice still had an edge to it.

"We mostly just play at the Navy base. There are different clubs there. We are a big hit at the Tiki Lanai."

"Oh, I bet you are," smirked Arlene.

"How big is your band?" I cut in before Arlene could continue.

"Well," he ticked off on his fingers, "there's me of course on drums, then we have Steve on piano. There's this colored guy, Trevor, who plays a mean yakkedy-yak tenor sax, and then Bruno on the electric guitar, and, oh yeah, I got Annie to take up bass guitar."

"Your wife is playing the bass?" Arlene asked astonished. "I didn't know she was even musical!" I wondered if Arlene was remembering her own attempts at the bass.

Bill smiled mischievously. "She's not, but I needed a bass. And for rock and roll, bass can be pretty simple." He hummed a boogie-woogie bass line.

"How does she like show business?" I asked.

"She doesn't," he said in an offhand manner. "But I said that is what I wanted, and if she wanted to see me more, then here was her chance."

Arlene and I didn't know Annie very well. I had visited a couple of times with Mom when they were first married and stationed in San Diego. I had gotten the feeling that Annie cared for Bill more than Bill did for her. On one of my few visits, I found Bill sitting around one early Sunday morning, unshaven in a ratty bathrobe. Annie, on the other hand, was in the bathroom and didn't show herself until she was fully dressed—hair done and in full makeup. Was she trying too hard?

"You also made her get a nose job too, I hear," said Arlene, breaking into my thoughts.

"I heard that too," I said, jumping back into the conversation. "Just what was wrong with her nose?"

Bill shrugged his shoulders. "Oh, nothing really, I just thought she would look better."

As I remembered, Annie was nice looking—fresh and natural with dark blonde hair. She did have slightly large teeth, but her nose was fine. Yet, Bill was not satisfied and had gotten her to dye her hair platinum and, as Arlene said, made her get a nose job. The new nose was a little turned up thing and seemed lost in Annie's new face.

Changing the subject before Arlene could further berate him, I asked about Hawaii. "Tell me all about living there. Isn't it beautiful?"

"Yeah, yeah, it's beautiful, I guess, but after a while you get tired of it. You can feel sort of trapped. There is nowhere to go that is different. It's all beautiful but all the same."

Now wasn't that just like Bill? To not appreciate living in paradise! I wondered too if the trapped feeling was more about being married to someone who wasn't *the one*. Yet again, I wasn't sure about Bill's feelings. Maybe it didn't matter if he didn't find *the one*. There was always something a little stoic and detached about Bill.

YOUNG BILL

Maybe it happened on that car trip across the country to Florida with Harry, the one I had missed out on because I always got carsick. Maybe that was when it started. When Harry pushed Willie, as he called him, into a mud puddle. Bill told me later that he knew right before it happened that Harry was fed up with the trip, and with him especially, when they were walking by this mud puddle. "I saw the puddle," he said, "and could see Harry behind me out of the corner of my eye. It was then I thought, 'He's going to push me in,' and right then, Harry's hand reached out and wham I was in the mud." Harry didn't apologize afterward either. He just made a joke of the whole thing.

But what did Bill mean by "Harry had had enough" of him? Did Harry sense that Bill was not part of the Harry the Hipster happy team anymore, and the dunk in the mud was payback? If so, just when had Bill lost faith in our father? Maybe it was the day a year earlier when we all went to the zoo at Griffith Park. Harry was into his new hobby of taking candid pictures of the whole family, so the entire day is documented. It started out fine. The pictures show us looking at the animals and eating and drinking treats. Then, a snapshot shows us walking home along the side of the highway. In one, Mom is carrying her high heels in her hands, walking barefoot; some of us are next to her or trailing behind.

What had happened to change our happy day? It was simple. Harry had lost another car. It had been repossessed from us right at the zoo, thus stranding us there and making us walk five hot miles home. At the time, I thought it was a great adventure, but Bill, I remember, was angry. One photo shows him in a boxer's stance with his hands curled into fists in a "put up your dukes" attitude. Was that the day Bill stopped wanting to please Harry?

Yet, had Bill ever been fully accepted by our father? For the most part Harry thought my brother's juvenile antics to get his attention were silly. He called him "Willie the Goofball," and that wasn't all. Harry was nervous about his firstborn son. "He lives with too many females," Harry would declare loud enough for all to hear. Bill at thirteen, with his high-pitched voice and pretty looks, did not quite live up to Harry's manly standards. Whenever Bill played along on his drum set with Harry's piano, my father would inevitably call out at some point, "Hey, Willie, you're dragging the beat!" Bill would smile away the tears welling in his eyes and try harder, until one day he didn't try anymore. Then after the zoo episode and the trip to Florida, my brother was different. I guess he lost heart.

THIS IS THE NAVY

Arlene didn't bring out the best in Bill either. Even now, I could feel the tension between them. Bill was still jiggling his leg and had started to hum to himself under Arlene's harsh stare.

Poor Bill, except for Hawaii, he never did see the world like the Navy promised. The Navy soon caught on to the fact that Bill was smart and clever with his hands. As a kid, he was something of a boy inventor; he could fix anything—clocks, radios, toasters. After being trained in Navy technology, the only time Bill was ever on a ship was when he was sent out to calibrate all the gears and dials and buttons and switches on those big boats. When it was done, he was ferried back to base again.

Echoing my thoughts, Arlene burst out, "Well, how is the Navy? Are you still making all the bells and whistles and gears go round and round?" It was strange how Arlene could make ordinary statements seem like insults.

Bill stopped shaking his leg for a second. He leaned back and smiled. "Well, when I'm not on a ship fixing it, I'm on duty as an MP."

Arlene gasped, "You're a policeman?" Then, rather teasingly, and with a sarcastic giggle escaping from her lips, she added, "Well, of course, you always did like guns and playing at war." She sat back with a superior smile on her face.

It was true. As a kid, Bill loved to play with his war gear that he bought at the Army Navy Surplus store. Back then, it really *was* War Surplus from WWII. Bill had a beat-up steel helmet with camouflage netting on it. He would strap on his real ammunition belt with empty bullet shells still in it around his shoulder and trudge off to play in his camouflage pup tent. He played soldier way into his teens. He really got into trouble though when he fired off his BB gun and accidentally shot Jeff out of a tree one day. He liked to shoot birds too. I caught him roasting a dove on our BBQ one day and didn't talk to him for a week.

So I, too, was not surprised that he later joined the Military Police. Was he still playing at war? Still, did Arlene have to tease him about it? Bill, however, was above being hurt by Arlene anymore. He just sat there drinking his now-lukewarm coffee and jiggling his leg.

When Bill left, Arlene said with finality, "He isn't like us anymore! He's turned into one of those hicks in the Navy. He even has a kind of twang to his voice. Did you notice? He's turned into another Bob." As far as Arlene was concerned, that was the ultimate insult. I knew that the real reason Arlene had washed her hands of Bill was that he had left the family to live his own life.

CHAPTER 40
FROM THE GRAY NOTEBOOK
DEMOLITION

LOVE LOST

Mom made up the couch for me as a bed with crisp sheets and a soft pillow. Every so often, I'd stay overnight at the apartment with Mom and Bob. It was quiet and clean and nice to have my mother fuss over me a little. I was up late playing records. Their collection was mostly Count Basie, but I also found an album of ballads by my favorite singing group. Every song was about losing love. One called "I heard you cried last night," made me blubber a bit listening to the sad breakup. It didn't help either to remember that The Four Freshmen had also been the favorite singing group of my ex-boyfriend. Might *He* even be listening to this very song right now missing me and thinking that he had made a big mistake letting me go?

It took a few moments to remind myself this kind of thinking was not helping me do what I came here to do. I wanted to work on the new story. With the record player switched off, I turned my attention to the gray notebook. I had lugged it here in order to finish what I had started writing the other day and I had better get to it before I got distracted again. Sometime later I put down my pen and closed the notebook. It was just a short piece, but I liked it. I reread it one more time.

DEMOLITION

Laughing and bubbling with excitement, the three children plunge ahead to the end of the sidewalk and, waving their brown arms and legs, frantically teeter on the edge of the curb like tightrope walkers. The golden day is sending out rays of sunlight to play with the children. It bounces off their bodies and glows behind their heads, turning them into dandelions—blonde fluffs dancing at the curb before me. "Don't cross," I warn, and obediently, they wait for me to catch up and sweep them across the busy avenue, depositing them safely on the corner bench to await the bus. We are going to the movies.

Not far from the bus stop, a small crowd has gathered to watch the demolition of a nearby building, abandoned for more than a year now. I have passed it many times on my way to the store or trotting to the beach but have never taken much notice of it before.

Held together by cockroach-infested walls, it sags, yellow and rotting now. Through the punctured windows, I can see the carpet of dust that holds organic smells and damp sea air. Recently, the rankness has begun to penetrate the walls and greet the people passing by.

"Look at that big tractor," Lindee remarks, standing on the bench for a better view. Donnie and Laurie J. scramble up after her, following their older sister. The big machine's shovel-like jaws make it look like some sort of prehistoric monster as it roars up to the shack and gnaws voraciously at the vulnerable wood, grinding the broken splinters beneath its rubber tread feet.

Freed from its sleep, the settled dust rises up in a cloud of beige from between the papery walls. The old frame shifts sideways as if cringing from the ravenous engine that tears at it. The small crowd stares at the carnage, thrilled and fascinated as if the orange tractor is part of themselves, smashing with abandon at their own dark secret terrors.

The air is sick with dust at each crash of the tractor. Now one wall is completely gone, exposing a bathtub on the second floor. It looks lonely and naked as it pauses for a second then falls into the growing mountain of wood and plaster. Section after section groans to the ground under the charge of the raging machine—old wood collapses quickly—brittle and crackling. Next, a wall falls, taking with it a closet and part of the roof.

At last, only one wall remains. Like a stubborn tooth hanging on by one single strand of root, it refuses to collapse. Again and again, the great jaws close in, tearing away, biting down, and spitting out the flimsy fabric of resistance. It will soon be over.

The watching faces show anticipation and a longing to kick down the last boards themselves as they silently encourage the mutilation. All watch as the last wall falls gently and quietly onto the mountainous splinters.

I notice Donnie. The boy is staring at the wreckage, his lips a-droop. "It's dead now, isn't it," he states calmly yet he is close to tears. "Why did they kill it, Lorraine?"

"Why? Oh, Donnie . . . Well, because it smelled. Yes, and it had bugs, and . . . and . . . it was old, useless, it was in the way, that's why." But I could almost cry too.

*A small crowd had gathered to watch
the demolition of a nearby building.*

CHAPTER 41
FAME, SORT OF PART I
BEGINNINGS

JEFF

After mid-morning cleanup, it was time for a coffee break. I happily propped my broom into a corner where I had already collected a good-sized mound of dust and debris—I would pick that up later. In her bedroom, my sister, hearing the tinkering noise of coffee being made, stopped her sewing and slowly ambled into the dining room. Seeing her plunk herself down at the table, I automatically took another mug from the cupboard.

Arlene was working on a new dress and although the material was thick and the sewing needles often broke, she knew she could make something wonderful. It would all be worth it in the end, she told me. The dress had been inspired by a remnant of upholstery material discovered in the scrap box at Logan's Fabric Store.

She had fallen in love with the pattern. "It looks like one of those tapestries crafted back in the old medieval days," she enthused. "Like something on a castle wall embroidered by those once-upon-a-time noble ladies and their handmaidens sitting for hours during long, boring winters with thimbles and needles and silver and golden threads—their lily-white hands dripping blood from the pinpricks and all to bring beauty and warmth to the barren walls of those cold and drafty castles." Only my sister could be inspired like this by a piece of material. When I looked a little blank after her heartfelt soliloquy, she added, "You know, a tapestry like the one Polonius was hiding behind when Hamlet stabbed him?" I decided later some of the credit of inspiration also belonged to the drama classes my sister was taking because Shakespeare, too, seemed to have had a hand in the new dress design.

In the kitchen, I moved around automatically. Did we have enough milk for coffee? I opened the refrigerator. If not, we would have to make do with the powdered kind that always involved lumps. As I pondered this dilemma, I watched the water in the pot begin to boil and blow bubbles.

Suddenly, there was a loud fumbling and jiggling at the front door. When it burst open, a more-rumpled-than-usual Jeff staggered into the dining room. "Oh my God, Jesus, Mary, and all the Holy Ghosts!" he yelped. "What I have to sacrifice for my art!" After staggering a few more steps, he collapsed at the table beside Arlene. His head plopped down on his arms. "Oh, what I've been through!" his muffled voice moaned. It was strange that he had come in through the front door since he usually came tromping up the back stairs when the smell of coffee wafted down to him.

"What? What happened?" I asked, leaving the boiling water to hover over his bent head. "Why did you come in the front door?"

"Yeah, where were you?" Even Arlene looked surprised.

"Coffee, coffee!" Jeff whimpered weakly, peeping up at me from his arms. In the kitchen, I added more water to the pot and prepared one more cup.

"But where were you?" Arlene repeated.

Jeff straightened up in his chair. "Well, it was like this—I was arrested last night."

"Arrested!" Arlene gasped. "We didn't even know you were gone until this minute."

Now I really was confused. "But what happened, Jeff? Last night I saw you go downstairs to your room."

"Yeah, well I did go to my room and was dead to the world, but I woke up and couldn't go back to sleep, so I decided to do a little practicing. I've been working on this solo. It's one of the Monk tunes that the group at the Blue Horn plays. They have this great version of ''Round Midnight,' and we all take a solo."

"I don't see how this leads to a night in jail," Arlene butted in impatiently.

"Well, if you just let me finish," said Jeff, exasperated. "Did you know that jails are really cold at night?" He shivered remembering. "I didn't sleep a wink!"

"Sorry, go on, go on," Arlene said in an exaggerated voice, putting her palms together and bowing her head in contrition.

"Thank you so much," Jeff replied in a fake magnanimous tone. He cleared his throat noisily. "Well, as I was saying when I was so rudely interrupted, I knew the kids were sleeping right above me, so I very thoughtfully took my sax and went out into the dump. I found a nice cozy slab of cement near the railroad tracks to sit on and started to practice. I was really getting into it too, making headway with my solo when all of a sudden, I hear a siren and see these lights flashing and two bulky-hulky type policemen are surrounding me. They drag me into their car with the flashing lights. Off I go to the lockup, the slammer, the hoosegow, the clink, the . . . the . . . !" Jeff ran out of colorful words for jail, so he continued with, "They booked me for disturbing the peace. They just let me go this morning. Whew!" Jeff's head flopped back down on the table, exhausted by his long speech.

The police in Hermosa Beach loved to hassle people, especially young ones. There was an eleven o'clock curfew for minors they strictly enforced. They were nasty about it too. I guessed that night they had nothing better to do, so to make their quota, they took our little brother to jail.

Jeff's head rose up again when I put the steaming coffee mug down in front of him. Leaning back in his chair, he took a big gulp. "Eee yow! That's hot!" he said, fanning his mouth with his hand.

"Oh, dear," I said, sitting down with my first cup of coffee of the afternoon, trying not to laugh. Even though Jeff's story was really serious, it was hard not to laugh at the way he told his tale. "That is some story!" I said, as he now gingerly took a cautious sip of his coffee. But to tell the truth, I wasn't too surprised. My little brother always seemed to get into trouble one way or another. He just looked odd, and that was enough.

The three of us sat quietly for a few minutes and drank our coffee, then Jeff said, "Well, one interesting thing happened. There was a reporter hanging around the station house and he interviewed me." He suddenly brightened. "I'm going to be in the newspaper!" he said with a shy smile. After finishing his coffee, Jeff stumbled downstairs to finally get some shut-eye, as he called it. Even the coffee didn't keep him from sleeping way into the next morning. Two days later, a small article appeared in the *Daily Breeze*.

HEREAFTER HORN BLOWS AT MIDNIGHT

Hermosa Beach police stopped a man from playing his trombone yesterday morning. He was playing at 3:00 a.m. in a vacant lot. Officers said Jeffrey Gibson 19, of 326 Culper Court Hermosa Beach, apparently was seized with musical desire, picked up his trombone and carried it to

a lot near Second Street and Valley Drive. Police immediately received complaints from persons who don't like trombones at 3:00 a.m. Officer Fred McAllister said he asked Gibson why he didn't do his practicing at home. "I don't want to disturb my neighbors," Gibson said.

Jeff cut out the article, pasted it on a piece of paper, and stuck it up in his room right next to Thelonious Monk's cigarette butt. I thought it was curious that such a short article had so many mistakes. First, it was a saxophone and not a trombone that Jeff was playing, and they got his age wrong—Jeff had turned twenty in April—and they had gotten the number on our house wrong too, but for that we were grateful.

CHAPTER 42
FAME, SORT OF PART II
MUSIC . DRAMA . ART

STRIKE UP THE BAND

A staccato, yet tentative, knock at the front door broke into my self-imposed music lesson. I was still trying to master all the inversions of the major, minor, and diminished chords. I stopped playing for a second and listened. The staccato rapping repeated. When I finally opened our troublesome door, a young man with a mop of floppy brown hair falling over his forehead stood smiling at me.

"Ah," he said, the smile turning into a crooked grin. "I think I got the right house at last. The piano tinkling was a tip off."

I was confused. "Can I help you?" Mr. Floppy Hair seemed enlightened, but I was still in the dark.

Finally, the young man said, "Jeff Gibson *does* live here, doesn't he?"

"Yes, he does. I'm his sister," I said.

"Oh, that's obvious," the mop of hair responded. "Can't miss the big sad eyes and dark eyebrows."

Now it was becoming clear, it was another of Jeff's new friends. I wondered what this guy played—bagpipe? I wouldn't be surprised. Jeff encountered the strangest musicians and was willing to play with all of them.

The young man turned back to the street and called out, "OK guys, we finally got the right place!" Then he turned to me. "Jeff said we could rehearse here."

I hadn't noticed the old car before, but now I could see that it was filled with a bunch of guys. The doors opened and they began to file out, each carrying a musical instrument.

"I'll just get my axe too," the mop-haired young man said and stepped back off the porch. He immediately had to skip around the line of musicians and instruments that were already coming up the narrow brick walkway. One by one, as each person walked through the door, they introduced themselves. A stocky blonde carrying a horn approached. He smiled shyly. "Hi, I'm Harvey Lane, tenor sax." I stood by the door like some kind of usher and directed each person into the music room.

An older guy with a bald head and hollow cheekbones was hanging on to a snare drum and some brushes along with a large cymbal. "Ed Cassidy, drummer, do you happen to have any bongos?"

After him, a rather short fellow with a snub nose and brown curly hair moved up the walk, carrying the stand to the snare drum. He nodded as he passed, then he said, "Ricky Luther, vibes, but the piano will do for now."

Bringing up the rear was the fellow who had been at the door first, but this time he was lugging a bass. "Gary Marker here, bass," he said, as if that wasn't obvious as he held the large instrument in his arms. Giving a little bow to me with the scrolled neck of it, he plunged through the door and across the living room to join the rest in the rapidly filling music room.

Already, I could hear the sound of instruments being tuned up to the piano. "I hope there is enough room in there!" I called back at Gary's receding figure. *I guess that is the end of my music lesson for today*, I thought, then busied myself with the crowd. It turned out that some rearranging of the room had to be done to accommodate Jeff's new friends. The desk had already been moved against the wall, and the apple-green wicker chairs with the Indonesian scrollwork on the top were ejected into the living room. Back in the noisy music room, I tried to explain to his friends that Jeff had taken my sister to the market, and I wasn't sure when they would be back.

"No problem," Gary waved me away. "Jeff said to drop by any time," and he went back to tuning his bass.

I was relieved when I heard the rattle of Jeff's van pull up in front of the house. It idled for a while, then after a gasp or two, the engine stopped. A few moments later, Arlene and Jeff came in carrying bags of groceries. Jeff's face beamed in surprise as he walked in. "Hey! The band is here," he said to me, as if I didn't know. Still holding his bag of groceries, he moved over to the music room. "Hey, man! Hey great! You made it! I'll be with you guys in a sec."

I heard calls to Jeff of "Hey, man!" and "What's happening, man!" And someone said, "Nice pad you got here." Arlene looked surprised when she first came in, then just shrugged and moved into the kitchen.

PRACTICE MAKES PERFECT

In the weeks that followed, more people showed up along with the Blue Horn Group from Santa Monica. There was the dark-haired ex-girlfriend of the former piano player. There was Cookie, Gary's young wife. She was small and delicate with soft brown curls and an elfin face. Soon, she would become fast friends with my sister. Then there was long, lanky David Feller, who wasn't a musician at all but was tight buddies with the tenor sax player, Harvey. Sometimes they came with the group, sometimes they didn't. After a while, David and Harvey started showing up to drink coffee and talk with us late into the night.

The retinue grew larger or smaller at will. They came in the mornings, they came in the afternoon, they came in the evening. Actually, they came at all times to practice. Once, around two o'clock in the morning, I woke up in my loft suddenly to a cacophony right under me in the music room. The group was experimenting with free jazz along the lines of one of their heroes, Ornette Coleman. It was an exercise in spontaneity and liberation, they said. I had heard Jeff go at it many times along with Ornette's recordings, but this was the first time I had experienced a live group right under my bed in the early morning.

I later found that all this rush and hustle was to get ready for the Annual College Jazz Festival Competition at the Lighthouse Nightclub only a few weeks away. Jeff, of course, was in heaven playing with a real group of young musicians who thought the same way he did about music.

It was an exciting time for jazz. Jeff and his new friends felt that they were on the cutting edge of this innovative direction music was taking. No more uptight West Coast jazz for them, they said.

I was to find out later that West Coast jazz meant California, white musicians, and cool sophistication. East Coast jazz meant New York, Colored musicians, and a liberated, earthier sound. Yeah, Monk and Miles and Coltrane were great, but newer even more free-sounding musicians were inspiring Jeff and his friends now: Ornette Coleman, inventor of free jazz on sax; Charlie Haden, bass player; Don Cherry, trumpet; and Billy Higgins, wailing drums. These were names I heard the Blue Horn Group toss around. For Jeff, things couldn't get better, and to top it off he would actually be playing at the Lighthouse, one of the most prestigious jazz clubs on the West Coast.

THE PLAY IS THE THING

The school year was almost over. In a few weeks, the kids would be off to their Grandma Pauline's house. Arlene's drama class was in its final weeks. I had to hand it to Arlene; she hardly ever had to take the bus to El Camino. Jim Bishop, Bill Connelly, Rita, Paul—anyone stopping by—would be corralled into being her chauffeur to her drama classes.

For the finals, Arlene said that Mr. Ferguson's students had to perform a scene from a famous play. Arlene had chosen *Cat on a Hot Tin Roof* by Tennessee Williams. The play was all about mendacity, sexual desire, repression, and death, I was told. A rich Southern family has problems. Big Daddy is dying and the alcoholic son, Brick, and his sexy wife, Maggie, are having trouble in the bedroom. Brick is mourning the death of his best friend and resists the affections of his extremely unfulfilled wife, sometimes called "Maggie the Cat." Arlene, of course, was going to play Maggie, and she had picked a good-looking guy, who she had a sort of crush on anyway, to play Brick.

They chose as their scene the most dramatic part of the first act when Brick attempts to hit Maggie with his crutch after being confronted about his lack of desire and his relationship with the now dead Skipper. Arlene even incorporated Lindee into the act, coaching her to play one of the bratty nieces. Every few nights, Brick (I never did catch his real name) came over with his crutch, and all three would rehearse in the living room. Busy in the dining room or kitchen, I could hear indistinct voices saying their lines. I could hear even more when the dialogue got intense.

"Maggie, shut up about Skipper!" Brick's voice would ring out.

Or at other times my sister's voice with a heavy Southern drawl would burst out, "Ai cain't stop myself! This thang has got ta be told and you never let me!" Here Arlene's Maggie would burst into hysterical sobs.

Lindee, waiting outside the living room door, took this as her cue to enter the scene, loudly yelling, "Bang! Bang! Bang," pretending to shoot off a cap pistol. Lindee's part was brief but funny as the little niece who taunts Maggie because she isn't pregnant yet. She got to stick out her tongue and jut out her stomach in mock pretense of being pregnant. I was told later that Arlene and her co-actor worked very hard on getting the physical part just right. In the scene where Brick tries to hit Maggie with his crutch, Arlene and her Brick practiced tirelessly trying to get it as realistic as possible without Arlene actually getting bashed in the head.

Finally, the night of the finals came, and Brick picked up Arlene and Lindee for their debut. They came back in a glow of triumph. Lindee had gotten lots of laughs for her part and Mr. Ferguson was impressed overall. Arlene had put a lot of emotion into her part, he had observed, and did a very good job, but he gently cautioned her not to let her voice get too screechy in the emotional parts and, also, to try to control her body a tad bit more because when she furiously threw herself around the stage, it tended to look like a ragdoll flopping around with comical results and not tragic ones. Yep, that sounded like my sister all right.

After her triumph in Mr. Ferguson's class, Arlene was seriously bitten by the acting bug and started reading plays. She finished all of Tennessee Williams then started on Arthur Miller. Theater was in her blood, she would say. She had loved acting since she was twelve and had seen June Allison play Joe in the MGM version of *Little Women.*

Another part of the finals with Mr. Ferguson had been to recite a speech from Shakespeare. Always one to go for the hardest challenge, Arlene set out to tackle Hamlet's soliloquy. She had the kids practice and recite it with her over and over until she was letter perfect. It was strange sometimes when weeks later after the class had long ended, to walk by Laurie J. and hear her lisping to herself, "To be, or not to be, that is the queth-thion."

THERE'S NO BUSINESS LIKE SHOW BUSINESS

Paul was delighted to have a new partner to join him in his love of theater and encouraged Arlene to pursue this new dream. Together, they went to several auditions for small theaters that were gearing up for their summer productions. Arlene would come back from these tryouts and mimic the other audition hopefuls for us. "Hey, watch this," she would say, moving to the middle of the living room. "This is what this one girl did for her audition." Then my sister would do a perfect imitation of someone trying their best to sound like Betty Hutton in the movie *Annie Get Your Gun*. She had us rolling on the floor as she strutted around the room like a plucked chicken, her eyes bugging out as she twanged "You Can't Get a Man with a Gun" in a thick hayseed accent. After the demonstration, Arlene would make clear how different her audition was and how the song she sang— something more melodic and hip—was so much better. "I just sang straight out with no ridiculous movements." She dropped her arms to her sides to emphasize her point. "I just wanted to let the quality of my voice speak for me."

"Well, did you get the part?" I asked expectantly.

"No, damn it, the other girl did!" Arlene said in an aggrieved voice. "Some of those directors have no taste at all!"

After a while, my sister got a little depressed with the hunt for a play. But one afternoon she and Paul crashed enthusiastically through the door, leaving it swinging open behind them. "I got a part! I got the part! I'm going to play Pearl in *Tobacco Road*. It's at the Drawing Room Theatre." Arlene stood there hugging herself, smiling the biggest smile, and showing all her small white teeth.

Paul beamed next to her. "Rehearsals start next week," he said, "and I have a place working on the set and props."

I was surprised to find that our mother knew all about *Tobacco Road*. It had been a tremendous hit on Broadway in 1933, when she was a teenager in the Bronx. "Everyone was talking about it," she said. The play told the story of a family of poor white trash scraping by on their worn-out farm during the worst of the Depression. Mom said it had even shocked the sophisticated theatergoers by simulating public urination in the first act, and it was actually banned in Chicago and L.A. In the 1940s, however, the play became a Hollywood movie starring Gene Tierney.

As rehearsals began, Arlene became more and more excited about her part as Pearl. The director had told her that her character was essential to the story. Whenever my sister talked about her part, her eyes got bright and shiny. "You see, Lorraine, there is this beautiful young girl, and her father just ups and sells her to his neighbor for seven dollars, or was it a sack of turnips?" Arlene was not sure but "Pearl really is the catalyst for all the action," she said with conviction.

"Wow, impressive," I said, and added a note to myself to look up the word "catalyst." Each day, Arlene came back with stories of how the play was progressing, about her scenes and the other characters that played opposite her. She had some big scenes, she said and some problems to overcome; for instance, she was supposed to hate the husband she had been sold to and cringe in revulsion every time he touched her, but in reality, Arlene thought her co-star was really cute and had a bit of a crush on him. It took all her acting skills, she said, to act repulsed. In another scene, she, Pearl, was to run to her mother and cling to her. Arlene said how embarrassing it was to embrace Connie, a middle-aged woman who played her mother. "She is really boney, and the costumes we wear are so thin. I can feel all her ribs when I hug her. It's weird."

Yet all in all, Arlene was having the time of her life at rehearsals and at home discussing how to play her scenes. For several weeks now, she had been talking in drama lingo. "There is this one part where Connie, I mean, Ada Lester, my mother, tells Jeeter he is not the real father of Pearl and I have to play it just right. First, I have to figure out my motivation, then my reactions." Arlene talked a lot about motivations and reactions.

Paul, for his part, told us about the difficulty of finding props for a farm in the Deep South at a beach town. "Somehow, I have to replicate an old broken-down shanty of a house and a well, as *well*," he added, then laughed at his pun. I mentioned that an old house on the corner had just been torn down and if it hadn't been carted away yet, there must be plenty of old boards and even some cedar roofing that could be used for the shanty. Paul's eyes brightened. "Really, I'll go look later, thanks."

Getting out a small notebook, he started to make a list of the items that he had already found and the props still to be obtained. The Goodwill, he said, was an excellent place to look for out-of-date clothes—old dresses, shoes, hats and gloves, even jewelry. Now if he could just dig up overalls for the men. "I might have to buy them new," he said. "That would be more expensive and then I would have to age them by washing them in bleach and rolling them in oil and dirt. I need some burlap material too, for your costume, Arlene."

Arlene made a face. "That stuff is really itchy. I made a dress out of it once. What a mistake. The only way it can be worn comfortably is to line the whole inside. Can you tell someone to do that for me, Paul?"

Paul looked dubious. "Well, if I have time."

"I'm going to need a tree too," Paul mumbled, "but that can be a dead one, so maybe a nursery has one they want to get rid of. Money is pretty tight. It will be more like beg, borrow, and steal to bring this show in under budget." By this time, Paul was talking more to himself than to us, and Arlene took over the conversation again.

"Did you know that some of the actors have already done

professional work? Colette, who plays my sister, Ellie, just acted the same part in Los Angeles with John Carradine, no less. He had done a revival of *Tobacco Road* on the New York stage some years ago."

"Was it on Broadway or off Broadway?" Paul asked.

"What's off Broadway?" I wanted to know.

Arlene supplied the answer. "It just means that it isn't a big production. It's a little theater, like what we are doing, only theirs has more prestige because it's in New York. Of course, they have a low budget too, but sometimes an off Broadway theater can get a success, and move on to the Broadway stage."

"Really?" I said.

"Yes, and Connie, the woman who plays my mother, once starred in a Broadway play, but it only ran for three days. It was a flop!"

Arlene and Paul suddenly looked at each other and became silent.

Wow, I thought, *I guess it must be bad luck to even talk about a flop while you are in a play opening soon. Actors are so superstitious!*

A moment later, however, Paul piped up happily, "And guess what! The guy that plays the lead of old man Jeeter Lester in our play is almost famous!"

"Yes," Arlene cut in, "he is Frank Lovejoy's brother!" She said this with great satisfaction and waited for my reaction.

I knew of an actor called Frank Lovejoy from old movies from the '40s and '50s. He was what you call, a kind of "everyman." He never got the girl and mostly played the police detective or army sergeant or the guy next door, or the best friend of the lead. Some of this celebrity must have rubbed off on his brother because, after that, whenever anyone asked Arlene about the play, she would promptly declare that Frank Lovejoy's brother was taking the lead role, which in her mind must have been the most impressive thing about the whole production.

BACK TO SCHOOL

As Jeff pulled into the tight space in the El Camino parking lot, the truck gave a final lurch before settling into a stop. Here I was again at my old college. It looked pretty much the same after—what was it, two years?—the same red brick buildings, the same green campus with crisscrossing paths and small shade trees, only now they were bigger.

At my high school back in Riverside, we had had "career day." Students from the prestigious Art Institute of Los Angeles came and showed us their designs of snazzy cars and refrigerators and toasters—all modern and sleek. I was told that when they graduated, they got jobs as top artists and art directors—the school was *that* good. I wanted so bad to go there and become a commercial artist, maybe do illustrations for books or magazines, but the tuition for a year was four thousand dollars. Gosh, our house in Riverside cost that much, and Mom was still paying it off.

EL CAMINO COLLEGE

It was Arlene who got the idea of my going to the junior college in Torrance, which was almost free and just a jump away from Hermosa Beach where she had just moved. It took a long time, but she had managed to persuade her then-husband, Don, to relocate there. I could live with them, she said, and help out with the children. Well, that didn't last long; Don kicked me out after a couple of months. He said as long as I lived with them, Arlene would never truly bond with him, so I had to go. It turned out all right though because Mom decided to rent out the house in Riverside and move to the beach too. She found an apartment, and soon I was back living with my mother and little brother again.

At El Camino, I took as many courses in art I could and hoped it would be enough to start me off in a career. I could work my way up after that. As it turned out, there were some extraordinary teachers in my new school: Mr. Bluske of the Design Department and Mildred Walker, who taught figure drawing, figure painting, and art history. My problem was the commercial art classes were not as good as the fine art classes. By graduation, my portfolio was filled with great sketches of naked models but not enough slick renderings to get me a job in an art department, but that was all water under the bridge now. I was here today to have fun, with no pressure about the future.

VAN GOGH PLAYS ALTO

Sara Lee had kept me informed for months about the alumni exhibition that she and Chris were organizing at the Annual Art Show. Even her new baby had not stopped her from drumming up former graduates and soliciting their best paintings for the exhibit. In that vein, Sari had pestered me for something to submit to the show, until I finally dug up an old painting I had some pride in. I was lucky to still have it.

Some time ago, I had given it to Arlene right after my graduation from El Camino. I couldn't drag all my paintings to Hollywood, so I gave several of them to her. She had begged me to furnish her with something to brighten the dreary apartment she and the kids were moving into with her husband. It was yet another attempt at marriage with Don, and it turned out to be the last time they were ever to be together.

It wasn't even an apartment Don was setting up in Venice Beach. This new dwelling was no more than a huge cement space—more like a warehouse or garage. Arlene said that having my paintings around would make it "at least bearable living in that cavernous gray hole." Don had built makeshift areas of a bathroom and kitchen and had constructed against one wall a rustic three-tiered bunk bed for the kids. Sure enough, there was a big blowout within a few months.

When Arlene and Don fought, Arlene screamed insults, and Don retaliated by destroying things she cared about. This time he chose my paintings and chucked them into the alley where they were carted away with the garbage—all except for one painting, the painting of Jeff. Don didn't like me, but he liked Jeff, so he didn't throw that one out, and this was the painting I now gripped in my arms.

The portrait was a rendering of my brother playing his alto sax. Van Gogh had inspired the painting. Maybe because I thought Jeff had some of the same qualities and problems that van Gogh had. They were both shy and inarticulate yet in a way, bigger than life. The result was primitive and stark—the colors straight out of the tube, applied in thick impasto—yellow for Jeff's hair, cobalt blue for his eyes, a brighter orange yellow for the saxophone and cadmium red for his shirt. The background was just swirls of thick white paint that made the primary colors of red, blue, and yellow stand out even more. Jeff's fingers, playing the sax, I had dashed in quickly and they looked almost disfigured, which somehow gave the impression of fingers striving and moving fast over the keys of the instrument. I think it was the shortest time I ever spent on a painting, so it had a fresh spontaneous look. I was proud of the results.

THE ART DEPARTMENT

Feeling around with my foot for the running board, I clutched my painting tighter as I scrambled with one arm out of Jeff's truck. Turning the canvas side of the painting inward so no one could see it, I called back to Jeff. "Are you coming with me?" I asked through the rolled down window.

"Naw, you go on. I'll just do some woodshedding till you come back." Jeff reached behind the front seat and grabbed his alto and started to play. As I picked my way out of the parking lot, I could hear a series of arpeggios coming out of the van, getting softer and softer as I directed myself toward the Art and Design Department.

Flanking a courtyard, the buildings were a separate complex of about five or six studio rooms connected to each other. High windows ran along the back of the rooms. Outside each classroom was a display window that showed student work. I remembered how proud I was whenever one of my designs made it into the window outside of Mr. Bluske's class. The front doors of the studios led directly outside into the courtyard. A big rectangular brick planter stood in the middle filled with large green leafy plants and bushes. I used to sit there between classes and talk to the other students about art. Seeing it all again, I realized that my time here had been the happiest two years of my life. To begin with, college, even junior college, was unlike high school, where I felt different. The art group people were like buddies. I was comfortable. For the first time I didn't worry about who I was or who I talked to. And there was that other reason that it was the happiest time. I had fallen in love; something I never thought would happen.

A taped sign on one of the doors read: "Drop off artwork here for Art Show." With my free arm, I hefted it open. There was an excited buzz in the room and I could see a lot of hustle and bustle going on. Students stood a bit impatiently holding their artwork. They formed a queue that led to a long table with teachers in chairs sitting behind.

Some teachers were talking artwork and talking to students, some were writing down information on square pieces of paper while others taped the information on the backs of the paintings and stacked them against the wall. I recognized a few teachers. There was Mr. Suzuki, one of my painting teachers, who had refused to show me how to paint clouds and water; when I asked him, he said, "The way to learn to paint is just to paint!"

There, next to him, was Mr. Neice, another one of my design teachers. He always looked more like a football coach than an art teacher with his crew cut and burly frame. I had taken lettering with him. On the first day, he told the class that learning to letter was a waste of time, so he lectured about modern design. He loved the Charles Eames chair and the Buckminster Fuller geodesic dome. He never wore a tie because "They were useless ornaments." He believed in the "less is more" concept and at his own home, he said, he had removed his front lawn and filled the space with pebbles that he raked like a true Japanese garden. The neighbors weren't happy.

There, next to him, was Miss Walker. Good old Miss Walker, she actually taught me a lot. I didn't see Mr. Bluske anywhere, and I didn't recognize the other two teachers, but one had a sticker nametag *Mr. Gadden, ceramics.* I thought it was strange that in my years here, I had never bumped into any ceramics class.

CAMERA SHY

On the other side of the room was another familiar face. He looked more like an artist with a delicate build and longer hair. I had only taken one class with him. Now, what was his name? Standing next to him was a guy with a serious looking camera. He was saying something to my unnamed teacher. Mr. What's-His-Name paused and looked thoughtful for a second; then he looked around the room and spotted me. He smiled then and wiggled his finger in that sign that means "come here."

Oh no, now what was his name? It was something simple like Jones or Smith. As I got closer, I read *Mr. Clark Art Appreciation* on his nametag. When I reached the two men, Mr. Clark put a hand on my shoulder, then turned back to the man with the camera.

"I think this young lady will do very nicely, don't you think?" he said.

The man nodded and looked at me. "I'm from the L.A. Times, the Bay View section," he said, adding, "I need to take some photographs for the article we are doing for the show. Do you mind coming with me and taking some pictures?"

"But I have to check in my painting," I blurted out, lifting the Jeff portrait up a bit and turning it around for the first time.

"I'll just take care of that," said Mr. Clark, taking hold of the frame and gently removing it from my hands. "I see you have already taped all the information on the back of your entry . . . and written your name, er . . . Lorraine," he said, looking closer. "And you also have the name and category of your painting—very good, that's all we need." He quickly walked away toward the long table. Then Mr. Clark turned around and called back to us, "I think a good place for a picture would be in Mr. Gadden's ceramic class, room two-twenty-two." The cameraman nodded and started moving to the door. As I followed him out of the room, I wondered if Mr. Clark realized that I was not in his class or the school anymore.

Eventually, we found the ceramics room. It was filled with pottery and blocks of clay and a few pottery wheels. I had never seen this place before. I didn't recognize any of the students either. The kids were bustling around organizing tables that displayed their earthenware for the show. The cameraman stopped in front of one table. "This looks good," he said. Some students paused in their busywork, curious about who we were and why we were in their class.

"OK," the cameraman said to me, "can you move over here?" I moved to the middle of the table and stood waiting for more direction. The cameraman was in full artistic mode. "If you could look at the ceramics that would make a nice shot," he said. I moved in closer and tried to examine a small bust of a woman. Slowly, I became aware of a subtle buzz of voices around the table as the cameraman cleared some of the people out of range and concentrated on organizing his picture.

I heard a girl somewhere to my left saying in an acid voice, "She's not in the pottery class!"

Another hissed, "I never saw her before."

"Yeah, who is she?" said another terse female voice.

I cringed a little inside. There it was again, the old high school thing, that feeling of not wanting to stand out too much, the vibe I got from girls sometimes—a kind of hostility, like I was some sort of threat—no, no it wouldn't do to be too smart, too talented, or too pretty. Others didn't like it—must not ever blow my own horn too loud either. All this time, the cameraman was positioning my fingers around a very large vase. I stared at the strange pot with the tiny opening at the top and wondered what could even fit in a jug like that.

"No, no. Look off into the distance," the cameraman said, "over a little to the left. Yes, that's it!" He adjusted my head a bit with his finger.

I wondered, *Shouldn't I be looking at a pot if I was touching it?* But the cameraman was still giving instructions.

"Now, raise your chin a touch," he said, as he readjusted my fingers for the second time.

The pose felt awkward and unnatural. *This must look pretty stupid*, I thought—my finger brushing up against a weird pot and me gazing off into the sky.

"Now raise your eyebrows a little and lick your lips." I complied. Flash, flash, flash! "Got it!" he said. At the door, the man smiled at me now, no longer the domineering cameraman. Thanks a lot for your help," he said. "Look for the picture this Sunday."

They probably won't even use the photo, I thought, as I made my way back to the truck, where Jeff was still practicing.

NEWSWORTHY

That Sunday, we all trooped down to Hermosa Avenue to the convenience store where we usually got our pinto beans. Inside, Arlene ran up to the stack of *Los Angeles Times* newspapers and grabbed the first one off the top of the pile. Keeping the paper to herself, she flipped through the sections until she came to the Bay View segment. Holding it up, she let out a yelp. "Oh, my God, Lorraine, you look beautiful!" Then she flipped the paper over so we could all see. The photo was really big and surprisingly, my pose didn't look weird or awkward at all.

The caption on the photo read:

Coed Lorraine Gibson inspects artwork to be displayed at the Annual El Camino Art Show.

This time the newspaper made only one mistake: I wasn't a coed anymore.

CHAPTER 43
FROM THE GRAY NOTEBOOK
THE DAYS OF WINE AND WASHING

The traditional day for washing usually comes on a Monday, but it is a Friday summer evening that finds me and my sister on our way to the all-night Laundromat. The wheels on our cart kick and bump and bumble along the narrow street, making a clumsy erratic rhythm like a cement mixer with hiccups. The rubber on the left wheel has come off, and the wooden wagon jangles unevenly on the asphalt. Down the hill we go in the warm summer night. There is no moon, and the sky is black against pinholes of stars. The bundle of damp laundry weighs down heavily on the wagon and sways threateningly.

Without Jeff's van, our transportation depends on one bike and this wooden wagon. Each week, the little buckboard carries groceries, but every two weeks it serves as our laun-dry truck. I secure the quivering load with one hand, while juggling a box of IRIS detergent (the cheapest brand) in the other. My free pinky is painfully hooked through a half-gallon jug of bleach.

"Don't go so fast, Arlene," I call over the noise of the wagon. "I'll drop the bleach!"

Arlene is guiding the rope that pulls the carriage with our gargantuan load. She is skipping merrily down the hill with a pillow sack of wash thrown over her shoulder. "I'm gonna wash that man right out of my hair!" she carols, still skipping, unmindful of the half-gallon jug slipping from my little finger.

It must have been the wine we had before we left the house because I joyfully join in with harmony on the last chorus and somehow also hold on to the bleach. What a way to do wash, I think as we turn the corner on Second Street. A few cars screech and swerve to avoid the ghostly procession of two dancing girls balancing an outsized bundle of laundry and singing in two-part harmony.

Strange as it may seem, we make it to the Laundromat without so much as a dropped pair of dungarees or a lost leotard.

We have forty minutes to kill while the laundry goes through its acrobatics in the graying bubbles, so we gallop back home, the wine still in effect.

We make our way, faster this time up to Culper Court. The inky night has changed our house into a dark reddish shadow, and the glowing lights shining from within through the cracked and broken windows are a deep yellow. Our funny little cottage seems to smile like a droll jack-o-lantern complete with missing teeth. Its amused grin welcomes us.

Music is still pouring out of the house, and through the French windows you can see that the jam session is still in full swing. Gary is on bass, Jeff is blowing his sax, while Ed Cassidy, having left his drums at home, is keeping time with hairbrushes on a telephone book, occasionally hitting a spoon on a tinkling glass of water in lieu of a cymbal. They have been playing a variation on a Thelonious Monk tune for the last thirty minutes. Finally there is a five-minute break for more wine.

While the band starts up again, Arlene and I, fortified by more wine, merrily prance back to the laundry just in time for the drying and folding. Twenty minutes later, we repeat our trip back up the hill in the same manner as before, with the now beautifully washed and folded clothes piled high in a neat swaying skyscraper.

So, here is my advice to one and all. If you have washday blues, why not try it accompanied by good jazz, a gallon of cheap red wine, a wobbly wagon, and a warm summer night? You can even do it on a Monday.

*The rubber-less wheels clanked and bumped
along the street like a cement mixer with hiccups.
Down the hill we went in the summer night.*

CHAPTER 44
FAME, SORT OF PART III
TOBACCO ROAD

THE WRITE-UP

Arlene stood, both arms raised in triumph, a ragged scrap of paper in one hand and a large pair of scissors in the other. Always a little shaky, her hands now quivered with excitement, and Arlene *was* excited. My first thought was that I had caught my sister in an act of some sort of violence. There she was wielding a weapon, hovering over the victim with a jagged hole cut out of its innards. It reminded me of a scene from an adventure movie where, atop an Aztec pyramid, a warrior priest has just cut the heart out of a sacrificial victim and is holding the still-beating organ up for the gods to see. Arlene's eyes *were* glittering true, but her mouth was spread, not in a maniacal grin but in a wide joyful one.

"Lorraine," she gushed, "look at this." The *Daily Breeze* was spread out on the dining room table exposing the arts section. "It just came out today about the play and my name is in it! A reporter came yesterday and interviewed us. Read! Read!" Her still trembling hand shoved the news clipping at me. I took the gouged out piece of newsprint that somewhat resembled the shape of Florida and examined it. Arlene, in her excitement, had cut half the headline off at the top and several letters and words on the whole right side of the column, but she was looking at me expectantly, so I read it as best I could.

CAST AWAITS DEBUT OF "TOBACCO ROAD"

"This is great!" I said. "But you've cut your own name off. Now it says 'Arl . . . Brauer will play Pearl,' and why were you using your married name anyway? And, of course, they spelled it wrong."

"Lorraine, you are so picky, picky, picky. But aren't you excited? We open this Friday night."

"Well, what time?" I retorted. "'Cause you cut that off too, along with the price of admission."

Arlene squinted down at the rest of the paper. "Uh, Friday at 8:00 p.m., and admission is . . . is . . . well, I can't read it so good. Just bring a couple of tens; that should be enough for you and Jeff. Anyway, Mom will be coming too, so she can cover it if you don't have enough." Arlene looked satisfied that she had cleared up all the problems. "And remember keep this Friday free. I want you and Jeff and Mom to be right there in the front row on opening night to cheer me on."

"And the kids, who will be with the kids if we all come?"

"Such a stickler for details you are." And here Arlene almost smirked. "I got that all covered. Rita will mind the kids and then come to see my performance on Saturday. You see, Lorraine, you are not the only one who thinks ahead." Arlene started to gather up the paper, folding it haphazardly. "Well, I'd better go next door and give Betsy back her paper," she said.

OPENING NIGHT

That Friday, Arlene and Paul left early in the afternoon to drop off the kids at Rita's and get to the theater for costume fixing and makeup and any last-minute changes in the play. The kids were excited to bunk in the attic with Rita's kids. Arlene had laid out one of her dress creations for me to wear. It had an Empire waist-line, which I always thought made me look taller, or maybe it just made my short legs seem a little longer. The top was a midnight blue of velveteen cloth and the bottom and sleeves, an olive-green faux suede material. The dress was formfitting, and I had to shimmy myself into it before I did my hair and makeup.

Bob dropped Mom off at the house just as I was finishing the Cleopatra slant to my eyes. Jeff was going to take us to the the-ater later in the truck when he came back from Santa Monica. The Blue Horn Group was squeezing in as many rehearsals as they could before the Jazz Festival at the Lighthouse the following Sunday.

Mom wore a dark taffeta sheath dress. I had never seen her look so glamorous. She was even wearing eye makeup. "Oh, I thought I would never get it on," she confessed. "I was blinking so much, but Arlene told me she wanted me to look stunning for a change, and I didn't want to let her down."

"And the new coif too!" I motioned at her newly cut hair.

"Yes, I went to that salon on the corner. They said it was the newest thing." Mom turned her head in profile, showing her perfect nose and patted at the puffed-up curls. "They call it 'The Artichoke.'"

Sometime later, Jeff rumbled up in his truck just as Mom and I were beginning to get worried. He beeped his horn, and we scurried out. In spite of our worrying, we made it to the theater with time to spare. After finding an easy parking space, Mom and Jeff got out of the front seat, which allowed me to scramble forward from the back of the truck. I stepped out gingerly onto the running board and took my first look around as the other patrons were ambling into the theater. A sign above the entrance said, "Drawing Room Theatre" and under that *Tobacco Road*. I felt excited. *So this is small theater*, I thought. *I wonder if we should call it off, off, off Broadway, since we are so far from New York.*

As we came into the foyer and were given our programs, I noticed several glossy 8 x 10 photos of the cast pinned up on a board. Arlene's name was there but not a picture. Was that a bad omen? I remembered again how the theater was all about luck—good or bad. Then, some more people came in, so Mom, Jeff, and I made our way toward the raised stage. The crowd was still sparse enough that we could claim three front-row seats that turned out to be folding chairs that sat about twelve abreast and twelve or fifteen rows deep. I looked around as the last of the patrons wandered in and took their places in the dimly lit playhouse.

As I readjusted Arlene's snug dress that had hiked up a little in the truck, I studied the closed vermilion curtains, wondering if there was some kind of rule or tradition that all stage curtains must be made of red velvet. Maybe it was another one of those luck things. There were still several empty seats when the house lights dimmed, then darkened. I quickly looked over at Mom and Jeff. We grinned at each other. We were going to see Arlene on a real stage.

THE PLAY

There was a spatter of applause as the curtain opened onto the set. A deep orange light of early morning illuminated the scene. On my far right, in shadow, was an old shack, battered and shabby, with a sagging porch and shingles missing from its decrepit roof. On the far left was an equally dilapidated well and rustic bench. Paul had really done a good job with the leftovers from that demolished house on the corner. I wondered if he had also painted the canvas background that showed a dusty road running off into the distance to nowhere. There was the dead tree—I had almost forgotten about that. I was squirmy with anticipation.

The orange light started to get brighter and more yellow then white, and as the dawn turned to morning, I realized there were two figures frozen in time on the stage. I could make out a young man standing by the side of the house and an old man sitting on the sagging porch. When the light was at its brightest, they came alive. The young man started throwing a ball against the wall of the house with a steady bonk, bonk sound. The old man with a gray patchy beard and slouch hat was fiddling with an inner tube for a tire. The play had started.

That old man must be the famous Frank Lovejoy's brother, I thought. On stage, the father and son were talking in the twangy accent of poor country folk. They complained, bickered, and traded insults until they were interrupted. A small dark figure carrying a gunnysack crawled painfully out of the shanty and onto the porch. Could that be Arlene? I could feel Mom beside me rise up a little in her folding chair. No, the figure on stage was too old and bent, and they called her Grandma. Mom and I sank down again.

After teasing and tormenting the poor grandmother until she crawled painfully off into the woods, the two men went back to arguing again about how to get some money. The door to the shack jiggled then, and another figure came out of the house. I couldn't see Jeff on the other side of Mom, but Mom and I rose up again. A moment later, we settled back down. It was just the thin gaunt figure of Ma Lester, only middle aged but not a hint of youth left in her bony figure and faded, outdated dress. She and Pa Lester had nothing good left in their life together, so they bickered about money and being hungry.

Umm, I thought, *now that we have Ma and Pa and Grandma and son, Daughter Pearl must certainly be up next.* And sure enough, a young woman stepped out of the shadow of the creaky old house, only it wasn't Arlene. Her figure was stocky, her hair jet black, and she even had a harelip painted on her upper lip. It was the other daughter. We were deflated again.

Oh, but wait, the cast was now talking about Pearl. I gave a quick encouraging look at Mom, and she smiled back. This must mean Arlene would be coming in soon, but the discussion didn't last, and the actors went on to other topics. When the "public urination scene" came, I was ready and not shocked a bit like the audience of 1933. It consisted merely of Pa Lester going off to the side of the shack and fiddling with his pants. A timid titter rippled through the audience.

After that, the old couple was alone again and talking about Pearl for the second time—how pretty she was, her silky "yeller" hair. Then, when one of the characters suddenly called out that someone was coming down the road, Mom, Jeff, and I were all in expectation again. This had to be Arlene's entrance cue, but sadly it was someone else. This time it was Pearl's husband, Lov, who had come to complain about his new wife. Arlene (Pearl that is) had refused to sleep with her husband even though he was good to her and "bought her fair and square." There was further talk of how Pearl was so pretty and had pretty "yeller" hair. Meanwhile, our group in the first row had to console ourselves with the idea that at least Arlene's character was the center of the conversation even if she wasn't there yet. I looked down at the program and concluded that almost every cast member was or had been on stage now but my own sister. I heard Mom give a little sigh. Jeff rustled his program. Act I ended and the curtain closed with no sign of our Pearl.

The lights came up, and Mom and I looked at each other with questioning faces. Even Jeff was wiggling in his folding chair. "Mom, what's going on? When does Arlene get to come out? Don't you know?" I asked.

Mom got that defensive look she got when she thought her children were asking for too much from her. "Now, Lorraine, I didn't see the play on Broadway. I was only fifteen and when they made the movie, they changed things and enlarged the part of the sister with the harelip. They had Gene Tierney play the part. Of course, they didn't give her a harelip. So, I know as little as you do about this play."

"But Arlene said it was such an important part."

Mom just sighed at me and shrugged her shoulders. By this time, Jeff was humming a song under his breath while his fingers ran over imaginary keys. I just studied the playbill again. Maybe the cast was listed in order of appearance. I searched for Arlene's name.

Right before the second act started, the director came out on the stage. He was smiling but in a slightly strained way. "Hi, folks," he said, forcing his mouth into a toothy grin. "The cast backstage has sent me out here to have a little chat with you." I was sorry now that we had claimed seats right in the front row because the director seemed to be looking straight at us before sending his gaze out to the rest of the audience. He paused for emphasis, then said, "Now we've noticed that you are a pretty quiet group. You're just not laughing enough! The cast wants you to relax and have a good time, so enjoy the rest of the show." There was a ripple of embarrassed laughter from the audience as the director stepped back off the stage again.

What! I thought. *He wants us to laugh? I didn't realize this was supposed to be a comedy.* Why, these people were dirt poor, and what about that talk of starving their own granny to death? And . . . and their youngest daughter . . . her father sold her to a neighbor for a sack of turnips. Laugh at that! *What's going on here?* First, there was no Arlene in the play yet and then this guy just told us that we didn't know how to be an audience. A quick peek at the cover of the program, however, confirmed the director's speech. It said "Tobacco Road: a comedy in three acts." I showed the program to Mom, but she still looked confused. Jeff on the other side of her was making grunting noises like he did when he was embarrassed about something. I was a bit embarrassed too that the director had to come out and tell us how we had failed as an audience.

After the lights went down again, the red curtains opened onto the second act. It was another morning with another amber light. There were three actors on stage now. When the light got bright enough, I could see Arlene was not one of the three. They were not even talking about her this time. In this scene, a stout older woman, "The Preacher Lady," they called her, was sermonizing about redemption and God, but what she really wanted was to marry the young and lanky Duke, Jeeter's son. She finally convinced the not too bright boy to oblige her by bribing him with a shiny new car that she promised to buy. She would even let him honk the shiny new horn on it too, she said. Then Duke and the Preacher Lady exited left off the stage. The two love birds were gone, but we could still hear the sound of young Duke in the distance hooting and tooting like he was already in his new car.

Ma came out of the house and sat on the porch next to Pa. There was a quiet scene where she and Pa Lester reminisced about all their children who had gone away to Augusta never to return. I waited for more talk about my sister but there was no mention of Pearl this time at all. During a lull in the dialogue, I took a cautious look at Mom next to me. She was starting to sit a bit stiffly in her folding chair with her hands clasped together and her face kind of closed down. A sure sign she was becoming dispirited, but my attention quickly turned back to the play when Pearl's husband, Lov, in great distress rushed onto the stage.

Now, what? I wondered gloomily as the actor stood in the spotlight. After getting his breath, we heard the news that Pearl had run off! I wasn't expecting this. Was this good or bad? Did it mean we would see Arlene soon? Maybe not, if her character had gone to Augusta like all the other children. At least they were talking about her again.

On stage, Lov was bemoaning the missing Pearl—how pretty she was, how pretty her "yeller" hair was, and how he wanted to touch it; finally, he exited stage left. I was starting to give up ever seeing my sister in Act II now and started to pin all my hopes on Act III. Then, somewhere past the middle of the second act, Pa Jeeter wandered off the stage. *Is he going to take another leak behind the shack again?* I wondered vaguely. A short time later, however,

I heard cries. They got louder and louder until Jeeter appeared and . . . it was . . . yes! At last, it was our own Pearl, finally on stage for the first time, and what an entrance! Arlene, kicking and whimpering like a caught rabbit was frantically resisting old Jeeter as he dragged her across the stage.

Mom and I, even Jeff, sat bolt upright in our folding chairs. My sister was wearing a shapeless burlap sack as a dress. I wondered if it had been lined like she wanted, or was it as itchy as it looked. She was barefoot too, and her blonde hair, always a bit unruly, was now all snarled and tangled. Suddenly, seeing the character of Ma Jeeter sitting on the porch, my sister finally pulled away from her captor and uttered her first line.

"Ma!" she cried in a strangled voice as she ran to the far end of the stage and threw herself into the arms of the actress playing her mother. *At last*, I thought, *her first line, well* word *really.* As the scene progressed, my sister's character clung to her mother and remained mute, nodding only yes or shaking her head no and looking back and forth as Ma and Pa Jeeter quarreled.

Finally, the squabbling couple came to the part in the play Arlene had been telling me about for weeks. *This must be where Pearl finds out that Jeeter is not her real father*, I thought with rising enthusiasm. *Here is her big scene.* I looked closely at my sister for the reaction-acting she had been telling me about during rehearsals. I waited for some hysterics from Pearl, but apparently, Arlene's Pearl didn't understand or just didn't even care that she was a bastard because there was just a blank look on her face and a slight shrug of her shoulders.

Finally, Pearl was alone with her mother, and I was ready for some heartfelt dialogue between them. Ma had a lot of long speeches to deliver about how much she loved her daughter and that she must run away to Augusta like the other children, meanwhile my sister answered briefly with three short lines. Number one, "Don't leave me, Ma!" Number two, "I don't want to go back to Lov," and, finally number three, "I'm scared to go to Augusta."

At this point in the play, the mother exits into the shanty, perhaps to pack Pearl's bags, and all is quiet. Arlene, on the stage all alone, pensively sits by the defunct well brushing the tangles out of her hair. I suddenly felt very proud of my sister because with the light shining down on her like that, she truly was as beautiful as Pearl's character was said to be. I guess she *was* a catalyst after all. Now, I waited for something to happen, even wondered if Pearl would break out into some sort of soliloquy like Hamlet, but she stayed silent and just kept brushing her hair, unaware that the character of Lov had come onstage, and was creeping up behind her.

When he grabbed her by the arm, there was a long struggle. I had to admit my sister did the fighting and struggling parts in this play very well. She gasped and cried and fought, but she did not say anything. Lov, however, never stopped talking about how he loved her and her purdy yeller hair and that he would do anything for her. *His* soliloquy lasted a long time, again, no response from our Pearl. Finally, she pulled away and disappeared into the wings. I wondered if we would ever see her again. As the play continued, there were more characters and more dialogue before the end of Act II, and Arlene did not come back. *She must be in Augusta by now*, I concluded morosely. Mom and Jeff looked dejected too, sitting stiffly on their folding chairs.

Act III opened on another orange morning and like all third acts, all the various plots and subplots got resolved. For the Lester family, it resolved in the worst possible way. For starters, old Grandma never came back from collecting wood in the forest and was casually presumed to have starved to death or been consumed in a brush fire. The bank man came and told Jeeter he and his family would have to leave the farm, and, as if it couldn't get any worse, Jeeter's son, Duke, crashed his brand-new car to pieces and as a by-product had run over his own mother, who lay dying by the porch. I thought for the second or third time this evening, that if *this* was a comedy, it was a very dark one.

There was one bright spot, however. My sister appeared again. Pa Jeeter, for the second time, dragged her back onstage to do a big scene with her dying mother. Again, Arlene clung furiously to the actress playing her mother. In my sister's one speech, if you could call it that, she declared loudly, "Ma, I swear I will get you a new dress to be buried in!"

Now, I must stop here and say, that for someone who had just gotten run over by a car, this worn-out mother sure had a lot of breath left in her for the very long speech that followed. On she went at great length, tenderly telling her daughter how much she loved her, urging her to be brave and to get away from her old husband and . . . "Leave the ruin of this worn-out farm!" And just when I thought she was finally at the end of her soliloquy and about to die . . . a most surprising thing happened. That old Ma Jeeter riled herself up and attacked her husband, biting down hard on his hand.

With a yelp, Old Jeeter had to let go, and Arlene, I mean, Pearl, was set free. At least Arlene got the last line. "Goodbye, Ma!" she calls out as she runs behind the shack, presumably toward Augusta.

As the stage lights started to dim into orange again, Jeeter sits down on his porch all alone, except for the dead body of Ma of course, and picking up the inner tube, starts to fix it again. And just as the light faded into blackness, a rotten shingle let loose from the roof and fell to the ground as the curtain closed.

Arlene told me later that she didn't go completely off stage but stayed behind the shanty until she got the cue to toss the shingle over the roof right before the curtains closed.

CHAPTER 45
FAME, SORT OF PART IV
THE LIGHTHOUSE

MEETING UP

It was Sunday, and the jazz concert would be starting at twelve noon. The Blue Horn Group was ninth or tenth in the lineup, but we wanted a good seat and to hear all the other groups, so we told everyone to meet up before twelve, and the first ones to arrive at the Lighthouse were to save seats for the others. Arlene and I would walk together over to Pier Avenue, and Mom was to meet us at the club.

I hoped that seeing Jeff play at the Lighthouse would raise everyone's spirits. Arlene had been strangely quiet since the opening of *Tobacco Road*, a play that had for weeks previously consumed so much of her attention and conversation. She seemed to be licking her wounds from this debut into the life of the theater, and I was hesitant to talk about it unless she brought it up. There had been that sparse turnout on opening night, and some lackluster reviews, maybe even something bad said about her part. I didn't know, but I thought it best, at least today, to let it go.

Even at the opening night party after the performance, there had been a general atmosphere of gloom. No one was laughing and chattering. The cast and crew stood glumly around the fold-out table that was set up backstage. They ate their Ritz crackers and drank their wine in paper cups with a grim determination. For my part, I thought Frank Lovejoy's brother had turned out to be a pretty good actor. I let go of my disbelief (as they call it in the theater) and did believe he was Jeeter Lester. The other actors were OK too, but I just couldn't accept Arlene to be anyone other than my sister. Who was that person up there on a stage wearing a gunnysack and not talking at all?

Walking to the Lighthouse, I realized I hadn't seen Jeff all morning. He was not there when I woke up. I assumed he had left early to meet up with the band or had stayed with them last night for more rehearsing. Well, we would be seeing them all later on the bandstand. The doors were already open at the Lighthouse when we arrived. As usual, the Dutch door near the stage was half open, letting afternoon light into the dim interior. Beachgoers walked by in their bathing suits and flip-flops, carrying towels, kids, and baskets of food for a day at the beach. Some stopped to peek over the Dutch door into the club, wondering about the sign outside that said "Annual Jazz Festival this Sunday featuring California City Colleges." A special crowd was already arriving at the entrance, talking and collecting in a bottleneck at the open door. It was nearing twelve, and the place was filling up fast.

Cookie had said she would try to come early and save us some seats. We were not disappointed. She had commandeered a table right next to the stage and was waving as Arlene and I walked in. Ever her bubbly self, today, her eyes were even brighter and shinier in anticipation of seeing her husband play his bass. As we sat down, we congratulated her on her skill in grabbing up such great seats. If I reached out, I could touch the bandstand. I looked around at the fast-filling room and, before anyone else sat down at the next table, surreptitiously pulled over an extra chair for Mom.

"Oh, I'm an old hand at this," Cookie was saying, "I've been at all the important gigs since I met Gary, every one of these concerts at the Lighthouse, the very first one, in fact, when Gary and Cass played with Martin Eagle. Back then, they called themselves The New Jazz Trio." I remembered that Martin was the name of the piano player that had left the group for a try at success in New York.

Echoing my thoughts, Cookie further explained, "Yes," she said with a little sigh, "back then, it was just the three of them but when Martin left, Ricky and Harvey stepped in and here we are again," she finished brightly.

"And now Jeff," I added, "so that makes them a quintet." Arlene was looking around, smiling, picking up on the excitement, and I relaxed. We had been told there were ten to twelve different bands and they were to play two sets. I also discovered it was not just a concert but also a competition for best college jazz band. I looked around for Mom, then around at the club. The ceiling was painted a flat black. It was strange to be in a nightclub during the day. During the day, they always looked a bit dingy, yet at night they came into their own with everything in deep shadow, the air cloudy with cigarette smoke and the spotlight on the stage gleaming off a polished piano or splashing off the gold of a trumpet.

Arlene and Cookie started talking about fashion. Cookie was interested in seeing some of Arlene's creations. They soon had their heads together, giggling about clothes or as it turned out, the lack of clothes. "I'll show you the rest after the concert but look at this." Cookie handed an 8 x 10 sized photo to Arlene. "Gary and I wanted to have photographs taken now that we are officially married. We wanted to have it done professionally and we knew this guy . . . I guess we were a little crazy that day. I don't know who got the idea, but we decided that we should get into bed for the photos. So, what do you think?"

Arlene was smiling. "This is pretty wild," she said. As I peeked over her shoulder, there was Cookie and Gary smiling happily, neatly tucked into bed with just a sheet covering their naked bodies. Cookie giggled again and took back the picture and put it into the manila envelope. "Some of the other pictures are more daring!" she said with an elfin grin.

Just then, a young man trotted over to the stage and started arranging things, putting a tenor saxophone on a stand and moving the drum set around a little. I spotted Mom at the door and waved her into the seat next to me. Before she sat down, we introduced her to Cookie. The club was now completely full. The show was about to start.

APPLAUSE

There was a hush as Howard Rumsey moved through the crowd and stepped up on the bandstand. He was a little guy with dark hair and ferret-like features. Today he wore a dark suit with a skinny tie. My old boyfriend and Lenny always made fun of Howard Rumsey. They thought he was a little too self-important and would do imitations of how he played the master of ceremonies like he was king or something, but Mr. Rumsey did deserve all the credit for turning a seaside dive bar into a world-famous jazz club. Even so, I had to repress a smile when he picked up the microphone, because I knew pretty much what he would say and the way he would say it.

"Good afternoon and welcome to the Annual Collegiate Jazz Festival. This year we have several jazz groups competing from fifteen junior colleges around the Southern Californian area. But before I introduce the first group, from Santa Barbara, I want to tell you that today we are recording the session live."

Here comes the lesson now, I thought.

"So, before we start," Mr. Rumsey continued, "I'd like to give you a little tutorial on how to clap." I had heard this many times before when I happened to be in the audience when the Lighthouse was taping a session, usually when a prominent musician was booked so I could almost recite the speech along with our master of ceremonies.

"First, I'll show you how *not* to clap." Mr. Rumsey said, as he held his hands stiffly not very far apart and clapped. A muted clip, clip, was the result, and there was laughter from the audience. Mr. Rumsey continued, "Now, we don't want any stingy applause here. Here is how you do it." He cupped his hands and held them at slightly different angles. Then, by holding them a little farther apart, he clapped forcefully, making his applause sound more like thu-whap, thu-whap, thu-whap! "You get the idea," he said. "So let's hear it now for our first group, from Santa Barbara City College!"

The audience thu-whapped correctly, and some people (probably family and friends) even gave a whistle and cheer. The Santa Barbara group made their way through the crowd. Four guys jumped on the bandstand and proceeded to pick up instruments. One had been the same guy that had been moving things around before. After a bit of adjustment, the piano player leaned over to his microphone and introduced the members of the band one by one. Polite clapping followed after each was named, then the ensemble broke into an up-tempo song.

After each group finished their set, Howard Rumsey wiggled back through the crowd and onto the stage to introduce the next group of players. There were trios and quartets and quintets for the most part. Usually a piano led the group, but sometimes the lead was a guitarist or, in our case, a vibraphone. Some bands played straightforward jazz, some had a more Latin flavor especially when the main horn was a trumpet, a sort of tribute to Dizzy Gillespie who brought an Afro-Latin sound to jazz. Some groups had a Dave Brubeck-Gerry Mulligan kind of cool sound to them with hints of Bach and counterpoint. Other bands fell back into bebop, playing fast and furious, like early Charlie Parker. They were all very serious and all very good.

Finally, Mr. Rumsey jumped onto the stage and introduced our group as a quintet from Santa Monica City College. I had to smile a little because Ed, the drummer, definitely didn't look like a college kid with his bald head, and Jeff had not even finished high school. Maybe Ricky or Gary had gone to the Santa Monica school.

From the back of the club, The Blue Horn Group wove their way through the crowd. Gary was carrying his bass. One by one, they got onto the bandstand and took their places. Ricky pulled out the vibes from somewhere in back of the piano. Ed Cassidy sat on his stool rearranging the drum set, tapping on all the cymbals and finally tightening the snare drum. Gary plunked a few notes on his bass, then looked satisfied and stopped to wait for the others. By this time, Ricky was rippling his mallets back and forth over the vibes.

Harvey and Jeff, like a kind of ritual or ceremony, stood at the front of the stage nodding and bowing to each other as they played a few notes in close harmony. All this took less than a minute. Then Ricky took the microphone and introduced the members. Our table clapped hard using the Rumsey technique.

"We would like to play," Ricky continued, "two original compositions. First 'Tiana,' by Gary, our bass player, and a composition of mine called 'Ostrich Head.'" Cookie whispered quickly to our table, "Gary wrote 'Tiana' for me. It's my real name." The song started with the bass alone. A few bars later, the drums picked up a slow rhythm and soon Ricky joined in softly on vibes until Harvey and Jeff came in to echo the theme. The audience responded favorably when the song ended.

Arlene and I smiled at Cookie, and then I whispered to Mom that it was a song Cookie's husband wrote for her. Mom smiled, I was glad she was relaxed and comfortable. Maybe she was identifying with Cookie having a musician as a husband.

Early in her own marriage, my mother went to most of my father's jobs just like Cookie did. There is a picture in our album dated 1944 taken during World War II, which was when Harry went to a lot of factories and shipyards entertaining for the war effort. He even got a commendation from the War Department for his service. This picture, though, is not about that. I used to study it occasionally because it was the only picture of my mother all dressed up.

She is perched on a barstool in a nightclub. You can see the bartender in the background mixing drinks. Mom wears a dark dress with a big corsage of flowers pinned to her right shoulder. There is another, even larger flower fixed in her hair, perched onto her dark pompadour like a bright crown. The rest of her hair is long and curling to her shoulders. The picture is unusual for two reasons. First, my mother is the main interest. The person taking the picture has put her in the middle. She is center stage. Harry stands near her in a dark suit and bow tie with his hand in his pocket, for once taking a back seat. The second is because Mom is looking directly at the camera with a big smile on her face. My mother usually ducks or blinks when a camera is nearby, but here it is different. Her eyes are shining. She looks beautiful. Arlene is always going on about how our mother is beautiful, but I can never really see it until I look at this picture where she is glowingly happy.

On the bandstand, all was ready, and Ricky called out, "One, two, three," and on the unsaid "four," the group charged into Ricky's composition, "Ostrich Head." It was quite amusing. Jeff and Harvey started it off with several dissonant notes that made you think of quarrelsome birds, then the melody line began in a waltz time with the vibes, drum, and bass taking the next several bars alone. Now I remembered that Jeff had been humming that same melody around the house for weeks. After a while, he even put words to the song. Let's see, how did it go? "Time of the ostrich, hide your head in the sand." And then there was something that rhymed with sand—I never quite got all the words. After the bridge, the group took their solos.

Ricky clamped his lips together in concentration; his two mallets with the white pompoms on them flew swiftly over the metal bars. A lot of piano players start to hum loudly and tunelessly when they take a solo. My father, in particular, was a prime example of that. I wondered if vibe players were the same, but Ricky remained mostly quiet except for a huff or two.

Next, Gary took his solo, intently bending over his instrument, almost caressing the bass as he concentrated, his floppy hair touching the strings. It was pretty far-out free jazz that he was playing, but if vibes are mellow, the bass is the mellowest of all, and the audience was not unduly disturbed by the new sound the group was making.

During solos, I always looked around at the other musicians. Cass on drums reached around for his sticks and got them ready for his solo. Ricky, arms folded, nodded his head in time to the music. Harvey was taking this moment to clean his horn out with a handkerchief on a string, and Jeff, who didn't quite know where to look when he wasn't playing, looked with great interest into the bell of his horn. After Gary, Cassidy ripped into his solo running through all the acrobatics of drum percussion, hitting the snare and cymbals in various patterns of syncopated rhythm, while keeping a steady beat with sock cymbal and bass drum. Sometimes his drumming quieted down, almost stopping, only to explode loudly into another cadence altogether. Drum solos usually bring out spontaneous applause.

At our table, Cookie was smiling, Arlene had a slightly bored look (I think she felt the same way I did about drum solos), and Mom, well—she looked a bit tense. I thought she must be counting down the soloists until Jeff played. Only he and Harvey were left to perform now.

When Cass finished his solo, Harvey moved into his, working through some chord progressions in a smooth and dexterous manor. A few eyebrows went up when he threw in a riff or two of free jazz, but that was all. These people were knowledgeable fans and they expected some innovation. At the end of his solo, Harvey got the usual scattering of applause.

JEFF'S SOLO

Jeff had been standing quietly, hardly moving, but now, as Harvey stepped back from his solo, Jeff stepped forward and closed his eyes. Taking a big breath, he plunged into his solo. It started with a run of notes going up and down the keys of his alto at lightning speed, ending in a high squealy note. Immediately, everyone jerked up their heads. The man at the table next to us jettisoned out of his seat and a moment later, hurried out of the club. The audience was in for it. It was a free-for-all. It was free jazz. Jeff was throwing out every rule in the book of music. All those hours of practice were paying off for him as he continued to wail into his solo, fingers flying and flickering over the keys, sometimes making fluttering noises on one note, which required strength and control. He honked and wailed, at times going at a super-fast pace, then slowing like a 78 record played at a lower speed. He made guttural growling sounds. He made high-pitched squeaks and squawks in between the fast triads running forward on the scale and circle of fifths going backward. At one point, he leaned over and put his knee into the bell of the horn, emitting a sound similar to a drunken foghorn.

At first, the audience was startled and frozen in their seats. Then, after the next few notes hit them, the people nearest the bandstand, jumped up and hurried out of the club. The second row of tables was the next to pick up and leave, some gulping down the rest of their drinks before quitting the scene. After that, random people all across the room left. Some were even running.

Jeff played on, oblivious to the sensation he was causing around him. I looked over at Mom who was sitting stiffly with that closed-up look again—poor Mom! Arlene had a kind of half smug, half angry, holier than thou expression. Cookie just looked amused; maybe she had seen something like this before. I turned back to Jeff. With his eyes still closed, he finished his solo with several notes that sounded a lot like a collision of a truck and a train. Instead of applause, there was total silence. The room was completely empty except for our little group by the bandstand. We almost forgot to clap ourselves; the pitiful applause must have sounded sparse and hollow in the recording that was going on. I wondered what Howard Rumsey was thinking now. Finally, Jeff opened his eyes and looked around. He didn't look upset or anything. He just had his regular embarrassed smile on his face. I suddenly felt a surge of pride and clapped harder. I mean, how many people can clear a room in five minutes like that?

We stayed for the whole round of second sets and when the Blue Horn Group came up again to play their version of "'Round Midnight," as before, Jeff's solo cleared the house in record time. When I asked my brother later at home if he felt bad, he just shrugged and said that when Ornette Coleman played *his* free jazz, the audiences threw things at him and he was often attacked, mostly by other musicians. "I figured I got off easy," he said, ambling back into the music room. A moment later, he was practicing again.

CHAPTER 46
FAME, SORT OF PART V
ART SHOW

THE STAGGS FAMILY

It was the day of the Art Show, and I was dressed and ready when Sara Lee and her husband, Chris, picked me up around one o'clock. As I squeezed myself into the back seat of their old car with Neisha and Inger, I was glad to see that Inger had fully recovered from the trauma of visiting our house. She sat, happily contented to stare out the window at Hermosa Avenue going by. Neisha was a bit more antsy, jumping and sliding down on the back seat, then standing up and repeating the whole thing again.

Chris, who was driving, turned around at a stoplight and in a chiding voice said, "Now, young lady, calm down. Remember last week when you almost put your foot through my design poster that we are taking to the art show?"

Neisha slammed down on the seat and froze—stiff arms clamped to her sides. Her eyes rolled back then and only the smallest telltale giggle escaped from her lips.

"All right, all right, that's enough," said her father, turning back and resuming his driving. Chris was good-looking by all standards, with his thick brown hair and even features. He was a talented artist and intelligent, yet he was a bit too perfect for my taste and sometimes seemed more like Sara Lee's mother than her husband. He invariably started his sentences to her with "Now, Sari!" as if she was a child and he had to teach her the right way to do things. Meanwhile, Sara Lee seemed not at all bothered by this. She sat calmly in the front seat, occasionally turning around to smile at us in the back.

With Chris, I got the feeling that underneath all his good looks and talent, he was basically timid. Was there a tinge of insecurity I was picking up? Like those kids in high school who stand on the edge of the popular crowd and laugh too loud. Chris may have been the star of Mr. Bluske's design class and lord of the Staggs family but . . .

As we came to the intersection of Hermosa and Pier Avenue, where most of the downtown stores were, I stopped my analysis of Sari's husband and noticed the block was being decorated for the Fourth of July festivities next month.

"Oh look," I said, "they are putting up American flags." I gestured to the banners flying from streetlights and the red, white, and blue bunting inside store windows.

Behind the wheel, Chris looked up and grunted, "Such bad colors!"

Inwardly, I had to laugh at his response. Only a Mr. Bluske student would say something like that about his own country's flag. It was well known that Mr. Bluske loathed bright colors. He would loudly proclaim, "Whenever you use any color, *always* mute it down with its complementary color, and when you use a bright color like red or orange, be stingy, too much will overwhelm a design." In Mr. Bluske's class, I learned that a complementary color was the hue directly across from it on the color wheel—green is the opposite of red, purple has yellow, and orange is the reverse of blue. If you use the same amount of opposite colors together, eventually you get brown, and brown seemed to be Mr. Bluske's favorite color. He was particularly partial to a greenish brown he called "bilge water green," although I had also heard it referred to as "monkey vomit green" by someone in the class. I suppose if Chris or Mr. Bluske had been asked to design the American flag, it would have turned out to be a banner with a field of bilgy-green with one tiny bright orange star on it. That thought made me smile for several blocks.

By now, our happy group had left the downtown area and was nearing the beginnings of the El Camino campus. In the parking lot, we spilled out of the car and headed for the room that housed the former student's exhibition. I remembered it as my former figure drawing and painting class that I had taken with Miss Walker. Now, the space was filled with artwork on the walls and on easels around the room. One oil painting was so big and long that it ran across one entire wall. It was (Oh, my, gosh) *The Crucifixion of Christ on the Cross*—complete with three weeping Marys, Roman soldiers, and maybe I could even find Pontius Pilate if I looked closely.

"My, my, that *is* ambitious!" breathed Sara Lee—a slightly sardonic smile playing on her lips.

Chris turned away. "Let's see where they put our entries." He found his design on the other side of the wall. It had a tasteful wooden frame painted black. I think if it hadn't been pointed out to me, I would still have known immediately it was done by Sara Lee's husband. Squares and rectangles covered the surface all neatly assembled in an intricate pattern—some big, some small, some vertical, some horizontal, and each shape a different color of brown—dark brown, light brown, greenish and pinkish ones. Some verged into the golden spectrum, while others moved more into the blue and purple hues, yet—they were all *brown*—it was quite attractive really.

After we had all properly admired it, we moved on to find Sara Lee's contribution. The children were happy to run around the room looking for it. "Here it is, Mommy!" they both chanted, jumping up and down in front of a large sized drawing. "It's Rita!" they squealed.

The chalk sketch was impressive. There sat Rita with her untamed hair flying wildly out around her head. She sat proudly and solidly dressed in a ruffled blouse and a big full skirt like some mystical gypsy or priestess. Big swaths of colors in burnt sienna, umber, and ocher colored the background and parts of her skirt.

MOM

Moving on, our group looked around at the other entries. I didn't see my painting of Jeff, so after awhile, I said I had better go look for it because I had promised Arlene and Jeff I would meet them by my painting. "And my mom said she would show up too." I added, "I'd better go search for it before anyone comes."

We were to meet around two o'clock, so I didn't have much time. Mom would be at the proper place at the proper time, but there was no telling when Arlene and Jeff might show up. I took a quick look at the other artwork as I searched for my own. I really couldn't go very fast anyway. This morning, Arlene had insisted I wear one of her latest creations. She said it was the perfect outfit for an artist at an art show.

Actually, the dress was pretty special, simple but ingenious. It was made from a light stretchy jersey material. One long tube formed the main part of the dress, then two smaller tubes were inserted as sleeves. Another tube structure fashioned above the sleeves acted as a hood. When put on, the material fell in grace-ful, natural folds around the body, sort of like that funny dog with all the loose skin.

I had to take small little steps because I had on heels and the bottom of the dress, though stretchy, was tapered. The fabric had come in only one color and with the hood up, it was sort of like being in a chrysalis, a bright orange chrysalis. The dress was getting some attention too, and I hoped I wouldn't run into Mr.

Bluske, who would probably not approve of such a large amount of orange.

Soon, I forgot about the dress. There was so much art work to look at. The first room held figure drawings. Forgetting to hurry, I pretended to be a judge deciding which work was best and awarding imaginary ribbons. The judges had already been here. Some artwork had ribbons pinned to them. In the next room, the category was oil figure painting, and sure enough, in the middle of the room, I spotted my mother bent over examining my contribution to the show, her forehead wrinkled in a quizzical expression. Mom always tried to like the art of her children, but sometimes it was hard for her. I knew my painting of a vase of flowers on a table in the spirit of Vermeer was easier for her to praise than this expressionistic one before her, even if it was a picture of her son.

"Hi, Mom," I said, making her jump a little. "I see you found my entry."

The judges had already been in this room too. Three or four works had ribbons. I wasn't really surprised my painting had none. Yet, I did feel a bit let down. As if Mom read my thoughts, she said, "I think your painting is very original."

I smiled at her effort to try to comfort me. "Have you seen Arlene or Jeff yet?" I asked, changing the subject. "They said they would meet me here by my painting."

Mom looked concerned. "Was that wise?"

I laughed. "No, I guess not." They could show up at any time or no time, but I thought the art department wasn't that big, and I figured I would have to bump into them even if I missed them here. "They did say they would take me home."

"Well," Mom said, "if it doesn't work out, Bob and I could take you. He is picking me up in an hour." She glanced at her wristwatch.

"In the meantime," I said, "let's look around."

We strolled through the show, and I tried to explain to her which pieces were good and why. I showed her the ceramic room and the big pot that had shared the spotlight with me in the newspaper photograph. I even modeled Arlene's new stretchy dress creation for her by striking a high fashion model pose that I had seen often in *Vogue* magazine.

Mom's comment on the dress was, "Of course, it is very inventive of Arlene, but I do wish she had put more time into getting the seams straight, and look here, there is a loose thread just hanging from your hem." Mom opened her purse and got out some tiny scissors and kneeled down to clip off the errant strand.

I was glad Arlene was not here yet. She was always looking for Mom's approval and would not like to hear that her creation would have been better if she had just done it properly.

My mother usually gave people the impression that she was a hard worker in a family of talented people, but had no talent herself. She saw her role as the woman behind the piano genius of her husband and the mother helping her children with their artistic attempts, sewing curtains for Arlene's theater productions, getting Harry to shell out money (at least for a little while) for drum and piano lessons for Bill and me. Harry was a big believer in raw, untutored natural creativity. He thought lessons would pervert Arlene's singing voice, so he vetoed them when Mom brought it up.

As usual, my mother sold herself short. In truth, she was very creative and always resourceful, especially if she had little to work with. She could take almost nothing and make it something special. One summer when I was away for two weeks, she made over my bedroom for zero dollars. She dyed my old chenille bedspread and curtains a deep forest green, then scrounged up some material in a different green and reupholstered the fabric on the headboard of the bed (which she always called "The Hollywood Headboard"). What was left over was made into a flouncy ruffled skirt around the kidney-shaped dressing table. The dark green colors matched the green leaves in the wallpaper of pink roses. When I got home, the new room was a lovely surprise—not bad, for someone who claimed to have no artistic talent.

More people were milling around now but there was still no sign of Arlene or Jeff.

THE COURTYARD

Later, Mom and I sat on the edge of the large cement planter in the outdoor patio area where she got out her tiny scissors again and cut off more threads from the orange dress. I thought back to the last art show when I was a student. I had gone that year with my boyfriend. The art show had been before our breakup, and even then I sensed something was wrong. It seemed the closer I got to graduation, the more distant my boyfriend became.

It suddenly occurred to me that he and I had done the very same things Mom and I had just finished doing. We had walked around looking at the art, especially mine. I was surprised to find two of my works had winning ribbons on them. One was a third prize for a poster design and the other a second place, for an oil in the figure painting group. Dizzy with success, we had taken a break in the courtyard at this very spot. *Well, so what!* I quickly told myself. *I'm not going to let that spoil my day*, and turned my attention back to my mother. She had finally finished her cleanup of threads and had put her scissors back in her purse.

It wasn't long before Sara Lee and her family also wandered into the courtyard. The girls were hopping up and down with excitement. "Tell Lorraine what happened, Mommy!" they squealed together.

Sara Lee was beaming in spite of herself. "Well, someone liked my picture and just bought it for a hundred dollars! I put that price on it never thinking . . ." Her voice trailed off as her smile got bigger.

Chris put in, "Well, now aren't you glad you took my advice? I told you that the drawing of Rita was the right pick for the show." Yet, Chris didn't look half as happy as Sari and the kids.

"That is just great," I said. "And now you can up your price when you sell to that old art-connection man who thinks your drawings are only worth twenty-five dollars."

Chris added, "You know, if we do bring in more money, we will be able to buy the Eames chair I've been thinking about. It would be a good investment too."

After more congratulation and more jumping up and down, Chris broke into the celebration with "Now, Sari, I think it's about time to go home. Your mother is not the best babysitter, you know, and I have some work to get to."

It was time for Mom to be picked up by Bob as well, so we all ambled over to the parking lot. The Staggs family pulled away in their battered car with the rope still holding the door closed, and I found myself thinking that an investment in a car might be a better idea than an investment in a designer chair.

LATE ARRIVALS

Mom was soon picked up by Bob, and just as I was debating whether to go with them, Jeff and Arlene rambled up in the van. Jeff wore his usual casual clothes, but Arlene had on another one of her eye-popping creations. This time, she had taken a fancy to a white lace tablecloth (another Goodwill find) and fashioned it into a long robe like a Catholic priest might wear at high mass.

"Sorry we took so long," Arlene said, smoothing down and rearranging her vestments, "but my ex-mother-in-law was late picking up her own grandkids for their yearly summer vacation with her in Beautiful, Hot as Hell Riverside." Arlene was always happy to point out anything that was not perfect about Pauline. It was partly payback for all the times her mother-in-law had pointed out Arlene's child-rearing and housekeeping flaws over the years, and it also reinforced Arlene's claim that "Perfect Pauline" couldn't be perfect because she had raised a son capable of abandoning his own children.

"I'm a free woman now, for two weeks." Arlene threw up her arms in elation and spun around in the parking lot. When she stopped spinning, she looked at me and her eyes glinted. "What shall we do, Lorraine? Let's have an adventure! What say we do something wild and crazy, like bike down to Tijuana?" She paused. "Or how about we go to Las Vegas for a few days? Bob even said he would pay for our tickets on the train. He thought Mexico was too dangerous for two young women when I brought up the biking trip."

"But we have no money to gamble," I said, "and isn't it expensive?"

"Oh, gambling is just for suckers and I heard that everything there is dirt cheap—food, lodgings, you can just stroll through the casinos and catch all the acts for free or with just a drink or two, and we can sneak into the back doors of the big shows I'm told. It will be fun!"

"Well, uh . . ." I ventured. Things were never quite as uncomplicated as Arlene made them out to be—like how I would live with her and Don and go to El Camino at night. It turned out no buses ran at night, and then Don chucked me out and I had to scramble for a place to stay. And there was that other time when Arlene persuaded me to give her most of my paintings and Don threw them in the garbage . . .

Arlene's voice broke into my thoughts. "Don't worry, we'll talk all about that later." By now she had grabbed my arm and was pulling me out of the parking lot. "And now, my dear, lead us on to see your masterpiece of Jeff."

Soon, we were making our way back to the art department. "There it is!" Arlene said, a little too loud, running over to the tripod holding Jeff's portrait. "Jeff, Jeff, come over and see yourself."

Jeff stumbled over, turning bright red with embarrassment. "Oh, don't worry," Arlene assured him, laughing. "Without your horn, no one will know it's you."

"I think it looks better here than at your old apartment with Don," I said teasingly.

"Don't remind me of that time. Nothing could have made that rattrap of a place look good," said my sister through clenched teeth.

Jeff was looking shyly around the room. He mumbled, "Hey, how come you don't have a ribbon? I see some others have them."

"Yeah! Why?" Arlene repeated, again, a little too loud.

"Well, I really shouldn't even be in this room. I'm not a student anymore. I guess Mr. Clark made a mistake when I gave him my painting. I should be in the room for former students. Things must have gotten mixed up. It's fine, really." And yet, I was a little disappointed. It was one of my best works.

Our group looked around the room some more until I finally said, "You know what? Why don't you guys see the rest of the show? I've already seen it twice. When you're finished, just go to the courtyard outside. I'll be by the plantings. I'll wait for you there."

DRESSING FOR SUCCESS

Ten minutes later, I was sitting in the same spot as before, watching the art lovers crisscross the courtyard and disappear into the various rooms. Before long, I was reflecting back to that one day in Mr. Suzuki's class. Some of the kids were asking him if *they* had the makings of a real artist. His answer had been sobering. He said that one shouldn't even have to ask that question. You should just know it! "Something inside just has to paint!" he said gravely, and added, "An artist has something to say to the world, and it just has to be expressed and shared." At the time, I knew I didn't have that kind of burning desire or something special to say to the world, and I certainly didn't have the ego that would go along with those other traits. I was a good artist and I liked to draw and paint, but that was all I knew.

Lost in my thoughts, I almost didn't see Mr. Bluske bearing down along one of the corridors outside the classrooms. I recognized the green smock he always wore. *Oh my gosh, my old design teacher! What if he recognizes me?* In a few moments he would see me in a flagrant orange outfit. I could still remember when I wore my blue and green plaid jumper to class. I had paired it with a bright green sweater. Mr. Bluske pointed me out to the whole class. "Never wear that again in my class, Miss Gibson!" he boomed.

I feebly defended myself, saying, "Well I like it," but I never did wear it again. Now here he was yet again coming closer and closer, and just when I was ready to duck behind one of the plants with leaves the size of elephant ears, I realized it wasn't my old teacher after all. What a coward! I wasn't even in his class anymore but old habits die hard, I guess. I was still musing over my cowardly reaction when a boisterous voice called out, "You there in the orange dress. I'd like a word with you!" I jumped, thinking it might really be Mr. Bluske this time, but when I turned around, there was big and bulky Mr. Neice smiling at me. I recovered enough to greet him.

"Hey, are you in one of my classes? You looked familiar."

"Yes, I was your student a few years ago—er, lettering?"

"Oh yes, hand-lettering—a waste of time. But hey, I wanted to talk to you about your dress. Where did you get it?"

"My sister made it," I said, looking around to see if Arlene and Jeff were nearby.

"Well, it's a great design! Do you mind standing up?"

I stood up and explained how it was made. Mr. Neice was impressed as I told him about my sister and her ideas.

"Look, I'm writing a book for next year's design class and yes," he chuckled, "the students will all have to buy it. It's all about what is good design. I'd like to include your sister's dress. It is a perfect example of what fashion can be—elegant, beautiful, and easy to wear. Now, if you wait here for a second, I'll just get my camera." He sped away even before I could say anything. Within minutes though, he was back again with the camera. As he posed me, he explained more about the book. "I'm almost ready to go to press, but a dress design is the perfect finishing touch. Oh, how about a pose that shows the folds of the hood. Turn that way a little. Yep," he said, repeating himself, "good design is simple— form follows function."

"So, less is more?" I added.

He smiled. "I'm glad you remembered your lessons. All right, just one more full length but I'm not including the high heels. They are about the worst thing the fashion world has ever done to women—almost as bad as the Chinese binding the feet of their little girls. OK, we are done now." He put down the camera and briskly took a little notebook out of his pocket. "Now, what are your names—you and your sister? If you give me your address, I'll send you copies of the pictures. The book will be in print September for the fall semester." He tucked the little book into his pocket and grabbed up his camera. "Bye, and thanks for the help. Look for a package soon." He walked back to his classroom whistling.

CREDIT WHERE CREDIT IS DUE

We hardly ever got mail, so it was nice a few weeks later, to see a rolled up manila envelope wedged into our mailbox. I carefully unrolled the envelope, which plainly said in large letters "Photos!

Do not bend!" I wondered if rolling qualified as bending. I guess not. At least the address was correct, and it got here.

I opened the packet and pulled out several photographs of me in the dress. Mr. Neice had also included a rough mock-up of the book itself. I skimmed through pages of pictures and text about Charles Eames chairs and Buckminster Fuller's geodesic dome until I came to page ten, and there I was in the stretchy dress sitting in front of the big elephant leaf. Underneath, it said: "Tube dress by Arlene Gibson." *Won't Arlene be pleased?* I thought, and I put the pictures and book on the table in the dining room where she would see it when she came back from the Laundromat.

SUMMER

CHAPTER 47
A WALK ON THE STRAND

AND

FROM THE GRAY NOTEBOOK
WARNER TOBE

LINDEE

After Arlene and I returned from our great adventure in Las Vegas, it took several days to get back into the habit of sleeping at night and staying awake during the day, but by the time the kids got back from their Grandma Pauline's house, Arlene and I were pretty much back on our old schedule again. Our strange adventure in Las Vegas seemed like something out of a dream now, and it wasn't long before I started again to mull over my situation. What should I do with my life? What was my next move? So much had happened in the last month. I needed to think.

I had just crossed Hermosa Avenue when I heard the scuffling noise of little sandals. I turned to see Lindee, her light hair flopping up and down as she scooted to a stop behind me. "Lorraine, Lorraine! Wait up!" she gasped.

Had she just crossed the avenue by herself? I looked at the traffic casually whizzing past. It wasn't exactly a freeway, but there were no traffic lights and Lindee had never crossed it alone before. "You came over by yourself?" I demanded, scanning the street again.

Lindee looked at me and smiled proudly, "Yes, I wanted to go with you."

"But Lindee, I'm not going to sit on the sand. I'm just going for a walk."

"I can walk too." She looked up at me with an eager, pleading face. She was so pretty, her silver hair, not flopping now, was like a shiny cap. Any other day would have been fine, but today I wanted to be alone.

"Look, I'm going to walk fast. You won't be able to keep up."

Lindee looked determined. "I can keep up. I just want to be with you," she said.

This was not good. Today I needed to get away from the house and the people there. I needed to think things out.

"Lindee, I really have to be alone right now. I'm taking you back across the street," I said firmly. "I want you to go home, and don't cross that street alone ever again! Do you understand?"

"But I want to be with you!" she repeated. She looked like she was about to cry, which made her even more beautiful. All this was breaking my heart, but I took her hand and ferried her back across to the other side of the busy avenue and watched as she marched up Second Street toward home—her shoulders hunched. She didn't even turn around, which made me feel even worse.

FAMILY TALENT

I crossed the street again and soon reached the Strand. Turning north toward Manhattan Beach, I started to walk at a fast clip. I wanted to think about the last couple of weeks, the weeks before we rushed into our crazy trip to Vegas. Was it significant or just a coincidence that Arlene, Jeff, and I all had gone through a test recently? To put it another way, we had a brush with fame—well, sort of fame. It seemed significant somehow.

I walked a bit slower, to start out, it was important to acknowledge one thing about the Gibson family and that *thing* was talent. Our father had it and he always told us that we were special too, not like other families, who were square. We had natural talent and talent was everything . . . Well, did we have it, and was it everything?

There had been such a buildup about the play, the jazz festival, and the art show the month before. We had all gone through some attempts to prove him right. We all had the experience of having an audience and being judged. So how did we do? Actually, we hadn't done all that well, but did that matter?

Did art really need verification and did we personally need recognition and approval to continue on? Jeff had driven his audience right out of the room. Arlene had very little audience and a very small part, and I had submitted a painting that got no special attention. We certainly didn't get recognition, much less fame. Should we stop doing what we were doing? To look at it in another way, there was some success. Jeff got to play with a true jazz group at the celebrated Lighthouse. Arlene, at her first try at acting, had gotten chosen for a part with professional actors and had performed it in a real theater, and I got to take one of my best paintings and have it seen by many people.

As for recognition, all three of us had gotten our names—and in my case, picture—in the newspaper. That was some sort of fame, even if Jeff did get in for disturbing the peace, and let's not forget that Arlene's dress creation was singled out to be the epitome of good design in Mr. Neice's book. Maybe it was all small potatoes, but it was some satisfaction nonetheless. All in all, I decided we didn't do too bad in our first attempts.

The question is, do we need fame and why do people want it? All those young men and women in Hollywood when I lived there all wanted to be the next Marilyn Monroe or Marlon Brando. They wanted to be stars, and if they didn't make it, they thought they were failures.

FAME

I thought about my father, who had actually been famous for a time in the 1940s. I always got the feeling that after getting it once, he couldn't let go of the idea of not having it anymore. By the mid-'50s, his "fame" had died down quite a bit. He was still popular in nightclubs, but there were no more record hits or guest appearances on radio shows. He wasn't on the cover of *DownBeat* anymore and there were no more cartoon jokes in the *New Yorker* magazine about his boogie-woogie records and no more characters based on him in the funny papers like those in the *Dick Tracy* Sunday comic strips. All that would probably not happen again. There were fewer glowing reviews or memorabilia to be pasted in his scrapbook of triumphs that my mother had carefully made for him over the years.

The way I saw it, my father was always trying to get back what he had before. He seemed almost desperate about it . . . It ruined him because he could never settle for anything less. Every time he got a job in a new nightclub, he would become elated at first and talk endlessly about how he would pull in the crowds and how the owners of the club wanted him so much that they were going to do everything he wanted just to have him stay for a long engagement. They would rearrange the stage and the lights, provide a great piano, and get super publicity.

Opening night would arrive, and Harry would come home and brag about how the crowds loved him and wouldn't let him leave the stage—and Harry would not leave, not while people still clapped and laughed. Every night, my father sweated through six white dress shirts, each shirt embroidered with "Harry the Hipster" sewn in red thread above the pocket. Harry had gotten Mom to hand sew his signature on every dress shirt he owned, and before every performance these shirts were washed and ironed to a white stiffness by my mother.

At first, all would seem well at the new gig. Then, after a while, my father would start complaining: the owners of the club were not doing enough for him, the spotlight was bad, there wasn't the right publicity. He would quit or lose the job, and with the end of each job, there were longer times between them, and they would not be as good as the one before and the owners, in turn, did less, and fewer people came to see him. I stopped walking abruptly and turned toward the water. It was a hot hazy day, the sky and sea, the same dull gray. A tiny white triangle of a sailboat far out in the water was moving slowly south.

I thought again about Harry. He started out wanting to be a great jazz pianist like Art Tatum or Fats Waller. My mother said that after he became "Harry the Hipster," the crazy jive- and drug-talking funny man, he changed. She thought it ruined Harry Raab, the serious musician she had married and believed in, the one who won a music scholarship at Julliard and played at Carnegie Hall. Over time, Harry started calling himself an entertainer and not a jazz musician. *He wanted his fame*, I thought soberly. Somewhere along the way he confused it with love, and he sure wanted to be loved by everyone.

MORE ABOUT FAME

I continued to look at the hazy seascape, my mind drifting along with the tiny boat and skimpy clouds hardly moving in the sky. In no other occupation are the stakes as high as they are in the arts. You are a failure if you don't make it to the big time. You wouldn't say that about a plumber or an electrician or a schoolteacher.

Jeff had his audience run out the door, but still, he was just happy to play his music. He would probably always be that way. Bill seemed content with his band, but I'm not sure about Arlene. Early on, Harry had claimed she was a "chip off the old pill." He told her she would be a great singer. Maybe *fame* is what she was after too. My sister could be good at so many things. If only she could just pick one and stick to it. She had tried singing, bass playing, clothing design, acting. What would be next and what about me, did I have to have fame? The answer for me was no. The best thing I knew was to do what makes you happy and not get hung up about praise from other people. That was success, and fame was just a by-product that happened sometimes. I could be happy in an art department making enough money to get by and maybe someday write and illustrate a children's book.

While I'm listing people who want fame, what about Lenny! I turned from the gray waves in the distance and started walking again a bit faster. Lenny wanted not only fame but money. He was willing to write teenage surfer songs that he knew were crap just for a chance at it.

I stopped again and leaned my elbows on the wall . . . and what about *Him*? Today I wouldn't push it away. Maybe this was what I wanted to think about all along. *He* was caught up in this fame thing too, wanting so badly to be the next Frank Sinatra and not settling for anything less. It was the biggest reason he had cited for needing to break up with me.

THE NIGHT WE CALLED IT A DAY

When we first got into the car that evening, I had a feeling something was about to happen, yet his words still caught me by surprise.

"The fact is, we met each other too young!" This was how he began. It was starting, I thought. He was breaking up with me. For a while now, he had been moving away and now it was here. I was glad the light was dim inside the car—a kind of barrier against the words that were going to be coming. Now he was saying something about needing to sow wild oats, then he stopped talking. Had he rehearsed all this before?

Sitting forward with a serious look on his face, he continued. "We were nineteen—that's way too early to settle down with one person." His experience with sex, he said, had been limited to a few older women before he met me, and he wasn't going to get more if he stayed with me.

On my side of the car seat, even with the sinking feeling, I could still find a part of me that could mock him. I mean, who says "sowing wild oats" anymore? Even so, the words hurt.

When I didn't say anything, he continued. I was the marrying kind, he said, and if he married me in a few years there would be kids. He would have to get a real job to support us. I managed here to mumble something about wanting to work in art, and that I hadn't thought about kids, but he interrupted.

Well, maybe I hadn't thought about them yet, he insisted, but if we married, well then, I *would* want them and then . . . then he would have to give up his dream of being a singer. "I'll wind up playing piano in a bar," he announced gravely, "like my father—a failure!" Sitting back in the car seat he waited for me to say something.

What could I say? I was losing him and couldn't stop it from happening, and yet a part of me was still laughing at him. All those dramatic statements, how silly of him to declare that he would end up playing piano in a bar like his father! How ironic, because all the time I knew him, he had patently refused to even consider learning to play any instrument. Even when I told him it made sense because then he would always have an accompanist.

"Sinatra doesn't play an instrument!" he would declare staunchly. "He doesn't even read music!" (As if that proved anything.) Even when I brought up Nat King Cole, who could play great jazz piano, yet was known mostly as a singer, he wouldn't budge from his idea that a true singer never touched an instrument.

There was a long silence. I could dimly see the dashboard and the different dials and gauges. Some I knew didn't work, like the full-and-empty gauge. We had often run out of gas. It was an old car and leaked oil. The battery had often run down too, mainly because the radio was always on when we were parked, but this time the radio wasn't on.

He started talking again in a low voice, sounding more serious this time. I felt a sadness surround me, trying to find a way in. If I stayed still maybe it wouldn't seep in too fast. My soon-to-be ex-boyfriend continued to talk, and I wondered why he made it seem like his problem was somehow my fault, that I was the one holding him back from success.

I still hadn't said very much so far. He must have been waiting for an argument, but my throat was so very tight and dry. In my mind, I was defending my side of the story fiercely. I had never thought about marriage. Yes, I always assumed that when you found love it was forever, but I never thought much beyond that. All I knew was that he had cut through my self-imposed isolation. He had pursued and pursued. He had climbed the tower; he had cut through the brambles of the castle and had won the princess—me! And that meant "happily ever after," not "I want to date other girls."

I was aware of the distance between us now as we sat in the car. He was sitting behind the steering wheel, not next to me as usual. His words became a low droning sound, and I thought about two years earlier.

I was in love for the first time. He was funny and smart. He was there every day to pick me up after my classes to take me home. I liked that he felt intense about things. He told me once he accidentally ran over a puppy and killed it. He got out of his car and kicked the fender until it caved in. He was passionate like that about his music and about me. He even liked my quirky family.

I did have some qualms. He still lived at home. When he needed cash for singing lessons or to fix his old car, which continually broke down, he worked for a few weeks as a busboy or delivery driver, then he would quit. A steady job would interfere, he said, with him becoming a singer. Once he told me that if a sack of money fell off a truck, he would keep it. I was shocked. The next day, he told me he was kidding. He wasn't perfect, but I was committed. I had said "I love you," and I wouldn't take it back.

With him, everything was about music. We mostly talked about his career. I wanted to believe in him. Could he really make it? He had a pretty good baritone voice, he was good looking enough to be a star, and others with far less talent became famous, so who was I to doubt?

THE BEGINNING OF THE END

I readjusted my arms on the wall. They were starting to get bumpy imprints from the grainy cement. The sailboat was now a tiny white dot moving toward the cliffs of Palos Verdes. I started walking again. Did I really want to continue going into my sad love life? But trying not to think about it hadn't worked.

The first sign there was something wrong was about a year earlier. My cousin Billy-Boy was getting married. He had moved to California with my aunt and uncle when they first came from New York. He had finished his education at El Camino, studying some sort of engineering in tool and dye (whatever that was), and now he was ready for matrimony, he said. It wasn't going to be an expensive wedding; Uncle Billy was a frugal man and did not lavish gifts on his children, but Billy-Boy's older, married sister, Kathy, had flown all the way from the East Coast just to be there for him.

Kathy was still unpacking when my boyfriend and I dropped in to see her at my aunt and uncle's apartment in Torrance Beach. After an enthusiastic greeting, she told us in a hushed voice of her secret surprise. Knowing that it was to be a penny-pinching wedding, she had brought her very own wedding dress with her in case the bride might want to wear it. Kathy was animated with excitement as she dragged her long white dress out for us to see. It was lovely. The crinoline and full satin skirt under the lace gown rustled as she held it up.

"Oh," she said suddenly, "I was so skinny when I got married; I bet this dress would even fit you, Lorraine! Come with me into the bedroom and we'll try it on." I followed, curious, I had never owned or worn any kind of fancy dress, much less a full-length gown. With Kathy's help, the dress slipped over my head smoothly and except for being a little long, it fit perfectly. Kathy pulled me out into the living room.

"Now look at Lorraine," she said with satisfaction to my boyfriend. "Doesn't she look beautiful?" I sensed something wrong by the silence even before I looked around. Instead of smiling and complimenting me, he just stared, saying nothing. Was it my imagination, or did I see barely contained panic? Later, at the wedding, he was back to his old self, laughing and joking with Arlene and my mother, taking pictures of all of us.

There was another time, almost a year later. As a hopeful, would-be singer, my boyfriend hung out at various piano bars at the beach and in Hollywood. He would come prepared for the night with a list of songs he liked to sing and the keys he sang them in. Most of the pianists—many were also singers—knew him well and would let him sing a song or two. One night, in Hollywood, I was introduced to a guy at a new piano bar. He was small, with thinning fair hair. When he found out that my name was Lorraine, his face lit up and he promptly turned to his piano and rolled into the introduction of that old Nat King Cole favorite "Sweet Lorraine." In a slightly thin voice, which he intertwined with rippling piano arpeggios, the man sang my song, occasionally smiling over at my boyfriend and me as we sat directly across from him at the piano bar. This was embarrassing, but what happened next was worse.

When the song ended with the last words, "I can't wait until that lucky day when I marry sweet Lorraine" and a last arpeggio from his piano died down, the man gave me a final smile, then turned to my boyfriend. "Well, I guess that means you, kid. Just when will you marry this Sweet Lorraine?" Again, there was that look of frozen panic.

There were other signs. He asked me to wear more makeup, claiming it would make me look sexier and then said I was too quiet and should speak up more because his agent had called me "that girlfriend of yours who doesn't talk." Well, I was quiet, but that was what he used to like about me.

FROM THE GRAY NOTEBOOK
WARNER TOBE

Mr. Warner Tobe, a successful talent agent, was an old friend of my boyfriend's family going back to the forties when they had all been in a band together. For the last few years, Mr. Tobe had taken my boyfriend under his wing and believed, with a little luck, he could make him into a star—the next teenage heartthrob. Mr. Tobe, however, was a busy man, and I was told we mustn't waste his time.

We usually met at a coffee shop on Hollywood Boulevard. My boyfriend and I ordered rice pudding and waited for the Great Man to show up. Sometime later, he appeared looking polished and immaculately dressed, and, sliding seamlessly into the leather seat of our booth, gave us fifteen minutes of his time before zipping away to meet a real client, like Angie Dickinson. A few minutes would be given over to how he had spent the weekend "on the yacht" with June Allyson and Dick Powell. Then, for the rest of the time, we listened as Mr. Tobe gave his sage advice. Of course, I never said a word.

THE FINAL NOTE

That my boyfriend wanted to change me was just one of the small signs he was pulling away. He didn't show up for my graduation from El Camino, and soon after, we were having that talk in his car.

The droning voice became intelligible again as my boyfriend repeated for the second time his reasons for breaking up. Finally, he confessed, "One night, I looked over at you and I said to myself I don't love her anymore."

There it was, that something I had been trying to keep from knowing. The dull ache tightened slowly. I'm not sure if I said anything. What could I say? "I understand"? I didn't. How could he love me then just stop? You don't stop loving someone because they are inconvenient, do you?

For me it was different. I had let him into my life, and he had become part of it, like my family. That doesn't go away. The ache that was tightening finally dropped down and closed in around my stomach. How funny, Mom always told me that my stomach was my weak point, and I guess she was right because that was where the hurt was now. Arlene got headaches, Bill broke his bones, and with Jeff it was nosebleeds. For a moment, the picture of my little brother having a massive nosebleed while breaking up with a nonexistent girlfriend distracted me—how can I still think of funny things in the middle of . . . I was puzzling this out when my boyfriend (can I still call him that?) startled me by suddenly blurting out, "I'd marry you if you were pregnant, or if the draft was after me. I would marry you then too!"

My stomach eased as I felt anger suddenly well up. Was I supposed to feel grateful he would marry me if I saddled him with a kid? I could see how that would play out. If he didn't become famous, he could blame it on me? My pride was now in full swing. Oh no, I wasn't going to go that route to use sex to get him to marry me or the other route of crying and begging or threatening to commit suicide like other girls I knew about.

Anger had loosened the tightening grip in my gut, but eventually it returned more like a dead weight. I realized all I had left was my pride, and it wouldn't let me beg. I would let him go. I must have been crying a little because he sighed sadly and deeply. "Oh, you are so simple!" he said. The remark made my anger return, but he was right. It was that happily-ever-after thing I believed in—the idea that we were special. Yet, he had proved me wrong: we were just like everybody else and were breaking up just like everybody else. There was more silence as I accepted the fact that we wouldn't be sitting in his car talking like this after tonight. I would not be seeing him after this, and if we did it would be different. Then, just when it seemed that all was settled and done, *He* suddenly broke the silence. "Well, now that *I* have let you go," he said in a voice both sarcastic and begrudging, "you will probably be getting married to someone else within a year."

Now I *was* offended, and for the first time had something to say. "What an insult," I sputtered out. "As if I'm so desperate I'd marry just . . . just anyone! You don't even know me at all." After that I don't remember our last words or getting out of the car or going into the house or how I felt just then, but somehow the night ended and we had broken up.

BREAKING UP IS HARD TO DO

Maybe it was because I got mad or acquiesced too easily but a week or two later, *He* popped up at the house one night. He claimed to be worried. "I thought I would just come over to see how you are," he protested. This became a pattern. He would come over. We would sit and talk. Eventually talking would lead to a kiss, then another, then another. Then he would leave, and I wouldn't see him for a while. Were we broken up or not?

And now, because I *was* insecure, I *did* want to get married if only to prove he loved me. I strategized. I would move four hundred miles away to San Francisco. San Francisco was a big town. I would surely get a job in the art field. That would show him! I wouldn't even tell him where I was. If he really wanted us to be together, he would have to somehow find me. This would be a test, but somewhere along the way, I changed my destination to a cowardly twenty-mile distance to Hollywood, his perpetual hangout, where I might bump into him at any time or turn of a corner.

At first, I was busy finding an apartment, looking for a job, and meeting new people, but as the weeks went by, my confidence lessened and I called him. As before, he would stay away for weeks, then knock on my apartment door. I always let him in. We weren't together, yet we weren't apart either. One night, he told me that Warner Tobe had lined up a job with a singing group. They were going on tour for two months. He never wrote. A few weeks later, I moved back to Hermosa Beach.

MOVING ON

Does this rehashing everything do any good? I asked myself, stopping and turning to the wall again. I had been so sure, so confident—so arrogant! I was going to succeed in love where my sister and my mother had failed, but I had failed too. He had left me, just as Harry had left Mom and Don had left Arlene. So, what had I figured out? That pride doesn't keep you from feeling hurt, sad, humiliated, and ashamed? I took a deep breath. I had just admitted I was ashamed that someone didn't love me. There, I said it! And was I also ashamed I was still waiting for him to change his mind and come back to me? Was that why I couldn't move on? I took another breath and realized suddenly that I had walked almost to El Segundo. I should probably turn back now, but I wasn't finished thinking yet. Now that I was down from my Rapunzel tower, I really couldn't go back up there again. If you look at it in a certain way, he actually had done me a favor by getting me down from my tower of isolation. If he hadn't, I'd still be up there growing my hair! I had to laugh at the image. Nevertheless, I was not about to thank him for it, not yet anyway.

It was strange, but I actually started to feel better, somehow lighter, as if I had gotten rid of a dead weight I had been carrying around. The afternoon was coming to an end, and I turned and started walking back toward Culper Court. Maybe I could find Lindee and make it up to her with a game of checkers.

CHAPTER 48
POPPYTRAILS TO YOU

AND
FROM THE GRAY NOTEBOOK
JEFF

THE NEW JOB

I was not the only one who was getting restless. Jeff was off most of the time with his musician friends in Santa Monica, playing at dive clubs into the early morning and sleeping extra late when he came back. Sometimes he didn't come back at all, staying away for days at a time. I had gotten used to not seeing him. Another reason I didn't see him was because I had gotten a job at Metlox Poppytrail, a local pottery factory in the next town that made dishware. Their famous signature design, I was told, was of a red rooster crowing. Every morning, I got up early and biked to Manhattan Beach. My job was in the glazing department. I told myself I would at least be painting and holding a brush in my hand again.

On my first day after punching in at the time clock, a bell rang and I followed a long line of women into the workroom. It was an enormous space, more like a huge shed or hanger with great rolling doors. Banks of fluorescent lights above gave off a bluish glare. The room was filled with row upon row of long tables and straight-backed chairs, lined up to the tables with precise regularity. Everyone moved quietly and deliberately to their seats at the tables. I was shown to an empty chair and sat down.

Against the wall, another long table was filled with stacks of soft brushes and jars of different color glazes. I was told to collect the colors and brushes to be used that day, then immediately return to my chair. Until the bell rang for the first break, I was only to get up to go to the bathroom, refill my pots of colors, or get a drink of water at the water fountains. When we were all seated, as if on cue, a huge door on casters rolled open and several young men burst into the room pushing large metal trolleys stacked high with chalky white plates. The boys moved up and down the aisles of the tables, stacking a towering skyscraper of chalky dishes before each woman.

A picture of a crowing rooster was stamped on each plate. The job was to paint in the colors with the special glazes. It was important to stay within the lines of the image, and it was also important to be fast, I was told. The women set to work immediately. There was no laughing or chatting in the big room. Each woman worked silently and diligently. The trolley-wielding boys traveled up and down the long tables, picking up the finished stacks of dishes and wheeling them out of the room to the kiln to be baked into a glazed finish. Other carts cruised the aisles and replaced the empty spots on the tables with more chalky white dishes. The only noise was the dull scraping sound of the trolleys as the boys pushed them back and forth over the cement floor.

Everything was gray—the walls, the floor and ceiling, the tables we sat at, and the boys in their gray aprons pushing the carts. Was it really gray or just the fine covering of clay dust settling on everything?

Hours later, a bell rang and my shift was over. I punched out at the time clock. Outside the sky was blue and the sun was sparkling on the water of Manhattan Beach. I had to blink several times to realize that just a moment ago beyond those doors was a completely different world.

BROUGHT BEFORE THE CARPET

About three weeks into the job, I was called into the office. The room was quite plain, just a desk and a leatherette couch. One high window was covered by a closed venetian blind. As I entered, two men and a woman were looking at me with serious, sober faces and asked me to sit down. I sat on the plastic couch. What did they want? The man at the desk started to talk.

"We have had some complaints about you, Miss Gibson."

I was puzzled. "Complaints?" I echoed.

"Yes," said the other man, who was standing. The woman said nothing and just stood with her arms folded.

The second man went on. "Several people have told us about you!" Still perplexed, I wondered who those "several people" could be and looked warily at the woman who still had her arms folded.

The desk person took over again. "Our man at the kiln said you have been asking him to put some of your own pottery through to be fired with the usual batches."

It was becoming clearer now. "Oh . . . I didn't think I was bothering him," I said. "There was always plenty of room in the kiln, and he told me the pottery I used was just going to be thrown away and . . ." My voice trailed off.

"We don't do things that way here," the man at the desk retorted through tight lips. "Some of the women said that you don't leave the room when the break bell rings—you sit there, I'm told, and paint your own pottery."

It was true; I used the break time to paint my own designs. So far, I had painted two coffee mugs, covering them with graphic daisies, and I gave the breakfast bowl with a large sunflower on the bottom to Rita. It had come out very well. I started getting lots of ideas. My next project was going to be an even bigger strawberry on a dessert plate. I looked around the room now. "But it was my break," I said. "Shouldn't I be able to do what I want on my break?"

"You have to leave when the bell rings, like everyone else," he snapped. "You can't just do what you want here. We can't have that!"

I looked around then at all three of the inquisitors; their faces were so serious.

"But I don't see what it hurts—"

I was interrupted by the standing man. "You know you're not a fast worker," he sneered. "You're not producing even enough product for us to break even on you yet."

The woman still said nothing but looked vindicated when the standing man said that. I began to wonder who she was.

Hey! I thought to myself. *That remark was uncalled for.* There was no reason to make me feel bad. Of course, I wasn't fast yet. I was new.

"The reason we called you in here," the man at the desk took over again, "was to warn you that if you continue to stay at your seat and paint when the break bell rings and continue to do what you have been doing, you are jeopardizing your employment here."

What were these people afraid of and why were they afraid of *me*? I wasn't a troublemaker. They seemed to think I was some sort of rabble-rouser—me, "Miss Goody Two-Shoes," as Arlene sometimes called me.

The man at the desk wasn't finished. "So, young lady, if you want to continue in this job, you have to behave like everyone else. Otherwise, we will have no recourse but to let you go."

I had been fired from many jobs, but this was different. I sensed a certain hypocrisy. It wasn't about rules really. They didn't like that I was different. I could feel an old stubbornness creep over me. I had rights too, didn't I? Besides, the only thing that made this deadening job bearable was being able to paint on my break time.

Later, as I was picking up my very last and final paycheck from the cashier at the little window with the bars on it, I almost had a smile on my face. At least this time I was not "let go." I was the one who chose to quit. I felt vindicated at last.

NO GOODBYES

Jeff was gone—left, split, vamoosed! He had flown the coop of Culper Court. He had lit out to New York with the boys in the band, well, part of it. Nobody told me, and I didn't know until Arlene showed me the postcard. She had found it in the mailbox just that morning. On it was a picture of the Brooklyn Bridge with a short message in Jeff's strange angular handwriting. "Finally got here!" he scrawled. "All is well. Crashing at Martin's loft! Jeff." Arlene placed the card in front of me.

I looked at the image of the famous bridge, then the message on the back. I hadn't realized my brother was even gone and now he was far away in New York City. I had lost track of him while I was busy working. Still, I was taken aback; he never said anything about his plans, but then again, he had hardly been around for weeks.

Arlene sipped her coffee and took back the card. She looked again at the old bridge with its web of cables strung onto two Gothic stone arches. "Yeah," she said, "I didn't know he was going either. I just didn't believe him I guess, when he said that Gary and that drummer Cassidy were going to try their luck in the Big Apple and that he thought he would like to see it too. Yesterday Harvey and David came over and told me the whole story."

Still a bit stunned, I realized how out of touch I had been these last few weeks I had been working. Suddenly, I needed coffee and went into the kitchen to pour myself a cup while the pot was still hot.

Back at the table, Arlene took a deep breath. "The whole thing started because of Martin Eagle. You remember, he was the piano player that had been in the first band with Gary and Ed Cassidy."

I nodded, yes, now I did remember Gary telling me about the first group called The New Jazz Trio with him on bass, Martin on piano, and Cassidy on drums. He looked wistful when he told me of the close bond that gave them their special sound. Arlene, sensing that I was drifting off, snapped her fingers in front of my face. "Hey, pay attention," then continued her monologue, "Now Harvey told me The New Jazz Trio only broke up because the piano player left to try his luck in New York a year ago, and it was only then that Gary and Cassidy hooked up with Harvey and Ricky. It turned out that this Martin guy had been pretty successful at getting gigs and, yes, is actually surviving in New York!" Arlene took a breath. "Of course, Martin still longed for the old group, and the upshot was that he convinced Gary and Cass the old trio could make it in New York if only they would just come. He even had an apartment they could stay at until they found their own place. Cookie would join them later when Gary got set up with his own apartment." Arlene paused here for emphasis. "Well, they fell for the bait, and two weeks ago set out for the big city. Jeff must have just gone along too." Arlene finished and sat back with a wry smile on her face, satisfied she had explained everything.

"What about the rest of the band?"

"Oh, of course they are bummed out losing the whole rhythm section all at once. It had all happened so fast."

I tried to picture Jeff in New York City. Would he be more likely to get into trouble there? Maybe he would be better off than he was here, where the police hassled anyone the least bit different. He was probably in heaven right now, there in the thick of all the nightclubs and stars of jazz. The greats all lived in New York—Sonny Rollins, John Coltrane, and Thelonious Monk, who I was told practically lived at a club called The Five Spot.

I was glad for Jeff. Still, I felt a bit hurt. He didn't even say goodbye . . . Yet, maybe it was better that way. I hated goodbyes; it was never like in the movies where everyone got emotional and hugged and kissed and cried on each other. Mostly, people just stood around looking uncomfortable—I finally decided Jeff had been too embarrassed to say goodbye.

YOU'VE GOT TO BE CAREFULLY TAUGHT

Will I miss him? I wondered. When I was a kid, others would tell me how homesick they got when they went away to summer camp. I wasn't like that. In my house, we never knew when our father would come home. Harry could be away for months crossing the country on his tours, and we never gave it a thought, although I guess Mom did. One night I heard her crying.

Then one day we would come home from school and Mom would be sizzling bacon at the stove and there would be Harry sitting at the kitchen table eating breakfast, knife and fork in hand, digging into his sunny-side up eggs, slopping up the runny yoke with his toast. It was always a surprise when he arrived in another new car or with another pet. We went through a lot of animals over the years. There would be weeks of excitement—fun trips to the mountains and the beach, then, just as suddenly, I would come home from school and he would be gone again. The dark drapes in Mom and Harry's room that helped him sleep in the daytime were pulled open again. There was no warning, he was just gone. This was the way it was. So, I was not too upset when Jeff just up and left the way he did—really I wasn't!

Unemployed once again, I was soon back with Lenny, traveling in his sports car to Hollywood and the Goliath Records office. While Lenny "wheeled and dealed" on the phone, talking his usual, "hit record," "hot thing," I was in my corner at the shaky table—the gray notebook open to what I had scribbled into it the night after Jeff left. I rolled a fresh piece of white paper into the typewriter and started.

FROM THE GRAY NOTEBOOK
JEFF

Jeff is my little brother. He doesn't talk much and to look at him you might not realize he is thinking much at all, but behind those droopy eyes lies a private world humming with musical tones, pitches, and dissonance.

Jeff knows one thing for sure. He is going to be a musician. It is as simple as that. Fame or recognition isn't considered, he just wants to blow sax. He believes jazz is as meaningful as a Beethoven symphony and has no respect for the slick commercialism of West Coast jazz. It is pure schmaltz to him. His ideal is free jazz—the theory of playing pure emotion not hampered by chord changes, keys, or measured bars as expounded by saxophonist Ornette Coleman.

He said once, "Sometimes you play and find something special—a communication between the musicians, everyone thinks with one mind and spirit. It may be for just a few seconds, but the audience catches it too and comes with you, after that you always work for that feeling every time you play, to capture the magic again so the moment will come back."

For Jeff, this was quite a speech, and he never talked about it again. At twenty, Jeff doesn't have a steady job, but there will always be someone to look out for him. They do it automatically. My mother provided him with money, Arlene with a place to live and practice. His friends supply him with instruments, cigarettes, and entertainment.

Jeff is the type of person who can dig into a garbage can in broad daylight without embarrassment. He is the type of person who can sleep in a damp cellar with snails clinging to his nose. He's the person who plays the blues in a vacant lot at two o'clock in the morning or walks into a restaurant wearing just a bathrobe and beret and orders coffee. He is the person who sings jazz fairy tales to the kids while they scramble on his lap.

CHAPTER 49
LEAHDELL

YOGA NIGHTS

It was Sara Lee's mother's idea to start the yoga parties. Leahdell had not forgotten the lessons she had learned at the health retreat in Mexico Sara Lee had told me about last summer. Leahdell may have fallen off the detox diet—and it was hard to give up cigarettes too—but she had kept up her yoga exercises. She was a teacher, after all, so it was natural she would want to instruct and edify others in this healing and healthful practice.

The sessions would be held once a week at Sara Lee's new home. Sari and Chris had moved from their cramped apartment to their new adobe house in Manhattan Beach. There were drawbacks to living in a real adobe house. The walls of the bathroom tended to disintegrate when one took a steamy shower, and vegetation sprouted from the walls when the weather was damp. Yet, the advantages outweighed the drawbacks. The house had a big kitchen, a roomy living room, and three bedrooms. It was the perfect place to do yoga. There was even a patio for outdoor cooking and a place to play for the gaggle of kids that would be coming along with us at these gatherings. It was agreed Sunday evenings would be the best time.

We at Culper Court didn't know much about yoga, but we thought it might be a fun thing to try. Obviously, Arlene had forgotten the short shrift she had given to her own "health kick" resolutions back in January and now was enthusiastic about this new exercise. Rita, always into health, was on board and persuaded her new boyfriend to join in too. Terry O'Shea was an artist and at least a decade younger than Rita. He was jolly with curly auburn hair and round, cherubic features. With the group complete, there evolved some rules. As Leahdell explained it, during the week we were to fast or eat sparingly, then after our yoga session we would all partake in a fantastic meal. It sounded great, especially the fantastic meal part.

THE GROUP

For several weeks now, Rita or David Feller had ferried us to Sara Lee's house for the yoga sessions. Long, lanky David was now a regular at Culper Court, whereas his friend Harvey had dropped away weeks ago, deciding, I guess, to spend more time rehearsing with what was left of the band.

At the sessions, I wore my black leotard and tights. Arlene and Rita had similar versions of this, but Rita wore a long skirt over her scarlet leotard and added a festive red headscarf. Arlene, as usual, was rather ragtag, with her seams beginning to split. Sara Lee wore a long skirt too. For some reason, she didn't do much yoga but fussed about in the kitchen preparing the food or dealing with the children when needed. I wondered if she was pregnant again.

On the first day, when we all found our spots on the rug, Leahdell stood in front of us like a plump pumpkin in her dark tights, coral smock, and orange curls, which all added to the pumpkin effect. She launched into the history of the ancient practice of yoga.

"It can be traced back five thousand years ago to India," she said in her low, gravelly voice, beginning to walk back and forth while we, her students, listened and tried, for the most part unsuccessfully, to sit in the lotus position. "Yes, my dears, it started out as a strictly spiritual thing," Leahdell continued. "Yoga was a way to find peace and reach enlightenment, through self-knowledge." Now warming to her subject, our teacher paused and smiled benignly. "And for us, it can be a way to strengthen and cleanse the body and mind."

While Sara Lee's mother talked, I managed a rather painful half lotus. My sister, just sitting in a cross-legged position, squawked in pain while David Feller, next to her, was serene and comfortable with his long legs entwined in a perfect lotus pose. Rita also managed the position, but poor Terry O'Shea's plump legs couldn't even sit cross-legged. We were a motley bunch.

As Leahdell walked before us, I noticed that for an older woman (she had to be in her fifties and definitely on the roly-poly side), she had unusually slim and beautiful legs. Then I remembered Sara Lee had told me her mother had grown up taking dance lessons as a child and majored in it along with art, drama, and poetry at Berkeley. Leahdell was considered the most promising and talented student there and with her perfect skin and copper red hair, also the most beautiful.

The rotund Leahdell before us now whipped through several demonstrations of the poses we would take. One by one, with perfect balance and what I thought must be bones that were double-jointed, she performed each pose while describing the effect it was to have on our bodies. We scrambled into our own version of the plank, the triangle, the tree, and the downward-facing dog, while our instructor watched and rearranged our bodies if needed. Rita and Terry were not always serious and giggled a lot. Arlene continued to moan, but David, Chris, and I were attentive disciples and did well.

One position, called the bridge, had us lift up our bodies into an arch over our heads while our shoulders, arms, and backs were firmly pressed flat on the ground. Only then did Leahdell, while in the same position herself, caution us that this pose encouraged the release of flatulence. At the end of the session, we each got a massage from the person sitting behind us, then reciprocated by giving one back to them.

THE FEAST

By the time we finished our exercises, we were all famished. Out of the kitchen came Sara Lee with the food. Everyone enjoyed the meal, and I had to admit I really stuffed myself, mainly because I knew I wasn't going to eat much the following week until our next yoga meeting. So, instead of thinking about my future, I was wondering what the next meal would be and when we were going to learn the "Salutation to the Sun" position. Thinking about my future could wait a bit longer, at least until the summer was over.

CHAPTER 50
REDONDO LIBRARY

ART CLUB

I was trying not to think about the itch on my right shoulder, but it was becoming impossible to ignore. Yet it was almost time to take a break, so I decided to hold out a bit longer and scratch at my leisure. The first time I modeled for the Redondo Arts Painting Society, they had me in a black leotard straddling a cello. I guess their paintings had turned out well because they had called me back again. Being an art model, I found, had turned out to be a quick and easy way to pick up an extra ten or fifteen dollars for a few hours work, and I didn't mind coming back to the library. The art group liked to rent this special large room whenever they got together. I wondered what other things it might be used for—lectures, movies, maybe even weddings. It was quiet and cool, and as I said before, a library always gave me a quiver of excitement. This time, Laurie J. was to model with me. I worried at first that she might get squirmy and antsy—she was only four—but I was soon impressed with how long she was staying still. *Just like a professional*, I thought proudly. We had been posing for almost fifteen minutes. For the modeling job today, Laurie J. and I both had on our velvet dresses that Arlene had created. Mine was long-sleeved and black velvet. Laurie J. was wearing the one she got for Christmas—blue with a trim of white lace down the front. Members of the painting club had given out murmurs of appreciation when they saw that we were to be their models. That had made me feel more confident that we would do well.

We were posed on a wooden platform. I sat on a chair while Laurie J. lounged against my knees with her arms in my lap. My right hand rested lightly on her shoulder while the other held her small plump hand. I glanced at the painters standing before their easels, their eyes flickering back and forth between us on the dais and their canvases.

Rita, once more, had come through with a job. She had modeled for the group several times, and they loved to paint her. I can just imagine her selling the idea of the "Culper Court crowd" as their next models. "Oh, I know of the most gorgeous family!" she would declare enthusiastically. "The women are all beautiful blondes and the children dazzling towheads all. I'm sure they would make the most wonderful subjects for your group to paint."

FINE ART

The fifteen minutes ended, and I got to scratch my itch. Laurie J. stretched and yawned. During the break, we walked around looking at the paintings that were emerging on the canvases. Many of the artists were very accomplished, and I could imagine one of these paintings hanging in a smart gallery. *With our velvet gowns, Laurie J. and I would look very much like rich patrons having a family portrait done*, I thought.

Back on the podium, Laurie J. and I took our positions. Again Laurie J. stood still like a champ. As the youngest of her three siblings, she was the quiet one. She did not prattle on or ask questions. It was not that she was shy—not like my brother Jeff who at the same age was too embarrassed to look at people, much less talk to them—Laurie J. seemed to be quiet by choice. She just didn't see the need to babble. She got enough attention from adults who found her freckles and chuckling laugh adorable.

The rest of the sitting went by pretty fast after I decided to recount all the jobs I'd ever had. I lost track at about fifteen, so I tried to remember how long I had retained each one, starting at age eighteen with my first employment at McDonald's Hamburgers. They gave me one day, and I was "let go" on the second, I recalled. I guess that was the record to beat.

ALL ROADS LEAD TO HOME

Later, after we were paid, Laurie J. and I were lucky to catch the bus that ran along North Harbor Drive. A few minutes later, North Harbor Drive changed its name as it entered Hermosa Beach. I thought again how silly it was that each beach town had a different name for the same road that ran alongside their one or two miles of beachfront. In Redondo, it was North Harbor Drive, in Hermosa, it was Hermosa Avenue, in Manhattan Beach, it took a little jog to hook up with Ocean Drive before succumbing to Vista Del Mar in El Segundo. I lost track of it after that. I wondered again why didn't they just call it El Camino Real and be done with it?

It wasn't long before we were trudging up the hill to Culper Court. I noticed as we got close to the red house that the front door was hanging open. When it wasn't losing its doorknob or locking us out, our door had a tendency to drift open. It usually meant someone had been visiting and didn't close it properly.

Inside, Laurie J. ran off to change her clothes. A minute later, I heard the back door slam and heard her footsteps pounding across the deck and down the stairs. Only then did I notice that the house was silent—no music was playing, no pots banging in the kitchen, no sewing machine humming in Arlene's bedroom. It was very quiet.

ARLENE

Everyone must be outside, I thought, until I heard some rustling coming from the music room, and there, as I stepped down into that large space, I found my sister hunched and curled up in the big green Indonesian wicker chair with the scrollwork on top. She was clutching a mug of coffee in her lap. It looked like she was trying to warm her hands with the steamy cup, an odd thing to do on a hot day in August. Every so often, she released one hand to take a drag on her cigarette. After sucking the smoke deeply into her lungs, she replaced her hand back onto the warm cup again. I watched as the steam of the coffee and the smoke from the cigarette combined into one long stream. Arlene continued to sit huddled until she noticed me.

"You know," she said slowly, not looking up, "I don't think Jeff is ever coming back." A grimace passed over her face.

I cleared some music books off a chair and sat down next to her. "Why do you say that?" I asked, somewhat frightened by the expression on her face. "What happened?" When she didn't say anything right away, I prodded. "Was someone here?" I was thinking about the open door.

"Cookie and Gary came to see me. They just left," she said in a quavering voice.

"Are they back from New York? And Jeff, where is he?"

"He's not in New York." Arlene's voice continued to quaver. "He wasn't even there when Cookie arrived a month later after Gary sent for her."

"But . . . then where is he?" I was starting to get nervous.

"They didn't know, but they heard that he somehow got hooked up with Harry."

"Harry, our father—Harry?" I was surprised, yet maybe I shouldn't have been. As a child, Jeff idolized his father. Whenever he came home, Jeff would jump into his arms, not like me who usually stood back a little. Being the youngest, Jeff didn't have as many years with Harry as the rest of us did and was only in elementary school when Harry basically disappeared from our lives. Mom always said Jeff was the one who needed a father the most.

"I guess he has a father now," I said softly.

"Oh, yeah, some father Harry will make." Arlene sounded, more angry than sad now. I felt relieved. I was used to an abrasive Arlene, not a brokenhearted one.

I spoke too soon, because after that outburst, my sister fell back into her funk. "Do you think Jeff will get in touch with us?" she asked bleakly.

"Oh . . . I think so." I tried to sound assured. "Didn't he send us that postcard when he first got to New York? I think we will hear from him when he gets settled." I was not really sure myself, but Arlene perked up enough to tell me about what Gary and Cookie said about their adventure in New York City.

NEW YORK, NEW YORK, IT'S A (NOT SO) WONDERFUL TOWN!

It was a long story of hopes and dreams disappointed. Cookie said they had zero money, so they got an apartment in what people were calling the *East* Village below Fourteenth Street. At the time, some were trying to pretend that the Lower East Side was the next Greenwich Village, but it was just a slum, Cookie said. They lived in a five-story walk-up riddled with cockroaches.

I interrupted Arlene here by reminding her of what Mom used to say to us whenever we speculated on the idea that we might want to move back to New York City when we grew up. Mom's mantra always had been, "You'll never get rid of the cockroaches!" Arlene perked up at this and laughed, so I retold the old story we both knew so well of when Mom, struggling at the time with three little children, had finally found a great apartment with a small garden and a landlady who loved us, but had to move because she could—

"—never get rid of the cockroaches," Arlene repeated the last line with me and almost smiled. "Gee, Lorraine, you were just a year old and as cute as could be and poor Mrs. Murphy loved you and cried like a baby, Mom said, when we left."

There were a few seconds of silence as we contemplated poor Mrs. Murphy's sadness and what must have been Cookie's and Gary's hideous introduction to New York City.

And it wasn't just the bugs that drove them to come back; Arlene picked up the story where I had interrupted. It turned out that the whole rosy dream that they would set the town on its end with their talent once the old band got together again in New York, was just that—a dream—and a pipe dream at that. The trio only got a few gigs, and then everything went zip. As Cookie put it, "the writing on the wall" told them that breaking into the New York jazz scene was going to take more time and energy than they were prepared for, and after a month, Cookie couldn't take New York City one minute more. Where they lived were raggedy alcoholics who panhandled up and down the streets and they would just pass out and sleep anywhere, right there in the middle of the sidewalk and sometimes even the vestibule of their building. Then there were the crowded subways where Cookie got groped and pinched. She told Gary in no uncertain terms she was going to leave and go back to L.A., and if he didn't go with her she would go home without him. This is where Gary broke in, Arlene said. "He told me they decided to come back before winter set in because, 'if you were going to be a starving musician, you may as well starve in a warm, sunny place like Southern California.'"

Arlene had been animated as she talked, but now she slumped back down again in the green Indonesian wicker chair with the scrollwork on top and looked up at me with a little smile. "Well, maybe Jeff is better off not being in New York after all." Then she took another drag on her cigarette before she downed the rest of her coffee from the now tepid cup.

CHAPTER 51
A DAY AT THE CLIFFS

LUNCH ON THE ROCKS

Rita got us excited about the picnic. She knew a great "secret place," she whispered conspiratorially to the children. It was a special cove, she said, below the Palos Verdes cliffs. She used to go there when she was first married to her second husband, Roger Mackey. They had discovered it one day while looking for a place to skin-dive.

Lindee, Donnie, and Laurie J. were excited to learn we would be building a fire right on the beach and cooking over it, and as we did for our yoga class, the picnic lunch would be a potluck. Everyone was to bring a special dish.

"I hope no one is afraid of heights," Rita giggled, as she jumped into her car and waved. "Ta-ta! See you next Sunday!"

The kids had questions. "What will we bring to eat? How far away is Palos Verdes? How tall are the cliffs?"

I explained that Palos Verdes wasn't that far away. You could see the cliffs rising up in the distance when you went to the beach and looked south. In fact, Torrance Beach, where Mom lived with Bob, was the last town before the cliffs, so it wasn't very far at all.

As for what we should bring to the picnic, Arlene had already decided on hot dogs for the fire and potato salad—perfect for any picnic. Now, with the menu decided and all questions satisfied, the kids went out to play picnic in the landfill. I hoped they wouldn't try to build a real fire. Luckily, we were out of matches again.

THE TRAIL

The next morning, we parked on the side of the roadway at the top of the Palos Verdes Hills and from there, started the long climb down the cliffs. At first, we wandered through some gently sloping hills, through rows of what looked like a farmer's garden. Later on, we came to more rocky terrain with a few sparse patches of scraggly grass and bushes. Green succulents and scrubby pines were dotted here and there clinging to the hillside. Very soon, however, there was a steep drop off with just a narrow trail to lead us down to the sea below. The path looked treacherous, so at this point all the adults instinctively grabbed the hand of the nearest child.

I looked back at Arlene, holding Laurie J's hand. My sister had never been the athletic type, and now there was a steely grin on her face. "My, this is exciting isn't it," she said through clenched teeth. I didn't know if she was being brave for Laurie J.'s benefit or her own. In front of the pack, Rita was gaily skipping down the trail like a sure-footed mountain goat, as if every step was familiar to her. With one adult holding on to one child, we marched down the winding path until finally reaching the bottom. As we descended, I checked out my fellow travelers. There was Rita, her family of four, and her boyfriend, Terry. On our side, there was me, Arlene, the kids, and David Feller, who seemed to be around even more these days.

AT THE BOTTOM

At last, we came to the end of the trail. All around us, like a half bowl, were the steep cliffs of the cove. All around the cove were large rocks and dark jagged boulders on the shore and in the ocean. It felt raw and isolated with no people or houses about, and, unlike the soft sandy beach near our house, the ground here was covered with pebbles, many the size of golf balls. They had been chipped off the jagged boulders and rounded smooth over time by the tumbling tides. They were strange and unstable to walk on. The children ran off to look for sea animals in the tide pools. Rita called after them, "Don't be surprised if you run into an octopus or a moray eel or two." I had to shiver at the thought of slithery creatures sloshing about in this lovely cove.

Soon, I turned my attention to setting up a place to put our blankets and towels. Terry was off to look for firewood, and Arlene and Rita sat close to the water on one of the smoother rocks talking animatedly. I hoped they wouldn't have a fight today. They were both so used to claiming most of the attention they were apt to be competitive in mixed company.

David, however, just stood by sort of smiling and taking it all in calmly. I liked David. He had this funny voice that sounded a little like a creaky hinge so whatever he said sounded amusing, and he always seemed so tranquil, so comfortable in his own skin. He reminded me of a cat relaxing in the sun with that satisfied grin on his face and his eyes crinkling into slits. I wished I could be more that way, relaxed and calm, living in the moment, not always so cautious and worried about what was going to happen next.

THE KETCH

I turned away from Arlene and Rita and their battling wits and looked out at the ocean against the dark hills of the cove. The water lapping near us against the shore was bright and clear, the sand underneath turning it a light turquoise. It became bluer as it got farther out to sea until finally ending as a dark blue line on the horizon. It was a perfect day—sunny with a brisk wind. I tried to make out if that gray hazy mass way out in the water was Catalina Island. There was an old song about it that started out with the words, "Twenty-six miles across the sea, Santa Catalina is the isle for me."

As I squinted out into the distance, the prow of a sailboat came slowly into view from behind the dark cliff of the cove. It was beautiful and silent, moving straight forward like a swan moves through the water. I didn't know much about what kind of sailboat it was, but it was large enough to have two masts and several sails. The triangular smaller sail in front was puffed way out. I could see the wind blowing a curve in it, like I had seen on my mother's white sheets when she pegged them onto our clothesline on windy days.

I watched the ship as it sailed past the cove, but once it got completely into view, the beautiful boat stopped and sat bobbing—its front stick-thing going up and down. I tried to remember what that stick-thing was called—the bow? No, that was the front of the boat. The . . . bow . . . bowsprit—yes, that was its name and it was exactly like a fairy wand, I decided. I could see the ship gaily dancing up and down, up and down like a kind of water sprite. I could also see small dark figures moving around on the fairy deck.

Again, I remembered my favorite book. The one I had seen again that day in the Redondo library. I had been in love with sailing boats ever since I read *Seabird* and saw its beautiful illustration of a clipper ship. It had been given a whole page to itself, and it was rendered in full color. A few grades later, my favorite book was *Judy of the Islands*, about a girl who lived on a sailing boat in the South Seas. Oh, how I wanted to be that girl and go island-hopping with the old captain as Judy did. Now, looking at the graceful sailboat gently bobbing in the distance, I was mesmerized all over again.

Behind me I heard Rita exclaiming, "Oh, my God, I don't believe this! It's my ex-husband, Roger Mackey. That's his ketch out there. Lorraine, Lorraine, *do* go out and tell him we are here. His son is here!"

But Rita didn't have to urge me because I was already knee deep in the water and had been moving toward the beautiful sailboat without realizing it. Her encouragement was all I needed to take a few more steps, then plunge into the rather cold water. I forgot about octopuses and moray eels. My only thought was that I was going to get to be on that boat.

Roger Mackey's sailboat must have been several hundred feet away, and somewhere after the first hundred feet, I remembered that I wasn't the best of swimmers. I had forgotten that in my enthusiasm to see the boat up close. *Maybe this wasn't a good idea after all and I should turn back.* Then I told myself not to panic. After all, I did complete the mandatory swim test in my sophomore year in high school. To pass, one had to keep afloat in the pool for fifteen minutes, and I had done that. With that in mind, I thrust forward again. The ketch was getting closer, and I could see that the hull was lovely wood and not just some kind of fiberglass.

Yet even with my enthusiasm lifted, I was starting to tire. Doing my usual doggie paddle wore me out very soon. Then I remembered my swim class training again. It hadn't been much as our school was on a half-day schedule due to overcrowding, and we had to bus into town to the local YWCA. What with changing and drying off afterward, our pool time amounted to a mere fifteen minutes. Still, I did learn to do the back float, breaststroke, and sidestroke. I never did master the Australian crawl which just led to water getting into my eyes and even more up my nose. I had passed the swim test mostly by treading water and floating on my back.

Newly inspired, I flipped over and started kicking to propel me forward. Now, I was making good time but couldn't see where I was going, so I alternated the back kick with the side-stroke and the breaststroke. Finally, I was getting close to the ketch. The people on it now seemed aware I was headed toward them. Reaching the side of it, I realized the deck was several feet above me. *How am I going to get onto this thing?* I wondered, but people were reaching down and somehow I scrambled on.

REQUEST TO COME ABOARD

On deck, for a fleeting moment, I imagined how it must look, a mysterious young woman in a fetching bathing suit climbing onto their boat, water dripping off her tan body, long blonde hair in tangled tendrils. *I must be making an interesting impression*, I thought happily. Yet the vision of my lovely self was quickly cut short by the realization that the bobbing of the boat that had looked so charming from shore, felt like I was riding a lurching sea creature. Then, even before I could deliver my message to Mr. Mackey that Rita and son were on the shore, I dropped to my knees—violently seasick.

As nausea hit, the faces around me turned into a hazy blur. One female voice told me to look out at the horizon. In desperation, I obeyed, but like the boat, the blue edge of the sea was being flung about too. I tried looking straight down at the deck; still, everything was reeling before me. I decided to just close my eyes, which helped a little, or so I thought.

Still on my knees, with my face so close to the wooden deck I could smell the varnish, I sputtered out the message I had been assigned to deliver. A low male voice—Mr. Mackey's, I presumed—laughed and said something like, "That Rita! My ex-wife would do something like this!" Which I took as an acknowledgment that he had gotten the information.

Now that I had delivered my message, I wanted off this boat. Somehow, I made it known to the people on board who were murmuring concernedly around me. Then someone said, "We can't throw her back in the water like this, she might drown." Hearing this, I suddenly felt like some unwanted flotsam and jetsam that had become a problem. I remembered reading about how people who died on ships were given a burial at sea. I pictured myself in a body bag being slid into the water.

A younger male voice said, "We'll put her in a life jacket, and then she won't drown." There were some scuffling sounds, then footsteps. I felt a smooth puffy vest being slipped over my arms and buckled around my waist with a clinking sound. I believe I whispered thank you. All I could really think about was how soon I could get away from this monster that was reeling up and down, bringing my stomach along with it. I had a momentary thought that if I had gone on more carnival rides as a kid, I might have fared better on a boat than this. The romance I had felt connected to sailing ships had completely vanished. All I wanted was to get off this boat, and quick!

REQUEST TO DISEMBARK

With arms holding me on both sides, I was lifted up from the deck. I squinted through my eyelids and watched my feet being walked over to the side of the boat and then seeing blue water slapping against the ketch. It looked like a much longer drop going down than it had climbing up. The arms holding me positioned my body away from the side of the boat then let me go. I had a few moments to think as I fell toward the water. With the fat vest ballooning in my midsection, and my arms and legs hanging down, I felt very much like some spider that had come onboard uninvited and was now being ignominiously dropped overboard.

Plummeting straight down toward the water, I realized I was going to land smack onto my stomach. Was it going to hurt? Luckily the fat puffy vest softened my landing. I made more of a plop than a splat on impact. After my splash down, which did not hurt at all, I hoped my seasickness wouldn't keep me from swimming to shore. To my relief, the motion sickness was completely gone, and I easily, if not awkwardly, made my way back to dry land. As the life jacket buoyed me up, it was easy to dog paddle all the way back to the beach.

Some fifteen minutes later, I straggled over to our picnic spot on the cove and awkwardly pulled myself out of the water, embarrassed about the bulky life jacket I was wearing. The rest of the day was a bit of a blur. I don't even recall eating anything, only that the kids came back from their playing cold and shivery, especially Lindee who had an encounter of sharing a tide pool with a moray eel. We packed up before dark and made the trek back up the hill and to home. It was an exhausting day. As a *Judy of the Islands* character, I was a bust, but at least I had been living in the moment.

ANOTHER CHANCE

Strangely enough, the story didn't end there. The next day, when I returned the life jacket to Roger Mackey at the new Redondo Marina, he actually invited me to sail to Catalina Island that weekend with him, his girlfriend, Lola, and Hank, who lived on the ketch and maintained it for him. Mr. Mackey had liked my pluck in swimming out to his sailboat, so while he and his girlfriend spent more time together, I was to be a sort of companion to young Hank, who, along with being boat caretaker was also cook, navigator, and solitary deckhand for the *Whatever Lola Wants*, which was the name of the ketch. We were to leave that Friday afternoon.

Strange as it may seem, I jumped at the chance to actually go out sailing for several days to an "honest to God" island in the Pacific, even if it was only twenty-six miles away. I told myself that surely I wouldn't get sick if the boat was moving and there was a fresh breeze blowing on my face. It wouldn't be like getting sick in the back seat of a closed-up car smelling of gasoline with the landscape whizzing past and my father pumping the brake every few minutes.

I was wrong. I spent the whole night's crossing lying below deck in the cabin's bunk eating saltine crackers and sipping ginger ale that Hank gave me. However, when I woke the next morning, a miracle had happened. The seasickness was entirely gone. Even though I could feel the boat, at anchor, bobbing furiously as before, it didn't bother me at all. The rest of the weekend was spent exploring and learning about all the parts of Roger Mackey's thirty-foot ketch. I loved all the beautiful wood of the deck and masts. I loved the cunning built-in compartments for gear. I loved going below deck to make coffee and smoked oyster sandwiches in the compact little galley. Hank turned out to be a very nice guy. Not my type, but we became friends. Except for a short bit of sunbathing on a nearby rock on the island, I stayed on the sailboat the entire time. After three days, the ketch almost felt like a part of me. I was delighted with my "sea legs," as Mr. Mackey called them.

On the way back to the Redondo Marina, the sea was choppy, yet even then I didn't get sick. I thoroughly enjoyed every dip and lurch of the ride. By dusk, the sea had calmed, and as we were slowly drawing near the mainland, I could see the tiny red lights of the marina blinking in the distance. I could sense the ship under me rocking. I had never felt so peaceful before in my life.

When I got home, it was late and everyone was already in bed. I was so tired I plopped down and fell asleep immediately on the couch. The next morning, still exhilarated with my triumph over the sea and wanting to tell everyone about my great trip, I jumped up and promptly fell flat again. I had gotten my sea legs, but now it looked like I would have to get back my land ones. I was on the floor, but I still felt wonderful. The main lesson here, I told myself, was that I had gone after something I wanted and had gotten it. A few days later, we got a letter from Jeff. I read it out loud to Arlene.

Dear closest relatives of the female kind and little Kidlets,

Qué pasa? How is it going in good old Culper Court? If you don't already know about it from the boys in the band, I didn't stay in New York very long. I really dug it there but you got to have mucho moola bucks to stay.

I got hold of the phone number of our father's dearest sister, Aunt Doris, and like a trooper she helped me hook up with my long-lost father. Harry sent me some scratch to take a bus to Orlando, Florida where he is now shacked up with a wiggy girlfriend called Zelda.

Orlando is no Miami Beach. It's fifty miles to the nearest ocean. All it has going for it are lots of little lakes that I don't dare swim in because of the alligators and snakes. And if you think Culper Court had bugs, you haven't seen the Godzilla cockroaches here.

I already found a bike so I can check out the local surroundings. It's nice that everything is flat here but it rains a lot. Instead of looking for junk, I look for food. I already spotted mango, kumquat, and banana trees growing wild.

Remember that hurricane when we lived in Miami Beach and the next morning hundreds of coconuts were lying on the ground? Well, there are not many coconut trees here inland but when I do find them, I like to put the coconut milk in my coffee. With all this bounty of free produce for the picking, I'm thinking of becoming a fruitarian.

Harry plies the piano keys at the local hot spots in town, which means that he plays for tips at bars. And when Zelda isn't shoplifting at the neighborhood stores, she sometimes takes a turn with the snare drum and brushes and gigs along with Harry but now that I am here, Harry says with him blowing piano and Zelda on cocktail drums, we can be a bo-no-fied band or at least a trio.

Harry hasn't let me play my sax yet because he says the folks in this hick town are not ready for my kind of jive, meaning free jazz and anyway he needs a bass player more so I am learning the bass.

Last night, we played "Tea for Two." If you don't remember, it is Harry's specialty number. He first plays the "Tea for Two" part with his left hand and in the second chorus adds the melody of "Cocktails for Two" with his right. It's a crowd pleaser, at least when people are drunk enough.

Harry says he hears that Washington (DC, that is) could be where we land next because he has some big plans and connections there. It would sure beat this here "alligator swamp town." So if you don't mind reptile humor I'll just close by saying—see you later alligator! And tell the kiddies, after a while crocodile.

Your boy,
Jefferoony

There was silence for a moment; Arlene broke it with, "What's with the Jefferoony handle? You see, Harry is already influencing the way Jeff is talking. He won't be coming back now that Harry has his hooks into him. Not when he can get a bass player for free anyway."

I was worried too. "I'm not sure he's getting enough to eat," I said.

"Well, why doesn't Zelda steal him some food while she is at it!" was Arlene's retort.

"At least we know where he is," I said, and I took the envelope with the return address on it and put it away in my loft, where it wouldn't get lost.

CHAPTER 52
FROM THE GRAY NOTEBOOK
HEAT WAVE

A strange wind is blowing in from the desert, breaking all records for the past eighty years. Imagine 106 degrees in September on the coast and 113 degrees inland. Southern California is falling into a suffocating choked mass under a pressing hot blanket of heat, and while other states are pulling collars up around their ears and puffing breath-vapors into the crisp mornings, the Sunshine State lives up to its name. Oh wait! It's Florida, not California, that is the Sunshine State? I've lived in both, so I get it mixed up.

The papers say thirty people have died of heat prostration so far. In this time of rising temperatures and high blood pressure, people wilt and faint. Babies and old folks suffer the most. The sale of soda pop and beer doubles and the price of ice cream goes up twenty percent.

Even Hermosa Beach is burning with this incessant avalanche of heat where a rare quiet kind bores into your head, drying your brain so you feel weak and dazed. The sky isn't blue anymore; it is white with the glare of the constant sun.

The nights, usually cool and breezy, now cause bad dreams on wet twisted sheets. The only wind that moves is the hot breath from the desert.

During the day, houses become human incinerators. The people crawl from their homes down to the sea like animals fleeing from a forest fire. Water is the only haven. Everyone's previous plans are dropped as humanity heads for its shores.

For us, it is four sweltering blocks to the cool ocean carrying towels and sand buckets, kids trailing the adults, crossing wide Hermosa Avenue—bare feet running fast—black asphalt melting into tar, burning like desert sands. "Kids, step on the painted white lines. It's a little cooler!"

Beyond the Strand walkway are the real burning sands of a few hundred feet to the relief of the water. Arlene and I each pick up a kid and start to run. It's a good thing Lindee has sandals.

At the water's edge, by design, we join up with Rita, her four children, and also Sara Lee and her brood. Sitting, wading, swimming, we are all in the water or clinging to the edge of it, letting the tide ripple over our bodies.

The beach, this windless day, is populated with dehydrated zombies. There are no cheers from volleyball games or the usual boisterous group roughhousing or the buzz of people lazing in the sun. Almost everyone is subdued and in the water. Only in the water do people recover enough to let out a laugh or a restrained shriek or two.

I am scanning this multitude of people encrusted along the water's edge with us. *Day-Trippers*, I think, as I look at all the pasty office legs and pale arms surrounding us. *They have probably not been in the sun all year*, I surmise.

When you live at the beach, you develop a bit of a covetous attitude about your little patch of ocean and tend to have a kind of snobbery about the "out-of-towners" who have to commute to get to the beach—your turf as it were.

Along with the disdain for their pastel skin, you find your-self also being dismissive about their endless hampers of food and gargantuan beach gear, but today, we are all suffering alike, and we have become a kind of loose community of fellow wounded. I feel sorry for their plight.

I am glad we stole the kids from school and thankful that the beach is our home and not the claustrophobic city. What are those people doing now? Dying in little rooms? Hanging over fans? Soaking in bathtubs? How many men quit their jobs, ran over dogs, or beat their wives today?

Rita, Arlene, Sara Lee, and I sit on the wet sand cooled by the translucent tide. Nearby, the children play porpoise style in the waves, shiny sun-bleached hair plastered wet to their cheeks.

With the sea soaking our bodies and our emotions released in chatter, the conversation turns to love, life, and happiness. How do you judge it, by the duration or intensity?

The white sun moves slowly across the sky as the adults talk and the children play. Sometime later, even they have had their fill of the ocean and one by one, flop on the sand—small chests pumping for air, torsos limp, sucked of energy by the heat and frantic waves, mouths hanging open, eyes closed in coma-like dreams.

This malaise reaches us older ones too; we take little sips of air, no big gulps or the lungs cry out in pain. Today isn't meant for action.

In a day of such heat as this, there will be no pretense or holding back. Emotions and tempers will turn to fire like the sun. All the things never said come out on this hot September day. The heat is antagonistic. Already this morning a feud erupted between Arlene and good neighbor Betsy, who has forever provided us with food, good talk, and coffee.

Finally, the now-orange sun plunges under the ocean. We say our goodbyes and trudge back up the hills to our separate homes.

The weather has still not broken, and night only brings dimness. Homes that had been hording the heat of day now breathe it back upon its owners in the night. We eat supper on the front porch, gulping pitchers of ice water, but our bloated stomachs crave even more water, not heavy beans.

Other families sit outside their houses escaping the heat, TV is forsaken, children play quiet games, mothers bring food on paper plates, fathers sit with newspapers stretched across their knees.

It's funny to live on a block and never see most of your neighbors. Many faces are strange and new to me. Probably the first time they have noticed us too. We are as one now, fugitives from the heat sharing the cool of dusk over a plate of beans.

CHAPTER 53
THE WANDERER

LATE ONE MORNING

The sun hit the back of the house, and shafts of light poured through the windows making dazzling squares on the dining room floor. The children stood in a row, silhouetted against this brightness. It was late September on a Saturday morning, and they were all dressed and ready for an occasion. Arlene was in some sort of dressing gown vaguely reminiscent of something Rita Hayworth might have worn in an old movie. Only Arlene's was rather tattered, with cigarette holes in a few places.

My sister stood behind the children, leaning over them one by one to brush their hair. Uncharacteristically, the kids stayed still, their heads bowed. I paused for a moment, taking in the pretty picture. Standing quiet and pensive in that glow of light, the group looked like celestial beings gathered in prayer—one angel and three cherubs. I tried to remember from my limited Bible studies the proper definition of a celestial being. . . . *and there came a host of seraphim and cherubim* . . . That almost sounds musical. I half expected a heavenly chord to ring out, like when Charlton Heston parted the Red Sea in *The Ten Commandments*.

Actually, the group gathered before me was not going to fly off on some holy quest but was assembled on this September morning to go downtown to a special matinee. *The Greatest Show on Earth* was playing at the Hermosa Theater. Who would have thought that old 1950 Technicolor movie was still making the rounds of theaters after all this time? I had seen it when I was a kid with my brothers. We all agreed *The Greatest Show on Earth* was the "greatest movie on earth." It was all about the circus—clowns and elephants and trainers and trapeze artists. The movie dazzled us with girls twirling from ropes by their teeth and performers and animals encrusted with sequins, spangles, and feathers. The kids, I knew, would love it. A half hour later, after my sister had finally put herself together, she grabbed her straw bag from the couch and, atypical for her, checked to see if she had enough money for the show.

"Do we have extra to buy some Milk Duds too?" Lindee asked hopefully.

"I think we can manage that!" said her mother smartly, herding the children out the door and into the waiting sunshine.

It was strange to have the house to myself. Since Jeff left, it could get quiet like this. I didn't realize before what continuous background noise he had made. Without him, there was no banging in the kitchen as he made his coffee, no radio tuned to the jazz station, KNOB, all day, no horn practicing scales or playing the latest version of "'Round Midnight."

I shrugged and let my mind run through the things I could or should be doing now that I had the house to myself. I could make a batch of cookies if I had flour and sugar. I could write in the gray notebook what had happened at the Palos Verdes cliffs and the sailing voyage. That seemed long ago now that we were coming to the end of September. Of course, I could get in some practicing at the piano. I hadn't done that for a while; or I could just make another cup of coffee.

A VISITOR

Before I could decide, there was a polite knock at the door. Outside, in the shade of the porch, was a young man. He was unfamiliar, but I was used to that by now. My visitor was thin and blade-like. His almost-black hair flopped over a long face with a sprinkling of pock marks, the remnants of a battle with teenage acne. He wore a not-too-white tee shirt and dark jeans. Over his shoulder was a pillowcase stuffed with some lumpy things.

"Is Jeff here?" The boy smiled big and wide, exposing his teeth.

"Is Jeff here?" How often I had heard that question before. My first impulse was to feel sorry for this rather unattractive kid and then also sad that I was going to disappoint him. "Jeff doesn't live here anymore," I said. "He's in Florida."

Instead of looking upset, the young man looked interested. "Hey, now, Florida you say? Do you have his address? I might just contact him."

I should have been surprised by this cheerful reaction, but Jeff's friends were usually surprising, so I merely responded that yes, I had my brother's address and would get it for him. I left the young man at the door and climbed to my loft. I had Jeff's address in a box of papers and old sketchbooks. When I came back to the door, the boy was sitting on the brick step of the porch in a pool of light, his back to me, his lumpy pillowcase beside him. The light had moved to the other side of the house now and the sunny step looked inviting, so I sat down next to him wondering how old this kid was—seventeen, eighteen?

"Here is where he is living now," I said, handing him the envelope.

The boy took an address book and a pencil out of the lumpy pillowcase and carefully copied the information down in tiny, neat letters, then carefully put the pencil and address book back in their place before handing the envelope back to me.

"Are you going to write him?" I asked. "Because we haven't heard from him in a long time now, and we're getting a little worried." After that first letter Jeff had sent, we received four more—one right after the other, full of funny and weird things that were going on—but the letters stopped coming and there had been nothing for the last several weeks.

Repeating my words, the boy said, "So you haven't heard from him in a long time, huh?" He absorbed this information for a bit. "Well, yeah, that makes it more interesting then."

"More . . . interesting?" I questioned.

"Yes, more interesting and, no, I'm not going to write him." He dug out his address book again and found Jeff's page. "I thought I'd just go out there to . . . to . . ." his finger ran down the page, "to Orlando. I've never been to Orlando before!" Then he smiled his wide smile again.

Somehow, I wasn't following. "You're going to Florida?" I asked stupidly.

"Well, I just got back in town and was planning to stay a while, but this is too good a destination to pass up." The kid's dark hair was flopping back and forth in his enthusiasm.

I still wasn't following his logic. "But Florida is about three thousand miles away," I remarked. "How are you going to get there?" The guy didn't look like he had much money.

"I guess I should explain myself," the young man said. "You see, I'm a poet." That didn't answer my question, but he went on. "I'm sorta like the troubadours of old, you see?" I still must have looked a bit blank, so he continued. "I travel from place to place and find inspiration to write my poems," he said. "It doesn't cost anything to travel because I hitchhike. In fact, when I hitchhike, I don't need any money at all. So I might as well go to . . . to . . . he looked at the address again, "Orlando." He got up at this point as if sitting in one place for too long made him itchy. "Hey, the day is so fine." He squinted up at the sun. "Do you want to take a walk on the beach with me, and I can tell you all about it?" Another wide smile followed. This kid liked to smile a lot.

Living in the moment again, I found myself following him down the brick path and down Culper Court toward Second Street. We turned and walked down the few blocks to the beach. At the Strand, I looked longingly at my familiar spot by the wall, but the young man was asking about where the long sidewalk would lead us. I pointed south and said if we walked to Redondo, there was a marina and a pier. The other way took us further into Hermosa where most of the stores were.

As we turned south toward Redondo, the stranger started his story. His name was Jerry Wassa-something-ski, a kind of Hungarian or Polish name, and he was nineteen years old. He didn't seem to have any family, but he grew up in Hamilton, Ohio, and dropped out of school in his junior year. The first place he ever hitchhiked to from his small town in Ohio was San Francisco, and it was such a total mind-altering trip, he said, that he just kept moving on, looking for other great places and people. He had been hitchhiking now for about two years.

As for knowing Jeff, he had met my brother the last time he had come through Los Angeles. He had wanted, he said, to check out the Venice Beach scene, and that is where he ran into Jeff, who was playing his saxophone under the Santa Monica Pier. Of course, they got to talking. "He's a great guy!" Jerry said enthusiastically, his face breaking into the now-familiar smile, "and he said if ever I was in Hermosa Beach to just look him up at the red-shingled house with the brick walkway in Culper Court. Say, Culper Court is not an easy place to find. It's only one block long."

I smiled, thinking of all the people who had had trouble finding us and had said that very thing. But at least the mailman knew where we were. I thought again about Jeff being so far away in Florida and was glad the mailman at least knew where we lived, but now Jeff had stopped writing. My stomach tightened at the thought that we might lose touch with him for good. He could wander off with Harry and never be heard from again.

Jerry was still rambling on with the story of his wander-lust as we came to the new marina in Redondo. I looked around, thinking I might see Richard Mackey's thirty-foot ketch, but there were so many boats I soon gave up looking and turned my attention back to the skinny kid. In the two years Jerry had been hitchhiking, he had crossed the continent two times. "So, I am ready for the third," he said with pride, "and this time I will hit Florida. Won't Jeff be surprised when I show up at his door?"

Past the marina, we met up with the sand and the beach again, so I edged over to a bench and sat down. I had more questions. "You said earlier that you didn't need money when you hitch-hiked and you also said you are like the troubadours. So how does that work?"

Jerry broke into the smile-thing again. "You see, it's like this. When someone picks you up, they want a few different things from you and it's your job to give it to them."

"And what's that?"

"Well, let's take the truckers first; they mainly pick you up so you will keep them awake. It's easy to fall asleep on a long haul, so you can't just sit there silent, that wouldn't be fulfilling your job. It almost doesn't matter what you say as long as you keep them awake—jokes are sometimes good here, getting the guy laughing is helpful. It's hard to fall asleep if you are laughing."

"I see."

"Then, let's say the next person to pick you up just wants company. They are on a long trip and just want someone to talk to. You have to be a little more skillful here. Sometimes you could tell your story of where you are going and why, but I have found that it works better to draw the driver out and let them tell you *their* story. They are usually grateful for the attention and buy lunch and even go miles out of their way just so they can keep talking."

What a funny kid this was. "Are there any other types?" I asked.

"Yeah, I call them the do-gooders. The others that pick you up are loners, but the do-gooders can be alone or come in groups like a family or a couple of friends, maybe. Now, with these people, it is important to have a good story—'I'm trying to get back home because I ran away, and I don't have any money.' You have to pluck at their heartstrings because they *want* to help you. Or here is another story: 'I have to get to such and such a place because I got a job offer, but there is a time limit.'"

"Isn't that lying?" I suggested.

"Naw, naw, maybe an exaggeration, I admit it. But if you didn't have a good story, the do-gooders would be very disappointed and feel let down. And with the do-gooder type, you usually wind up with five or ten dollars when they let you off."

I shook my head in amazement. "So that's what you meant when you said you didn't need money? But it seems wrong to take theirs."

"Oh, no, no, it makes them happy to give the money. It would be disrespectful of me not to accept. Take my word. Now, if you were to hitchhike to Florida, you would have the perfect *real* story." Here the boy clasped his hands together and rolled his eyes up to heaven. "Sister searching for long-lost brother who may be lost in the swamps of the Florida Everglades."

"It's Orlando," I corrected, "lake country."

"Whatever," Jerry shrugged, then brightened again. "The last time I did a cross-country hop, I started out with twenty dollars and ended the trip with fifty, and that didn't count all the free meals. With your story, I could probably end up with much more."

I was beginning to think Jerry was a bit of a con man and not the innocent lost child I had thought earlier. "So where does the poetic troubadour part come in?" I said, a bit acidly.

Jerry shook his head, "You don't get it, do you? Just like me, the troubadour of old went from town to town bringing excitement and joy by singing ballads of adventure and romance to the people stuck in one place. And the people didn't ask if the stories were true, they just enjoyed the excitement that the troubadour brought into their lives and they were happy to pay for it. What's wrong with that? And by giving the wanderer food, drink, shelter, and, yes, money—they were happy to do it just to have their drab lives enlivened for a short time."

"And the poetry, are you really a poet?" The acid was a little less when I asked this.

Here the kid looked a little shy. "Well, yes. Yes, I am. I sometimes give one of my picker-uppers a poem that I write on the spot if I think they would appreciate it. One time, a couple picked me up on a cold frosty evening and put me up in a hotel room for the night. I wrote them one of my best poems."

Jerry continued in the niceties of traveling by thumb. "Now, truckers are a different species. They don't give much money or free meals, but they do take you on much longer trips, and when they finally drop you off it will most likely be at a truck stop where you can usually parlay the stopover into a ride from another trucker, and speaking of long and short trips, sometimes a jokester will pick you up. They are all nice and friendly and tell you that you can ride with them until they get close to their home. So, you hop in all happy and grateful and are just settling down when the guy goes ten feet then stops with a jerk at the very next mailbox. He's already chuckling when he opens the door and says, 'Bye-bye, here is where I turn in!' And then he takes off laughing himself silly, leaving you in a cloud of dust."

"That's a mean joke!" I said.

"Yeah, it is," Jerry gave a little sigh, "but most people are not that way. They are usually kind." At this point, the kid took a big breath and looked thoughtful. "All in all, hitchhiking has been for me a way to learn about America. Forget about those dry textbooks we had to labor through in our social studies classes. I have seen the real America and not just the landscape either. It's the people I'm talking about. They are all different, but they are all the same. Do you get me? Just the way so many of them are willing to help a complete stranger like me . . ." Here the kid stopped and looked embarrassed. "I know it's corny but—"

"No, no," I interrupted. I was feeling warmer toward this "complete stranger" than I had since meeting him. "I think it is a very admirable thing to say."

Jerry relaxed then, and his smile was wider than ever. "You know, I have made so many friends that after two years of it, I have contacts all across the United States, people that I can stay with overnight or for several weeks." He smiled dreamily as he reminisced. "A hot shower, a good meal, and a soft bed really feels really fine after several days on the road where mostly you don't sleep at all. The best that can be found sometimes is that little place right behind the seat of a trucker's cab. It's kind of cramped but when you're dead tired, even that is a relief."

I had to hand it to him, the guy really seemed to enjoy what he was doing with his life and really believed that he brought joy to the people he duped. Well, maybe I was too harsh. In some sense he did give as much as he took. Maybe he did bring them happiness as he said. I wasn't quite sure. He was such an odd kid. I hadn't noticed before when we were walking side by side, but he looked odd too. Now, sitting on the bench, I noticed that when he got enthusiastic talking, beads of spit gathered and foamed at the edges of his mouth. And his eyes—they were everywhere but looking at me, or maybe it was one eye was looking at me and the other roamed independently. Poor kid, wall-eyed with a foamy mouth and bad skin, he must have been taunted a lot at school. No wonder he dropped out.

OLD FOLKS

Just then, an elderly couple came tottering up to our bench. The man had a cane, and the woman was holding him tight by the elbow, sort of propping him up. "Hello there," they said together, when they reached our bench. "We wonder if you two young people could help us out." The couple must have been somewhere in their late seventies, maybe even eighties.

"Sure thing!" Jerry said, and he jumped right up and gave the ancient pair our seats on the bench. "What can we do for you?" he asked eagerly, and threw them one of his widest smiles.

The woman opened the shopping bag she was carrying. Inside were three empty large glass bottles. They must have originally held juice or soda. "Well," she said, "we came here to get some salt water from the ocean. Dad here uses it to soak his feet. It's very good for the rheumatism, isn't it, Dad?" She looked affectionately at her husband, who was nodding and making himself comfortable on the bench. The woman continued, "Salt water is so good for him, but the ocean is yards and yards away, with all that deep sand to walk through. I don't think we could make it there and back."

"It's no problem at all for us, is it?" Jerry looked at me, then beamed his signature smile once more at the sitting pair. "Here, let me take those bottles. Do you have more? Because we could get as much as you need." A moment later, the kid and I were jogging across the long stretch of sand and filling the bottles with seawater, the tide swirling around our legs. Jerry's jeans soaked to the knees. A short time later, we loped back to the couple who were sitting close together on the bench. With the same gray hair and soft floppy clothing merging together, they almost looked like they were one person instead of two. Jerry frolicked over to them like a puppy bringing back a stick to his owner. "Hey now, there you are," he said. "Can we do anything else?" He stood there panting with a happy smile on his face.

"You're a good boy," the old woman said fondly, patting his hand.

And I thought to myself, *Yeah, I guess he is a good guy after all is said and done.*

The couple started collecting their stuff and slowly ambled away. Jerry and I turned and walked back toward Hermosa Beach and home. After walking in silence for a few minutes, I spoke up. "They were a nice couple. I wonder how long they have been together."

But Jerry had other things on his mind. "Hey," he said with satisfaction, "I just figured out the itinerary of my trip. Want to hear it?"

I nodded.

"Here's how it will go. The southern route to Florida from here would be to first go down to San Diego and hook up with US Eighty. It's one of the oldest cross-country highways. Hey, I learned that from a trucker going to El Paso. See, I can learn things even though I dropped out of school. So then that will take me through the Arizona and New Mexico deserts until we come to big old Texas. That will take a while to get through. In Louisiana, when I hit the Mississippi River, I'm going to take a short jog south for a stopover in New Orleans. They have the friendliest people there and Cajun food."

"And jazz too," I added. But Jerry wasn't listening much as he dreamed up his trip.

"If I'm lucky and find a place to stay in N.O.," he continued, "I can spend a few days there. After that, it is just a short jump to the Florida panhandle. Now, it gets trickier when you get close to your destination. It is sometimes just up to the rides I get as to what roads to take going south until I hit Orlando." Here, the kid stopped and looked at me. "Say, after I find your brother in Orlando, do you think he would put me up for a few days?"

I shrugged. "I guess so."

Jerry looked a little worried. "Hmm, Jeff might not remember me. We only met that one time. But you could write a letter, and I could take it with me and give it to him." The strange young man hesitated for a few seconds and then smiled his extensive smile. "Hey and while I'm there in Florida, I ought to at least go see the Everglades. I've never seen a wild alligator before." Jerry took a brief rest in his dialogue while contemplating the Everglades.

My thoughts, too, were in Florida. I turned to look at the ocean pounding away in the distance. I wondered what was really going on now that Jeff was with Harry. Was Harry fulfilling any fatherly duties?

Jerry erupted in talk again. "So, after Florida, I'll just make my way up the southern coast—Georgia, the Carolinas, Virginia—kinda easy like. I might even stop off in DC if I get a ride close to it." He turned to me. "You see, that's the thing with hitchhiking, you have to be flexible, ready to change plans and take advantage of who you're hitching with. Eventually, I want to end up in Boston, because there is this professor in Harvard giving lectures that everyone was talking about in San Francisco. He has some cool and unusual ideas about how certain drugs can enhance the mind. But, you know, before that I'll stay with some friends in New York City."

All the time this kid had been talking, I had been dreamily picturing his trip in my mind, going through the desert and the prairie lands, stopping at western-type towns with wooden sidewalks in New Mexico or Texas, crossing the Mississippi like Mark Twain, hitting New Orleans to look for Basin Street and Cajun food (whatever that was), seeing Memphis and Beale Street, then at last suddenly hitting the tropical setting of Florida, where everything would be full of colorful flowers and birds—pelicans and flamingos. But when Jerry mentioned New York City, I perked up. "Oh, it all sounds just wonderful," I burst out. "I was born in New York, you know. I still have relatives there!"

THE KID GETS AN INSPIRATION

Jerry stopped walking and turned to me. "Hey, you don't say!" He had his grin-thing going again. "I have a great idea. Why don't you come with me then? After you see your brother and father, we can go up north, and you could look up some relatives and stay there for a few weeks while I'm off to see Professor Leary in Boston."

His words had a familiar ring . . . as if he was saying . . . *Why don't you come with us? We're off to see the Wizard, who lives in the Emerald City. I'm sure he will give you some courage. All you have to do is follow the yellow brick road.*

This funny kid did remind me of the Scarecrow, but would that mean I was the Cowardly Lion? I thought I was faithful Toto. Maybe I have been some of the others all along.

Jerry was looking at me expectantly while my thoughts tumbled around. I found myself saying, "I couldn't leave . . . I . . . couldn't . . ." Then I found myself saying, "But it would be wonderful to travel. I always wanted to cross the United States slowly, stopping off at interesting places. I crossed the country on a train when I was little, but it's not the same as having your feet touch the ground—to walk the roads, to eat at some local diner . . ." My voice trailed off as Jerry looked at me expectantly.

I still felt a pang of regret when I remembered that car trip from San Francisco to Miami, Florida, in the Cadillac that I didn't get to take. Everyone else got to go with Harry, even Jeff, who was only eight, two years younger than I was. Mom had held me back with the excuse that I got carsick. I wanted to go. I should have spoken up, asked for what I wanted, but I was the "good, obedient girl"; I whined a little, then gave up. Well, I did get carsick back then. As for now, didn't I just get over terrible seasickness a short while ago?

DECISION

"I'm going!" I found myself saying out loud.

Jerry was pleased. "Atta girl. You have a great story—sister looking for lost brother. Wow, it will get us far. But you haven't heard about the trip back yet."

I plunked down on the nearest bench, not believing what I had just committed to. It felt euphoric. "There's more?" I asked.

"Listen to this," Jerry said. "Since we will be up north, we will take a different route back to California. After I go to Boston, I will pick you up in New York City. Then we head west. I want to go to Saint Louis. I know a family there. They are of the Baha'i faith and beautiful people. I'm sure they will put us up for a couple of days."

"What is a Baha'i? I never heard of it. It sounds foreign."

"I'm not really sure myself—it's some sort of combination of all religions, but they would give you the shirt off their back. And before we hit Saint Louis, we will be going through Ohio. I have a friend in Hamilton from school and his mother, who is great. That could be another stop off if we need it. I told you I have contacts all over."

"It sounds exciting," I said, really meaning it. I had never been to Saint Louis. I pictured a quaint, old-fashioned town like the movie set in *Meet Me in Saint Louis*.

"And from there we just take Route 66 all the way back to California."

For the second time I perked up. "Route 66! You mean like the song?"

"There's a song?" said Jerry. It was obvious that this kid had not connected with Jeff over music or jazz in particular.

I explained that there was a song called "Get Your Kicks on Route 66." "And it explains the whole route."

"No kidding, how does it go?"

"Well, the song starts out telling you to take Route 66 if you are traveling to the West Coast and that it is two thousand miles from Chicago to L.A. Then it names some of the cities that you pass through like Saint Louis and Oklahoma City and Winona. It's the whole route." I paused for a second. "You have to sing it to remember the order of the names of the towns." Then, I surprised myself by starting to sing out loud, right there on the Strand, the familiar Bobby Troup song.

After I finished, the kid clapped his hands and laughed. "That's great! We will never lose our way, and maybe you could sing to some of our rides when we get on the road."

"I don't know about that," I said, abruptly going quiet. Everything was happening so quickly. I couldn't believe I had just spontaneously committed myself to this trip. Was I actually going to see all those places this weird boy talked about, and was I going to see it all up close and not from a plane or a train window?

By now, Jerry and I were approaching Culper Court again and the red cottage. The young stranger, who was changing my life, stopped at the brick walkway and was suddenly serious. "Look, here is the plan," he said. "I will come back here in exactly one week at 8:00 p.m. to pick you up. So be ready! You will need some sort of identification, so the cops won't think you are an under-age runaway and stop us." He was all businesslike now.

"I have a copy of my birth certificate," I said. "They accepted it when my sister and I went to Las Vegas."

He nodded. "I guess that will do. The trick is to travel light." Here he held up his pillow sack. "Get a pillowcase and only pack a couple of changes of clothing, something for hot weather and something for cold weather, also some underwear, a toothbrush. You get it? Keep it light." He started to move back down the hill, then stopped. "OK, then so long, I'll be at your door eight o'clock sharp next week. Be ready!"

"I'll be ready!" I said, and breathlessly ducked inside the house with the tune of "Route 66" still in my head.

The house was empty. Arlene and the kids were not back yet. I realized the matinee must be a double feature. Should I tell them about my trip plans when they got back? I was hesitant; I didn't want anything to spoil my day and decided to keep my traveling plans to myself for the time being. With nothing to do, I ambled into the music room and started to pick out the melody to "Route 66" on the yellow piano.

CHAPTER 54
THE PARTY

GETTING READY

Rita was having another one of her parties. They were usually casual affairs that could start as early as six o'clock if you had children and end late at night if you didn't. The reason for the parties varied. It could be to celebrate something big like a part in a play or the fact that she had just painted her walls a deep pumpkin orange, or it could be just a spur of the moment thing.

This party was being held next Friday night, and right away Arlene went to her eclectic wardrobe to decide what to wear. I quickly decided on my new wine-colored velour top, on which I had splurged a whole twenty dollars. Mostly, though, my thoughts were focused on my departure on Saturday. I was glad the party was this Friday and I would be able to go before I left.

I HAVE A RE-THINK

For the first few days after my decision to go hitchhiking—to throw caution to the wind, to have a great exploit, to do something I had never dared before—I was euphoric and almost smug, hugging my special secret plan to myself. I was going to have the adventure I craved, and no one was going to stop me this time because they wouldn't know about it. I was not going to be dissuaded by my mother or a boyfriend. And wouldn't everyone be surprised when I left?

As the days passed, I began to think a little more about what I was actually going to do. By Wednesday, I ran through possible problems. Hitchhiking could be dangerous, especially for a girl. I had heard stories of young women who went hitchhiking and disappeared, never to be heard of again. Could "the kid" protect me? He was just a skinny teenager. Was he smart enough to keep us out of trouble?

My guide-to-be had made no mention of danger, except for one story of riding in a beat-up pickup truck with some old geezer in Flagstaff, Arizona. Halfway down the steep mountain road, Jerry realized the thermos of coffee the old guy was chugging away on was laced with rum. All and all it had been dicey, he said, as the man swerved and dived down the mountain—the road and pickup on an almost vertical plane most of the way and the geezer getting drunker as they descended—his foot on the gas the whole time. Jerry had breathed a sigh of relief, he said, when the mountain abruptly ended at a wide flat desert.

I started thinking about other possible problems as the end of the week got closer to Saturday. The kid was a complete stranger. Could I really just up and go off with him? It wasn't a good idea, I knew. By Thursday, I was reluctant, and by Friday I had convinced myself that what I was about to do was completely ridiculous! What had I been thinking anyway! To go off hitchhiking with someone I only knew for a few hours! It was insane to hitchhike, period. I would have to tell the boy when he showed up on Saturday that I had changed my mind. I wasn't happy about this decision, but I told myself it was the only sensible thing to do.

FRIDAY NIGHT

Arlene and I took turns showering in our swampy bathroom. After Arlene finished and it was my turn, the room was a steamy sauna, and it took a long time for my hair to dry. I had been letting it grow for two years now, and it was almost to the middle of my back. Later as I sat on the porch deck to further dry my hair, I called in the kids to take their baths. They would be coming to the party too. After applying eye makeup and lipstick in the still foggy bathroom mirror, I moved up into the loft and squirmed into my black capri pants and soft velour top.

Arlene emerged from her room with her hair piled in a desultory upsweep. She was wearing one of the remaining dresses from her Renaissance Fair Collection. She liked to call it her "Anne Boleyn Decapitation Gown." The bodice, which had a low-scooped neckline, was made from that special piece of material she had found in Logan's Fabric Store. The embroidered tapestry could have easily graced the walls of Hampton Court. The skirt and great puffy sleeves were of dark green velveteen with the unique tapestry of the bodice echoed again in the stiff cuffs on the velvet sleeves.

After their bath, the kids dressed themselves. They wore their regular play clothes, as they would mostly be up in the attic with Rita's kids or downstairs secretly spying on the adults, hiding and suppressing giggles behind couches and doors. Lindee was the most interested in what grown-ups had to say. Arlene had, more than once, during an intimate conversation, discovered her daughter crouched nearby in an effort to know what the adults were saying.

We walked the short distance to Rita's house. The door was open and we could already hear the murmur of conversations that got louder as we entered.

EARLY BIRDS

Inside Rita's living room, Chinese paper lanterns of different colors hung from the ceiling or were suspended over lights. Indian
block print cotton throws were draped over couches and chairs.
A few people were milling around with glasses and cups of wine
in their hands. A phonograph in one corner was playing something that was mostly drowned out by the milling people. Rita
was nowhere to be seen, but high-pitched laughter came from
the bedroom.

The kids spotted Mary and Fallon and rushed over to their
friends squealing with excitement. Before they all scooted away,
I saw Inger and Neisha ducking through the crowd toward them,
which meant Sara Lee must be somewhere around too.

Arlene drifted away and I moved on, discovering Sari and her
mother, Leahdell, in the kitchen inspecting a huge pot of chili
simmering on the stove. A stack of rustic-looking earthenware
bowls were being stacked next to the pot of chili by a young
woman in a rumpled shirt and lumpy pants of a dusty dun color
that exactly matched the color of the pots. Without looking at
anyone, she emptied her load of bowls, then left, returning with
a new stack. I found out later this elusive person was Flavyn, the
potter, mostly called "the mud hen" by the other ceramic mak-
ers. Now I knew why. *So, it was she*, I thought, *who made all of
Rita's funny bumpy coffee mugs that take the skin off your lip, and
now here are new bowls.* I wondered what effect they would have.

On the counter were two large bottles of wine, one red and
one white, with several of the aforementioned earthenware
mugs lined up next to them. People came up to the bottles of
wine, looked around for a glass, then cautiously poured themselves a drink using the rustic cups.

At the stove, Leahdell gingerly took one of the lumpy bowls
and, with a wooden spoon, put a big dollop of chili in it. After
a taste or two, she nodded her approval to her daughter. I was

impressed that Sara Lee's mother could eat chili standing up and still manage to smoke her cigarette at the same time. Leahdell was dressed to the hilt for the party in a flowing earth-colored caftan of soft homespun material from her favorite boutique. Her arms were banded by many bracelets and as many rings encrusted her fingers. A chunky necklace of amber that brought out the high-lights in her red hair encircled her neck. I was surprised to dis-cover she was heavily made up as if she was just about to go on stage to play a Gypsy fortune teller.

Sari, on the other hand, wore no makeup, relying only on her newly washed hair to make a statement. She wore a long paisley shirt over loose fitting pants. The shirt was not tucked in. Only if you looked closely could you see her pregnancy was starting to show.

"Is Chris babysitting?" I asked, surprised.

"It's all right," replied Sara Lee. "I fed and put Val to bed, so there is nothing for Chris to do but stay put."

I didn't know how Sari did it, balancing kids and kid-to-be and having time to make art too. "How are things with that man at the Furniture Mart that you sell your stuff to?" I asked. "Have you raised your prices yet?" I thought it ridiculous he gave only fifteen or twenty-five dollars for an original "Sari" drawing.

Sara Lee was beaming now. "I have so much to tell you. So much has changed. As you know, 'Furniture Mart man' was pay-ing peanuts for my work."

I nodded and leaned back on the refrigerator to listen.

"Well," Sari continued, "one day a woman came into the showroom with drips and slops on some brown paper and tried to sell them as watercolors." Here Sara Lee took a big breath. "So, when I saw them, I told 'Mr. Mart' that if he wanted watercolors, I could do something much better for the money she was asking for. The next week I came back with some large flowers on good paper. He loved them and wanted more. So now that I am doing only watercolors, I upped my price to sixty dollars, and he went for it!"

"Wow, that's great," I said. But Sara Lee was not finished.

"I also have a designer in Tustin who had me making poster-type theatrical watercolors, like portraits of Chaplin and W. C. Fields, that kind of thing. Now he is asking for something Western, you know, like cattle and horses, sagebrush and cactus, cowboys and Indians."

"Oh, I love Indians!" I blurted out. "When I was a kid and we played cowboys and Indians, I always wanted to be the Indian. My mother even made me an outfit with fringe and everything. I'd go into the backyard and make bows and arrows out of sticks and sit in my tepee I made out of an old blanket."

Leahdell, who had been quietly eating her chili, piped up in her gravelly contralto. "I agree, the ayes have it for the Indians. Long live the Indians! Sari, did I ever tell you that I think we just may have some Indian blood?" Sara Lee looked at her mother skeptically, then noticed something.

"Mom," she said, pulling out a tissue from her pocket, "your makeup is melting again!" She started dabbing at her mother's bosom with the tissue. "Why do you wear your theatrical makeup here? You're not doing plays anymore."

Sure enough, when I looked at Leahdell, the makeup on her cheeks was slowly dripping down onto her chest in little rivulets.

Leahdell grabbed the tissue herself now and dabbed her chest. "Well, why is it so damn hot in here?" she said. "And, and, didn't Shakespeare say 'all the world is a stage'? This is a party, the lights are dim. I didn't want to sink into the background," she explained, a little sheepishly.

Sara Lee laughed. "Mom, you could never sink into the background, believe me!" After we all chuckled about this, I went to look for Rita.

Back in the living room, I spotted Arlene in a group, talking excitedly and waving her hands. *She could usually gather an audience around her; a combination of her beauty and intensity*, I thought, *must draw them to her.* She seemed nicely occupied, so I milled around holding my pebbly Flavyn cup carefully while sipping the strong wine.

THE PARTY MOVES INTO SECOND GEAR

Rita finally emerged from the bedroom dressed in a spectacular white gossamer gown. The sleeves were long and almost as wide as the flowing skirt, which made them look more like wings as Rita moved and gestured. Rita's hair, newly washed, stood out around her head in a frizzy white halo. Behind, her daughter Diane had on something that reminded me of a Hawaiian grass skirt except that it was made from string.

Rita saw me and called out, "I see that the lovely Dolly Sisters are here!" I vaguely remembered that the Dolly Sisters were identical twins famous in vaudeville and . . . As I pondered this bit of trivia, Rita clasped me purposefully by my neck and like a puppeteer, propelled me around the room introducing me to different people.

"This is Lorraine. She is a wonderful writer!" she said, as we moved from one group of people to another.

A writer! I was amused to remember at an earlier party Rita had introduced me as "Lorraine, she is a wonderful artist." I definitely never told Rita I was writing anything. Obviously, my life was not safe from the scrutiny of Arlene and Rita when they got together. At least this time, Rita didn't say anything embarrassing, as she was wont to do in a crowd situation. Being alone with Rita was wonderful. She was smart and understanding, but in a crowd . . . well, something just happened to her. I was glad she didn't tell anyone this time the cup size of my bra or about our recent cockroach invasion. She might if she thought it would be entertaining.

She once told a crowd of people that Arlene's feet, with her funny square toes, were so adorable that she wanted to cut them off and suck on them. That was bad, but I also had to admit that Rita was not above making fun of herself. She liked to tell the story about once overhearing some women gossiping about her in a public restroom while she was in one of the stalls.

"I don't understand why everyone makes such a fuss over her," one woman had complained.

"Just tell me what is so wonderful about her?" said another.

"She's not beautiful!" remarked a third, whereupon Rita stepped out of the stall to say, "I don't know what it is either, guys. I have a nose that looks like a potato!"

I smiled remembering the story. So now I was the wonderful writer, and Sara Lee was still the wonderful artist and her mother, the wonderful actress, and Arlene would be, by turns, the wonderful jazz singer, actress, dress designer, or anything else.

Left alone again, I wandered around and after a while started to recognize people. There was Bill Connelly at the bar counter filling up his lumpy cup. The bar was now quite crowded with other bottles of wine and whiskey that people had brought. I heard the bubbly voice of Terry O'Shea across the room. Rita's boyfriend, I noticed, was growing a beard, and it was coming in a brighter red than his hair. I wondered if it was to look more like an artist or to look more mature. He was talking to a man who was a bit older, in a corduroy jacket with those leather-covered buttons that always reminded me of acorns. They were deep in discussion.

In a corner, I recognized Jared, the filmmaker from UCLA, in a tight knot with his film friends—a tall young man and his equally tall girlfriend. I remembered some of them from the student film festival Rita took me to at UCLA, where I got to see the film Jared had made at Rita's house. It was strange to see Rita pretending to be someone else's character in her own home. The film was interesting, but I sensed the people there were somehow disappointed and felt sorry for Jared.

On the opposite side of the room, I was a bit surprised to spot Lenny hovering over the record player and leafing through a pile of records. I hadn't seen him since he took me to Hollywood, weeks earlier, when I typed up the short piece about the heat wave.

Moving across the room, I sidled up to him at his post by the record player. "Hi, Lenny," I said. "I didn't expect to see you here!"

"Well, I don't know why." He almost looked hurt, then recovered. "I've known Rita for years and years if you know what I mean?" Here he couldn't resist giving a lascivious Groucho Marx leer.

I was used to this banter, so I just sighed wearily and said, "Lenny, will you ever stop turning everything into a sexual innuendo?"

He grinned like a naughty boy. "Not when I have a chance to shock a little mouse like you." Eyeing the record he had in his hand—and to change the subject—I asked what album he was about to play. It turned out to be one he had brought himself. "Hey, I'm glad you are here. I want you to listen to this. You have some taste in music," he said as he lovingly took an LP out of an album with a girl's face in dark shadow singing into a microphone. "Now listen," he said, putting his finger to his lips before I could comment. We both leaned close, trying to block out the sound of the party around us.

I heard a strong vibrant voice of a female singing. It was an old song popular during the Depression. "Happy Days Are Here

Again" is usually bouncy and boisterous, but the singer sang it as a slow ballad, giving emotion to each word.

"She was only twenty when she made this record!" Lenny breathed excitedly, looking at me in expectation.

I was impressed. "Sounds a bit like Judy Garland without the wobbly vibrato!" I responded, "She sure is a belter, maybe torch-singing is coming back in style."

Lenny smiled in a self-satisfied way. "I predict Barbra Streisand will become a big, big star," then sighed. "If only I could discover someone like that!" I left Lenny then to sigh over the rest of the LP and rejoined the party again.

As the night progressed, more people arrived and the murmur of voices became a louder drone, then moved on to a controlled roar interjected by laughter and the occasional squeal, usually emanating from Rita greeting more people. Every few minutes, another kind of squeal or bellow was heard as people became aware that the bathroom door had no lock on it and were caught with unzipped pants and hiked up skirts.

SOCIAL MIXING

Tonight, I was finding it easy to talk and mingle. Maybe it was because people came up to me first. Mostly, they wanted to talk about Rita and how they met her. There was an older couple somewhere in their sixties, Ross and Delia, who had just met Rita that very day on the beach. They had struck up a conversation and here they were at a party their first day in California. They had come from New York City. Hearing the words New York City got me excited until I remembered I wouldn't be seeing it or Florida or any of the other places now that I had decided not to take the cross-country trip.

Sometime later, I discovered the man in the corduroy jacket with the leather buttons was an artist and also an ex-student of

Mr. Bluske. We got into a heated discussion about our former art teacher.

"He is full of hot air! He's nothing but an old fart, a humbug, he browbeats his students. He isn't a good teacher," Draper spouted.

I had to disagree. "He may have been those things, but he was a good teacher if only because he changed us!" I stated firmly. "He had startled us out of our everyday torpor and woke us up to what beauty really was!" I think I made my point, because Mr. Draper went back to talking to Terry again.

Making my way across the room, I spotted Jared the filmmaker topping up his drink at the bar counter. He spilled quite a bit and made more of a mess when he tried to clean it up. He looked up as I passed. "Hello there," he lisped, trying to enunciate his words. "Shay, don't go away. I have somepin' ta tell you." I stopped then and stood politely as he stood up shakily. "I just want to tell you that I am a fan-tas-tic lover and I've been watchin' you all night and I wanna ravish you right here and now!" He fell back heavily on the barstool.

I really didn't know how to respond to this. He must have had a lot to drink. "I know, I know, you are a virgin and all that," he continued, "but lizen, it would be sooooo good for you because I can feel my juices flowing through me. I would be terrific for you." Slowly I backed away from inebriated Jared, as he talked on, trying to entice me into a moonlit walk on the beach. At the proper distance, I quickly ducked into the crowd and moved on. Goodness, he sure was drunk! I never would have expected any-thing like that from him judging from the first time I saw him that day, studiously measuring Rita's house for his film project.

Later, I watched as Bill Connelly, dressed in his sober suit and tie, wandered through the crowd of people. He would stop and have a short conversation with one group, then move on to another, then another. Judging from the laughter emitted every few minutes, I assumed he was wearing his Superman tee shirt under his suit and had at a certain point in the conversation whipped off his glasses and pulled open his shirt to expose the Superman crest and his true identity.

SOCIAL EAVESDROPPING

A short time afterward, I found Arlene talking to the filmmaking friends of Jared, who was now sleeping nearby. The tall couple bent over her as she talked. When I moved closer, I heard my sister say that she had seen *The Virgin Spring* two times. "The second time I made my sister go with me," she said. "I told her that she had to see it since she was still a virgin."

I cringed a bit. Did everyone have to know? I turned away but could still hear the conversation; the tall couple were now explaining that their final for a class had to be an original story written, directed, and filmed by themselves.

"Really," Arlene responded. "You know, I always wanted to write for the movies, but first I want to write a novel. If it turned out to be a bestseller, then I'd be asked to do the movie version too. I even have the title—*Blood of the Plums*. It's about my horrible childhood!"

Blood of the Plums, horrible childhood—really? We did have a plum tree in Burbank. I guess Arlene was going to concentrate on the more dramatic parts of our childhood, like when Harry went to prison and we lost our house.

I moved away from my sister's conversation and drifted around talking to the other party goers. Rita was eclectic in her taste of people. The guests were all different. Many were actors, artists, writers, or musicians. Usually there was something in their dress, manner, or posture that told you that they came from the artistic side of Rita's life. Then there were others who looked more regular, like the old couple she met on the beach. One younger couple had been her neighbors long ago. Standing there, big, solid, and blonde, they looked more like Scandinavian farmers from a Willa Cather novel than someone who would show up at a "Rita party."

For a time, Arlene and I stood together, talking to Howard K. Small with his girlfriend, Gillian, hugging close by his side. "Hey, man," said Howard, his eye tic winking along with a quick jerk of his head. "Nice party, huh? Any record producers here by chance?"

Gillian grimaced. "He's joking, of course."

"Actually, there does happen to be someone who produces records," I said, and pointed to Lenny, who was across the room trying to listen to another record he had put on.

Arlene then added, "Yeah, the last record he produced was called *Our Surfer Boys* by the Surf Bunnies! His company is not exactly a jazz label."

Howard blinked again. "Well do you think he might want some ballads or maybe a novelty song? I'm working on a tune now called 'Christmas in Hollywood.'"

"You know what," I said. "Lenny is a singer too. He can sing like anybody from Nat King Cole to Dean Martin."

"Oh, yeah, is he a baritone?" Howard looked interested. "I have lots of ballads for a male singer. He might want to record one himself." At this, Gillian looked tense, and I thought she was probably remembering that most of the titles of Howard's ballads were named after girls he had known.

It was getting late, but the party was still growing. I looked around; the kids must have grown tired and left for the attic. I didn't see them winding and giggling through the guests any- more. At one time, I saw Arlene talking to Sara Lee. Judging from her gestures—cutting motions toward her neck—I concluded my sister must have been explaining the inspiration of her dress design.

In the dim light, I saw Leahdell talking to a middle-aged man with a beard. I pretended he was a stuffy philosophy professor or maybe a silk screen artist who became morose when his silk screens didn't come out as he wished. He wasn't talking, but Leahdell looked animated as she simultaneously smoked her cigarette and read his palm.

It was fun to watch the partygoers connect and disconnect into different groups and listen to snippets of conversation.

Sara Lee and Arlene talking to Flavyn, the dusty potter:
Arlene: "I think I would really like the feeling of clay oozing between my fingers."

Terry O'Shea to a still-drunk Jared, now awake, and a guy in a cape with an impressive Salvador Dali mustache:
Terry: "I'm sick of oil paints. I got this idea about plastic."

Lenny and Howard K. Small in deep discussion:
Lenny: "I do imitations too." (He said in his Jerry Lewis voice.)

Arlene to the guy in the cape and Terry O'Shea:
Arlene: "I know I could make money being an art model like Rita, but my mother brought me up to be such a prude. I could never go nude."

Sara Lee to the old couple, Ross and Delia, from the beach:
Sara Lee: "Now picture this, an old Indian chief in full headdress—feathers all a blaze of brilliant colors—his face, deeply lined but strong, done in a simple ink line."

Sometime later, I found myself in a group discussion about existentialism. Names like Kierkegaard, Sartre, and Camus were tossed around. The Theatre of the Absurd, *Waiting for Godot*, *The Stranger*, and other avant-garde literature was sprinkled liberally into the conversation too. Words and phrases like "freedom," "disorientation," and "confusion in the face of a meaningless world" abounded. I can't say that I was following it all too well, but if existentialism was about how nothing really mattered, then why bother writing about it, I wondered vaguely.

I was giggling about this to myself when I heard my sister's laugh. Arlene was only a few feet from me in a group of her own, surrounded by a small assembly of amused people. "Oh no!" she exclaimed loudly, and shook her head for emphasis. "My *little* sister would never do such an adventurous thing!" Then there was that trilling laugh again while others joined in. Why was Arlene talking about me? She must have been answering a question someone posed, but why did she laugh and use that tone? Is that what she thought, that I was so inhibited or unimaginative that I could never do anything exciting or dangerous or spur of the moment? Yet I knew that was exactly what my sister thought and had been saying.

Other voices entered my mind—my mother telling me I would only get sick if I went on the car trip to Florida; my boyfriend happily sighing over my passivity; Lenny saying, "I like a little mouse sometimes"; and now Arlene informing a group of strangers her sister had no spunk, no spark! I stood for a long moment taking it in, then, standing up a bit straighter, I made my decision. The hitchhiking trip is back on!

CHAPTER 55
EL CAMINO REAL

PREPARATIONS

It was Saturday—the big day—the day of my departure. I moved in a kind of haze, going through the motions of doing all the regular things like any other day, but my thoughts were focused on what would happen at eight o'clock, when I would be leaving.

By late afternoon, I was up in the loft ready to pack. Stacked in a neat pile on my bed, I had already chosen what I would wear: my tennis shoes, a striped long-sleeved pullover, my most comfortable jeans, and clean underwear and socks. That finished, I took the pillowcase off my pillow. It would be filled with the essentials I would need as dictated by my junior guide. The gray notebook went in first. It would be heavy, but I couldn't go without it. I hoped it wasn't a bad omen. I had already broken the first rule of the road: "travel light."

With that settled in my mind, I continued to pack: a pair of sandals, extra socks and underwear, one pair of cutoff jeans, two short-sleeved shirts, and another long-sleeved pullover. On impulse, I grabbed a dress from the pole that held my better clothes and carefully folded into the sack a beige sheath, just in case I needed a dress in Orlando or New York City. I tightly wrapped my toothbrush, comb, and a lipstick in a washcloth and, as a second thought, added a fingernail brush. I didn't use it much here, but I figured since I might not get to take a real bath for days, at least my fingernails would be clean. All was wedged into my bag. Satisfied, I scuttled down the ladder to help with dinner.

After a distracted meal—I hardly tasted the spaghetti—I took a precautionary bath. Again, there was no telling when I would be able to take another, and I was unusually thorough. Finally finished, I wrapped myself in the old terrycloth bathrobe, noting that it was getting threadbare. We would need a new one soon, I thought, before I realized I wouldn't be worrying about things like that for a while. Reaching for the last towel, I wrapped it around my wet hair and left the bathroom.

DONNIE

Maybe it was the hot steamy bath or my state of mind, but I suddenly felt very strange and sat down heavily on the lumpy couch in the living room, completely drained. I must have had an odd look on my face because a few moments later, I felt a little bump as Donnie sat down next to me.

"What's wrong, Lorraine? Are you going to cry?" he asked, looking up at me with his quizzical Charlie Brown expression.

There was a break in my voice, and I croaked out, "No, it's OK. It's just that I am going away for a while, and I feel a bit anxious."

Donnie did not ask any questions. He was quiet for a while, then said, "Well, I guess you have to go then," and gave a little sigh.

Wasn't that just like him to say that? *What a little philosopher,* I thought. *Now, would that be a fatalist, a realist, or a stoic, maybe even an existentialist?* I hadn't read very much of the philosophy book Howard K. Small had given me some time ago. If Donnie was OK with me going away, then I would not be timid about it either. It suddenly occurred to me that my sister's children were great kids and that I really loved them a lot. It would be so easy to just stay with them here in this bungalow by the sea.

Slowly, I stood up. "Thanks, Donnie," I said. "You really helped me." Then I made my way up to the loft to dress. Slipping off the bathrobe, I quickly pulled on the long-sleeved polo shirt and jeans, then brushed my hair until the tangles were gone. As my hair dried, I checked the contents of the pillowcase for the third time. Eventually, I gave up waiting for my hair to dry and braided it into two damp plaits, tying them off with rubber bands. Finally, I put on my shoes and socks.

At the last moment, I rummaged through the cardboard box near my bed. I had almost forgotten to take my ID and some money with me. Reaching far down, I found the money and my birth certificate, then a small clinking sound caused me to feel down to the bottom of the box. My fingers closed onto something, and I pulled out a string of black beads with a small cross with an even smaller crucified Jesus attached to it. Months ago, I had found the rosary while I was cleaning. I assumed it was left by the Bird Lady and had put it away here, then forgotten all about it.

The ID, I put into my back pocket. The five dollars was carefully folded and stuffed into the bottom of my shoe under my arch. After a brief hesitation, I lifted up the rosary and put it over my head, dropping the beads under my polo shirt. I could feel the metal of the cross hitting my breastbone. Maybe it was silly, but I felt protected. I was also vaguely uncomfortable. After all, I was a lapsed Catholic and hadn't gone to church since I turned ten. Now I wondered if it was still OK to ask for help and, besides, wasn't it some kind of sin to even wear a rosary? I thought I remembered a rule about it from somewhere in the past.

Ahida Corona who lived down the block from us in Burbank was only twelve but a fervent Catholic. She had a long list of things that were sins. I knew the biggies, like don't steal or kill, but Ahida knew all the little sins like going to a church other than a Catholic one. I never knew that biting down on the Holy Communion wafer was a sin either until she told me. Probably wearing a rosary on one's body was a no-no too.

I think God will forgive me this one time, I decided, as I gathered up my traveling pillowcase and cautiously climbed down the ladder and before anyone could see, stashed the pillowcase in back of the couch where I had earlier placed my car coat. With everything set and in place, I casually wandered toward the dining room where I could now hear a murmur of voices.

LAST CHANCES

Rita and Bill Connelly were sitting around the table deep in conversation, their hands clasping their cups of coffee. Arlene was just bringing in one for herself when I joined them for a last cup of coffee. It had been dark for some time, and the kids were already in their bedroom. I could hear them talking and laughing quietly. They would be asleep before I left. *And I didn't say goodbye*, I realized. I had been so secretive. I wondered if Donnie could explain it to them tomorrow.

I greeted Rita and Bill Connelly as casually as I could, then went into the kitchen to make myself coffee. It would be a good idea to stay awake and alert. I wondered about the time and tried to surreptitiously check out Bill Connelly's watch. Giving up, I sat down and joined the conversation. It was hard to follow when half my mind was listening for a knock at the door or picturing Jerry trudging up the hill to Culper Court.

When I did hear the knock, I jumped and fairly flew to the door. Out of curiosity, Arlene followed me. "Who could be coming now?" she said, looking over my shoulder as I opened the door. There on the porch was the same thin, dark figure I had first seen a week ago, only now, instead of a bright afternoon, it was a starry night. Jerry smiled. "Hi, are you ready to go?" he said. He made no move to come inside, and I made no move to invite him.

"Who is this?" Arlene called over my shoulder. "Are you ready to go where?" she demanded, turning me around so I had to look at her.

I turned back to the dark figure in the doorway. "Um, Jerry, can you just wait out here for a minute?" I said hastily, almost slamming the door in his face. Turning to Arlene, I said boldly, "He is here because I'm going on a hitchhiking trip to Florida to find Jeff. He is a friend of Jeff's," I added a bit lamely.

By this time, Rita and Bill Connelly were standing in the dining room archway taking in the whole situation. Arlene was speechless for a few moments, trying to understand what I had just said. Then she sputtered out, "You're going on a hitchhiking trip with that . . . that guy outside?"

"Yes, it will be an adventure. I'll be going to New York too." I was standing my ground, I thought.

"No, no, no! Wait a minute, wait a minute!" Arlene had caught me by the arm and was pulling me back through the dining room and into the kitchen. There, she spun me around to face her. Her hands clutched my shoulders, and her eyes locked onto mine. Our heads were almost bumping into each other.

"You can't go with him," she said through gritted teeth. "He's creepy. No, listen, that guy will ravish and rape you by the side of the road somewhere in the middle of nowhere. Then he will kill you and leave you for the coyotes." Her fingers were digging into my shoulders, and I could feel her breath hot on my face. She looked terrified.

I pulled away and walked back into the dining room. Rita and Bill were still standing, watching quietly. I was torn. I didn't want to upset my sister. I did have to admit that Jerry was kind of creepy looking, and I didn't want to leave with her so upset. I looked around at everyone. They were expectantly waiting to see what I would do.

Rita was standing nearby now looking at me seriously. Maybe she thought I might be backing down because, when I caught her eye, she said in her calmest voice, "Lorraine, if you don't go on this trip, I think you will regret it for the rest of your life." She was right and I knew it. It was like down at the cliffs that day when I wanted to swim out to the sailboat. I looked over at Arlene, still quivering in the kitchen. "I have to go!" I said finally. "Look, it will be all right."

Rita was scribbling on a piece of paper. "Here is my address. Write to me and tell me where you are," she said, sticking the paper into my hand.

"I will. I promise I'll write every day!" I said, and pushed it deeper into my jeans.

Bill Connelly came up and shook my hand. "Goodbye, little one," he said in his quiet voice. "Have a good trip." I felt some money being discretely pushed into my palm and quickly put the bills in one of my last free pockets. By this time, Arlene, looking completely wilted, came over and hugged me. I hugged her bony shoulders, then turned toward the door.

"Goodbye," I called back, not turning around as I strode into the living room, stopping only for my coat and pillowcase beside the couch. When I opened the front door, the kid was sitting on the brick step of the porch, his back to me just as he had been on that sunny day a week ago.

He turned around then. "Ready?" he said, grabbing his stuff and getting up.

"Ready," I said, putting on my coat. Then, hefting our pillowcases over our shoulders, we moved out into the cool night, off the porch, across the short brick path of the small front yard, and out onto Culper Court.

It was strange to be going down the familiar road, turning right on Second Street as if nothing was different. It was strange to be walking the same short blocks to Hermosa Avenue as if it was any other evening, and it was strange to be following this young man across Hermosa Avenue to where the cars were moving south.

"OK, here we go!" the kid said, as he stepped out into the street and leaned toward the oncoming traffic with his thumb out.

"You mean we are starting right here?" I called out questioningly. It seemed odd to be on Hermosa Avenue and not be waiting for a bus or picking up a loaf of bread at the convenience store or just passing by on my way to the beach.

Now I pulled the hood of my coat over my head and purposefully stepped into the street. Cars were whizzing by, their headlights flashing past, one after the other. *You know,* I thought to myself as I took a few more steps forward, *if one can believe in folktales, I'm not standing on ordinary Hermosa Avenue, which can only take me to the next town. No, I am really standing on a vestige of the old El Camino Real, The Kings Highway, The Royal Road, and it can take me anywhere!* Then, mimicking Jerry, I leaned forward and stuck out my thumb.

FLOOR PLAN OF CULPER COURT

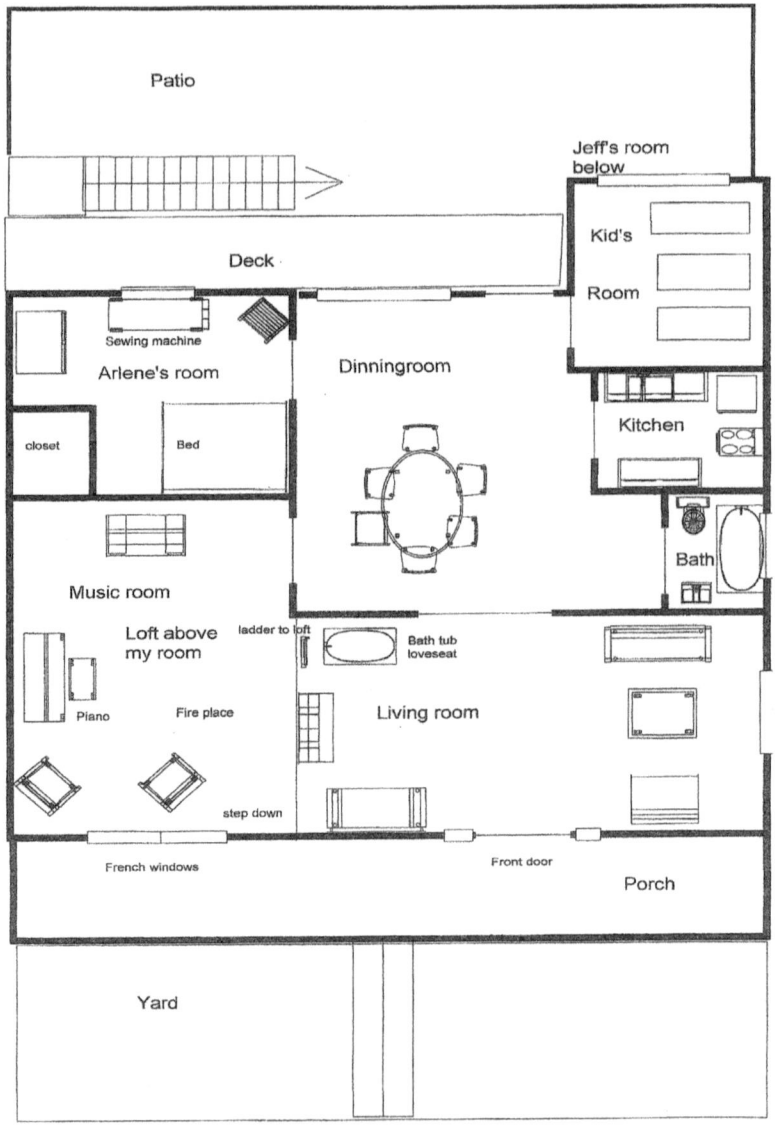

CULPER COURT

FAMILY AND FRIENDS PHOTOS

The front of the red cottage on 230 Culper Court, 1961.

The back of the red cottage. Arlene and Jeff are doing some fixing up. Note the old washing machine in the far lower right corner. Jeff had not yet put in the big window in the children's room or built his bedroom under it.

Florence, 1947. This is the only picture my mother likes of herself.

Florence with a new haircut called The Artichoke, 1961. I posed her against the door showing her perfect profile.

Florence and Harry just married, 1935.

Florence and Harry at a nightclub on her twenty-sixth birth-day. Doesn't she look beautiful?

Arlene at sixteen.

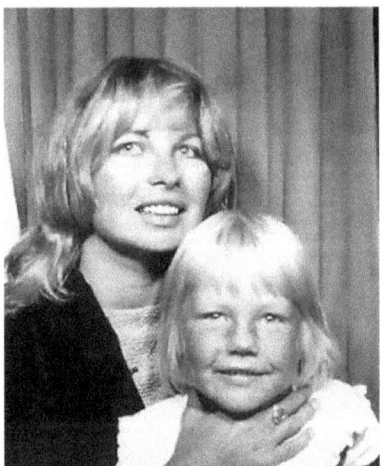

Arlene and Laurie J., 1960s. I don't know
why Arlene has her hand on Laurie J.'s neck.

A few years later, after I left for New York, Arlene has let her hair go straight and is wearing her own dress design called the Anne Boleyn Decapitation dress. She is also pregnant with Flavyn.

*Lorraine in the orange tube dress designed
by Arlene and worn to the Art Show.*

Lorraine with hair getting long.

Pensive Lorraine in bathing suit.

Lorraine with unknown bike in front of Culper Court.
Notice the French door/window is left open.
Maybe the front door has lost its doorknob again.

*Jeff and his first saxo-
phone, a C Melody, 1950s.
I took the picture and
somehow cut off his head.*

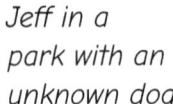

*Jeff in a
park with an
unknown dog.*

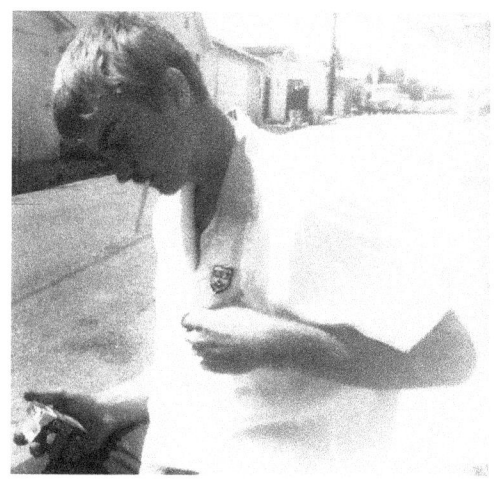

Jeff needs a light. Culper
Court in the background.

Jeff and friend talk as Jeff has another smoke as he
relaxes on the running board of his self-decorated van.

From left to right: Laurie J., Donnie, Lindee, 1963.

From left to right: Laurie J., Lindee, Donnie, 1962.

Pretending to be an old-fashioned family from the 1890s. From left to right: Front row, Donnie and Laurie J.. Second row, Lindee and Arlene. Top row, Jeff.

Bill, just after joining the Navy in the 1950s.

Harry's new powder-blue Cadillac on the front lawn. Arlene, Jeff, and Bill with new Christmas bikes. (Notice Bill's is stripped down for speed.) Lorraine is not in the picture due to throwing a tantrum about taking a family photo.

Harry with Bill and Jeff, 1949.

We posed for a mock family band. In order from left to right: Bill and his mother-of-pearl drum set, Lorraine pretending to play Harry's fife, Harry at the piano, Jeff pretending to play a clarinet, and Arlene (hair in pin curls) sulking about taking a family picture.

Harry makes the cover of DownBeat Magazine in 1947.

Harry at the piano.

A signed photo to a fan.

Dig that checkered suit!

Glamorous Rita.

Rita in a bulky knit sweater. It must have been a cold day.

Sara Lee and her mother,
Leahdell, in the adobe kitchen.

Sara Lee in front of her drawings.

This is the card Howard K. Small gave to Arlene. He sometimes wrote her poems under the name Paul. I don't know what he wrote on the other side.

A postcard sent to me in New York City by Bill Connelly, wearing his Superman shirt and holding Fang.

Cookie (Tiana) in a dress designed by Arlene.

Cookie in a dress by Arlene made from a lace tablecloth.

*From left to right: Ed Cassidy, drums,
Gary Marker, bass, Ricky Luther, vibes.*

Gary Marker with a puppy.

EPILOGUE

The hitchhiking trip was everything I thought it would be. I felt I was seeing and experiencing the people and places of my big, wide country at last. After days and nights of riding in everything from cars and pickup trucks to eighteen-wheelers, we finally met up with Jeff and my father in Orlando.

After a week there, we traveled to New York City, where I stayed with many of my relatives for a few more weeks. My young guide and I finally returned to the West again via Route 66, ending up back in Hermosa Beach, California. Jerry and I went our separate ways, and I never saw or heard from him again.

I had been gone almost six weeks and had many adventures, mostly good and some not so good, but I made it home safe, except that I had fallen in love with New York City. The following year, I went back there to stay.

In New York City, I got an apartment and started looking for a job, any job. Early on, I worked as a temp, filling in for filing clerks, typists, and receptionists. Later, I worked in several different art departments before finally becoming a package designer for the JCPenney Company.

Early on, through my first roommate, I met George, who was a college student. He went into the Army in 1968. In 1970, after his return from Vietnam, George and I married and had three children: Galois, Brandon, and Blake.

After my children came, I spent a good part of my time volunteering in New York Public Schools doing projects with the children in art, film, and writing. I continued to paint and write short stories on and off through the years. In 2015, I wrote a children's book based on my brother Jeff called *Jeff, the Jumping, Jiving Jazz Musician and His Continuing Adventures*. In 2016, I started writing *The Hipster's Legacy*.

My husband and I still live in New York City on the Upper West Side with our cat Miss Fatty Fat. One of our children lives nearby in Brooklyn. The others have branched out to Toronto and Japan. I have two grandchildren: Nora and Luna.

A few months after I moved to New York City, Rita wrote me a letter to tell me that **Bill Connelly** had committed suicide by jumping out of his apartment window. He had been so funny and kind to our family. I was sad that he couldn't find happiness.

Not too long after I left for New York, **Arlene** moved from Culper Court to Topanga Canyon with David Feller. They had a child, naming her Flavyn, born in 1967. Some years later, Arlene and David split up.

Harry and Arlene, by the middle 1960s were working together writing and recording new songs. Arlene continued to experiment in life and art, working in many different media. She sculpted in clay and wrote several plays, all the while continuing to design clothes and sing on occasion. She also became an art model and co-modeled with Cookie. That led to her becoming an artist—she specialized in big oil canvases of gods and goddesses. Arlene went back to school and got degrees in filmmaking. She and her daughter, Flavyn, a film editor, made a documentary called *Boogie in Blue*, about their father and grandfather, Harry (the Hipster) Gibson.

David Feller went on to be a loving father to his only daughter, Flavyn. He explored healthy lifestyles by becoming a vegan, studying Zen, meditation, and Aikido. He made his living writing articles for men's magazines.

My brother **Bill** stayed in the Navy for twenty years and retired at forty as a chief petty officer. He and his wife divorced soon after. He opened his own business as a mobile disc jockey, playing at parties, weddings, and school reunions. He married again but later divorced. He has a daughter, Amber. Retiring again twenty years later, Bill now spends his time finding his ancestral roots, making a family tree and going back and forth between his home in San Diego and his rustic hacienda in Jocomba near the Mexican border, where he can ride his dune buggy to his heart's content in the desert.

My brother **Jeff** stayed with Harry for a while, then eventually moved to France, where he met and lived with our younger half brother, Jimmy, who had a rock band, and watched out for him. In France, Jeff played with several groups who were interested in free jazz. After that, he traveled the world busking on the streets of Europe, Africa, Mexico, and islands of the Pacific and Caribbean, returning to America every so often to live with our mother or other family members—only to leave again for other places with his saxophone slung over his shoulder. Jeff has a French daughter, Dorothee, who came to America at nineteen in 2000 to find him. She became a prop master and works in movies and TV. She lives in New York City with her partner Jason and daughter Joyce.

Linde (I added an extra E to her name in the story for easier pronunciation) lived with us in New York City in the early 1970s, in her last year of high school. Later, she studied dance at Cal Arts in California and after that danced with the Colorado Ballet Company. After her second marriage, Linde searched out her father and lived near him in a houseboat in Sausalito, California. Later, with her boyfriend, Don, she sailed to Hawaii on his sailboat and got shipwrecked on the Big Island. Linde still lives on the island, with her third husband, Patrick, and various cats, dogs, and other pets while they build their own house. She is a wellness expert and is a licensed MELT practitioner.

My nephew **Donnie** grew up in Topanga Canyon. He joined the Navy for a few years, then got into construction and became a jack-of-all-trades with his tools and his pickup truck. He now lives near Linde on the Big Island of Hawaii. Recently, he had to move because of an oncoming lava flow. He is now building himself a cabin in the wilderness.

My niece **Laurie** (in the story I use her middle initial to differentiate the girls' L names) continued her interest in makeup and beauty, first as a manicurist, then as a hair stylist. She now has her own salon in the Southern California hills. She is married and has a son, Jamie, and a grandson, Benny.

Florence and Bob moved back to our old house on Mission Boulevard in Riverside. They separated five years later. My mother went back to work at the Mission Inn as a chambermaid, then retired at sixty-five. She lived in Riverside until physical problems made it sensible to move to San Diego nearer to my brother Bill. Five years later, she came to New York to live with me and my husband. During all this time, my brother Jeff would come back from his trips around the world to live with my mother, wherever she was, for a few months or a year, until he moved on again.

My father, **Harry**, reconnected with Arlene and her family a few years after I left California. He and Arlene made music and wrote songs together. Later he organized a couple of bands and recorded two or three record albums before he retired and moved to Brawley, California.

Rita continued her acting career, including parts on *Happy Days*, *Knots Landing*, and *Dallas*, as well as several prestigious local stage productions. She earned a degree as a psychiatric technician and worked many years in the mental health industry. Moving to Santa Monica, she continued to be interested in music (including heavy metal), arts, and politics. She took long walks, handing out coats and soup to the homeless and talking to strangers who caught her smile. She wrote prodigiously to her many friends and admirers and was an acupuncture devotee.

RITA'S CHILDREN:

Diane, Rita's oldest daughter, was a generous soul with a sweet smile and a wicked sense of humor. She found herself part of essential California culture in the '60s and '70s, including dancing and running with the infamous Freak Out Dancers, who often performed with the Mothers of Invention. Stock footage of her dancing at love-ins can still be seen. She also was a topless dancer during its heyday in the North Beach area of San Francisco. Diane struggled with drugs and alcohol and passed away in 1995 at the age of forty-seven from an accidental overdose.

Christine became involved in the entertainment business on the production end and worked for The Comedy Store, ABC, Lorimar Productions, and 20th Century Fox. She was a casting coordinator for *Dallas* and other shows and the assistant to the producer of *Knots Landing*. She was also assistant to James Preminger in a literary agency. She now runs a musical instrument repair shop with her husband, Jay, a musician; the two share a home with their four cats.

Mary Elizabeth worked for twenty-five years as an engineer, researching semiconductors. She then traveled and wrote books for a decade before going back to school to become a lawyer, working mostly to help the underprivileged. Mary has many patents and has published papers on law and in her field of science.

Thomas Fallon lives and works in Santa Cruz, California. An artist and photographer, his work may be seen at www. tfmackey.com. In 2014, he published a collection of poetry, *Point Lobos Underwater and Other Poems* (available on Amazon).

Terry O'Shea, Rita's boyfriend, became a recognized artist known for his work in resins.

Sara Lee had one more child, a boy, **Dana**, then separated from her husband, Chris. She went on to paint with great success. She lived in Wyoming for a time to paint, teach, and run a gallery. Back in California, she opened a studio in L.A., known mostly for her figures, flowers, and paintings of Native Americans. Her work has been seen in galleries in California, Wyoming, and online under the name **Sari Staggs** (saristaggs.com).

SARI'S FAMILY:

Leahdell continued in her happy carefree way, enjoying food, drink, smoking, and a casual lifestyle. Even heart trouble didn't slow her down.

Sara Lee's oldest child, **Inger**, went to Berkeley and Harvard and became an architect. She has a business called Brooklyn Greenroof and designs and installs gardens on rooftops in New York. She is married and has three boys.

Neisha, the most active and fearless one, became a dedicated swimming coach. She lives near her mother in Southern California.

Val attended trade school for ten years to become an expert welder.

Dana, the youngest, is an athletic coach specializing in swimming, cycling, and running.

Chris went on to have two more children, but not with Sara Lee.

Howard K. Small finally married **Gillian** and moved away from the beach. He taught high school English and continued writing and performing music. Later, he developed an interest in photography—taking pictures of pretty girls.

I lost track of **Tad**, and the last I heard of **Lenny** was that he had to marry an eighteen-year-old girl, and they moved to Hollywood.

Miss Beek (The Bird Lady) kept in touch with my sister and the children for several years as they moved from place to place.

Cookie now goes by her real name Tiana Lee. She and Gary divorced but remained close friends. For a while, she and Arlene worked together as art models. Then for twenty years ran a clothing store in Guerneville and Duncan's Mills on the Russian River in California. After belonging to the local theatre group, River Repertory, for several years, Tiana took a leap of faith, and with her friend Judy DeRosa, started Tribad, a lesbian-themed theater group with Judy as producer and Tiana as artistic director. They had great success and for five years put on several productions, including a holiday show each year. Tiana now lives near Palm Springs.

Gary, Ricky, and Harvey formed a new band with a few other musicians and called themselves "Fusion." They recorded an album called "Border Town" in 1969 that was called a combination of blues, rock, jazz, and folk.

Gary married again. He went on to join the Rising Sons and over the years played with numerous bands and with many performers. He also became a sound engineer/producer.

Ed Cassidy is best known for being the drummer in the band "Spirit" and made twenty albums over a period of thirty years. He also acted.

Harvey formed a band called New World Jazz Co., then teamed up with Ricky in the bands Fusion, Luther, and Red Hill.

Ricky continued to play vibraphone and other keyboard instruments, sing and write music for the various bands he played in.

As for **Him**, I couldn't locate his name on the internet so I guess he didn't become the next Frank Sinatra after all.

A FINAL NOTE

According to **Betsy**, when Arlene and the kids moved out of 230 Culper Court, the owner of the house pulled up in his car and looked at the cottage. He didn't even get out but shook his head and pulled away down the hill. A week later, there was just an empty space where our home used to be. Culper Court was torn down.

ACKNOWLEDGMENTS

If it takes a village to raise a child, bringing a book into the world is not that different. I may have started alone writing in an attic in an old gray notebook but that in time morphed into a computer of who's contents was sent out chapter by chapter to friends and family for scrutiny. When *The Hipster's Legacy* was finished even more people came onto the bandwagon by the way of copy editors, proof readers and book and cover designers not to mention a website designer and finally a marketer to spread the word of my words.

I learned many new things about the world of book publishing. I was particularly bowled over by the knowledge of the English language, sage advice, painstaking accuracy and kind encouragement shown by the work of Jenny Burman, Lauren Alexander, and Kharysa Watt. The beautiful visual presentation and style of the book and its dynamic cover is due to Jan Westendorp of Kato Design and Photo.

Closer to home, I'm grateful to my niece, Linde Kanahele, who shared her early childhood memories, which added more depth to the story and to her sister, Flayvn Mendoza, for her advice and steadfast belief in the book. Much thanks are due my husband, George, who laughed in all the right places as I read each chapter aloud as they were finished. I also need to give a heartfelt hug of gratitude to my "Computer Guru", Kae Chang, who patiently talked me though the pitfalls and disasters that I got myself into trying to learn about connecting on the internet.

And finally, a special thanks to Gayle Christian the good friend who started me on the journey of writing this book in the first place.

ABOUT THE AUTHOR

Lorraine Gibson Cohen is an artist turned writer. She was raised in Southern California, a stone's throw from Hollywood, and after studying art a El Camino College returned to her birth place in New York City, eventually becoming a package designer for JCPenney.

Her first book, *The Hipster's Legacy: A Story about a Family* is a memoir based on her life growing up with her father, a zany entertainer and jazz musician better known as Harry the Hipster Gibson.

Lorraine lives in New York City with her husband on the upper west side, with a view of Central Park if she leans far out the window and looks east.

To find out more about *The Hipster's Legacy* and read the lost chapter, please visit: plumtreetales.com